BLITHE SPIRITS

About the Author

S. D. Tucker is an author who writes the regular 'Strange Statesmen' column in *Fortean Times* magazine, and whose articles have appeared in print in the UK, US, Ireland and online. He has published six previous books with Amberley. His two books with CFZ Press, *The Hidden Folk* and *Terror of the Tokoloshe*, also touch upon the topic of poltergeists. He is a very learned man, but in all the wrong areas.

Also by S. D. Tucker

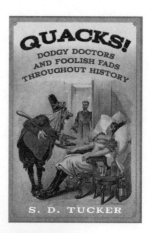

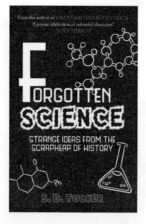

BLITHE SPIRITS

AN IMAGINATIVE HISTORY OF THE POLTERGEIST

Do Ghosts Have a Sense of Humour?
A Comparative Study of Mythical Trickster-Figures and
Real-Life Poltergeist Hauntings

S. D. Tucker

AMBERLEY

I've got a book about the paranormal. I didn't buy it – it just appeared...
Paul Merton

I wrote a book about poltergeists. It flew off the shelves.
Jack Dee

If the soul is not destroyed, what becomes of the souls of idiots?
Camille Flammarion

First published 2020

Amberley Publishing
The Hill, Stroud
Gloucestershire, GL5 4EP

www.amberley-books.com

British Library Cataloguing in Publication Data.
A catalogue record for this book is available from the British Library.

ISBN 978-1-4456-6728-7 (paperback)
ISBN 978-1-4456-6729-4 (ebook)

Typesetting by Aura Technology and Software Services, India.
Printed in the UK.

Contents

INTRODUCTION
Acting Like Little Children

I do not see why we should imagine there are no fools or naughty children
in the spiritual world; possibly they are as numerous there as here.

Professor Sir William Barrett

We do not think of ghosts as being funny. Scary, yes. Mysterious, of course.
Some may even find them rather magical and awe-inspiring in their nature.
And yet we are not accustomed to thinking of them as being humorous –
unless you want to laugh to express your lack of belief in them, perhaps.
When it comes to that specific well-known sub-category of noisy spirit we call
the poltergeist, this feeling is if anything heightened. Poltergeists smash things
apart, set fires, keep households up at night with loud bangings and rappings,
throw stones at people, even on occasion physically assault them; and there
seems nothing very funny about any of that.

Then again, think of Hallowe'en, and trick-or-treaters. They smash things
up, throw eggs at cars and houses, strew toilet rolls across trees and gardens,
hurl stones and shatter windows, shove unpleasant substances through letter-
boxes and even, occasionally, go so far as to set things aflame. This also isn't
terribly funny – if you're on the wrong end of it. The kids responsible would
disagree. It's funny to them. Maybe it is to the poltergeist, too?

When we read of a case from 1649, when parliamentary officials sent
out to survey a property in Oxfordshire witnessed a stinking tub of green
and foetid ditchwater flying into the air and then upending itself onto their
heads, it is hard not to visualise the scene and laugh. It is pure slapstick.
When we then read that horse-bones began materialising from thin air and
whizzing around the place, and that someone glimpsed 'the similitude of a
hoof' disappearing through a doorway, and encounter the possibility that,
just perhaps, it was *a dead horse* playing all these tricks, we are apt to snigger
again. It just sounds far too absurd for words. When we later discover that
the parliamentary agents were so disturbed by such ridiculousness that
they fled the house, more amusement arises; agents of authority have been
undermined, pomposity and power pricked. Even if the Woodstock haunting

was all just a very human fraud, as has been suggested,[1] then it is still a comic story, whether a real ghost lay behind it or not. One contemporary account spoke of 'Strange *Pranks* plaid by the Devil' and you can certainly see why.[2]

Perhaps you are unconvinced. We readers may find the tale funny, but the original victims were scared half to death by it. Was *this* not, therefore, the true motive of the poltergeist at Woodstock – to terrify, not to cause mirth? Perhaps. There seems a curious acceptance in the popular mind that ghosts may well exist purely in order to scare us. But if so, then why? Surely it would be just as odd for any given spirit to desire to alarm us as to amuse us.

Woodstock was no one-off. Many poltergeist hauntings on record are far more silly than scary. Take the case of the Canberra-based prostitute Liz Fleming, who during the early 1990s was followed around by an invisible ghost which liked to draw love-hearts and write 'I love you, Liz!' on mirrors at the brothel where she worked. The spook was helpful, not malevolent, retrieving keys which Fleming's clients had accidentally locked inside their trucks to aid her levels of customer-satisfaction, or making a torch drop out of thin air when somebody needed one. One distinctly comical facet of this haunting was that Liz was constantly being followed around by warm potatoes. They would fly through the air in her presence, or roll along the floor from nowhere, settling at her feet. One day in 1994, while Liz was sitting inside a hairdressing salon waiting to get her hair done, certain unmistakable signs of poltergeistery began to appear. A child's pram repeatedly tipped itself over when nobody was near it. Then, from the deserted street outside, came rolling in two strange objects … another pair of potatoes, a tasty gift just for Liz, provided by her wannabe lover on the Other Side.[3] The salon staff were somewhat disturbed by this event, though I would question why. It is hardly the stuff of Hollywood horror; I personally would love to see a Liz Fleming biopic called *Potato-Geist*, though I doubt many others would. It all just sounds far too surreal to be taken as anything other than one big, daft joke… doesn't it?

Maybe it *was* a joke. We can find several poltergeists which have audibly laughed at what they were doing, suggesting humour may indeed lie somewhere among their intentions. The following example was recorded in a book of modern Irish fairy lore, and concerns a farmer named Mickey O'Mahoney. One cold October night in 1957, having stayed out long after midnight supervising the birth of a valuable new calf, O'Mahoney wanted some nice hot tea to warm his bones, but found his kettle empty. Modern plumbing not yet having reached his corner of rural Ireland, Mickey grabbed a bucket in one hand and a lantern in another, setting out across the fields for water. Reaching a nearby pool, he dipped down his bucket, whereupon his lantern was suddenly kicked away by forces unseen, sending it right into the middle of the pond where the coldness made its glass shatter. As O'Mahoney stood there bewildered, he heard a 'low mischievous chuckle' coming from the night air beside him. 'Oh, ye rascals,' he muttered, to the fairy folk. 'Sure, you're the divils for tricks.' On his way home, the farmer heard another peal of laughter from behind him. He swung around sharpish, but again saw nobody there to account for it. The only thing he could do was sound a threat of defiance every bit as empty as were the surrounding fields: 'I wish to glory

I could catch ye, for 'tis the switch ye want and no mistake and gladly and soundly I'd give it ye.'[4] He never did manage to catch them, though.

Look at what happened here and wipe the idea of fairies from your brain – essentially, an inanimate object was kicked around by an invisible agency. Whether polts or pixies, what is important to us here is that they actually laughed at what they had done. They sound less like terrifying demons, and more like mischievous little children; which is why the medieval writer William of Auvergne called such beings *joculares* and *joculatares*, meaning 'pranksters'.[5] It is also why such colloquial phrases as 'laughing like a kobold' and 'laughing like a pixie' were popular across pre-modern Europe; fairies and spooks, of whatever breed, were traditionally imagined as having a distinct sense of humour.[6] The French poet Pierre de Ronsard catalogued such facetious *follets*' foolish fancies thus:

> Upon our stomachs they probe and prod,
> At night they move benches, tables and stools,
> Locked doors, gates, cabinets, beds, chairs, step-ladders;
> Or count our treasures, or crash against the ground
> Sometimes a sword and sometimes a glass:
> However in the morning nothing broken can be found
> Nor any furniture moved from its normal place.

Inveterate *joculatares* are they all, always game for a laugh. The verb *lutiner* – meaning 'to behave like a *lutin*', a type of oft-unseen French fairy, by playing jokes on people such as filling their shoes with pebbles, or shaving sleepers' beards off – survives even today in the modern French tongue.[7] According to the occultist Montague Summers, such *follets*, or 'spirits of folly', would:

> … make their presence first known in a house by various silly pranks and idle japeries. Trinkets and knick-knacks belonging to the house and more especially to the person whose attention the *lutin* wishes to attract vanish from the place where they had been laid down, only to reappear shortly afterwards in another spot. These Tricksters next annoy people by hiding in dark corners and laughing suddenly, or calling aloud as one passes; they will even pluck the sheets off the bed from sleepers, or tweak one's nightcap … Very often they beset tender girls, to whom they manifest themselves as handsome gallants, hot young amorosos, who pursue them with obscene suggestions, whispering in their ears the most indecent words at unguarded moments.[8]

In other words, these polter-fairies spent their days (and nights) very much having a laugh.

Another poltergeist which laughed repeatedly at the tricks it played infested the fairy-tale villa of one Homem Christo in the Portuguese town of Coïmbra in 1919. One prank affected a friend staying the night at the haunted house. As it was cold, the guest closed the shutters in his room. Lying there in bed, he was at length awoken by moonlight streaming in through the window; the shutters, which he had carefully bolted, were now standing wide open, keeping him from his sleep. Thinking they must have blown open somehow, even though there was no wind, he got up to pull them back shut – but he could not. He raised the window's lower pane, grasped the shutters and tried to pull them closed; but they refused to budge. Suspecting trickery, he stuck his head outside, shouting threats to ward off pranksters. However, 'almost instantly' as he did so, the spring which held up the window-pane let itself loose, sending the glass shooting down onto the man's neck with such a 'furious blow' that he became choked and struggled to get free. He didn't call out for aid, however, as he 'feared the ridicule of my position'. Eventually extricating himself from this cruel trap, the man looked around (through the closed window-pane this time) to see if there was anyone outside. There was not. Rationalising it had all been an unhappy accident, the guest once more closed and bolted the shutters – 'very methodically', this time – and returned to bed. Glancing at the window again, all thoughts of sleep quickly disappeared; the shutters had unbolted themselves and were standing open a second time. Then, the man heard a 'horrible grinding like a muffled laugh' followed by a series of heavy blows being struck upon the walls, floor and furniture. Overcome by his fear much like the parliamentary agents at Woodstock had been several centuries beforehand, the guest said he 'bolted into the garden like a lunatic and ran straight before me, without a hat, without even shutting a door' until he reached the safety of his father's house across town.[9]

Given such puerile japes, it is unsurprising that many eruptions of poltergeistery have been attributed to the actions of mischievous and discarnate deceased children; after all, they do continually insist upon acting like them. An alternative viewpoint, though, would be Frank Podmore's infamous assertion that all such outbreaks were simply down to the pranks of naughty *living* little children. Podmore, a significant early member of the original British SPR (Society for Psychical Research), did not necessarily take this view upon matters initially and, when investigating a relatively unremarkable haunting in Worksop in 1883 where various objects flew around, smashed and hit people on the head, he was not quite outright in his dismissal. Writing in the *Proceedings* of the SPR in June 1896, however, he had changed his mind:

> If my verdict on the Worksop disturbances in 1896 differs from that which I gave in 1883, it is because many things have happened since ... In the course of the thirteen years which have passed since I wrote my [original] report, we have received some striking object-lessons demonstrating the incapacity of the ordinary unskilled observer to detect trickery or sleight-of-hand; and we have learnt to distrust the accuracy of the unaided memory in recording feats of this kind, especially when performed under circumstances of considerable excitement.[10]

To Podmore, apparent poltergeist activity could always be attributed to a combination of faulty observation within an excited, abnormal situation and subsequent tricks of memory. But who was responsible for the *actual* tricks which took place in any affected home, if not a polt? Why, a naughty child of course. As he says, it was a fact that a young girl called Eliza Rose – 'the daughter of an imbecile mother' – was present at most of the Worksop disturbances. They began shortly after she came to stay at the affected cottage and ended when she left. Podmore therefore concluded that Rose herself, 'as a half-witted girl gifted with abnormal cunning and love of mischief', was probably 'directly responsible' for all that had occurred.[11] To Podmore, wherever a mischievous child is present on the same scene where mischievous, childish tricks are being played, the least complicated, most efficient solution is to blame that very same mischievous child.

Sometimes this is a wise assumption, but Podmore allowed the idea to colour his interpretation of other, more impressive, cases. His discussion of the Wem poltergeist of 1883, which appeared within a farmhouse where a teenage nursemaid called Emma Davies was employed, features the following apparently conclusive paragraph:

> On Tuesday morning … Miss Turner [a visitor] was in an upper room at the back of the house, and the servant of the establishment and Emma Davies were outside, Emma having her back to the house, and unaware that she was observed. Miss Turner noticed that Emma Davies had a piece of brick in her hand held behind her back. This she threw to a distance by a turn of the wrist, and while doing so, screamed to attract the attention of the servant, who … turning round saw the brick in the air, and was very much frightened. Emma Davies, looking round, saw that she had been seen by Miss Turner, and apparently imagining that she had been found out, was very anxious to return home that night. Miss Turner … asked the girl if she had been playing tricks, and the girl confessed that she had, and went through some of the performances very skilfully.[12]

Here, Podmore's opinion appears to be wholly vindicated. However, examined more closely, it actually begins to fall apart. Yes, the girl once threw a brick, but on another occasion a chair in which Davies was seated rose a foot into the air with her still on it – as witnessed by twenty people.[13] How did she manage to fake that? There are many suspicious elements to the case; when various items (including a baby's clothing) were found to be 'paranormally' afire, it was always Davies who discovered them. But we will also find such events being described as coal 'coming alive' and flying out from the hearth 'in various parts of the room', crockery leaping out of a cupboard while Emma, under close observation, stood apart from it with her arms folded, and various items rising up from the kitchen table of their own accord when Davies *was not even present on the property*.[14] Given this last fact, surely it is simply not possible for the child to have been responsible for absolutely *everything* that went on at Wem?

Podmore thought otherwise. Referring to a statement from a couple called the Leas that Emma was in their house when dinner-plates levitated from the table elsewhere, he had this to say by way of 'explanation': 'memory is apt to be treacherous on such matters as the presence or absence of particular persons at particular times, and the precise sequence of various events.' For Podmore the Leas were, quite simply, 'indifferent witnesses' and not quite 'first-rate' – an opinion largely based upon the fact that their testimony was inconvenient to him.[15]

Nonetheless, there remains Miss Turner's own testimony. How is that to be dismissed, if the whole affair is not to be written off as mere deception? Surely, it cannot be dismissed. Brick-throwing Emma Davies was, indisputably, playing childish tricks – and so, at the same time, was a poltergeist. Podmore and similar critics cannot seem to grasp the idea that the jiggery-pokery of some witnesses, whether conscious or not, may take place during a great many genuine poltergeist outbreaks, *alongside* the real phenomena. Sometimes, poltergeists stubbornly refuse to perform their usual routine in front of investigating visitors, for example, placing the person at the centre of affairs in an awkward position. Not wanting to disappoint, it is easy to see why a child might be tempted to throw a few things around on the sly, to avoid looking like a little liar. One sympathetic ghost-hunter aptly compared this to taking your car to the garage with intermittent electrical faults: 'they never seem to happen when the mechanic is looking at them and you feel somehow tempted to fake it just to show him what's wrong.'[16]

Now put yourself in a child's shoes for a minute, and imagine you are living or working in a polt-infested home; every day you see chaotic yet fun tricks being played, as windows are smashed, objects thrown and furniture upended. Wouldn't it be natural to start cutting some of these capers yourself? Naturally; to a child, such things are funny. If you didn't like making a mess and a noise when you were a child yourself, then you weren't much of a child, in my opinion. Children, far more than adults, appear capable of recognising the humorous elements inherent within poltergeist phenomena, and joining in with it all as a species of amusing game. Just because this occurs during any given outbreak, it does not *necessarily* mean that the polt itself is not real.

One of the first to realise this counterintuitive fact was Sir William Barrett, another early member of the SPR, Professor of Physics at Dublin's Royal College of Science, and the natural counterpoint to his colleague Podmore's sceptical views. Writing in Volume XXV of the SPR's *Proceedings*, Barrett had this to say:

> If upon the cessation of the disturbances, investigators appear upon the scene and ask for something to occur in their presence, and are sufficiently persistent and incredulous, they may possibly see a clumsy attempt to reproduce some of the phenomena, and will thereupon catch the culprit child in the act. Then we hear the customary 'I told you so', and forthwith the clever investigator will not fail to let the world know of his acumen, and how credulous and stupid everybody is but himself ... In cases of poltergeists, children are usually the centre of disturbances, and the superficial or prejudiced observer, knowing the love of mischief among children, and that in his and nearly everyone's experience, objects *don't* jump about without an assignable cause, naturally comes to the conclusion that any supernormal explanation is needless and absurd. But this *a priori* argument, which satisfies the man in the street, completely breaks down when a critical and historical study of the whole subject is made.[17]

Take a 1941 case from Cornwall, involving a nine-year-old boy. Some busy-body spied upon the child alone in the living-room, saw him throw a tin-can, and declared it was all a fraud – even though the very same tin-can then rose into the air and flew back at him by itself! As a test, his mother tied his hands behind his back with a belt and sent him into the scullery – whereupon pots, pans and chairs pirouetted around the room wildly of their own volition.[18] Via the selective use of evidence, Podmore and Barrett could each have made good use of this exact same haunting to draw entirely opposite conclusions. During one Indian case of 1928, in which stones were paranormally thrown in the presence of a young boy, his pockets were searched and found full of pebbles. Problem solved – except still the stones kept falling, even with the lad kept under close watch, with his pockets emptied out. His pockets searched again, they were full of stones again, even though he himself had demonstrably not put them there.[19] Tell Frank Podmore about stones being thrown in the presence of a youth whose pockets just happen to be full of stones, however, and what do you think he might deduce?

Undoubtedly, sometimes young scamps have been caught engaging in acts of definite hoaxing without any accompanying supernatural elements present. In 1857, a teenage girl named Baker was sent to prison for demolishing her parents' glass, crockery and furniture, simply because, by her own admission, they had grounded her. Her abortive attempt to blame the vandalism upon a ghost was unsuccessful in a court of law. Described as 'a very bad girl, exceedingly idle and dirty, and fond of wandering the streets to get into bad company', Ms Baker does sound like an archetypal Minnie the Minx-type who would indeed try to blame her actions on naughty poltergeists.[20] Beverly Allitt, the British nurse who infamously killed several hospitalised infants in 1991, had in her youth performed similar disturbed actions, setting curtains on fire and stabbing a knife through her bedroom pillow – both of which stupidities she tried to blame upon poltergeists.[21]

On the other hand, in May 1878 a fourteen-year-old servant girl named Ann Kidner was prosecuted by her employer, the Somerset farmer John Shattock. Loud knocking was heard upon Shattock's doors, a rick of straw was set ablaze, and items of furniture and crockery, together with a large pig trough, moved from their usual places. The lazy Podmore-esque assumption was made that Kidner, as a recent arrival on the farm, must have been behind events, and a court case was brought. Kidner did not plead guilty, however, and, as nobody had actually witnessed her performing any such actions, she was acquitted.[22] She was first accused of being the ghost by a policeman who happened to be passing by the blazing hayrick. Kidner was nearby at the time, so he marched her back to Shattock's farmhouse. Once inside, he witnessed dishes and loaves of bread 'wandering about the kitchen', and heard loud raps booming from inside the walls. Despite this, he still did not feel compelled to do anything but blame the child in the matter.[23]

Little thought is usually given to the feelings of the children who find themselves so unfairly persecuted. At Milwaukee in 1874 one particularly unlucky 'poltergeist-girl', named Mary Spiegel, was subjected to such unending scolding by her abusive parents after being dismissed from her position as a maidservant for attracting polt phenomena to her person that she was driven to attempt extreme measures. A contemporary report makes for particularly pathetic reading:

The girl cried and entreated, and finally hid herself in the woodshed, where her father found her, and by way of mending matters began to beat the unfortunate child. The next thing heard of her was that a man brought a poor, dripping, shivering creature up to the house, who turned out to be Mary. She had jumped into the river and tried to commit suicide. On being asked … her reason for doing this, she said she was hunted and hounded by everybody, and could not endure her life.[24]

During an 1835 haunting in Edinburgh, in the days before the term 'child abuse' had even been coined, a young and sickly girl named Jane Molesworth was tied up in a sack to prevent her from playing 'tricks' – to no avail. The scratchings, rappings, footsteps, rustlings and bed-movements which plagued her polt-haunted home continued nonetheless. As for Jane herself, she later died, 'hastened out of this world, it is said, by the severe measures used while she was under suspicion.'[25]

Another sad – yet also finally comic – example was an 1874 haunting from Illinois. Here, money vanished from a locked drawer, pictures fell from walls and stoves flung their lids at people. The resident housemaid, Margaret Corvell, was deemed responsible and, as a test, her hands were tightly held by investigators. While being held prisoner thus, a large crash was heard and the piano in the room went conspicuously walkabout. Still poor Margaret was accused of being the ghost. Under pressure she confessed to everything, even the thefts, 'except whatever had occurred when her hands were held.'[26] That's just beyond satire.

Historically, such correlations have been made most forcefully where teenage serving-maids are present during a haunting. The thinking goes that, being young and therefore inherently mischievous, and, furthermore, being disgracefully lower-class and wrenched away from within their family homes to labour away unhappily within an unfamiliar environment, they have quite naturally resorted to playing poltergeist either to draw attention to their plight, to get revenge against their snobby employers, or simply for the sheer devilish fun of it all.

The classic example occurred at Norfolk's Swanton Novers rectory in 1919, where strange showers of petrol, paraffin, methylated spirits, sandalwood-oil and water were pouring from inexplicable 'appearing points' on walls and ceilings before gushing down into the rooms below, a common motif of poltergeistery. As much as 50 gallons of oily substances were caught in buckets and eventually the vicar, the Reverend Hugh Guy, was forced to parcel up all his water-damaged possessions and evacuate home altogether; he described the oil-slicks as being akin to a 'downpour'.

Fortunately for the Frank Podmores of this world, the Reverend Guy had in his employ a fifteen-year-old housemaid, Mabel Louisa Phillipo. When Oswald Williams, a stage-magician, and his wife went out to Norfolk to investigate, they rapidly declared the house unhaunted. Mrs Williams hid in one of the rooms after her husband had left a glass of water out as bait, and, she said, saw Mabel come in, pick up the liquid and throw it across the ceiling. Triumphant, Mrs Williams jumped out and confronted the miscreant red-handed, with her husband later telling reporters: 'She admitted that she had done it, and finally the girl, after first denying her hoax, made a clean breast of the matter in the presence of the whole party, and burst into tears.'

According to Mabel herself, though, she had made no such admission. In her version, Mr and Mrs Williams had simply accused her of tossing water onto the ceiling when a wet patch had suddenly appeared there in the room before them: 'I was told that I would be given one minute to say I had done it, or go to prison. I said I didn't do it.' A few months later, Phillipo brought a legal case against Mrs Williams, claiming that she had 'time after time' struck her in the face and demanded she admit she was the ghost. Mabel's face, still bruised, was pointed to as evidence in court, but still the case was dismissed. Despite the fact that no little girl, poor enough to be working as a housemaid to a vicar, could possibly have afforded to buy 50 gallons of oil and petrol, and then made them cascade down – in a 'downpour', remember – inside a house which was before long swarming with architects, chemists and geologists, and in which *she was not even present* when all such flows occurred, it was still considered acceptable for her to be made the scapegoat.[27]

Once the Williams shouted 'hoax!' that was, officially, the end of the matter; even the SPR neglected to send any representatives out to investigate. But why, if the sensational details given above are in any way accurate, was it considered so plausible to so many that they were dealing with nothing more than the mischievous antics of a naughty adolescent, not those of a spook? Surely it is because, at root, their actions are the same. If they are distinguishable, then it is only in terms of scope and of scale. Little girls might well throw tumblers of water at ceilings for fun; but only poltergeists could pull a similar stunt with gallons and gallons of oil and paraffin. But if you don't believe in poltergeists, then this option is not open to you; and so, however implausible the feats are as being the acts of mere children, they simply *must* be attributed to them if you wish to be able to successfully uphold your pre-existing world-view.

* * * * *

It is not only sceptics who can fall into such traps of false-logic; many ghost-believers do so, too. Advocating the literal existence of disembodied souls after death, some theorists have naturally drawn the obvious conclusion that dead, invisible toddlers are responsible for the many childish pranks of poltergeistery. Consider the wonderfully outré haunting of a Scottish garage at Innerleithen between 2005 and 2009, where much of the phenomena centred upon the child-friendly sweets on sale; hundreds of Smarties would go whirling through the air like a swarm of chocolatey bees, while water would appear in mid-air before splashing down onto people's heads (or else fall to the floor in the shape of *square* puddles). The unseen ghost would frequently laugh at the trouble it caused, and make animal-noises on the forecourt like a boisterous toddler. It also developed an 'articulate, child-like' disembodied voice, all of which led understandably to the on-the-spot conclusion that the polt was the returning spirit of a five-year-old girl called Beth.[28]

Sometimes, actual visible child-like apparitions are witnessed, as at a Cardiff engineering workshop which was haunted for several years from 1988 onwards. Here, small items such as stones, nuts and ball-bearings would fly around, striking people but causing no harm, with keys of unknown origin repeatedly turning up about the place too. Phenomena even followed workers home, with cutlery being laid out on their tables while they were out, fruit disappearing from bowls overnight, and pairs of strange scissors being found embedded within curtain-racks and stuck into cornices. Often, the ghost would cause objects to materialise in response to requests. When someone said they could do with a pen, one might simply plop down out of thin air, while when a desire was expressed for some planks of wood, two heavy such articles were thrown instantly into the workshop. Naturally, the entity was asked to fetch some free cash – which it did, sometimes in shape of antique pennies and crowns, sometimes in spendable, current-tender notes.

The spook enjoyed rising to challenges. Workers would set it specific tasks, such as leaving a carburettor-float out overnight and daring the ghost to move it. When the worker who devised this test then went to a shop to buy cigarettes, he found the very same float handed back to him in his change! Given the nickname 'Pete the Poltergeist', the ghost became a minor local tourist attraction, a neat way to attract passing trade. Potential customers would arrive and ask to 'play with it'; the idea was to toss a few pebbles into a designated 'ghost corner', and ask the spook to return them, which it generally did. It would also drop 'clouds of fertiliser' onto customers' heads, causing them to run away without waiting for their change. If this sounds like a child at play, then perhaps it was. The shade of a small boy, wearing old-fashioned short trousers and peaked cap, was seen sitting on a shelf, while a rubber ball and teddy-bear kept in the workshop disappeared, only to later be found stashed away within a ceiling cavity after sounds

The Italian poltergeist-medium Eusapia Palladino causes a table to come to life and begin goose-stepping its way around the room, in the same basic manner as experienced by Sir William Barrett during the Kingstown haunting.

were heard emanating from within. The ghost-boy seemed to have no visible head; amusingly, one sceptical Podmore-like parapsychologist guessed this was because he was actually a tiny local prankster from an ethnic minority, whose dark skin just *looked* invisible under poorly-lit conditions![29]

In 1876, Sir William Barrett investigated a haunting at a country-house in Kingstown near Dublin. Here, ghostly bangs and raps centred upon the ten-year-old daughter of the household, Florrie. At first her parents thought Florrie was playing jokes, but circumstances speedily conspired to convince them this was impossible. In broad daylight Barrett, Florrie and her parents sat around a dining-table where they heard 'a sort of rubbing', then blows on the back of their chairs. The hands and feet of Florrie were closely observed; they were found 'perfectly still', even though sounds as if 'someone were hammering small nails into the floor' rang out all around. Curiously, 'The blows became louder when we began a cheerful song, or when there was music; they then beat time in a most amusing way and changed into a rhythmical scratching, as if a violin bow were being rubbed on a piece of wood.' Or, in other words, whenever the group were having fun and enjoying themselves, the phenomena increased in intensity. Eventually, Barrett tried communicating with the poltergeist:

We repeated the alphabet slowly, and the invisible intelligence knocked at each letter required to make an answer to the questions asked. We learnt in this way that the communicator was a little boy named Walter Hussey. Mrs C [Florrie's mother] told me later that when she went to say good-night to her daughter she often heard knocks and found Florrie chatting animatedly with her invisible comrade by means of this system. I made a note of some of the answers obtained, and they were such that Florrie herself could have made – merry and unimportant, the invisible intelligence corresponding to that of the child, also the spelling.

Given these facts, Barrett admitted some might say all such phenomena had simply been 'concocted by a mischievous child to make fun of a professor', but opined that the force he saw at work was 'much beyond' Florrie's childish capabilities. Sir William had some curious experiences with a large and heavy mahogany table, which began levitating to such a height that he could pass his feet beneath the gap between its legs and the floor. So weighty was this table that it could not be lifted 'without much difficulty, even by a clever and vigorous man', and certainly not by a small child. Another table-trick was even more remarkable. After it had begun jiving sideways of its own accord, Barrett requested the wooden quadruped raise its feet into the air. It did so; first with two feet, then the other pair, rearing up a full 8 to 10 inches above the floor. More remarkably yet:

I moved back to my chair and it advanced towards me (nobody touching it), and finally got right in front of my chair, so that I could not leave it. When it was under my nose it rose up several times, and I could convince myself by touch and sight that it did not rest on the ground, and that no human being could be directing its movements.

These activities of the living table, it seems to me, were essentially comic in nature; we can picture the scene quite vividly, with the eminent professor trapped there in his chair while it bounds towards him like an over-eager guard-dog. We can well imagine what young Florrie's feelings must have been when confronted with such a sight; no doubt she was delighted. Certainly, at no point does she seem to have been scared of her 'pet ghost'. These displays finally convinced Barrett of the reality of some kind of supernormal world. There was 'no doubt' in his mind that there was a 'hidden intelligence' behind these manifestations. 'This is an extraordinary affirmation,' he wrote, 'which destroys all the foundations of materialism.'[30] Indeed so. But in what precise way?

Barrett was a Spiritualist, one of twelve sitting on the SPR's first-ever Council in 1882 (there were six non-Spiritualist founding-members, too)[31] and he took the existence of the young and playful spook who called himself Walter Hussey for granted, in a literal sense. The disturbances at Kingstown seemed proof, to him, that the human spirit survived the death of the body – this was the sense in which 'the foundations of materialism' had been destroyed. Some unseen force plays silly little tricks at a country-house in Ireland – it can't be the actions of the only living child present, although she does seem to be a *spirit-medium* – and so it must be down to the actions of a dead one working through her, Barrett concluded. Obligingly, the poltergeist even specifically claimed to be just such a character, Walter Hussey; but was it telling the truth?

I think we tend to construct 'explanations' for the poltergeist largely by fitting observable phenomena in with certain pre-existing *a priori* assumptions we already hold about the world. For example, a materialist sees the tricks, but knows already (he thinks) that there are no such things as the spirits of the dead. Therefore, he says, the phenomena are all down to childish knavery. A Spiritualist, however, sees those very same phenomena and, knowing already that there *are* such things as the spirits of the dead (he thinks), says that, therefore, they must all be down to the invisible ghosts of young children. However, neither option might be true.

An alternative view, going under the label of RSPK, or 'Recurrent Spontaneous Psycho-Kinesis', holds the more moderated opinion that, while poltergeists *do* exist, they are *not* the spirits of the dead, whether under-age or otherwise. Instead, they are bursts of psychokinetic (often abbreviated to 'PK', the word meaning 'causing movement at a distance') energy, emanating from within the mind of a nearby individual, or 'focus', which they direct outwards, quite unconsciously, moving objects around, setting fires and so forth, much like in the film *Carrie*. A teenage American focus-figure named Tom Ross independently figured out a variant of the RSPK hypothesis for himself during his own early 1980s outbreak of poltergeistery, when he noticed he could successfully predict which objects were about to be moved next by virtue of them suddenly developing a 'halo' which made them 'pop up and kind of stand out from the background' and appear 'hyper-real' to him. This made Ross guess *he* was really behind the haunting, not a true ghost. He now tried deliberately causing objects to teleport via conscious willpower, but the experiment didn't work. Instead, once Tom realised what it really was,

A levitating child; the association of poltergeists with such juvenile 'focus-figures' has been jumped upon by sceptics to argue that all such hauntings are simply due to childish knavery.

the spook just faded away. Ross admitted to feeling strong urges to fake further phenomena via throwing things around by hand, not PK; another indication that such desires can potentially be expressed both paranormally and non-paranormally concurrently.[32]

The fact that the focus-figure often seems to be a teenager going through puberty, or perhaps with certain unresolved mental or emotional issues, is held up as the main reason why the poltergeist expresses itself in its characteristically immature and antisocial way. In the view of the parapsychologist Professor A. R. G. Owen, in his landmark 1964 book *Can We Explain the Poltergeist?*, such spooks are a form of 'conversion neurosis', wherein a troubled adolescent, standing confused upon the cusp of adulthood, seeks solace in the unconscious performance of psychic tricks which hark back somehow to the safer mental world of their childhood. This is what Owen has to say about the topic of poltergeist humour in light of this idea:

> ... its status in the hierarchy of wit is necessarily at the lowest level – that of the practical joke. Perhaps it can be understood as aggressive action of a mild kind. The victim is put in a comic situation and made ridiculous in some degree. To this extent we perhaps understand the pranks of the poltergeist as rebellion by the poltergeist-medium, so often the foster or stepchild, the servant-girl from a far place, or the misunderstood adolescent, isolated and resentful. Like neurosis itself, the practical joke represents regression to the small-boy level of behaviour. Some of the more unpleasant phenomena – jokes in bad taste, such as the flinging or smearing of dirt [i.e. shit] – possibly represent neurotic regression to yet more infantile levels.[33]

Some hauntings support such notions. In one modern-day London-based case, allegedly polt-penned notes appeared, saying things like 'look at me' and 'can't you see me, I'm here all the time'. Adults in the affected household, viewing the childish handwriting, interpreted this as meaning the resident schoolgirl had acquired a Walter Hussey-like ghostly pen-pal her own age. Investigators, however, noting the girl had been forcibly transferred to a strange new school by her mother and forced to live with a step-family instead of her own real father, felt such messages' contents were simply RSPK-produced 'cries for attention from her own subconscious' – the poltergeist complained about being invisible because that's how the child who conjured it felt too.[34]

The wife of Professor A. R. G. Owen, Iris M. Owen, was understandably a big fan of the RSPK hypothesis, so much so that, during the early 1970s, she and a mediumistic circle in Toronto made use of their own latent psychic powers to summon up the ghost of an entirely fictional person called 'Philip', conceived of as being an Oliver Cromwell-era aristocrat who committed suicide after his gypsy-lover had been unjustly burned at the stake for witchcraft. Amazingly, their experiment, as chronicled in Owen's oft-cited 1976 book *Conjuring Up Philip*, worked – a rapping, table-animating poltergeist claiming to be the wholly non-existent fellow did indeed emerge from the very ether.

For Mrs Owen, therefore, the Kingstown spook was not the ghost of a small boy named Walter Hussey, as it was to Professor Barrett, but, rather, a personified emanation of RSPK abilities from little Florrie, just like Philip was in relation to her own mediumistic circle. Mrs Owen compared Walter to an invisible childhood friend, observing how the ghost delighted in enjoying itself in the very same way a child Florrie's age would, beating out its raps in time to jolly music, for instance. She was further intrigued by how Walter had a similar spelling ability to Florrie's own, as the Toronto circle had also frequently noted that 'Philip is limited to the joint knowledge and experience of the group in his answers to questions'.[35] For Iris M. Owen, poltergeist phenomena reflect some facet of the immature mind of the generally adolescent or pre-adolescent focus-figure because, essentially, the 'ghost' *is* that mind – or some aspect of it – externalised.

Among most parapsychologists, this is now the standard first-option explanation, not the discarnate spirit hypothesis. In 1998, a polt appeared in the home of the Cobb family of Savannah, Georgia, overturning photographs and piling up stuffed toys in the middle of their fourteen-year-old son Jason's bed. The Cobbs, amused, dubbed the spook 'Casper', and left it crayons to communicate with. The friendly ghost obliged, saying its name was Danny, that it was seven years old, and that in 1899 its mother had died in the antique bed Jason had been bought immediately prior to the haunting's outbreak, and that as such the lad had better show some respect and start sleeping elsewhere. When Jason disobeyed, Danny threw an ornament at him. The bed was soon sold, but Danny stayed behind, scrawling out more infantile messages like 'Danny sorry' or 'Tell story'. He also gave Mr Cobb official written notice to stop smoking and filled in noughts-and-crosses grids, scribbling 'Ha ha! Beat you!' on them afterwards. When parapsychologists descended, the idea that Danny was who he claimed to be was instantly dismissed. Noting Jason would infallibly know just when Danny was going to pull another prank, it was quickly concluded the spook was living not within Jason's old bed, but within the RSPK-addled brain of the boy who had lately slept in it. As the ghost also sometimes claimed to be Uncle Sam, a figure no less imaginary than Iris M. Owen's Philip had once been, this conclusion may have possessed some merit.[36]

There are problems with the RSPK hypothesis providing any total, all-encompassing explanation for poltergeist phenomena as a whole, though. Children and adolescents aren't *always* present during polt-hauntings, although to listen to the deliberately misleading way some investigators speak you could be forgiven for thinking otherwise. Some have no focus at all, and are what is termed 'location-centred'. This is when we speak of 'haunted houses' rather than 'haunted people' (although in practice the two can often be difficult to separate).[37] Other spirits show knowledge of past and future events and possess impossible information which the focus-figure could have had no normally-acquired awareness of whatsoever. How are these facts to be accounted for?

A bizarrely ingenious variation upon the Owens' theories came from their colleague Dr Joel Whitton, a qualified psychiatrist. He had the curious notion that poltergeist phenomena typically occurred in such a childish fashion because they represented a regression back to infantile forms of 'magical thinking' on behalf of the focus-figure. As a small baby's mind will not yet have developed any capacity for rational or abstract thought, various mundane household events could very easily be misinterpreted by the infant as being down to mysterious supernatural forces, said Whitton:

> ... a baby may hear the footsteps of someone walking on a bare floor above his head. Looking toward the sound, nothing is to be seen. Not able to conceptualise the fact that the sound is simply due to someone's footsteps on the floor above the ceiling, or to someone moving furniture around, the memory remains in the baby as a strange, unexplained [poltergeist-like] experience.

If the baby is alone during their initial uncanny encounter, they might wish for the presence of their mother, thus experiencing what psychologists call 'separation anxiety'. This whole complex would then lie dormant and repressed inside the child's mind until he or she reaches adolescence, when poltergeistery is meant most typically to emerge. At this age, the focus would probably be suffering more anxiety about the rapidly approaching end of childhood. Subconsciously, this new fear becomes associated with long-forgotten events like the invisible footsteps once heard on the ceiling during babyhood and the focus' desire for maternal protection from such scary things. At this point, says Whitton, the original infant memories of the focus are 'relived or acted out, or externalised in the physical world' through RSPK, with genuine phantom footsteps now appearing around the family home. Such hauntings are thus no more than a form of anxiety-driven infantile regression.[38]

Whitton cites a case involving a twenty-two-year-old girl named Annette and her sister Joan, who was both younger and more attractive than Annette, and, unlike her, had a boyfriend. The relevant poltergeistery occurred when the girls' parents were away from home. During the adults' absence, phantom footsteps were heard, together with heavy breathing sounds appearing in Annette's bedroom, the door to which slammed shut and inexplicably could not be opened, before Joan's hair was tugged back by invisible forces. Whitton interpreted all this psychologically. Sibling envy over Joan's sexual success served as motive behind the ghostly hair-pulling, he said, while separation-anxiety directed towards her absent parents, particularly her sick mother who was shortly due to undergo a serious medical procedure, combined in Annette's mind to subconsciously dredge back up those long-forgotten spooky terrors of earliest babyhood. Instead of facing up to her looming fears consciously, they were realised by Annette in the outside world symbolically, through the RSPK-enabled performance of various regressively immature acts. For Whitton:

> The psychic ability to close the bedroom door, and the actual closing of it, is an event that can be used by the ego to symbolise and externalise a sexual conflict. The theory predicts that sometime in [Annette's] past the closing of a door, or some related event, became associated with this conflict. When the conflict is re-experienced or renewed, as it was during that week, the memory of the door closing is also renewed and that causes the individual unconsciously to actually close the door if the individual has PK ability.

When the stressful situation ends, the need for this curious symbolism to be expressed externally also ends, and the poltergeist, as it so often tends to, simply disappears, argued Whitton.[39] It's an ingenious theory; but, like much Freudian thinking, it has its flaws. How can it be *proven* that a closed door symbolised sexual conflict for Annette? And what of more elaborate polt-pranks than producing footsteps, slamming doors and pulling hair? How does Whitton account for those? He doesn't. While his theory might seem vaguely plausible in this particular case, for most other hauntings it would appear to have next to no relevance at all ...

* * * * *

In attempting to explain the poltergeist, in any universal sense, it may be that you are actually attempting to *explain away* the phenomenon. I do not think that poltergeists are, in any complete and literal fashion, the spirits of the dead, fairies, RSPK-events, demons or devils, or the funny tricks of naughty little children at all. You can find some individual cases wherein any of the above categories seem to explain events quite fully. And yet, you will never be able to shelter *all* outbreaks of poltergeistery under any such narrow single umbrella. As one poltergeist caught on-tape once admitted, 'I'm a mirror';[40] that is, the individual theorist can very often end up seeing little but himself and his own theories being reflected reassuringly back to him in such ghosts, as with the Freudian Dr Whitton.

Whatever they truly are, these things should not be trusted. In 1990, the McWethey family of the tiny Oklahoma hamlet of Centrahoma began suffering the unwelcome attentions of a stone-throwing spook which, after learning to speak English by watching TV shows (or so it said), developed a metallic-sounding voice. It made threats such as 'I'm going to paint your birds', before throwing food-colouring from the kitchen all over the McWetheys' parakeets, staining their feathers most motley. Then, it began claiming to hail from Saturn; the ghost had landed nearby in a flying saucer, it said, and been abandoned by its crew-mates. To 'prove' this tale, it pressed down some grass in the rough shape of a crop-circle, and drew the astronomical symbol for Saturn on mirrors with lipstick. And yet, for an alien, it gave an unusually Earthling-like name: Michael Dale Sutherland. How did the McWetheys account for such inconsistencies? 'Course, he lies a lot,' was the best explanation offered.[41] So do they all. Tricksters always have.

A surprising number of poltergeists develop disembodied voices, but the content of their messages is filled with conundrums, lies, contradictions, disingenuity and utter drivel – admixed confusingly with tantalising morsels of truth apparently derived from psi-powers of clairvoyance, precognition and telepathy. To cite an old Greek saying, 'Hermes leads the way or leads astray.'[42] The greatest of all Trickster-gods, Hermes was often said to be the guide of human souls, but the Greek word used to describe how precisely he *did* guide such souls means something more akin to 'lead on'; and, in English, to 'lead someone on' means to deliberately *mislead* them.[43] As such, it is remarkable, given some of the more loopily absurd identities poltergeists have adopted for themselves down the years, just how willing some still-living human souls have been to be so misled. In 1994, a family reported that a polt was plaguing their fourteenth-century Welsh home with phantom footsteps, ghostly smells of incense and sulphur, and a noise 'like a cat snoring', all while artificially inflating their electricity bills by methods unknown. They called in a vicar, who swiftly identified the unquiet spirit responsible. 'I've met a man who died at the end of the last century,' said the gullible clergyman during his visit. 'He's been stuck in a thorn bush ever since.'[44]

Communicating via spirit-raps, a 1950s poltergeist from my own neighbouring town of Runcorn once identified himself as a native African Devil-worshipper from the Impi tribe. He said his name was 'Jooker' – or 'Joker', in the broad northern accent of the region. Jooker quickly lived up to his name, soaking one victim with the contents of a comically exploding lemonade-glass until he was 'dripping wet'. Predictably, the spook did indeed become something of a laugh to many Runcorn residents. The local newspaper carried an advert showing Jooker as a bright and spotless white sheet-style spook, lingering outside his haunted home and remarking to an unwashed, greyer-hued companion, 'I use the new launderette in Church Street'.[45] *Joculatare* the ghost may well have been, but he was surely no African satanist.

*****

Some spooks' appearances are fantastic in the extreme – as we read on, we shall encounter the shades of a giant yellow three-legged dog, a man with the head of a cow, and a dead pensioner obsessed with the menstrual cycles of young women. When you read about them, you will be sorely tempted to laugh. Just like an alien called Michael, they are so implausible and unlikely that they seem almost designed to *make* us laugh at them, or even to deliberately undermine the notion of their own reality in the first place. Throughout, therefore, I will not be taking these blatant liars' words at face-value. Rather than analysing poltergeistery by reference to ghosts *per se*, I shall do so in light of a rather more obscure quasi-supernatural entity; that of the Trickster, a figure of world mythology whose vital importance to our field has been picked up on by disappointingly few.

But what is this Trickster? Is he a real paranormal entity mankind has somehow forgotten about? No. He is more a mythological personification of certain tendencies in the human mind – the strange combination of cunning and stupidity to be found within our species, for instance, or the uniqueness of mankind's sense of humour. A full explanation of what the Trickster is, and how he relates to poltergeistery, shall follow soon. Suffice to say right now that, if you recall characters from mythology, literature and popular culture as diverse as Hermes, Loki, Odysseus and even Roger the Dodger and Dennis the Menace, you will have some basic idea of what kind of personality a Trickster-god is. If a dead child or rebellious maidservant really were to go around creating chaos beneath the nose of authority, then they would be acting just like one.

Just to be clear, I am not claiming that the poltergeist *is*, literally, the Trickster. There is no *real* Trickster. Roger the Dodger clearly isn't real, but neither is Hermes. He simply provides a convenient mythological prism through which it can be useful to view such naughty ghosts; much as, say, people have often found it useful to interpret Hillary Clinton's life in terms of that of Lady Macbeth. Clinton is not *literally* her imaginative counterpart; but, by considering her in light of such a figure, we do learn something new and useful about her actual real-world personality nonetheless. This is what I shall seek to do with my own analysis of the poltergeist in terms of the Trickster.

I believe the stories detailed in this book show us that the figure of the Trickster is actually, quite contrary to expectations, still alive in the folk-beliefs of the twenty-first century – in the mutated form of the poltergeist. Nobody but a lunatic believes in Loki anymore; but quite a few *do* believe in polts. I believe in them myself. Many of these spooky yarns (or truthful accounts, depending upon your viewpoint) feature several motifs in common with early Trickster-narratives from world culture, and these shall be examined at length. Maybe Loki and Hermes have just changed their names recently, possibly even to such unlikely monikers as Michael Dale Sutherland, late of the planet Saturn? Perhaps it would be best to just dub them *all* 'Jooker' and be done with it.

CAVEAT LECTOR

How True Are These Tales?

I cannot say that truth is stranger than fiction, because I have
never had acquaintance with either.

Charles Fort

This book is about the *imaginative function* of the poltergeist as much
as about the spooks themselves; and their main function, I feel, is to be
humorous agents of Tricksterism. By playing tricks upon us, poltergeists
reveal our current world-view to be in some way incomplete, breaking the
accepted circle of logic and provoking laughter at their audacity in doing
so. Even if some stories should turn out to be just that – *stories*, false and
fabricated in their entirety – then, *as stories*, they still fulfil that very same
imaginative function, much as a fairy tale, while not literally true, can still
hold some profound moral, poetic or other truth in it.

As such, I take the vast majority of accounts presented throughout at
face value. I have made zero attempt to interview witnesses or hunt down
any polts myself. For the purposes of this present book, it is often almost
irrelevant whether certain specific hauntings detailed within it did or did
not truly occur. What interests me just as much is that they were *reported*
to have done so. Even if there were no such things as poltergeists, it would
still be a profoundly interesting fact that mankind has chosen to *imagine* that
there should be, and then to report ostensible instances of them appearing,
time and time again, over hundreds and hundreds of years. As the Victorian
folklorist Andrew Lang once put it, 'We do not so much ask 'Are these stories
true?' as '*Why are these stories told?*"[1]

So, even if you are the mental reincarnation of Frank Podmore himself,
I hope this book is still worth reading. You don't need to be a practising
Christian to understand the meaning of Christ's parables. For sceptical
readers, it could be approached less as a collection of 'true-life tales', and more
as a compendium of essentially fictional 'texts' to be read and interpreted for
what they show about their tellers, believers, and the wider societies which
produced and then either accepted or dismissed them. But what *do* these

The old American satirical magazine *Puck* – the rough US equivalent of *Punch* or *Private Eye* – adopted an image of the cherubic fairy-Trickster in question on its masthead, together with an appropriate quote from Shakespeare. The publication's contents perfectly captured the meaning of the term 'puckish humour'.

stories tell us, and why have they been so often told? It is my contention that the humorous aspect of such narratives – whether consciously recognised or not, as they often in fact aren't – are central to their long-lasting appeal.

* * * * *

One clear example of a noisy ghost's comic potential having already been successfully noted is that of the 'Drummer of Tedworth', the most quintessential English poltergeist narrative of all. The oft-told story centres upon the Wiltshire manor-house of a magistrate named John Mompesson which became infested with various extreme poltergeist phenomena following the magistrate's rather unnecessary confiscation of a drum from an itinerant beggar, busker, forger, thief, con man, conjuror, tinker, Trickster and general ne'er-do-well named William Drury in 1661. Sentenced to deportation, Drury escaped from captivity, but not before having sworn his revenge, which he unleashed upon his adversary in the form of an invisible 'Demon Drummer', which produced loud tattoos from the sky around Mompesson's home as if the beggar's impounded drum were playing itself to death in ironic retribution. Even though Mompesson had the item taken out and burned, still the rhythmical rapping continued.

The basic narrative fulfils many of the criteria for a typical Trickster-tale. The pomposity and conceit of a harsh, unyielding authority-figure in the shape of Magistrate Mompesson is fundamentally and humorously undermined, together with his dignity, while Drury himself can be viewed as an archetypal Trickster-type. Marginal and ostensibly powerless, eking out a precarious living on the very edges of society, he has sometimes been claimed, whether plausibly or not, to have had gypsy blood, or even to have been a Siberian shaman with the power to induce trance-hallucinations in his victims via the use of ritual drumming.[2] However he unleashed the extremely unquiet spirit, he certainly got one over on his oppressor in the end, in the cheering manner of the mouse that roared or David braining Goliath.

No known image of Drury survives but, interestingly, the print used by the most famous of all British ghost-hunters, Harry Price, to illustrate what he may have looked like in his comprehensive 1945 book *Poltergeist Over England* was of Richard Tarlton, a kind of celebrity court-jester to Elizabeth I.[3] Tarlton died in 1588, but his ghost soon returned to pull further pranks from beyond the grave – in pamphlet-form, at least, with *Tarlton's News Out of Purgatory*, a curious parodic document, being published around 1590. Described by the pamphleteer as 'a mad, merry companion, desired and loved of all', Tarlton, like a model Trickster, was known for being a cunning fool, always getting into antic scrapes against superficially more formidable opponents (here, Death himself) only to then improbably escape from them via a characteristic form of clever stupidity.

In the pamphlet, Tarlton invades the dream of a man dozing in a meadow, and urges him not to be scared by explicitly identifying himself with the known fairy-Trickster Robin Goodfellow, spoken of by Shakespeare in *A Midsummer Night's Dream* as enjoying spoiling butter and milk and removing stools from beneath people's rears when they sit down. As Tarlton's spirit, 'artificially attired for a clown', says, 'think me to be one

The Elizabethan jester and Trickster Richard Tarlton emerges from purgatory with his pipe and drum; the original model for the Drummer of Tedworth?

of those *familiars lares* [playful hobgoblins/fairy-poltergeists] that were rather pleasantly disposed than endued with any hurtful influence, as Hob Thrust, Robin Goodfellow, and suchlike spirits'. Tarlton then addresses a major theological controversy of the day by confirming, from direct personal experience, that Purgatory does indeed exist. It is within just such a realm he currently labours, working off his sins in the way deemed by the Judges of the Dead to be most appropriate. Namely, says Tarlton, 'because they knew I was a boon companion, they appointed that I should sit and play jigs all day on my tabor [drum] to the ghosts without ceasing.'[4] This makes him sound rather like Tedworth's own Tricksterish Ghost-Drummer, does it not? No wonder Price chose to use his image.

This whole comic nexus was later exploited by the writer Joseph Addison in his 1716 play *The Drummer, or, the Haunted House*. Although directly based upon the Tedworth incidents, Addison's plot isn't particularly true to life. Due to several unreasonably sceptical presentations of the case being made in print, the Drummer had become a byword for fraud, farce and fakery by the time of Addison's play, so he sets out to make it a Georgian version of *Scooby Doo*, with the drumming 'ghost' being but a human in disguise. To Addison, the very idea of a genuine ghost was, in his Enlightenment times, a matter fit only for humour in itself. 'Though with a ghost our comedy be heightened,' he promised in the prologue, 'Ladies, upon my word, you shan't be frighten'd.' To believe in the reality of the Demon Drummer was now a mere byword for regional backwardness among the metropolitan elites at whom the play was aimed. ''Tis the solitude of the country that creates these whimsies; there was never such a thing as a ghost heard of at *London*, except in the play-house,' one character says. Happily, Addison's work was a complete commercial failure.[5]

The Drummer provides an early example of how the literary and media industries have exploited allegedly genuine poltergeist hauntings for entertainment purposes. Financially successful Hollywood franchises like *The Amityville Horror*, *Poltergeist*, *The Conjuring*, *The Entity* and *The Exorcist* are all supposed to have been 'based on a true story', as they say, although not very closely.[6] You would think that, by promoting such films as being based on fact, Hollywood is simultaneously promoting belief in ghosts among cinema-goers, but actually, by massively exaggerating supposed real-life events to the extent of obvious absurdity, and then mis-labelling them as based upon literal truth, they actually subtly reinforce the idea that such things are *not* real.[7] Watch *Poltergeist* and, while you'll see reasonably well-reported things such as chairs being stacked on top of tables by invisible hands, you'll also see a little girl getting sucked inside a fuzz-screened television set, for example.

But the issue is even more complicated, as sometimes details from real-life hauntings are used in fictional films and then re-appear again in subsequent real-life hauntings too, due to their victims having seen these same fictional films featuring such motifs. The idea of a haunted house being built on an old Indian burial-ground is familiar to most people from the Steven Spielberg-produced 1982 movie *Poltergeist* but actually has its origins in a haunting which erupted in Tennessee in 1817 involving a particularly notorious polt known as the Bell Witch. This affair probably began as a genuine outbreak of poltergeistery but the tale became taller and taller with each retelling, eventually standing as part-fiction, part-fact; just like the 2005 film later based on the case, *An American Haunting*. The haunting upon which the movie *The Amityville Horror* was based was supposedly also a true one – although generally now thought to have been faked – and was blamed by certain ghost-hunters at the time upon the 'real-life' haunted house being built upon sacred Indian soil too. By the time *The Simpsons* got around to lampooning the whole idea with their very first *Treehouse of Horror* Hallowe'en special, the very notion had become parodic, a stereotypical Hollywood absurdity ... even though it was all based upon initial alleged fact in the shape of the Bell Witch. Indeed, there are still new US cases which pop up even today, in which dead Native Indians are in all seriousness blamed by their victims for causing poltergeistery – but, now the very notion has become a standard comic one, who would believe it? 'You just got that from *The Simpsons*,' a sceptic might reasonably scoff.[8]

Although unsuccessful, Addison's *The Drummer* has since had many imitators. From the earliest days of cinema, images of ghosts have been used to inspire a certain comic brand of scepticism among movie-goers. Prototypical *Scooby Doo*-like tropes can be seen in comedies and melodramas such as 1914's *The Ghost Breaker*, in which a castle is subjected to a fake haunting in order to aid theft of hidden treasure, 1916's perfunctorily-titled *Bogus Ghost*, or 1926's *Shivering Spooks*, in which a gang of kids unmask a fraudulent Spiritualist. The silver screen's most celebrated funny men quickly got in on the act too. Laurel and Hardy's *Habeas Corpus*, Buster Keaton's *The Goat* and Harold Lloyd's *Haunted Spooks* all feature the classic image of silent-movie morons being terrified by men dressed in sheets or covered in white substances like flour.[9] Once *Scooby Doo* himself later hit TV screens, some sceptics actually hailed the cowardly canine as providing a genuine public service to society; by indicating to children that all ghosts/vampires/werewolves/mermen/living skeletons/Egyptian mummies were really men in rubber suits, it was argued that the cartoon inculcated early belief in the materialist dogma of scientism.[10]

Every week, *Scooby Doo*'s villains proclaimed that they 'would have gotten away with it if it wasn't for those pesky kids' who accompanied Scooby across the USA in their flower-powered Mystery Machine; but in sceptical accounts of poltergeist cases, both in real-life and in the media, this situation has become reversed and pesky kids are now unmasked by courageous adults as being the true faces behind fake hauntings. If you choose to present a 'true-life' haunting in a comic or ludicrously sensationalised light on-screen or on-stage, it might be argued, as Addison did, then this fictionalised debunking effect is only heightened. But what happens if, while ostensibly real like the Drummer of Tedworth, a haunting is *already* somewhat comical, Tricksterish, unlikely and absurd in many of its respects?

Take the poltergeistery which supposedly played out after three newly-wed American couples, the Murphys, the Nelsons and the Chapmans, embarked on a communal honeymoon together in February 1917.[11] The couples rented a house in Santa Ana, California, for (as is customary in such cases) 'an absurdly small sum'. Quickly, phantom footsteps burst out and taps were turned by hands unseen, while doors slammed or opened of their own accord and ice-cold breezes blew about the rooms. One new bride was thrown to the ground by an invisible assailant, twisting her ankle. A summoned doctor, knowing the house well, said such incidents were not surprising.

The sounds of an unseen wagon, with shod hooves and jingling harnesses, were then heard, the invisible scene culminating in a fierce argument between two angry men, a real-life radio-play that was repeated across the airwaves constantly. The old rusted-up windmill at the back of the house began to emit a noise as if turning, though in fact it was not. The thud of a body falling down to the ground then rang out; a man had indeed descended from the structure to his doom years beforehand. In the basement, one husband was knocked from a box while reaching towards a high shelf, with some hidden thing 'sighing and panting like a giant bellows' down there beside him. The merely melodramatic soon became positively unbelievable. One day, the new Mrs Murphy's grandparents, the Woodruffs, came to visit. Mrs Woodruff was psychic. She could make furniture levitate. She could also speak to the ghost of a nice blonde lady whose portrait hung above the fireplace, who explained she had been poisoned in an upstairs bedroom. However, their chat was rudely interrupted by a horrid ginger beast which tried to strangle Mrs Woodruff on the floor, cutting her neck all over: 'It was as big as a man ... [with] orange hair standing out from its head, stiff and wiry. Its hands curved into talons. The arms were like a man's, but covered with orange hair.' After one bride nearly got her toes bitten off by a giant bat, which then escaped by smashing through a window, everyone finally decided to leave, and a good job too; the house promptly spontaneously combusted. But the ordeal continued. Many years after Old Mrs Woodruff had died, several family members went to stay on her old ranch. One, named 'Uncle Jim', came downstairs one morning and claimed he had seen a 'thing' with orange hair poke its head out of a storage room, before bothering him in his bed. Uncle Jim was laughed at; until, not long afterwards, he died.

In 1948 one of the original honeymooning couples, the Murphys, arrived on this same ranch for a holiday together with their nine-year-old grandson, Mike. One night at 3.00 a. m., Mrs Murphy awoke to find something shuffling towards Mike; it was the orange-haired orangutan monster. It had 'a grinning mouth with huge, yellow teeth' and its eyes were 'almost hidden in a series of mottled lumps'. It lunged towards Mike, and Mrs Murphy began wrestling with it. Mr Murphy turned on the lamp. The creature backed away from the light before stumbling away through the doorway, leaving behind a sickening stench of decay. As it did so, Mrs Murphy was just able to see the crowning absurdity of the entire case; the entity was wearing 'a light-coloured, tight-fitting one-piece suit of a thin material which ended at the knees and elbow.' It was never seen again – if, indeed, it had ever really been seen at all.

*****

This is total nonsense. And yet, taken element by element, each and every aspect even of this obviously invented story has its direct parallels within various other, apparently more plausible, hauntings. Phantom footsteps, slamming doors, self-operating taps, cold breezes, disembodied voices, violent assaults by invisible hands, the supernatural raising of fires – you can find all of these phenomena spoken of elsewhere. There is even one case on record in which another ghostly humanoid orangutan was supposedly seen; albeit not one wearing a tight-fitting one-piece suit.

This wonderfully odd tale comes in two parts, both centring upon a former Scottish Gas-Board worker named John Adams. Sometime during the 1970s, John was working at a gas-storage station in Kilmarnock, so he testifies, when stones flew around the yard and keys disappeared, later turning up hidden away inside cracks. At Adams' next workplace in Lanark, messages were scratched onto walls. They read 'Rocky' (Adams' nickname) and 'freend'. Intrigued, Adams asked the spook questions, ambled away around the site's gas-tank, and then returned back to where he had started; by now, an answer to his query would have appeared, signed either 'Jonathon' or 'JV'. Moving on to work in Motherwell, Adams was startled to see a newspaper float down from the sky bearing these same initials together with the image of a skull-and-crossbones – the ghost's new 'tag'. Milk-bottles and pick-axes were then hurled around, narrowly missing contractors, while every day as they drove home it felt as if some strange force was trying to pull the workmates' van backwards.

Back in John's Glasgow flat, curtains billowed out at ninety-degree angles on windless days, Rubik's Cubes solved themselves, furniture was vandalised, an iron flew into a visitor's face, a glass whiskey-bottle became ground down into grains of sand and a model pirate-ship made entirely from matchsticks materialised from nowhere, alongside notes bearing the word 'WHY?'. Uniquely, the polt tried communicating via foodstuffs, arranging piles of peas into question-marks on the kitchen floor, or causing spaghetti to flop onto table tops, tangled up into yet more piratical skull-and-crossbones. (To save time, why did Adams not just buy Jonathon a tin of Alphabetti Spaghetti?) Even when John visited his local pub, coins hopped around and fell into pint-glasses, making them foam. One of his friends bought some smokes from a cigarette-machine, opened the packet, and found a message from Jonathon inside, waiting to be read. Eventually, a series of loud hammer-blows rang out around John's place for hours on end one day before suddenly stopping, at which point the ghost abruptly disappeared.[12]

In October 1995 Jonathon returned, announcing himself with more mysterious bangings before dragging his victim out of bed and throwing him about, together with furniture. Via automatic writing, Adams made contact with various entities claiming to be demons, and even a group of self-professed aliens, who talked about a UFO crash in Arizona in 1961. One entity said he was an angel called Ibeza, warning Adams about the pirate-obsessed Jonathon. Eventually, Adams started seeing weird apparitions haunting his home, including a humanoid figure created from red-and-blue strands of electricity, and a repulsive orangutan … with a human face.[13]

Now, you can believe this story or not; the only witness testimony we have is that of John Adams himself, and it would hardly be unreasonable to conclude he was deluded. Again, though, we come up against the fact that, while taken as a whole it seems positively amusing in places, virtually each and every individual aspect of it has been reported from elsewhere, frequently by multiple witnesses who seem fairly level-headed and reliable in nature. There is, therefore, to the open-minded reader a real problem which presents itself when trying to assess whether or not individual poltergeist cases are real or simply a load of mad, made-up twaddle: that poltergeists, when you consider the full range of stories told about them down the years, can apparently do just about *anything*!

We laugh at tales of supernatural spaghetti forming pictures of pirate-flags, and yet consider the far more well-attested case of the Enfield poltergeist during which, as we shall later see, a teenage girl apparently passed through a solid wall in her bedroom one day. If a polt really can do a thing like that – and many knowledgeable commentators happily accept that they can – then why on earth should one not also be able to draw skulls with spaghetti? Which, really, is the more impressive feat? The problem is that if a poltergeist can do literally anything, than literally *anything* can be attributed to one, whether by genuine witnesses or outright liars. I must admit, then, that at least some of the stories discussed in this book are bound to be absolute rubbish.

Most standard small-scale poltergeistery is really rather easy to fake; anyone can drop a plate or throw a tea-cup. In September 2014, a French housewife named Chantel Hachette made headlines after a State Prosecutor appeared to accept her sensational claim that the ruination of her living-room had been perpetrated by a poltergeist. Mrs Hachette's husband heard crockery smashing below and came downstairs to find the living-room wrecked. The police being called out, puzzled *gendarmes* witnessed a TV set fall from its stand. Mrs Hachette spoke of ghosts, and the authorities seemingly believed her – until the fifty-eight-year-old housewife admitted to having trashed the room herself in a fit of domestic pique, before enlisting the help of her twelve-year-old nephew to push the TV over when nobody was looking, hoping to pass her own handiwork off as that of ghosts, not a violent temper.[14]

Some hoaxers can be both very committed and rather ingenious. The prominent SPR man Tony Cornell investigated one case in which a man went so far as to slice his body hundreds of times all over with razor-blades and set his own home on fire, before blaming both acts upon spirits in a misguided attempt to gain sympathy from his stepchildren. In another case, an elderly hoaxer faked poltergeist phenomena to scare off his unwanted daughter-in-law from the family home. By rigging up 'a noisy contraption' consisting of 'two tin mugs, an iron bar and a biscuit tin with two wooden balls in it' beneath some floorboards and then pulling on a hidden wire, the old man produced loud polt-like bangs in the despised relative's bedroom, in sure knowledge she had a severe phobia about ghosts.[15]

Further muddying matters is the way that, in certain pre-twentieth century cases especially, initially genuine events later came to acquire accreted layers of pure folkloric invention, as with the Bell Witch. Consider the 'Baldoon Mystery' of 1829–30, when a farmhouse in Baldoon, Canada, was bothered by a spook that specialised in hurling bullets, stones and other items through windows. Knives were thrown, burning fireballs flew about, dishes levitated and furniture tipped itself over, all while a sinister black dog appeared atop the haunted house's roof. Supposedly, all of the above is true.

What is categorically *not* true, however, is that a psychically gifted teenage girl subsequently visited the farm, had a vision, and announced that a shape-shifting witch was cursing the property in the form of a goose. This goose being shot in the wing, the guilty sorceress developed a broken arm, and the haunting ceased. The motif of the 'wounded witch' is a familiar one from global folklore (sometimes it is a werewolf whose true identity is revealed by such means) and was clearly only later invoked by locals as a neat way of providing the spooky story with a satisfying narrative conclusion. In reality, the Baldoon ghost, like most polts, just faded away at random.[16]

Throughout, though, I shall not dwell at any length upon which stories seem likely to be true and which do not. Instead it is simply presumed that, when the reader encounters stories of evil orangutan demons wearing one-piece suits and witches transforming themselves magically into geese, they will be able to operate their own judgement upon such matters. Take the prudish polt which haunted a house in Altrincham during 1984, where it delighted in arranging shoes and slippers in long rows when the householders' eyes were averted. The ghost itself was actually once seen; it was 4 feet tall, insect-like in structure and wore a black rubbery gimp suit stretching right over its body and face. Its domed head was far too large for its stick-thin neck – and, most bizarrely of all, it had a vastly extended chin, specifically described as resembling that of the late game show host Bruce Forsythe. Black Brucie disapproved of filth, however. When the man of the house played Scrabble on his PC, he liked to look through porn mags at the same time, to liven things up – but the computer would constantly produce words like 'NAUGHTY!' when it was its turn to make a word, as if to chide him.[17] Do you accept that? Even if it *was* true, most people still wouldn't believe it.

However, each particular report, even ones about porn-hating insectoid Bruce Forsythe-demons, has made it into the related literature, and so has, to some tiny degree, contributed to the wider *mythos* of poltergeistery. At the very least, many unsupported testimonies and anecdotes are interesting, entertaining or comic yarns; at best, their dissemination may have some influence upon how genuine poltergeist cases are subsequently perceived and then reported back to us by their experients. It is through hearing stories of polts at work, after all, that we learn to recognise one.

Which cases did I choose to include, then? Not *everything* could be mentioned, sadly; there are literally thousands of purported poltergeist hauntings on record, stretching back centuries, and from every inhabited land on earth. My solution was simple. I chose to address those cases which most interested me, and these were generally the most fantastic, weird and amusing, not necessarily the most reliably well evidenced. If I have the chance to talk about a trash-talking ghost-mongoose with human hands called Gef from the Isle of Man, or a haunted toilet in a dentist's surgery that starts telling people to move their fat arses off it when they sit down to defecate, then I would much rather take up those appealing opportunities than any others. You may not, as a result, accept absolutely *all* of the stories you are about to read – but, for that matter, nor do I.

* * * * *

This book should not be read expecting to find out the absolute truth about noisy ghosts; if the poltergeist fulfils any purpose, imaginatively, it may be to remind us that in an ultimate sense there *is* no truth. Whether you find this fact frustrating or amusing depends, I suppose, upon how well developed a sense of humour you have. While personally a believer, I couldn't care less whether or not you believe in ghosts yourself. I don't hide my opinions, but I am not a proselytiser, and many of my conclusions should be taken metaphorically, being *suggestions*, not definite *assertions*. Please, please, don't take all my ideas literally. Many are intended purely in the spirit not of 'This *is* true' but 'It might be interesting *if* this was true'. Being the god of language and interpretations, and from whose name we also derive the word 'hermaphrodite', Hermes the Arch-Trickster is largely what you choose to make of him, male, female, or something other in-between; spook or joker, true or false.

The biggest mistake we can make is in taking the Trickster literally – whether as a ghost, or as a god. He can only be approached in an ironic and participatory fashion if we hope to make any sense of him. No laws will hold him. To the historian of court jesters Enid Welsford, 'The Fool does not lead a revolt against the Law; he lures us into a region of the spirit where … the writ does not run.'[18] Our best approach towards understanding Trickster's ways is frequently just to laugh along with him and see whatever insights, alongside all the hilarity, this should turn out to bring. This is the participatory game into which we enter through our dealings with him. According to one view, 'Laughter, humour and irony permeate everything Trickster does. The reaction of the audience in aboriginal societies to both him and his exploits is prevailingly one of laughter tempered by awe.'[19]

Such an approach may be by far the most sensible method one could possibly hope to adopt when dealing with the paranormal. Unorthodox Zen masters – teachers of so-called 'crazy wisdom' – have sought to exploit this self-same similarity between absurdity and illumination. By subjecting their disciples to bizarre, ridiculous and pointless surprises and ordeals, or giving them amusingly paradoxical riddles called *koans* to solve, they seek to illustrate thereby the metaphorical similarity between the moment we suddenly 'get' a joke, and suddenly 'achieve' enlightenment.[20] Examined similarly, many poltergeist narratives, whether real or invented, can do much the same thing, functioning as a kind of uncanny philosophical *koans* themselves. 'Funny' and 'odd' are not partly synonymous for no reason, you know…

PART ONE

A Trick of the Imagination?
The Trickster and the Poltergeist

I never met with any question yet, of any importance, which did
not need, for the right solution of it, at least one positive and one
negative answer, like an equation of the second degree ... For
myself, I am never satisfied that I have handled a subject properly
till I have contradicted myself at least three times.

John Ruskin

The world is a comedy to those that think.

Horace Walpole

So much of our data is upon a godess that so much resembles idiocy
that to attribute intelligence to it may even be blasphemous.

Charles Fort

The poltergeist is a Trickster. The things he does fit perfectly into the template
of the kinds of things that Trickster-figures do all the time in the tales told
about them right across the world. When a spook or a fairy plays the clown,
it inevitably becomes the poltergeist. You can occasionally come across cases
in which a real-life polt is said to be the ghost of a puckish jester or clown
due to the childish nature of the tricks it plays, as in Muncaster Castle in
Cumbria, where even today typical ghostly japes are often attributed – with
some superficial logic – to the spirit of the sixteenth-century castle Fool, Tom
Skelton. I think this is too literal an interpretation of matters myself, but at
least it demonstrates that not everybody has always been wholly blind to the
humour of our subject.

I

The Haunted Mask

The Clandestine Insurgent Rebel Clown Army is looking for
fools and rebels, radicals and rascals, Tricksters and traitors, mutineers
and malcontents, to join its ranks.
Official recruitment page, ClownArmy.org

In 1920, the house of an Indian man named A. S. Thangapragasam Pillay was
persecuted by an invisible fire-raising spirit which left messages scrawled across
walls in the Tamil language. These largely consisted of threats such as 'Don't
you know that I am the King? I will not leave this house, whatever the inmates
do' and, most significantly, 'My name is Rajamadan. I will not leave you.'[1]
According to A. R. G. Owen, this Rajamadan was the 'chief mischief-maker in
the Hindu pantheon'[2] – in other words, a Trickster-god. Disregarding those cases
in which the spook implausibly professes to be the arch-Trickster Satan, I can
find no other direct parallels with this act of specific self-identification, though
I do sometimes wonder whether some truly ancient poltergeists may not once
have amused themselves by going around falsely claiming the names of Loki and
Hermes. It is an interesting thought; but what is a Trickster-god, exactly?

The term 'Trickster' was probably coined in 1885 by the American
ethnologist Daniel G. Brinton for use in his essay *The Chief God of the
Algonkins, in His Character as a Cheat and Liar*, although, Tricksterishly
enough, this etymology is sometimes disputed.[3] Whatever the label's origins,
the Trickster is that strange and rather wonderful figure found in all of
world folklore and myth, from the Norse Loki to the Greek Prometheus to
the Eshu Elegba and Ananse of Africa's Yoruba and Ashanti peoples to
Robin Goodfellow and Puck of the English to China's Monkey King and the
Raven, Blue Jay, Spider and Coyote of the various Native American tribes,
not forgetting Japan's Kitsune and Susa-Nö-o, and the *djinn*, or genies, of
Islam. We might also mention Brer Rabbit, Reynard the Fox, Odysseus,
the baby Krishna and the Devil himself, frequently depicted in folktales as
a paradoxically powerful simpleton just waiting to be fooled or cheated by
his intended dupes, the Prince of Lies himself successfully lied to by others.[4]

In later literature, in tales whose authors we actually know the names of,
he might be identified in the stock shapes of Pícaro, Harlequin and Machiavel,

or in the more specific guises of Melville's *Confidence Man*, Dostoyevsky's *Idiot*, or the titular *Crow* of Ted Hughes' own epic Native American-aping poem cycle of that same name. TV viewers may even have laughed along with him dressed up as Arthur Daley, Bart Simpson or Sergeant Bilko. Like the poltergeist, as with the travelling con man he so resembles, Trickster has many faces – and yet he is easily identifiable behind all these masks due to the essential way that he behaves. Often considered, in his original mythological shape, to be an allegorical personification of the mind of early man, he is a sort of half-human, half-animal creature, or often a talking animal with a human brain, who plays various half-hideous, half-amusing tricks upon both man and beast, commonly to his own ultimate disadvantage.

According to the psychotherapist June Singer, the Trickster fulfils an important psychological function in human affairs:

> He symbolises that aspect of our own nature which is always nearby, ready to bring us down when we get inflated, or to humanise us when we become pompous. He is the satirist *par excellence*, whose trenchant wit points out the flaws in our haughty ambitions and makes us laugh when we feel like crying ... The major psychological function of the Trickster-figure is to make it possible for us to gain a sense of proportion about ourselves.[5]

A mix-and-match list of common characteristics of Trickster-figures might include the following: they are liars, thieves and con men, engaging in habitual acts of deceit; possessing powers of prophecy, their predictions may be either true or false, or something in-between; they are outsiders, marginal to mainstream society; they display a sense of humour that is often of an extreme, bizarre or sick nature; they are part-human, part-animal in form, whether mentally, physically or both; they can be extremely, unpredictably, violent or murderous; they display an uninhibited or perverted sense of sexuality, being obsessed with scatological substances like shit, semen and blood; they are associated with magic, sorcery and shamans; they cross over into the lands of the dead and the gods; they are great crossers of boundaries; they display both extreme intelligence and extreme stupidity, often simultaneously; they violate taboos and disrupt the natural order of things, becoming situation-inverters, sometimes for good, sometimes for ill; they are inherently paradoxical and contrarian in nature; doing things in a somehow backwards fashion, they act as parodies of the natural order of things, embodying the old saying '*Demon est Deus inversus*', or 'the Devil is God upside-down'; they are associated with change and transition, not stasis and fixed order; they are frequently irreligious, having an avowed disrespect for authority; they are illogical in nature, not logical; they commonly seem insane and undifferentiated in their mentality; they are ambiguous, anomalous, oxymoronic and fundamentally confusing, often being two mutually contradictory things at once, kind and cruel, physical and non-physical, visible and invisible, male and female, real and non-real; they are shape-shifters and masters of disguise extraordinaire; they are greedy and have uncontrollable appetites, being in many ways quite child-like; they are both the messengers and the false imitators of the gods; they often have little regard for linear time, and may be able to alter or dissolve its usual rules; they are creative inventors with an innate facility for recombining things in unusual ways; they are kings of word-play; and finally, of course, they don't like obeying rules, so sometimes Tricksters might not possess too many of the above-cited qualities at all![6]

As archetypal figures, Tricksters are best thought of as being constellations of personality properties which cluster together; where one appears, you are more likely to get some of the others showing up too, thereby strengthening the overall archetype.[7] A con man has to be a good liar, for instance; and, habitually seducing people with his words, he may also transpire to be a good lover.

A basic definition of this inherently bewildering character can be taken from the American anthropologist Paul Radin, whose 1956 book *The Trickster* is a classic in its field:

> Trickster is at one and the same time creator and destroyer, giver and negator, he who dupes others and who is always duped himself. He wills nothing consciously. At all times he is constrained to behave as he does from impulses over which he has no control. He knows neither good nor evil ... He possesses no values, moral or social [and] is at the mercy of his passions and appetites ... Basically he possesses no well-defined and fixed form ... he is primarily an inchoate being of undetermined proportions, a figure foreshadowing the shape of man ... regarding his specific features we are, significantly enough, told nothing.[8]

As a simple working definition, Radin's words are both immensely useful and yet, to an illustrator, quite useless. You can't properly fully visualise him. Nonetheless, during various poltergeist hauntings, he may actually have been seen. Polts do manifest in visible apparitional form on occasion, although they surely come donning disguise. Many such motley costumes do sound rather Trickster-like in their nature. During one 1979 polt haunting in New England, the spirit appeared on the scene first in the shape of a small boy, and then in the more disturbingly inchoate vision of 'a humanoid ... a short, hunched, grotesque figure clad in black, with very large feet that seemed quite demonic' who taunted the affected family by talking constantly of 'really disgusting things' of a sexual nature and carving inverted crosses onto their backs.[9]

Even more reminiscent of what you might expect a real-life Trickster-figure to look and act like was the poltergeist haunting a converted Yorkshire farmhouse during the 1990s, where lightbulbs would explode, electrical equipment malfunction, inexplicable floods occur, doors open and close by themselves, locks be severely damaged and keys go missing, while pets died 'in mysterious circumstances'. According to chief witness Jackie Johnson, the spook responsible, occasionally visible in her bedroom mirror, was 'approximately 3ft 6in tall and hairy like a bear, but with human features ... Its back is hunched and its legs are piggy.' The polt produced 'a dirty, sweaty smell' whenever it was near, possibly because it was in a constant state of high arousal; Johnson would see its reflection, staring at her and bearing 'this great big erection' which it was attempting to push up into its mouth, seeking to auto-fellate itself. According to a visiting medium, the spirit – dubbed 'Beelzebub' – was 'a pre-Christian entity' and suffered from a bad case of schizophrenia, being nothing less than 'the manifestation of 101 souls'. Maybe this is why it also appeared on the property in a myriad of other forms, including a young boy 'with a strange glow around him and in ancient dress' and 'a man called Ted who carries a shotgun and protects the farm'.[10]

Tricksteresque talking animals, too, occasionally manifest during poltergeist hauntings – if Coyote or Raven were there, they could have a good gossip. A fine example might be the chatty cat encountered during the 1974 haunting of a home in Bridgeport, Connecticut. The polt-possessed feline, a family pet, sang songs and possessed three distinct separate voices, yelling things like 'Help!', 'Bye-Bye!' and 'Let me out you dirty Frenchman, you dirty Greek!' before going off on one, kicking doors and swearing 'like a sailor', allegedly. This same case also featured a swan ornament which talked to passers-by in a 'deep guttural voice' … and a lonely little girl who had developed the skill of ventriloquism. She would talk to her teddy bears, described as being 'her only friends', and then enjoy 'making it appear that they spoke back to her'.[11]

* * * * *

If the Trickster is very often a half-human, half-animal figure, then so occasionally is the poltergeist. When asked what it looked like, the 1950s Battersea poltergeist (both a habitual liar and an appalling grammarian) provided a handy written reply: 'POLT. BIG CLAWS, HAND AND FEET – MEN'S BODY'.[12] Whatever the ghost in question was, its tracks certainly weren't human; it once left behind four oversized handprints in a snow-covered yard, each with six fingers and one thumb.[13]

My favourite poltergeist of all time, Gef the Taking Mongoose, was also part-human, part-animal; his main victim, one James Irving, a 1930s farmer on the Isle of Man, once theorised of him that 'the body is animal, but the brain, or mentality, human', like Brer Rabbit or Reynard the Fox.[14] His front paws – or really, I should say hands – were certainly human. Irving once described the peculiar Trickster-animal apparition haunting his remote rural residence thus:

> Undoubtedly he is a species of mongoose, but whether a hybrid or not, I cannot say. He is light yellow in colour, [with a] long bushy tail, which is also light yellow, and the tail has a black or brown tuft of hair at the extreme end … His front feet resemble the human hand, and he appears to have three or four fingers and a thumb, and as he has taken hold of my fingers in his, I could tell that he possessed great strength.[15]

Head besides, of all the body parts to possess human-like versions of, hands are the ones which would allow Gef to set himself apart the most from the realm of beasts, as his opposable thumbs enabled him to grasp and manipulate tools, which normal mongooses generally can't; Gef is said to have scribbled his self-portrait using a pencil, and to have picked up small objects like pins and hurled them at Irving when 'vexed'. His hands were yellow, 'as large as a big doll's hands', possessed nails, and would wave through slits in the wainscoting, being 'very hard and cold to the touch'.[16]

This makes Gef sound like a solid, flesh-and-blood Trickster, but not very much like a poltergeist; but, when you consider that he was generally invisible, threw pebbles around, made rapping and scratching noises from within the walls where he lived and spoke in a disembodied voice, he clearly was and was not one simultaneously, just as he was both human and not-human at the same time. While sometimes admitting to being an 'earthbound spirit', or even 'the Holy Ghost', Gef disliked being called a poltergeist, but 'the greater the truth, the greater the libel' in Mr Irving's view.[17] In fact, Gef professed to be scared of phantoms and once requested a book of ghost stories kept in the haunted house be torn up; Mr Irving preferred to don a white sheet and spring a spooky surprise on his strange little pet. When Gef saw this 'ghost' appear, he screamed in fright then began sobbing with relief when Irving shed the winding sheet.[18]

Gef's actual mentality was possibly the most overtly Trickster-like of all the polts detailed in this book. His many bizarre, squeaky-voiced utterances have been likened to the catchphrases of an old-time radio comedian like Arthur Askey, with Gef shouting out comical nonsenses like 'Hard-boiled eggs! Nuts, crack them and eat them!' before bursting into song, cursing and laughter, then spitting on his audience and weeing 'a little stream of water' through holes in the wainscoting.[19] He was a childish attention-seeker who would keep the Irvings up all night 'with his talk, talk, talk, laughing and singing', but if told to be quiet would throw tantrums, shouting 'Nuts! Put a sock in it! Chew coke!' before thumping on the walls so loudly beds would shake.[20] At other times, he would spy on females getting undressed, providing humorous live-action commentary.[21]

Characteristically *joculatare*-like was his laughter, which was both constant and unhinged, like that of Batman's arch-nemesis The Joker. According to Mr Irving: 'Sometimes it resembles the tittering laugh of a precocious or mischievous child, at other times I would say it was the chuckling laugh of an aged person, and another … satanic laughter, or the laugh of a maniac'. He could beat his fist down in hysterics like a cartoon character, so strongly that plates would bounce up and down with the vibrations. Most peculiar was the time he decided to randomly list thirty to forty serious but amusingly named illnesses, from elephantiasis to gouty phlebitis and Barbados leg, each of which was interspersed with yet another hearty hellish giggle.[22] He would also dance noisily at the top of the stairs; play the mouth organ; ring gongs; eat chocolate, sweets, biscuits, sausages, bacon, potato pie, bananas and oranges; and throw balls and count the bounces.[23]

Gef was also a pathological liar – perhaps even to himself. His favourite fib was to claim he was telling the 'God's honest truth' on his 'word of honour', but he clearly wasn't.[24] Continually, he contradicted himself about who or what he was supposed to be. Sometimes he was a ghost, sometimes a physical animal, 'just a little, extra-clever mongoose'; sometimes he admitted to his actions but sometimes he said his minion spirit-servants, FEAR, FOE and FAITH, were responsible.[25] Gef's most recent chronicler Christopher Josiffe has suggested Gef may best be considered 'as a mirror who takes the various terms and theories used to describe him and throws them back at his inquisitors', being 'a shape-shifter in terms of identity, as well as of physical appearance'. Indeed, he only began claiming to be a mongoose in the first place in response to a letter suggesting he might be one, printed in a local newspaper![26] Earlier, he said he was a kind of man-weasel, or appeared around the farm in the shape of 'a very large [tail-less] cat, striped like a tiger' with 'an unusually large bulldog head' which vanished into thin air when pursued with a shotgun.[27]

While generally benign, Gef could also be capriciously violent, slaughtering hundreds of rats and rabbits which he then left out as offerings to his adopted human family, and when it was suggested another, more ordinary, mongoose might be brought to the house, he warned that 'I will kill it' as soon as it arrived.[28] He was also a thief, stealing biscuits from jars and leaving teeth marks in butter.[29] Maybe the dead rabbits, which the Irvings sold to local butchers for easy cash, were intended as recompense. Then again, said Mrs Irving, Gef 'likes praise and he has feelings'. When praised, he could be generous in return: 'He brought me a rabbit for my birthday.'[30] But if you criticised him, he could turn nasty on a sixpence. One neighbouring farmer implied Gef was a fake, leading to him calling the man a 'damned shit', and stealing away his turkeys and ducklings to slay. 'You don't know what damage or harm I could do if I were roused,' he squeaked. 'I could kill you all if I liked, but I won't.'[31] And, if Mr Irving ever tried to sell his haunted house to get away from this potentially murderous fiend, Gef boasted he would simply 'speak when the buggers are here' to scare potential buyers off by jabbering non-stop nonsense, rendering the home unsellable.[32]

Return to the inventory of common Trickster characteristics provided above, and you will observe that Gef ticks almost every category on the checklist, perhaps using a pencil held within his cold, yellow human hands. With typical paradox, he was both the most unusual and irregular, yet also somehow the most comprehensively characteristic, poltergeist of all time, a kind of 'Typical Freak', if you will. If you want a great insight into the classic Trickster-mentality, then you would be much better off simply buying Josiffe's highly amusing book about the funny little fellow than reading any more comprehensive academic tome of religious anthropology – and far more entertained, too.

*****

Equally suggestive in its part-human, part-animal shape was the bizarre entity (often sensationally described as a 'werewolf') seen during the much-retold tale of the Hexham Heads. There, a council-house in the north-east England town in question became bothered by poltergeistery after some small, and apparently cursed, stone heads of supposed ancient Celtic origin were dug up from the garden one day, unleashing a 'half-human, half-sheep' apparition into the haunted home. The excavated heads were actually non-ritual modern-day creations, but were sent off for examination by an expert in all things Celtic, Dr Anne Ross, who also received a free spook with her delivery. Strange noises erupted around the Ross household, the front door was found

The Native American Trickster Coyote in his characteristic form of a man with an animal's head; such an inherently hybrid creature was supposed to represent the intrinsically hybrid human-animal intelligence of early mankind.

unlocked and wide open for no reason, and both Dr Ross and her daughter saw what looked like a spectral man-beast lurking around the place:

> It was about six feet … high, slightly stooping, and it was black against the white door. It was half-animal and half-man. The upper part, I would have said, was wolf and the lower part was human. It was covered with a kind of black, very dark fur.[33]

To me, that sounds less like a werewolf, and more like a Trickster – namely, like the Native American Trickster Coyote, who is often depicted as being just such a man with an animal's head in illustrations. Such images are meant to depict the psyche of an animal trapped within the body of a primitive human being, a kind of Gef in reverse, but they also greatly resemble the stock images of werewolves used to illustrate the tale of the Hexham Heads in books about the paranormal.

* * * * *

Different classes of paranormal phenomena often blur into one another around the edges; you would expect nothing less from border-subverting Tricksters. Bigfoot-type 'manimal' beings, for instance, have sometimes appeared during poltergeist hauntings, as with an Australian case of 1946 in which a house suffered with heavy showers of stones and self-unlocking, self-opening doors, all while a bipedal humanoid entity described as looking like 'a bloody big gorilla or something' paid the property repeated visits.[34] Mysterious, out-of-place big cats, such as black panthers of the Beast of Bodmin variety, are also occasionally witnessed alongside polt infestations.[35] But then, Bigfeet and phantom big cats are also sporadically encountered in conjunction with UFOs too … as, indeed, are poltergeists. Are such things just coincidences, or yet more evidence of the inherently shape-shifting and multi-faceted Trickster archetype being at work?

Given its slippery and imprecise nature, what, therefore, is the point of the word 'poltergeist'? Well, you need a word for something in order to be able to think about it properly. However, the term is still somewhat nebulous. Rather like a Trickster, you can't quite define what precisely a poltergeist is, merely suggest a list of its common properties. A poltergeist is more a sort of roughly personified typology than it is anything else. A comment of the philosopher Bertrand Russell about the nature of electricity may help us here. According to Russell, as cited by the noted poltergeist expert Guy Lyon Playfair: 'Electricity is not a thing, like St Paul's Cathedral; it is a way in which things behave. When we have told how things behave when they are electrified, and under what circumstances they are electrified, we have told all there is to tell.'[36]

For Playfair, as for Russell, the poltergeist could oftentimes be defined as being 'not a thing, but *a way in which things behave.*'[37] Although Playfair did come to believe that evil spirits may be responsible for certain hauntings, here the poltergeist is seen by him more as a *process* than an *entity*. This is what Tricksters do; they blur the boundaries between things. Mankind's conceptions of invisible entities – or invisible processes, if you prefer – are constantly changing, and the poltergeist is our current envisioning of the ultimately ungraspable world of spirit. As one historian of the subject, P. G. Maxwell-Stuart, has put it, poltergeists 'form at once both a category of their own while belonging to several others.'[38]

The term 'hermeneutics' was coined eponymously after possibly the greatest Trickster of them all, Hermes, messenger of the Greek gods. Meaning 'the art of interpretation', hermeneutics allows anything to be considered a 'text' to be read, and its meaning thereby changed. This enables anything so analysed to become like the words in a poem, which embody both a literal meaning and a subjective, wider meaning beyond the literal. The poltergeist is similar; he changes his form and meaning too, apparently in response to the promptings and prejudices of his observers. If you want to develop your skills in hermeneutics then, outside of the realms of poetry and art, the poltergeist provides as good a test of your abilities as anything else.

The poltergeist is so rewarding in a hermeneutic sense because, as a whole, it stubbornly resists all attempts to impose a definitive identity upon it. Nobody has ever proved that *all* poltergeists are the spirits of the dead, or caused by the inadvertent emission of RSPK forces, and probably never will. Sometimes, ghosts can quite violently reject the identities people attempt to place upon them. Gef the Talking Mongoose himself once taunted his victims thus: 'Of course I know what I am, and you are not going to get to know, and you are only grigged ['vexed'] because I won't tell you. I might let you see me some time, but thou will never get to know what I am.'[39] For once, Gef was not lying!

* * * * *

One famous human Trickster was Odysseus, a direct descendant of Hermes according to Greek myth. He is sometimes dubbed *Odysseus polutropos*, or 'Odysseus of the many ideas', a description symbolic of the unique characteristics of man as an animal. Most other creatures only do one thing well – beavers build their dams, spiders spin their webs – but man alone can imitate the other animals, stealing and refashioning their abilities into ones of his own (the spider's web becoming a fishnet, and the dam the basis for a reservoir). Early man, when he evolved into 'man the hunter' became a kind of Trickster himself; his techniques for hunting were not his own, but stolen. His identity became what is termed 'polytropic'; it was constantly shifting. For primitive man, in the words of the perceptive Trickster-scholar Lewis Hyde, 'there is no real self behind the shifting masks ... the real self lies exactly there, in the moving surfaces and not beneath.'[40] 'Having no way,' Hyde adds, 'Trickster can have many ways.'[41] So can the poltergeist.

The polytropic nature of the Trickster-figure, for the anthropologist Paul Radin, is partially explained by 'vague memories of an archaic and primordial past, where there as yet existed no clean-cut differentiation between the divine and the non-divine', a period for which 'Trickster is the symbol.'[42] What Radin means is that Tricksters, in their many story cycles, seem to have inseparable qualities of gods, men and animals. In such legends, Trickster possesses so many wildly contradictory characteristics that he ultimately has no stable root identity of his own. He is 'undifferentiated' in nature; his personality is not stable, he is not yet fully 'man' as opposed to 'god' or 'beast'. Because of this, says Radin:

> The symbol which Trickster embodies is not a static one. It contains within itself the promise of differentiation, the promise of god and man [as separate beings]. For this reason every generation occupies itself with interpreting Trickster anew. No generation understands him fully but no generation can do without him ... for he represents not only the undifferentiated and distant past, but likewise the undifferentiated present within every individual.[43]

In a similar way, perhaps the poltergeist-Trickster is no more than some form of temporarily personified concept allowing us to see disparate connections between seemingly different things – between Bigfoot and ghosts, for example, or UFOs and hauntings. This undermines the idea that any of the specific purported universal identities for the poltergeist, whether fairy, demon or impersonal product of RSPK, are ultimately true. If the poltergeist's true reality lies not in the specific mask, but in the polytropic *shifting* between such masks, then he could be best thought of, overall, as being a nexus rather than as a discrete, separate thing in and of himself.

There is a marvellously symbolic-sounding story which might be cited here. On 1 November 1978, having just held a Hallowe'en party, one Reverend Harrison E. Bailey of Pasadena, California, was purportedly awoken by two 'white, humanoid forms' hovering outside his bedroom window. When they entered, Bailey reached for his camera. As he snapped away, an interesting phenomenon took place; the beings 'began to lose their humanoid form and become wizened, rather like deflated siren-suits made of muslin' or popped balloons. The clergyman's photographs appear to show the weird appearances 'in various stages of deflation.' To avert this catastrophe, the entities positioned two Hallowe'en masks from Bailey's party over where their faces should have been, trying, somewhat desperately, to stabilise their form! It was no use. Before long, both apparitions gave up the ghost and shot away through the ceiling in the shape of 'whirling globes of light'.[44] Masks – just empty masks, with nothing there behind them. Formless, the things tried to hide behind the nearest protective scaffold they could find; but the masks, as always, were false, and soon fell away.

However, if you choose to view the poltergeist as simply being a kind of spooky nexus, or an undifferentiated chaotic mass of opposing antinomies – as a convenient label for the ultimately unknowable, in other words – then such problems as faced by the Reverend Bailey's spooks (which he in fact thought were aliens) might somewhat disappear. Consider the ninety-nine names of Allah in Islam. There, God is also thought of as being essentially unthinkable other than as some kind of all-encompassing nexus. This is why some of His many monikers appear self-contradictory, such as The First and The Last, or The Manifest One and The Hidden One. Nonetheless, this incommunicable, necessarily self-contradictory notion of God is still, for ease of reference, personified by Muslims as Allah. Allah, however, is *not* simply the name Allah! A similar undifferentation can be found in the Jewish god Yahweh. His name seems not to have any plausible etymology. *Ehyeh ašer ehyeh* (I Am that I Am), is the explanation presented in Exodus 3:14, uncomfortably close to Popeye's declaration: 'I Yam what I Yam!'

The great psychologist C. G. Jung once described the Spirit Mercurius, a Trickster-figure often interacted with by Renaissance alchemists, as follows:

> Mercurius truly consists of the most extreme opposites; on the one hand he is undoubtedly akin to the godhead, on the other he is found in sewers ... He is ... named a unity in spite of the fact that his innumerable inner contradictions can dramatically fly apart into an equal number of disparate and apparently independent figures.[45]

This is also why the similarly nebulous figure of the Trickster can be so useful to us when trying to think about the paranormal. According to the American parapsychologist and innovative Trickster-theorist George P. Hansen, 'The Trickster demonstrates the power of personified thinking. He is a personified concept, and it is through him that common patterns in so many diverse areas can be recognised.'[46] It is the same, I have been arguing, with the poltergeist; each figure mirrors the other, and it is through examining the perplexing interplay and dance of their twin reflections that we can come to better understand them.

* * * * *

In his seminal book *Daimonic Reality*, the writer upon mystical matters Patrick Harpur talks similarly about crop circles, using such (human-made, in truth) phenomena to suggest that all strange anomalies are in some sense but alternative manifestations of one another. Discounting fakery, we have many competing natural or supernatural theories as to crop circles' possible manner of formation; whirlwinds, so-called 'plasma vortices', UFOs and fairies. But Harpur shows how these are all just reflections of reflections, as in a fairground Hall of Mirrors.

Whirlwinds are often associated in folklore with fairies – they were meant to travel in them. But fairies are also imaginatively related not just to whirlwinds, but also to UFOs, through their commonly perceived status as strange dancing lights in the sky, like jack-o'-lanterns and will-o'-the-wisps. So fairies can be said, in an imaginative sense, to mediate between whirlwinds and UFOs. Plasma vortices then complete this circular nexus – they are also a kind of whirlwind, imagined by their main proponent, Dr Terence Meaden, as being displacements of highly ionised air, creating a form of strangely lit, bright luminescence within a highly energised electro-magnetic field which then flattens crops and could very easily be mistaken by bystanders for UFOs. So, plasma vortices mediate between UFOs and whirlwinds. Thus, says Harpur, the different theories of crop circle causation are basically:

> ... variations of each other, forming a kind of nexus of images which represent the imaginative attempt to reconcile by analogy such contradictions as natural/supernatural, aerial/terrestrial, and so on ... they seemed at first to merge and overlap with each other, but now we see that they are better described as analogical *variants* of each other. Even the hypotheses which set out to explain them ... turn out to be variations of the [paranormal] event under analysis. To 'explain' UFOs as plasma vortices is to say no more than that fairies are fallen angels.[47]

It may be true to say, in imitation of Harpur, that to 'explain' away the poltergeist as being a mischievous, puckish spirit like that of a child (whether literally or in terms of an adolescent focus-figure's RSPK projections) is to say no more than that a mischievous spirit is also a puckish fairy – except when it goes too far in its mischief, in which case Robin Goodfellow suddenly becomes Beelzebub. Ultimately, all proposed blanket explanations for the poltergeist, just like all those proposed for crop circles, are little more than metaphors taken literally.

In her book *Phantasmagoria*, the cultural critic Marina Warner argues that when it comes to the supernatural, we have become blinded by analogy:

> Unseen phenomena – spirits like angels and cherubs, shades of the dead, ethereal or astral bodies, subtle matter – have been visualised and communicated so effectively that the conventions they rely on and adapt have themselves become invisible. The metaphors that enflesh them introduce them into reality. But that reality can be expressed only through metaphor.[48]

When it comes to the invisible realm, our analogies have inadvertently become our realities. It is as if the letters 'D-O-G' had become more real for us than an actual, flesh-and-blood canine standing there before our eyes, in three-dimensional actuality – the same thing has now occurred for many

One 1678 pamphlet blamed the Devil for creating what now sound to us rather like crop circles; many different classes of paranormal phenomena blur into one another around the edges.

with the letters 'G-O-D'. This is lamentable but understandable. We need metaphors to be able to comprehend the world around us. No theory of the world can ever take *everything* into account – it cannot *be* everything, in total and in sum – so it has to be, at root, a kind of incomplete metaphor. In this sense, we cannot ever finally see the world in any way other than the metaphorical and the analogical. According to George P. Hansen:

> Strong supernatural manifestations are frequently disorientating. There is a natural tendency to put the phenomena into some kind of framework, to reduce ambiguity, to understand them, and establish their limits ... ETs, spirits, demons, and the unconscious have common properties, and such attributions create frameworks that socially construct reality and make it easier to speak about anomalous events.[49]

It is a seemingly necessary peculiarity of the human mind to seek to demarcate between phenomena, and thence to place things into categories thereby the better to grasp them. While all categories are, ultimately, false, we must accept that we have to draw a dividing line somewhere – but, whenever we do so, it will unavoidably be to some degree artificial.

According to the whimsy of Charles Fort, the esteemed American anomalist, renegade philosopher and collector of strange facts about such disreputable and disregarded subjects as UFOs, spontaneous human combustion and impossible rains of fish and frogs, the universe is essentially one large organism. Fort spent years combing through journals and newspapers in the New York Public Library and the British Museum, in search of what he called 'damned data', coming eventually to conclude that all things in Creation were connected but that our limited human perceptions could not generally tell this fact, except when it was momentarily revealed to us in those astonishing events we term 'coincidence'. The coiner of the word 'teleportation' in 1931, and very possibly the first man to (humorously) propose that strange lights seen in the sky might have been alien spacecraft, Fort had a particular interest in poltergeistery, something perhaps not entirely unrelated to the fact that he himself encountered repeated instances of pictures falling from his walls for no apparent reason. Appropriately enough, following his death in 1932, Fort himself appears to have briefly returned to Earth in spook form, his widow Anna hearing his voice crying 'Annie! Annie!' while his unseen eidolon produced spirit raps on a door.[50]

Fort's idea of universe-as-organism is given its best outline in his 1919 *Book of the Damned*. Here, Fort argues that all things are constantly trying to break away from this universe-as-nexus and establish their own, final identity – to become fully existent in their own right, you might say – but this is impossible. Any single thing in the whole universe which tries to establish itself as a wholly independent entity can do so only by systematically blocking out all other possible identities which it may, conceivably, be said to partly possess. A human being may reasonably say he is different from the ocean – and yet both consist largely of water. There is, obviously, a clear difference between the two, and yet everywhere and in everything are subtle merging points. For Fort nothing truly exists 100 per cent, in any final fashion. Instead there is a universe of what he calls Continuity, a concept best illustrated with comic examples:

> In Continuity it is impossible to distinguish phenomena at their merging points, so we look for them at their extremes. Impossible to distinguish between animal and vegetable in some infusoria – but hippopotamus and violet. For all practical purposes they're distinguishable enough. No one but a Barnum or a Bailey would send one a bunch of hippopotami as a token of regard.[51]

Fort has a multitude of such lines. 'What,' he asks, 'is a house?' It seems an easy question – but no:

> A barn is a house, if one lives in it. If residence constitutes house-ness, because style of architecture does not, then a bird's nest is a house; and human occupancy is not the standard to judge by, because we speak of dogs' houses; nor material, because we speak of snow houses of Eskimos – or a shell is a house to a hermit crab ... or things seemingly so positively different as the White House at Washington and a shell on the seashore are seen to be continuous.[52]

We have to draw an arbitrary line somewhere, however – and so we claim, quite falsely, that a cardboard box lying neglected beneath a bridge isn't a house. Well, it might be to some poor soul.

Fort holds the idea that we can ever fully distinguish between any two things in our universe to be a flaw of the way that human reasoning – and particularly scientific reasoning – works. 'Every [branch of] science is a mutilated octopus,' he once quipped. 'If its tentacles were not clipped to stumps it would feel its way into disturbing contacts ... To our crippled intellects, only the maimed is what we call understandable, because the unclipped ramifies away into all other things.'[53] As Fort argues:

> If, upon the basis of yellowness and redness, science should attempt to classify all phenomena, including all red things as veritable, and excluding all yellow things as false or illusory, the demarcation would have to be false and arbitrary, because things coloured orange, constituting Continuity, would belong on both sides of the attempted borderline. As we go along, we shall be impressed with this: That no basis for classification, or inclusion and exclusion, more reasonable than that of redness and yellowness has ever been conceived of.[54]

Let us apply Fort's thinking to poltergeistery. Randomly, I chose to unearth an instance of the poltergeist manifesting as an inanimate electrical phenomenon, and a rival polt preferring to imitate an intelligent spirit of the dead. These both *sound* totally different. Painting the first such spook as 'red', and the latter as 'yellow', however, I set out to reveal their unexpected merging point by finding a third *geist* somewhere in-between – an 'orange ghost', as it were. It was not difficult.

Poltergeist as electrical phenomenon (RED)	Poltergeist as continuous phenomenon (ORANGE)	Poltergeist as a spirit of the dead (YELLOW)
'The Iverson Cottage Mystery' *A house in Somerset is plagued by electrically-centred poltergeistery in 1987. Bulbs explode, appliances are destroyed, battery-operated devices malfunction and electricity meters go haywire, even when the supply is turned off at the mains.*[55]	*'The Weinsberg Prison Ghost'* *An apparitional polt visits a German prison, begging for prayers so it may escape from purgatory, whose existence it thus confirms. It makes a noise 'like the discharging of a Leyden jar' and gives shocks when touched.*[56]	*'Alis the Ghost-Nun'* *In 1526, the spirit of a French nun, Alis de Telieux, speaks via spirit-raps with the living, requesting the wrong of her burial be redressed. Polt-Alis confirms the existence of purgatory, and asks prayers be said so she may enter Heaven.*[57]

A suburban English home full of malfunctioning electrical products in the twentieth century, and an invisible purgatory-bound dead French nun communicating via spirit-raps in a nunnery during the Reformation – there is scant resemblance, one would think. And yet, at Weinsberg Prison in Germany in 1835, another purgatory-bound poltergeist appears which seems not only to be a spirit of the dead, but also to some extent electrical in nature. A clear difference at the extremes – but at the merging-point? The German case acts as a Continuity-revealing orange bridge between the red and yellow hauntings. According to Fort:

> I should say that our existence is like a bridge ... like the Brooklyn Bridge, upon which multitudes of bugs are seeking a fundamental – coming to a girder that seems firm and final – but the girder is built upon supports. A support then seems final. But it is built upon underlying structures. Nothing final can be found in all the bridge, because the bridge itself is not a final thing in itself, but is a relationship between Manhattan and Brooklyn ... everything in it [existence] must be relative, if the 'whole' is not a whole, but is, itself, a relation.[58]

For the committed fortean, even a bridge is not really a bridge; and, in the end, an electrical prison-ghost is probably finally neither truly electrical, nor truly ghostly, in its nature.

Mistaking a bridge for a bridge is a surprisingly easy thing to do if you're *looking* for a bridge, though. In fact, it's pretty much unavoidable. Most of us aren't conditioned to see it as being anything else. And, in the Middle-Ages, it would be just as easy to mistake a demon for a demon; or, in Auld Ireland, a fairy for a fairy; or, these days, an alien for an alien and his spacecraft for a spacecraft. It's what we are conditioned to do by the 'Dominants' of our time. Dominants are what Fort called prevailing world outlooks, or methods of social interpretation – 'epistemes' in the dead language of contemporary academic thought. In the past, everything would have been perceived through the prism of religion, and a comet viewed as a sign of the wrath of God. Then arrived the scientific Dominant, and it became an astronomical phenomenon. Now, we live in a media age of endless trivialisation and that very same comet is no more than a big, pretty firework. Or, as Fort said:

> ... my own acceptance [is] that we do not really think at all; that we correlate around super-magnets that I call Dominants – a Spiritual Dominant in one age, and responsively to it up spring monasteries, and the stake and cross are its symbols: a Materialist Dominant, and up spring laboratories, and microscopes and telescopes and crucibles are its icons – that we're nothing but iron filings relatively to a succession of magnets that displace preceding magnets.[59]

It happens with poltergeists, too – in sixteenth-century France, we had a haunted nunnery, and so a ghost-nun. In twentieth-century England, there was a private home, full of electrical goods, and so we had a spooky electrical phenomenon. The German prison case took place in the nineteenth century, a point of transition between religious and scientific outlooks for many.

And there, we had a peculiar orange hybrid. The question then arises of whether it is the phenomena which adapt themselves to the Dominants, or the Dominants which adapt their interpretations of the phenomena? Possibly it is a bit of both. According to Fort:

> Though just at present I am no darling of the Popes, I expect to end up holy, some other time, with a general expression that all stories of miracles are not lies, or are not altogether lies; and that in the primitive conditions of the Middle Ages there were hosts of occurrences that now, considerably, though not altogether, have been outgrown. Anybody who broadly accepts the doctrine of relativity should accept that there are phenomena that exist relatively to one age, that do not, or that do not so pronouncedly, exist in another age.[60]

In our current hyper-materialist era, any remaining poltergeist spirits of the dead such as Alis de Telieux are increasingly seen by even sympathetic men of science as embarrassing epistemic throwbacks, with many theorists frequently now resisting use of the very word 'ghost' in their studies.[61] Little meaningful attempt is often made to properly define what energies are supposedly being extruded by the focus-figure's mind in such persons' cherished RSPK model, but this fact is effectively disguised by the sheer obscurantist technicality of the term. In hope of lending the poltergeist some small cloak of scientific respectability, many parapsychologists have seized the opportunity to denude the poltergeist of all trappings of anthropomorphism, thereby reducing them down to a more acceptably neutral state. A typical slave to the prevailing parapsychological Dominant once produced this choice sentence about the noted English 'poltergeist boy' Matthew Manning: 'Matthew's gifts are still fascinating, but the "spook" has gone out of them.'[62] This is just what many now want – to exorcise the *geist* from the poltergeist altogether. In the original German, *polter geist* means, literally, 'racketing/noisy ghost', and to subtract the 'ghost' from that phrase makes it become nothing more than an abstract noise, full of sound and fury signifying nothing.

Innumerable contemporary investigations of poltergeistery have been written up and accompanied by various graphs, tables, fancy new acronyms and reams and reams of proudly turgid prose. Temperature fluctuations have been measured; the brainwaves of victims assiduously tabulated. Such reports have their interest. Some data produced may be of some use, to some theorist, somewhere; and the RSPK hypothesis is definitely valid in many individual cases, possibly even the majority. But more spectacularly outré hauntings, like that of the Hexham Heads, are less amenable to such rigorously methodical analysis. How, precisely, might ill-defined energetic processes like RSPK make werewolves and sheep-men – let alone talking, singing, poultry-killing mongooses – appear? To avoid admitting they don't know, many avowedly scientific parapsychologists ignore such extreme and comic-sounding outbreaks and focus upon the more low-level and predictable (and even slightly boring) incidents instead. The classic instance is William G. Roll's investigation of the Miami warehouse haunting of 1967.

Roll, who worked for the Psychical Research Foundation in Durham, North Carolina, was probably one of the original coiners of the term 'Recurrent Spontaneous Psycho-Kinesis' (RSPK),[63] a phrase first popularised among the wider public in his 1972 book *The Poltergeist*, where he wrote things such as 'When I use the word "poltergeist", I mean "an apparent case of RSPK".'[64] Roll was undoubtedly a commendably thorough investigator. It is just that sometimes his approach can appear somewhat misguided:

> I do not know of any evidence for the existence of the poltergeist as an incorporeal entity other than the disturbances themselves, and these can be explained more simply as PK effects from a flesh-and-blood entity who is at their centre. This is not to say that we should close our minds to the possibility that some cases of RSPK might be due to incorporeal entities. But there is no reason to postulate such an entity when the incidents occur around a living person. It is easier to suppose that the central person is himself the source of PK energy.[65]

Surely this statement of Roll's ignores *much* evidence, but Dadaesque cases like those of Gef the Talking Mongoose or the Hexham Heads are not really discussed by him. Instead, his work is an elaborate attempt at what Fort called correlation; a project to rescue poltergeists from their old and now outmoded Spiritualistic Dominant and reclaim them as part of the new, updated Scientific Dominant. Poltergeists *do* exist, Roll argues – but only on the terms of science. The imposition of 'rules' upon the poltergeist is a key component of the intermittent sympathetic scientific assault upon it. Here is a 1970s interview with Professor Brian Josephson, a recipient of the Nobel Prize for Physics, who had his own side-line in investigating RSPK:

> We are on the verge of discoveries which may be extremely important for physics. We are dealing here with a new kind of energy. This force must be subject to laws. I believe ordinary methods of scientific investigation will tell us much about psychic phenomena. They are mysterious, but they are no more mysterious than a lot of things in physics already. In times past, 'respectable' scientists would have had nothing to do with psychical phenomena; many of them still won't. I think that the 'respectable' scientists may find they have missed the boat![66]

Professor Josephson appears unaware of the irony implicit in his thinking. He justifiably chides those 'respectable' scientists who simply will not countenance the validity of psychical research; but then attempts to make the phenomena he is examining more 'respectable' to the mindset of those very same blinkered persons by asserting that there absolutely *must* be some comprehensible physical laws present somewhere behind them. But must there? Mainstream parapsychology now seeks to reduce the poltergeist down to little more than a novel branch of the expression of the laws of energy. Then it could be comprehended by the mindset of the modern Dominant and rescued, somehow, from the unpleasant medievalistic world of witches, ghosts and devils in which it has for so long lingered like Alis de Telieux in her purgatory.

Roll's beloved Miami warehouse case, for instance, focused upon a possible RSPK agent named Julio, a nineteen-year-old worker around whom objects shot from their shelves, smashing onto the building's floor. Roll's exhaustive investigation unearthed clear patterns. The majority of object movements occurred when Julio was within a certain distance of them; the further away they were, the less subject they became to his RSPK 'field of influence'. Roll here invokes a well-known scientific law, the 'exponential decay function'. This common-sense rule means that, the further away from an energy source something is, the less effect that energy source will have upon it; sit right next to a fire and you will be hot, move ten feet away, and you will be less so, as over distance energy disperses. Roll's finding delights him, as: 'If we are dealing with an exponential decay function, then in one respect there would be method in the poltergeist madness. Poltergeist disturbances would then conform to an old and established rule: the principle of conservation of energy.'[67]

Method in the madness ... the observance of rules ... this does not sound like a typical poltergeist (or a typical Trickster). If the poltergeist is bound by rules, then it must be science, Roll suggests. But what about cases where there is no apparent focus? There are 'haunted houses' as well as 'haunted people'. And what of those occasional spooks allegedly able to operate over distances of several miles? Roll's conclusions stand up well in some cases. The Miami warehouse one, undoubtedly, clearly fits in perfectly with his theory – and so it should, as this is the case it was primarily based upon. But what about Gef the Mongoose? Would it fit in with him? No! Roll's book is noticeably light upon discussion of such outlandish cases, presumably for the reasons outlined above.

Roll's sometime parapsychological colleague D. Scott Rogo has anticipated me here, accusing Roll of deliberately playing down the weirder elements of poltergeistery and thereby creating a 'poltergeist myth' based purely upon the citation of a series of rather mind-numbing hauntings involving only the most minor of phenomena 'which, to my mind, are not representative of the poltergeist in general'. A classic example might be the Seaford poltergeist, another of Roll's yawnsome favourites, which liked to do little more than unscrew the tops off bottles; it was in a co-authored 1958 paper of Roll's on the Seaford polt that the term 'RSPK' made its first printed appearance. Rogo happily admits many spooks are as dull as this, but equally validly points out that many others are not.[68] He explains that, when another colleague named Raymond Bayless released his book *The Enigma of the Poltergeist* in 1967, arguing that some spooks might have more complex causes than purely focus-directed RSPK, his ideas were 'simply ignored' with the text receiving not a single review in a major parapsychology journal. Even the very title of Bayless' book could have been considered a slight by some over-sensitive souls.

For Rogo, mainstream parapsychology itself had become nothing but a misguided attempt to 'champion rationality by naturalising the supernatural', meaning that 'any renewed attempt to reimbue the poltergeist with mystery' now 'seemed untenable or intolerable'.[69] His conclusion about such trends was damning: 'It would seem that either poltergeist researchers are indifferent to this sort of critical re-examination of their favourite theories, or that parapsychologists just aren't very interested in poltergeists.'[70] Personally, I prefer to adopt the wise approach of Dr Johnson, namely that 'Human experience, which is constantly contradicting theory, is the great test of truth.'[71] And, when it comes to poltergeists, human experience surely encompasses both the Seaford case *and* Gef the Talking Mongoose.

* * * * *

Roll's pattern spotting in regard to the Miami warehouse haunting was exemplary, in a way ... *but only for that one case*! Imagine a theologian aiming to maintain that poltergeists were caused exclusively by troubled souls requiring release from purgatory. He could cite the case of Alis de Telieux and, ignoring most others, make a very good argument. And then, if he encountered Roll's Miami poltergeist, he would find himself defeated. But what if both hauntings were equally real? As two of the best-regarded writers on poltergeists, the SPR's Alan Gauld and Tony Cornell, once put it, 'The first problem which confronts the theorist is: to what cases should he address himself?'[72]

Gauld and Cornell were fairly critical of the RSPK hypothesis themselves, viewing it as an inappropriate extension of lab-based parapsychology findings out onto the world at large. As they said, nobody really knows what PK itself actually is anyway, and thus:

> ... to explain poltergeist phenomena by reference to PK is to explain the unknown in terms of the unknown ... [anyway] there is no obvious similarity between [standard PK-lab achievements like] alterations in the fall of dice or in the output of electronic binary random number generators and the sorts of happenings which are reported in poltergeist cases; nor do we know of any 'laws' of PK which would enable us to show that these seemingly different kinds of phenomena fit within a common theoretical framework. It is at least as likely that poltergeist phenomena will throw light upon the nature of PK as that the laboratory study of PK will illuminate poltergeist phenomena; and neither of these eventualities is, we feel, *very* likely.[73]

In reality, even Roll had to keep on adding further mini-hypotheses onto his own main premise in order to account for various anomalies which would not fit properly within it – anyone familiar with the historian of science Thomas S. Kuhn's *The Structure of Scientific Revolutions* will recognise this as a classic sign of a scientific paradigm approaching the point of crisis and ultimate collapse.

While Roll said that 'It was the Miami poltergeist which [first] pointed to the lawful basis of RSPK cases' (or 'poltergeist hauntings', for those stubbornly old-fashioned types among us) the opposite conclusion could also be drawn. Subsequent evaluation led Roll, with commendable honesty, to admit that not all the data backed up his theory. Although it was true that the closer young Julio was to an object, the more likely it was to move, those objects which were closer to him when they began their flight moved a *shorter* distance, on average, than those further away from him, the exact reverse of what you might expect. So, Roll re-analysed the data, discovering the vast majority of displaced objects travelled in a counter-clockwise direction. Roll's conclusion was that the RSPK field surrounding Julio orbited him in a circular fashion, in a sort of vortex pattern. Consulting with experts, Roll found that objects thrown out from near the centre of any vortex field would indeed often travel a shorter distance than objects at the edge of the field did, due to the specific way that the physics of such things worked, thus correlating with his Miami data.[74]

It's a clever idea. But how would such a theory account for the following testimony, gathered from a Russian case of 1870–71 during which phantom hands were seen crawling around, and strange balls of light flitted through the air causing fires? According to one Mr Shchapoff, his wife was the focus-figure here, in whose presence household goods would frequently whizz about. This led him to make the following probing observations:

> Our first and principal wish was to bring the phenomena under some system or known rule; however, as if in defiance (and no doubt intentionally!) they always contradicted us. For instance, right at the beginning, when we sat together at tea, we observed that various things – the tea-spoon, the lid of the tea-pot, etc – flew at random from the table, and all of them took the direction away from my wife. This made us think that some sort of repulsive power resided in her, shall we say a negative current. However soon afterwards exactly the opposite happened: my wife went to the sideboard, and the moment she opened the door the things came towards her.[75]

What kind of law-abiding vortex does that represent? I am reminded of Terence Meaden's plasma-vortices in the thought of Patrick Harpur, mediating between one form of supernatural manifestation and another. With the RSPK theory, parapsychology claims to have devised a fully plausible and comprehensive-sounding explanation for the poltergeist. But really it is no such thing. Characteristically for a Trickster-related phenomenon, Roll's particular brand of RSPK hypothesis would appear to be both correct and incorrect simultaneously. In some cases, like that of the Miami warehouse, the rule applies perfectly and yet in others, like that of the Shchapoffs, not at all. These latter examples will be politely swept under the carpet. Every Dominant demands its sacrifices.

II

The Living Dead

And yet it moves ...

Galileo Galilei

Sometimes when you read about a beast-man Trickster like Coyote in his relevant Native Indian story cycles, he seems to be a human being, at others an animal, sometimes a patchwork cavalcade of more subtle gradations somewhere in-between. Like the poltergeist, he is red, yellow and orange all at once, just as the word 'weather' can mean equally rain, cloud or shine. The classic Trickster-figure is a collection of contrasting concepts of a binary nature, kept perpetually in opposition and never coming out finally upon either side. We cannot fully know exactly *what* he is, whether cunning or fool, human or animal, ghost of the dead or RSPK. As such, the Trickster is the natural god of boundaries; in their various guises, Tricksters guide the dead up into Heaven or back down into Hades, and preside over the sites of crossroads.

Hermes (the Roman Mercury – naturally, he has many aliases) is the best example. Messenger of the gods, he wears the winged sandals and occupies a place intermediate between the heaven of Olympus and the everyday world of men down here below. Brother of the sun god Apollo, he provides the moonlight logic to his sibling's well-lit intellectual counterpart. He is the inventor of language and so of both truth and lies. He spins each concurrently, with his many outrageous fibs containing an ounce of countervailing veracity in the sense that, as Lewis Hyde has aptly put it, they 'undercut the current fictions by which reality is shaped' by our presiding Dominant – such as the currently prevailing social fiction that paranormal phenomena do not exist.[1]

In his later medieval and Renaissance form of the Spirit Mercurius of the alchemists, Hermes was depicted as being an agent living somewhere betwixt and between the realms of matter and of spirit – the spirit in matter, and the matter in spirit, you might say. He was thus invoked as being able to effect strange pathways, or transmutations, between the two, when alchemists sought to transform worthless dead lead into the golden, living source of all eternal life, the fabled Philosopher's Stone. Mercury, or quicksilver, is a solid, a metal, but paradoxically behaves like a living liquid. This is a very Tricksterish way to be; and surprisingly relevant to the notion of the poltergeist.

During poltergeist hauntings, too, inanimate matter becomes infused with some Mercurius-like living spirit; objects leap around of their own accord, and appear alive. Consider this description of a nineteenth-century haunting at Bayswater in London:

> ... the spirit of locomotion was not to be arrested. Jugs and plates continued at intervals to quit their posts and skip off their hooks and shelves into the middle of the room as though they were inspired by the magic flute ... An Egyptian vase jumped off the table suddenly, when no soul was near, and smashed to pieces ... Candlesticks, after a dance on the table, flew off, and ornaments from the shelves, and bonnets and cap-boxes flung [themselves] about in the oddest manner. A looking-glass hopped off a dressing-table, followed by combs and brushes and several bottles, and a great pincushion has been remarkably conspicuous for its incessant jigs from one part [of the room] to another.[2]

In her 1848 book *The Night Side of Nature*, this case was specifically compared by the popular Victorian writer Catherine Crowe to the celebrated Stockwell haunting of 1772 where, in the presence of a London maidservant called Ann Robinson:

> ... a whole row of pewter dishes, except one, fell from off a shelf to the middle of the floor, rolled about a little while, then settled; and, what is almost beyond belief, as soon as they were quiet, turned upside down! They were then put on the dresser, and went through the same a second time. Next flew a whole row of pewter plates from off the second shelf over the dresser to the ground, and, being taken up and put on the dresser one in another, they were thrown down again. The next thing was [one of] two eggs that were upon one of the pewter shelves ... flew off, crossed the kitchen, struck a cat on the head, and then broke in pieces.[3]

According to Harry Price, writing in his *Poltergeist Over England*, the Stockwell ghost was the one case 'that best represented the popular conception of what a poltergeist is, and does.'[4]

If this is so, then what the poltergeist does best is bring life into a universe full of dead matter, just like the Spirit Mercurius – and also just like Prometheus, the Trickster-Titan of Greek mythology who stole the life-giving fire of the gods and placed it within dead clay to gift true existence to man, thereby imbuing inert matter with properties of consciousness and mobility. Was it really they, through the more modern medium of the poltergeist, who made laces jump from their shoes before they 'crisped and curled' themselves around a maid's hand 'like a living eel' in the village of Spreyton in the 1600s?[5] Were they the true powers behind an epidemic of lumps of coal that 'hopped out of grates and sauntered along floors' in London in 1921?[6] Or the salt-cellar which 'began to do the Charleston' at Poona, India, in 1929?[7] Or the wooden clogs which, during a French case of 1865, 'jumped about as if attached to the feet of a person dancing', or the copper plant pot that walked downstairs 'step by step' at a house in the French village of Vodable in 1914?[8]

And what about the haunted soldier's jacket kept in a glass display case in the restaurant of Edinburgh Castle, which began acting 'as if it were being worn by a soldier beating a drum' in 2001?[9] Or the mattress that got up off its bed, walked downstairs 'as if on legs' and threw itself angrily against the front door, as witnessed during a Birmingham haunting of 1977?[10] Or the clods of earth which 'danced' 6 feet high in the air, 'in the presence of hundreds' in a field outside a polt-infested Indian home in 1906?[11] Or the pair of mining boots which walked underground at South Yorkshire's Goldthorpe colliery in July 1985, causing a miner to flee sobbing from the pit?[12]

What should we make of the quantities of salt and pepper that shot out of their receptacles and went 'whirling about like a swarm of bees' before returning, utterly unmixed, back inside them in a house in Westmorland in 1849? Or the clothes which, we are told, 'came alive' during the same case? Gowns 'puffed themselves out in balloon-like and in the hoop-petticoat style' and an old riding coat 'was agitated in an astonishing way, stretching the right and then the left arm out' before a pair of riding boots 'issued from a lumber room and came walking downstairs'.[13] And what about the seemingly 'possessed' ape-doll which hung above the bed of an eleven-year-old girl in her Berlin flat in 1929 and took to dancing around with 'all its limbs going strongly' and its head nodding about crazily whenever a mouth-organ was played? Creepily, when placed upon the little girl's bed, the ape-toy tried crawling beneath the bedclothes to join her.[14] Were these amazing instances, if true, also the work of Prometheus' divine fire?

Such animated items are often too lively to suppress. In 1885 at Ylöjärvi in Finland, two polt-possessed plates were fastened down to a table to keep them still. It didn't work; the table jumped up into the air instead. Then, a woman in bed nearby awoke with her body tangled all around with string; that which had been meant to tie the living objects down dead with had, instead, *itself* been made to live![15] Some affected objects appear actively intelligent in nature. One poltergeist victim claimed to have known a bag which had the wit to react physically when it heard it was being talked about. Her father pointed at said item and promised he'd take it with him on a journey – whereupon it 'suddenly jumped up in the air and turned a complete somersault' in glee.[16]

Even more remarkable was an event implausibly alleged to have occurred during a 1696–97 haunting at a monastery in Naples. Hearing a strange noise, monks entered a room to investigate. There they found 'a black robe with a sheet over the shoulder, which moved ... [it was] nothing other than a man, made up of pieces of cloth'. Performing an exorcism, the monks successfully made this oversized Promethean rag-doll 'disintegrate' – only for it to magically re-assemble itself and overturn a table with its hands. Eventually a prayer brought it on its knees in the middle of the room 'as though it had been ordained' and it fell apart into a pile of lifeless laundry once more.[17]

Doubtless the monks perceived the hand of Satan here. The tale of the 'Devil of Hjalta-Stad' also shows the hand of this particular Trickster-figure at work in impishly animating objects. Hans Wium, the Sheriff of the area, a place in Iceland, wrote a letter to Bishop Halldor Brynjolfsson in 1750 to tell him how one day this polt-like 'Devil' – who spoke in 'an iron voice' from within a door – had:

> … said he was going to play with the door now, and with that he threw the door off its hinges with a sudden jerk, and sent it far in upon the floor. The strangest thing was that when he threw anything it went down at once, and then went back to its place again, so it was evident that he either went inside it or moved about with it.[18]

Was this door-puppeting 'Devil' also really the Spirit Mercurius by another name?

* * * * *

Hermes was certainly once Mercurius by another name. The name 'Hermes' originally meant 'he of the stone heap', or boundary and crossroads-marking cairn, which structure, according to Lewis Hyde, is 'an altar to the forces that govern these spaces of heightened uncertainty, and to the intelligence needed to negotiate them.'[19] Hermes being the god of boundaries sounds counterintuitive at first, until you consider that he allowed those same boundaries to be broken and then recreated in some new and novel fashion. In this way, such Trickster-gods were also gods of creativity and the creative impulse itself. During his occasional role as *Hermes psychopompos*, Hermes acted as a guide for the souls of the dead crossing the border between this world and the land of Hades, often while wearing a special cap which,

Hermes/Mercury, the most significant and poltergeist-like of all Trickster-gods. His winged helmet and sandals speak of his intermediary status between Heaven and Earth.

like a poltergeist, made him invisible.[20] With the aid of his magical caduceus-like 'ghost-drawing' rod, the *kêrykeion*, he was able to summon, ward off, control and direct spirits, thereby becoming a shepherd of souls.[21]

Sometimes Hermes creatively rearranged this border between overworld and underworld by bringing the dead back to life. Thereby, he created something else new; the concept of returning ghosts. According to Lewis Hyde, such borderlands as lie between life and death are the natural home of Hermes. They are most emphatically '*his* world, the crepuscular, shady, mottled, ambiguous, androgynous, neither/nor space of Hermetic operation, that thin layer of topsoil where all ... things are not yet differentiated'.[22] Their being, to him, 'not yet differentiated' means Hermes considers all borders as essentially plastic. They cannot hold him because he is forever acting to redefine them for his own purposes. Even death itself isn't clear-cut to a Trickster like Hermes.

Poltergeists, too, are forever playing with barriers, whether between life and death or otherwise. There is a reason why books upon the paranormal often come laden with titles like *Creatures of the Outer Edge, Borderlands, The Indefinite Boundary, The Infinite Boundary, The Enchanted Boundary* and *Footfalls on the Boundary of Another World*. At a haunted home outside Madras in British India sometime in the early 1870s, one of the most startling of phenomena was how, one morning, all of the house's doors were found removed from their hinges and laid up against the walls. Another morning, the opposite problem appeared; none of the doors in the house could be opened. Calling out for help, the inhabitants were told that 'large boulders of rock which could not be carried by any man' had been 'carefully stacked' against all the doors. Men had to be hired to remove them.[23] Here, in the first instance, barriers were transformed into portals; in the second, portals reshaped into impassable barriers. Could there be any clearer case of the hermetic redefinition of boundaries?

*****

Another boundary-subverting poltergeist appears in a tract named *De Daemonialitate, et Incubus, et Succubis*, written around the end of the 1670s by Father Ludovicus Maria Sinistrari de Ameno, a theologian. The book deals with the question of sexual intercourse between humans and putative 'sex-demons' – incubi (male) and succubi (female) who reputedly raped people in their beds at night. One such narrative, from the Italian town of Pavia, involved a married woman named Hieronyma to whom a lustful incubus took quite a fancy, plaguing her bedside at night in the guise of a handsome and well-dressed young man who continually pleaded for enjoyment of her body. Good Hieronyma refused, so by way of revenge the incubus turned poltergeist, stealing and breaking precious items from within sealed containers. Barriers were no problem for this Trickster either, then. Instead, he once created a rather remarkable barrier of his own. After Hieronyma had told him yet again one night to keep his demonic dick to himself, the incubus-polt allegedly:

... returned with an enormous load of those flat stones that inhabitants of Genoa, and of Liguria in general, use to cover their houses. With these stones he built around the bed such a high wall that it reached almost to the ceiling, and … [Hieronyma and her husband] had to send for a ladder in order to come out. This wall was built without lime. It was pulled down and the stones were stored in a corner, where they were exposed to everyone's sight. But after two days they vanished.[24]

If you yourself should ever build a wall to keep Trickster out, however, then he will demonstrate an unerring ability to penetrate such petty human barriers at will. During a French haunting of 1921 apples were hurled against the closed wooden shutters of a window until eventually they knocked out one of the boards, creating a hole an inch wide. Through this tiny aperture, numerous other apples, arriving in a 'horizontal direction' with 'considerable speed' soon passed with a wholly supernatural accuracy.[25] More striking yet was the haunted house at the Rue de Noyers in Paris in 1860, whose occupant sought to debar the stones of Hermes smashing in through his windows by the simple expedient of closing the wooden shutters. It made no difference; his shutters possessed a series of long narrow slits, to let in air. No sooner had he closed them than the shape of the stones being flung changed instantly – into long, flat narrow ones, which could just about enter through the slits to smash up his mirrors, vases and clocks. It should have been impossible to successfully aim so powerful a throw through so tiny a gap – but not for the hands of Hermes.[26]

*****

Why do so many hauntings involve the tossing or temporary animation of stones? The Greeks used to speak of something called 'Hermes in the stone', a reference to the potential artistic shape a sculptor might envision and intuit within his block of marble prior to carving.[27] But does Hermes really sometimes live inside such inert substances?

'Lithobolia', as the act of paranormal stone-throwing is technically known, is a historical constant of poltergeistery; as early as 530AD, a physician to King Theodoric was bombarded by showers of stones within his own house, events attributed at the time to invisible demons.[28] A similar case occurred recently in the small Romanian settlement of Sohatu, where in July 2018 villagers took to gathering outside and watching in awe as rocks were pelted at homes from 11 p. m. to 4 a. m. every night, while armed police could only shine their flashlights around uselessly. The victims may as well have been living back in the days of King Theodoric; Sohatu's local newspaper blamed 'the whims of evil night-spirits, [the] terrible spirits of terrible men!' for the outbreak.[29]

The term 'lithobolia' means something like 'stone-throwing' in Latin, and was coined by an early English colonial settler in America named Richard Chamberlain for his odd pamphlet *LITHOBOLIA: Or, the Stone-Throwing Devil*, printed in London in 1698. The general contents of this tract are well summed-up in its introductory preface:

Being an Exact and True account … of the various actions of infernal Spirits or (Devils Incarnate!) Witches or both: and the great Disturbance and Amazement they gave to George Walton's Family at a place called Great Island in the

Province of New Hampshire in New England, chiefly in throwing about (by an Invisible hand) Stones, Bricks and Brick-Bats of all Sizes, with several other things, as Hammers, Mauls, Iron-Crows, Spits and other domestic Utensils, as came into their Hellish Minds, and this for the space of a Quarter of a Year.[30]

These lithobolic stones do often act as if they really are alive, being temporarily imbued with motive power in both senses of the term; observe an 1818 case from Münchhof, Germany, where flying pebbles doubled back around in a semi-circular course against a window, 'precisely as an imprisoned bird might have done.'[31] The classic instance would be the sentient falling pebbles encountered by one F. W. Grottendieck in Sumatra during 1903. Not only did these pass through matter, feel hot to the touch, descend abnormally slowly and make an unnaturally loud sound as they hit the floor, these particular lithobolic items were also demonstrably aware of Grottendieck's attempts to catch them, peskily changing direction in mid-air whenever he made a grab for one.[32] In a case from Sicily in 1910, the exact reverse happened; a stone detached itself from a wall and described 'a slow semi-circle' in the air before landing, with eerie accuracy, in a bystander's hand.[33]

Predictably, the essential similarity of lithobolia to childhood mischief has led many sceptics to accuse the nearest adolescent of perpetrating such annoyances, not spooks. Several court cases have arisen, with seemingly innocent youths being prosecuted for minor crimes which, considered objectively, they could never actually have committed – unless by paranormal means.[34] During one 1980s London case, the police were alerted to a complaint that unknown vandals were continually lobbing rocks at a house's windows. No other phenomena were at this point reported. Eventually, someone said it sounded more like an uncatchable poltergeist than vandals. The victimised family had no idea ghosts were meant to toss stones, and dismissed the notion. However, this mental seed being planted, the polt's activities quickly began to diversify, with furniture rearranging itself into piles, food smearing itself across walls and a meal inexplicably vanishing from within a closed oven.[35]

* * * * *

One of the few investigators to develop a coherent theory about why poltergeists might possess such a taste for stones was the American parapsychologist D. Scott Rogo. A prosaic explanation might simply be that pebbles are virtually omnipresent, almost everywhere, and so are easy for spooks to make good use of. However, Rogo's more elaborate proposal involved our old friend RSPK:

It is my opinion that stones are thrown because they have the potential to do the most damage. Freud has shown that our unconscious mind is a breeding ground for our more fundamental urges and desires. C. G. Jung, Freud's disciple, believed that the unconscious also houses the collective memories of our entire civilisation. The poltergeist is the direct expression of our primitive desires to lash out and express hostility, urges that are generally held in check by conscious restraints. Primitive man knew of the destructive power of rocks and from them he fashioned his first weapons and killed his first foes. In biblical times, those who broke the law were stoned to death, and this method of punishment is still employed in many primitive cultures. During mob violence stones are the most often and lethally used missiles. When the poltergeist is unleashed, it carries with it the primitive consciousness of humankind. Because it, too, exists to destroy, it employs that most ancient tool of humans – the stone.[36]

According to C. G. Jung, the distinguished Swiss psychologist with an abiding interest in occult phenomena, the psychology of the Trickster-figure still manifests in the psychology of human beings even today, with the archetype (as he called such stock mental typologies) being 'like an old river-bed in which the water still flows.'[37] Jung's follower Karl Kerényi preferred to say that the memories of such ancient archetypes as Hermes, while not literally existing as gods, nonetheless lived on through the recurrent recapitulations of their basic personality structures in the actual personalities and actions of living men, arguing that the gods of old 'create [their] reality out of us, or more properly *through* us, just as one fetches water not so much *out of* a well as *through* the well from the much deeper regions of the earth.'[38]

You can see what the Jungians mean by considering a 1960 case in which a Los Angeles car-lot attendant named Anthony Angelo was accused of vandalising the vehicles in his workplace by throwing over 200 rocks at them – even though these rocks 'flew in abnormal, unpredictable trajectories, cascading into the lot every three minutes from all directions ... usually moving horizontally' and actively followed people around like stony stalkers. If Angelo was indeed paranormally responsible, via RSPK, then the man's mother provided a possible motive for his unconscious crimes: 'he resents washing cars and working his arms to the bone and get[ting] no money.'[39] A similar case occurred in 1995, when the step-family of a fifteen-year-old boy named Çetin, the son of Turkish immigrants living in the Dutch town of Druten, became subject to the attentions of a stone and sand-throwing poltergeist which even pelted policemen when they were called out to intervene. Çetin was disturbed by both the clash of cultures between secular Holland and his native Muslim Turkey, and by his father's recent re-marriage, and it seemed this was the method his RSPK powers chose to express his latent hostility towards his new step-family. Interestingly, in light of Rogo's ideas, investigators noted how, in the traditional Islamic culture adhered to by Çetin's family, stoning was considered an appropriate punishment for those who had performed certain moral transgressions and crimes.[40]

In Rogo's quasi-Jungian view, therefore, when supernaturally-gifted people like Anthony Angelo and Çetin get angry, part of their psyche reverts back to archaic levels and starts lashing out at their enemies' property by proxy via RSPK-fuelled acts of lithobolia. The primitive psyche of early man, however, is just what the Trickster-figure is supposed to be the mythological personification of, so another way of putting it might be to say that, during such outbreaks, RSPK agents inadvertently unleash their inner Trickster to engage in a spot of light vandalism with stones.

* * * * *

Stones are, imaginatively speaking, the very deadest of dead matter – we speak of killing things 'stone dead', while plagues involve their victims 'dropping like stones'. Phrases such as 'stone deaf', 'stone cold', 'heart of stone' and 'sleeping like a stone' are common. When the ancient Greek myth-makers wanted to hymn the magical powers of Orpheus – another, like Hermes, who crossed the shady borderline between life and death when descending down into Hades' Halls in search of his dead wife Eurydice – they chose to depict his skill with music as being so great that his lyre had the power to make even stones dance. Possibly the tale can be considered a metaphor for the ancient belief in something called 'panpsychism'.

For the Milesians, the Hellenes from whom the earliest pre-Classical Greek philosophers like Thales, Anaximander and Anaximenes emerged between around 600 and 500BC, the world was in a sense alive as it was fundamentally composed of things that moved – the stars, the waves, the wind, fire. Movement was considered a sign of life, as in animals, and so it seemed to Milesian thinkers that matter (*hyle*) possessed life (*zoë*), hence the word 'hylozoism', an alternative term for panpsychism. This outlook has been described as a kind of 'materialist monism', in which everything in existence is viewed as a part of the same underlying root reality – shades of Charles Fort's Continuity. Hence, the separation between mind and matter was a somewhat artificial one. The recent parapsychological trend towards RSPK seems like an unconscious resurfacing of this same archaic Milesian mindset, another brand of 'materialist monism' in which the idea of evil spirits throwing pebbles around is replaced with a re-linking of *hyle* once more back to *zoë* in the shape of the focus-figure's living mind interacting with inanimate physical objects in the world around it.

To Thales, the soul or *psyche* was ultimately what produced movement in any given thing; even within supposedly dead stone itself. The ancient world's equivalent of a magnet was a lodestone, a piece of magnetically-charged mineral which might look like an ordinary lump of rock, but which possessed the power to cause metal fragments to move about. For thinkers like Thales, this meant the lodestone, or magnet, possessed a kind of soul within it, that it used to induce movement in other things which may have *appeared* fully inanimate, but actually weren't, as their own mineral-souls possessed the ability to respond to the lodestone-soul's seductive promptings.

This 'mind' inherent within the rock was considered an expression of the minds of the gods, which were coterminous with the world itself, meaning all the (un)dead matter surrounding us was actually as 'full of gods', or spirits, as are the jumping candles and flying pebbles in a Hermes-haunted house. There was a hierarchy of 'mind' present within all elements of Creation, with fully conscious entities like humans and animals obviously appearing higher up on this mental ladder, later dubbed the 'Great Chain of Being', than rocks were. But, given the ability of lodestones to influence the 'souls' of other rocks containing bits of metal, evidently even some stones were more conscious than others, occupying a higher rung upon this same Ladder of Life.[41] Nowadays, nobody believes in the existence of a Great Chain of Being anymore – except, possibly, men like D. Scott Rogo, according to whose theories some stones can also temporarily become more conscious than others.

Milesian modes of thought lingered on until the tail-end of the Renaissance. Even the English proto-scientific naturalist William Gilbert, author of the seminal 1600 treatise *On the Magnet*, spoke of lodestones as being endowed with such panpsychism-like qualities as reason, claiming that 'the magnetic force is animate, or possesses a soul; in many respects, it surpasses the human soul.' Besides conceiving the concept of magnetic poles, Gilbert saw nothing embarrassing in proposing that magnets and the things they attracted possessed a sort of 'friendship' for one another. Interestingly, when lodestones are rubbed against a rock containing iron, they can magnetise that, too, or 'awaken' it into life, in Gilbert's terms – just as, when the RSPK-agent's mind rubs up against the previously dormant flying pebbles, he or she awakens them into life, too. Gilbert therefore felt, just like many a modern-day parapsychologist, that soul or psyche could be lent from one object to another, being passed down along the Great Chain of Being. The magnetised Earth's soul from which all minerals were ultimately mined was imparted first to the lodestone, then via this natural magnet to the lump of previously inert-seeming iron, which was not dead at all, only sleeping. Gilbert, I think, would have understood the RSPK hypothesis perfectly.[42]

*****

What truly killed such thinking stone-dead was the work of René Descartes, father of the modern-day Dominant of materialist science, whose philosophy of 'Cartesian Dualism' argued that, unlike in Gilbert's worldview, there was a complete and total separation between mind and matter, with humans being conscious, yet the world around them totally inanimate. But some people, guessing what such an outlook might ultimately lead to, tried to rebel. Among them were two of England's earliest proto-parapsychologists, Joseph Glanvill and Henry More. More was a Cambridge scholar who foresaw that Descartes' idea of a 'dead' universe working by itself as if by clockwork implied one with no need for God to intervene anywhere within it. He feared such a materialist philosophy was really just the first baby-step in a plan to later kill off religion itself – turns out More was right. His fightback was twofold. First, he imagined something called the 'Spirit of Nature', a Mercurius-like animating force which God, like a lodestone resuscitating slumbering iron, or Prometheus awakening inert clay, could infuse into dead matter to make it live.[43]

More's second path of assault involved ghost-hunting. He was a member of the 'Ragley Circle', a kind of SPR-precursor which met at the Warwickshire mansion of one Lady Conway to swap reports of apparitions, poltergeists, miracles and other such staple *X-Files* phenomena. One attendee at Ragley was Joseph Glanvill, chaplain to Charles II. He was also the author, in 1666, of the first-ever printed account of the Drummer of Tedworth, a haunting Glanvill investigated personally, witnessing the demon's actions for himself. Following his death in 1680, his friend Henry More bundled many of the dead man's notes together into a new book, *Saducismus Triumphatus*, in which the Drummer's story jostled for space with tales of witchcraft, levitation, apparitions … and lithobolia, most notably a long account of

Nefarious materialist philosopher René Descartes, who sought to separate mind from matter once and for all.

the trial of an alleged Irish witch, Florence Newton, who in 1661 had been accused of cursing a servant-girl to be followed around by showers of mysterious pebbles.

More's purpose in publicising such stories in *Saducismus Triumphatus* was to triumph over the so-called 'Saducees' – an insulting term for Cartesian-minded sceptics, basically – who were seeking to rob the world of both its soul and its true religion. As More put it, 'no spirit, no God', so the reality of ghosts, witchcraft and the Devil had to be reasserted in order thereby to reassert simultaneously the reality of Christianity. As 'those that dare not bluntly say, there is no God, content themselves (for a fair step and introduction) to deny that there are spirits or witches', there was good reason to try and prove that stones could dance by themselves; for if Satan and his agents could infuse dead matter with life, then so too could Jehovah with his 'Spirit of Nature', thus proving Descartes and his army of sceptical scientific Saducees wrong.[44]

Currently prevailing conceptions of the poltergeist unknowingly echo Henry More by seeking also to restore missing links within this Great Chain of Being. One RSPK-related school of thought holds that dead matter is not always entirely dead at all, but often contains what might be termed 'emotional content' buried away somewhere inside it. When a loved one dies, many mourners hang on to one of their most treasured possessions, to remember them by. A mere pipe may thus no longer really be just a pipe, but a physical symbol invested with raw emotion, imbued with memories of your dear, departed grandpa who used to puff away endlessly on it every night. Likewise, if you hate your wife, every time you see her wedding-ring it could act as a focus for your loathing. So maybe, if grandpa's pipe begins moving about by itself, that's an expression of the RSPK-element in your own psyche trying to bring you some comfort by implying he's still around, keeping a benign eye upon you. Or, if your wife's wedding-ring starts being hurled violently across the room, that's you trying to tell her you want a divorce by rather oblique means. One Freud-aping theory even has it that the reason so many poltergeist pranks involve flying cups, bottles, cutlery, plates and food may be because the focus-figure is unconsciously re-enacting stressful meal-time related events from their forgotten babyhood, thus recalling the universal and 'powerful oral needs of infants'.[45] (Although an alternative perspective might simply be that such implements were once considered sacred to Hermes the Cook in his aspect of 'god of the kitchen' …[46]) The Winnebago Indian Trickster Wakdjunkaga was always speaking to inanimate objects – which, to him, weren't really inanimate at all – and calling them his 'younger brothers'.[47] They are younger brothers to the poltergeist too.

*****

Consider the case of Tina Resch, an Ohio teenager who shot to media fame following spectacular incidents of poltergeistery around her home in 1984. Resch was an extremely clumsy and accident-prone individual with apparent developmental problems relating to hand–eye co-ordination, who stumbled into walls 'like a bumper-car'. Diagnoses of conditions like Tourette's Syndrome and dyspraxia may not be inappropriate; according to one analysis, 'her poor depth-perception made it difficult for her to manipulate things [and] RSPK may have been a form of overcompensation' for this. Resch also had severe emotional problems, due to bullying at school and the appalling way she was raised by her unkind foster parents.[48]

Tina was sent for psychological assessment, with a parallel being drawn between her 'unpredictable, chaotic, [and] periodically very distressing' childhood and the similar chaos unleashed into the world by her pet poltergeist. According to analysis, she was very confused about 'boundaries between the self and others and between the self and surroundings' – also a key characteristic of the psychology of the Trickster-figure in the legends told about him. Apparently, 'the process of individuation where the child learns to distinguish itself from its surroundings had been disrupted' for Resch, facilitating the interpenetration of her living mind with the otherwise dead matter surrounding her in some way.[49] No hard-and-fast Cartesian Dualism for Tina.

Curiously, the objects most frequently affected by Tina's spook did indeed possess some apparent latent emotional content to them. In the opinion of RSPK-godfather William G. Roll, one particular chair she habitually used kept on spinning around because it 'was [Tina's] place in the family room, but she felt unloved by her family', while the frequently flying household telephone, which suffered from inexplicable loud screeches echoing down the line whenever people tried using it, 'may have been [the vehicle for] Tina's way of saying that she had no real connection with people'.[50] That mealtimes were constantly disrupted was also significant to Roll. Resch's guardians were rather obese and appeared engaged in a cruel attempt to get Tina to follow in their wobbly footsteps by forcibly serving her over-large portions of food before then hypocritically criticising her for getting fat. In private, the teenager would later vomit much of this junk back up, like a bulimic. It is no wonder sticks of fattening butter subsequently slid upwards on kitchen cabinets 'like two giant slugs', while eggs flew impossibly through the closed door of a refrigerator and broke messily all over the room when Tina was asked to help cook, nor that crockery finally had to be replaced with disposable paper cups and plates (thus excusing Tina from dishwasher duty).[51]

As Tina herself said, 'It usually happens when I'm really mad.'[52] And, when she did get 'really mad', her unconscious mind chose its targets carefully; it was not simply the closest small objects to Resch which started flying about, as with Julio during the Miami warehouse case. Instead, it was most frequently those which contained the most latent emotional content. Now modifying his views, William G. Roll summed it up like this:

> The electromagnetic energy that may underlie RSPK is not the impersonal energy of traditional physics. RSPK energy has an informational side that includes people's emotions. As the term suggests, *emotion* entails *motion*. The motion can be [simply] 'in the head', or it can take place in the external environment [too].[53]

And, when it does, plates can fly, butter can climb, cups can smash and stones can live! When Hermes in the shape of a poltergeist facilitates the crossing of borders between life and death, he does so not merely by enabling the dead to return to the land of the living in the shape of ghosts, but allowing that which was never alive in the first place to become animated too. In these days of the Cartesian Dominant, the most fearsomely policed border of all is that which separates the dualistic boundaries of mind and matter. By indicating these two poles may not always be as diametrically opposed as we are told they are, and allowing the officially forbidden interpenetration of one by the other – by, in Fort's terms, inserting some subtly shaded orange in between the broad primary strokes of the yellow and the red – the boundary-slipping poltergeist, just like the Trickster, really does remake our current world anew.

Fort himself – whose books were full of dashes like the ones surrounding this very clause as a conscious stylistic-ideological choice, as is mine – used to speak of creating a 'philosophy of the hyphen' in which 'an uncrossable gap is disposed of, and the problem rendered into thinkable terms' by asking not whether mind can really act upon matter, but 'whether mind-matter can act upon matter-mind'.[54] The poltergeist makes us ask this same question. It is no wonder Fort's wife thought he had once returned as one – although strangely enough, when he did, he chose not to toss around any pebbles. Charles Fort preferred to smash down glass walls and barriers via other means – with dashes, not rocks – with books, not boulders – his Tricksterish pen was mightier than his lithobolic sword. In a certain sense, he really was a vandalistic poltergeist, therefore, in spirit if not in literal deed. Those who refuse to live quietly within fragile glass paradigms have no need to throw any physical stones.

III

Breaking Down Barriers

We must not let in daylight upon magic.

Walter Bagehot

Many a poltergeist has enjoyed breaking barriers and boundaries in a more literal sense than the spirit of Charles Fort ever did. In 1924 at Penkaet Castle in Scotland, servants were continually bothered by bedclothes in a certain room being found disarranged after the beds had been made. All entrances and exits were locked, and bricks placed against the inside of the room's main door. The next day, these bricks were found moved and the bedclothes yet again disordered; it was supposed the vandal was a ghost with the ability to pass through doors, not a mere human being.[1]

During the haunting of Gef the Talking Mongoose, the father of the household, Mr Irving, decided to protect his daughter Voirrey's nerves by moving her sleeping-quarters into the parental bedroom. Gef objected, his voice ringing out from behind the wall-boards, warning 'I'll follow her wherever you move her.' Determined, Mr Irving barricaded his bedroom door up with dressing-boxes, chairs and a heavy weight to keep the spook out. Soon after, the top of the door bulged inwards, as if some great force was pushing against it. 'I'm coming in!' said Gef before, seconds later, a heavy pot of ointment crashed across the room and into the bedstead.[2]

The nineteenth-century haunting of Willington Mill in Tyneside featured a poltergeist unlocking and then opening the household's well-barred front door, much to the consternation of the Mill's occupiers, the Procter family:

On one occasion, when family prayers were being conducted ... a noise began in the room above, a heavy footstep descended the stairs, passed the room ... and then proceeded to the front door, [where] the bar was removed, the lock turned, two bolts drawn back, the latch lifted, the door flung open and the footsteps [then] pass[ed] into the front garden. Mr Procter ceased reading, went out into the passage – and behold, the door was wide open ... Mr Procter filled himself with gloomy reflections as to the opportunities which such ghostly habits would afford to burglars.[3]

In 1645, a pamphlet entitled *Strange and Fearfull Newes from Plaisto in the Parish of West-Ham ... in the house of Paul Fox a Silke-Weaver* was published in London. It told the tale of how a sword and a cane began dancing around Mr Fox's house, before 'a strange kind of rapping' came at his door. A 'soft hollow voice' identified itself as a spirit, which commanded the weaver to open up and let it inside because it 'must dwell there' for some reason. Fearing evil, Fox told it to go away. The spook slipped through the keyhole, across the threshold and into the building anyway, where it began shredding Fox's silk and smashing his windows with such projectiles as tiles, oyster shells and pieces of (presumably very stale) bread.[4] Maybe the ghost would have acted a little less wantonly if the unfriendly Mr Fox had simply opened up his door and let it in?

Then again, Tricksters can be maddeningly inconsistent, very probably on purpose. A South African poltergeist of 1906 manifested in no way other than by lifting up a latch, turning a knob, opening a door, and wandering throughout the haunted house, producing the sound of furniture being moved around and knocked over (while the actual furniture itself stayed exactly where it was, oddly enough). Contrary to everything that has just been argued above, the ghost was successfully exorcised by the simple expedient of buying the affected door a new lock.[5] Far more common, though, are cases in which locks are rendered useless. One recent haunting involved the disturbing detail of a man being unable to exit his home during a fire due to his front door inexplicably refusing to open, even though it was actually physically unlocked at the time,[6] while accounts of locks and door-chains being torn off and destroyed as if by invisible hands or claws are not unknown. Occasionally, these latter occurrences have been interpreted as RSPK-enabled expressions of a focus-figure's desire to escape from the unquiet home being helpfully facilitated.[7]

Doors are not the only barriers penetrated by polts. There is an astonishing phenomenon known as 'matter-through-matter', in which spooks contrive to get solid objects to pass through other solid objects via mechanisms utterly unknown. When neutrinos were finally proved to exist in the 1950s, it was as part of a series of experiments dubbed 'Project Poltergeist'; the point was that these particular subatomic particles, often described as being 'ghost-like', also possess the ability to penetrate solid matter without leaving any trace.[8] Particularly puzzling are cases involving manipulation of sealed packages sent via the postal-system. During one haunting, a workshop owner experienced the disappearance of small tools from his premises – some of which were then found lying impossibly within unopened parcels when they were delivered to him there by mail later the same day.[9] Presumably the parcel-firm responsible was Hermes.

Sealed letters are sometimes interfered with too. The 1990s plaguing of a house in Somerset by weird electrical poltergeistery caused much correspondence to pass between the house's owner and a case-investigator. When one of these letters arrived at the haunted home, however, the researcher's note had been removed from its envelope and replaced with a random missive intended for a Lt Col Brounlie of Dorset, concerning the obscure subject of a Festoon butterfly. The Royal Mail's explanation for this incident was simple – 'this can't happen!'[10] But it did ...

During a very notable haunting at Poona in India of 1928–29, one day eggs were counted out into baskets and stored safely inside a cupboard. Once the doors were closed, an egg shot past the witnesses from the same direction and smashed on the floor. Looking inside, they found one egg missing. Three more soon followed it – passing directly *through* the closed cupboard door. As a last straw, an entire basket, containing forty-two eggs, then vanished from the shelf, never to be glimpsed again.[11] During an equally famous poltergeist infestation at Amherst in Canada in 1878-79, according to the investigator Walter Hubbell, it was 'an almost daily occurrence' for items locked away inside trunks and chests to be brought out and displaced. Worse, when these trunks were opened, entirely different household objects nestled inside instead![12]

One of the victims of the Poona polt, a Miss Kohn, once decided to set the talented spook a challenge: 'At 3.30 p.m. I went out, leaving on my table a tightly closed screw-top aluminium 'safety' inkpot, containing a glass bottle of Swan ink. By this elaborate device I had hoped to surpass the cunning of the malicious spirits.'[13] It didn't work; returning home, Miss Kohn found ink from the bottle spread messily all over her room. The aluminium inkpot could not be found – until it suddenly materialised 6 inches below the ceiling. Examining it, Miss Kohn found it remained as tightly closed as she had left it. Notes of paper money were also stolen from inside locked containers by the spook before, puckishly, its exact value was returned in coins.[14]

Here, the poltergeist not only breaks barriers, but also acts as a *literal* 'agent of change' – as did Hermes. He was the god of commerce and the market-place, and his Roman tag, Mercury, was the origin of the Latin word *mercor*, meaning 'to engage in commerce'. Terms like 'mercantile' mean, in a way, to act like Hermes/Mercury, the master of change – if you buy or sell an item, then you are either transforming it into money, or money into it.[15] Maybe this is why coins are one of the most common of all poltergeist apports (the technical label given to supernaturally-materialised objects); during one Australian case of 1955-57, when two of the 'victims' came home from the local bakery, they would find the exact sum of money they had just spent on bread and cakes handily dropping down from nowhere onto their kitchen table in coin-form.[16] Lucky them – a gift straight from Hermes, the god of lucky finds.

Hermes was furthermore the god of thieves. It is surely significant that many people's first reaction to signs of poltergeistery around their home – doors wide open, locks picked, items disappeared, furniture disarranged, drawers and cupboards ransacked – is to presume they have been burgled. Sometimes, awoken in the night by suspicious sounds and phantom footsteps, victims have summoned the police, only for officers to discover the true miscreants were beyond the bounds of all earthly jurisdiction.[17] A presumption of burglars at work was actually the first reaction of the family of Magistrate Mompesson during the Drummer of Tedworth case. Literal-minded sceptics have now theorised the entire haunting was merely an elaborate attempt by the real-life drummer William Drury's fellow mendicants to steal his confiscated drum back again, in collusion with corrupt household servants. The way the Drummer left metal spikes and knives in the Mompessons' beds has even been interpreted as a warning from the criminal underworld, equivalent to the celebrated horse's head scene in *The Godfather*.[18] But genuine ghosts sometimes do imitate burglars directly; there are cases in which wallets have been stolen from within locked safes, never to be returned.[19]

Whate'er the Quarters of the Globe produce?
For Pomp and State, for pleasure or for use,
The God of Commerce lays at Britain's feet,
And owns her Mistress of the World complete.

Mercury, in his guise of the god of trade, presents ownership of the continents to commerce's new global goddess, Britannia, during the height of her highly mercantile British Empire.

During one haunting, the ghost appears to have rifled drawers, stealing a purse and leaving a boot print on bedclothes; another time, the same spook falsely warned of a prowler armed with a knife having entered the haunted house.[20]

Tricksters are imagined as being the very first thieves in several different world-cultures, not just Hermes. When he was still a baby, the Indian Trickster Krishna's mother, Yasoda, warned her son not to steal the family's butter from its pots. Krishna disobeys, getting ghee smeared all over his face, hands and clothing in the process. Caught yellow-handed, Krishna simply asks his mother 'How could I steal it? Doesn't everything in this house belong to us?' Amused by his shamelessness, Yasoda laughs and instantly forgives him.[21] A more ancient order, that of the fairy kingdom, has reasserted its ancient rights of tribute over more modern, material notions of private property. To Lewis Hyde, 'Our ideas about property and theft depend on a set of assumptions about how the world is divided up. Trickster's lies and thefts challenge those premises and in so doing reveal their artifice and suggest alternatives.'[22]

However, these deities do not barge into a place with all guns blazing like bank-robbers. Instead, argues Hyde, Trickster's thievery 'is usually stealthy, which means [he] moves from one sphere to another without actually disrupting the boundary ... Hermes doesn't break down the door ... he slips through the keyhole'.[23] In the *c.*420BC *Homeric Hymn to Hermes*, Hermes is famously depicted as transforming himself into a cloud of supernatural mist in order to seep in through a closed door's keyhole, rather like the sneaky ghost which later invaded Paul Fox's premises in West Ham to criminally shred his cloth during the 1640s. This then allows the floating Hermes to swear 'honestly' in self-defence that he never even *stepped over* the place's threshold – a lie in the form of the truth, exactly like those politicians peddle.[24]

When he picks locks, Hermes inherently subverts and reorders boundaries. During one Brazilian haunting, a thrifty girl put three banknotes into her handbag before locking it within a cupboard for safekeeping. When she opened it, naturally the notes had gone missing; the money subsequently reappeared stuffed inside a bottle rolling around on the floor, as if mocking her.[25] We may talk of things being 'hermetically sealed', but in practice whenever Hermes chooses to shift into the shape of a poltergeist, no such impassable, Hermes-proof barrier is even possible.

* * * * *

What does it mean to steal something? As shown by the scholar Norman O. Brown in his 1947 book *Hermes the Thief*, the issue is more complex than you might presume. Thieves do not only steal goods, Brown explains, they first have to steal *into* places in order to do so, just like the troops hidden away within the Trojan Horse by Hermes' human descendant Odysseus. The words 'steal' and 'stealth' are related. Hermes was not a mugger, one who robs people through open violence, more of a pickpocket, one who utilises sleight-of-hand and lightness of finger; there was a festival held in his honour at Samos, the 'Feast of *Hermes charidotes*', where pickpocketing was temporarily legalised.[26] The Homeric Greek terms most characteristically used to describe Hermes' inherent qualities as both thief and Trickster, Brown shows, are derived from common root words which also meant 'to remove secretly', 'to deceive', or simply 'secret action'. Thus, to the pre-Classical Greek mind there was no real difference between deceptive trickery and the act of theft, just as there is no meaningful difference between the two in the scams of a duplicitous pyramid-scheme operator today. To call Hermes 'The Thief' meant also to call him 'The Trickster'.

In addition, the original Homeric Greek root words for both trickery and theft carried within them real connotations of the use of magic. We still talk of magic *tricks* today, and when Hermes slipped through keyholes by transforming into mist, he was hardly breaking and entering by normal, non-supernatural means. In *The Odyssey*, Homer labels the sorceress Circe not 'magical' as such, but 'tricky'; Homer described the shape-shifting abilities of the character Proteus similarly. Magic, just like theft, was therefore conceived of as being a form of 'secret action'.[27] The very word 'occult' is derived from the Latin *occultis*, meaning 'hidden'; 'occultation' is the astronomical term for when one celestial body becomes obscured by another, as during an eclipse.

So, originally Hermes was viewed as a thief not simply in that he relieved other persons of their property, but in that he supernaturally stole into sealed areas and performed secret, or 'occult', actions of object-removal there via magical means … just like poltergeists impossibly stealing eggs from within locked cupboards. At a haunted pub in East Sussex, the landlord's son once discovered six bottles of Perrier water 'lined up in a slightly curving line with all the labels facing one way' in the cellar. They had been removed from a nearby cardboard box; one which was entirely unopened, *and could not have been opened* without tearing the cardboard.[28] What was this, if not a theft in the form of a magic-trick?

The parapsychologist Hans Bender investigated a 1968–69 haunting in the German town of Nickelheim, in which a poltergeist enjoyed cracking eggs over the heads of visitors and rearranging dolls into obscene positions so it looked as if they were having sex. Noticing that the *spuk* could apparently teleport matter-through-matter, Bender arranged several 'target objects' within a sealed cupboard to see if the ghost might possibly remove them. It capriciously preferred to steal his coat from within another closed cupboard instead, transporting it outside, where it was found 'carefully laid and folded' in a bed of snow – a bed of snow in which, quite magically, no footprints were anywhere visible.[29] Once again, Hermes the Magic Thief had struck. When asked how it was he performed his own tricks, Gef the Talking Mongoose once replied 'Ha! That's magic!' – which, readers may recall, was the specific catchphrase of Britain's top 1980s TV magician Paul Daniels![30]

*****

In 1881, a hundred years before Paul Daniels began to haunt the airwaves, a very strange book appeared in English translation. Called *Transcendental Physics*, it was written by Johann Zöllner, who was not a conjuror but a Professor of Physics and Astronomy at the University of Leipzig, and purported to lay out just how Hermes managed to perform his acts of matter-through-matter. By doing so, Zöllner not only broke the code of the Magic Circle, he also advocated breaking the known laws of physics. Zöllner had become involved with a prominent New York spirit-medium named Henry Slade, who was most famous for getting ghosts to write messages upon slates within a séance-room. However, he was also followed around by spontaneous outbreaks of more standard poltergeistery; spirit-raps, flying knives, moving beds, self-vandalising furniture, teleporting tables, small objects falling from thin air, all were observed to occur within Slade's presence.[31]

Slade also had a nice line in matter-through-matter. Under Zöllner's investigation, Slade was able to tie and untie knots within bodies of string sealed at either end, place solid wooden rings around the stems of solid wooden tables which it was physically impossible for them to be passed over the wider ends of, and get separate leather bands to penetrate one another physically.[32] Incredibly, it appears that Slade's attendant poltergeists did this by virtue of causing corporeal ghostly hands to appear on the scene, which were both seen and felt by Professor Zöllner, even leaving behind their imprints in flour at the scientist's request.[33] If these were illusions, they were convincing ones:

> While ... Slade's hands, continually visible to me, lay quietly on the table, there appeared suddenly a large hand close in front of me, emerging from under the edge of the table. All the fingers of the hand moved quickly, and I was able to observe them accurately during a space of at least two minutes.

The colour of the hand was pale and inclined to an olive-green. And now ... the above-mentioned hand rose suddenly, as quick as an arrow, still higher, and grasped with a powerful pressure my left upper-arm for over a minute.[34]

Most magicians perform their tricks via sleight-of-hand; but if, like Henry Slade, you had access to more than two hands to be sleighty with, the tricks you could perform would be even greater than those of Harry Houdini. Zöllner's conclusion was that Slade, as a powerful poltergeist-medium, was indeed performing his tricks at third hand:

To complete the account of the phenomena of visible and tangible hands ... on the morning of 15 December 1877, at half-past ten o'clock, while W. Weber and I were again engaged with Slade ... suddenly Weber's coat was unbuttoned under the table, his gold watch was taken from his waistcoat pocket and was placed gently in his right hand as he held it under the table. During this proceeding ... Mr Slade's hands were, it is understood, before our eyes upon the table, and his legs crossed sideways ... the foregoing experiments have afforded proof that there are, outside our perceptible world of three dimensions, things furnished with all the attributes of corporeality which can appear in three-dimensional space and then vanish therefrom.[35]

As a Professor of Physics, Zöllner concluded that poltergeists lived within a hypothetical realm termed the 'fourth dimension'. Nowadays, we think of time as being the fourth dimension, but within the late-Victorian era it was otherwise. The German mathematician Bernhard Riemann introduced the notion of 'higher space', which was then developed by his British counterpart Charles Howard Hinton who proposed the existence of 4-D cubes called 'hypercubes', which possessed a new dimensional axis of measurement humans could not see. These 4-D spaces may contain something called 'tesseracts', which were like folds or wrinkles in 3-D space, allowing what might seem uncannily like teleportation to 3-D eyes to occur. Imagine you have a long piece of paper, and there is a living 2-D insect on one end of it, a drawing come to life. By folding this paper over carefully, you can transport the 2-D insect instantly from one end of the sheet to the other without it even having to walk there; from its own limited 2-D perspective, it might seem to have flown there instantaneously.

Such tropes became so familiar to the Victorian and Edwardian mind that they began popping up in fiction, as in Edward A. Abbott's comical 1884 geometrical sci-fi novel *Flatland*, in which a 2-D shape is kidnapped from its 2-D world by a 3-D sphere like a higher-dimensional alien being abducting a human into his saucer one night, before taking him on a journey across the universe to demonstrate to him the limitations of his usual sense-perceptions. When the 3-D sphere's 2-D abductee is returned back to 2-D land, he is then imprisoned as a dangerous loony by other 2-D sceptics who refuse to believe his heretical 3-D tale.[36] These themes even later appeared in a 1932 short story by US horror writer H. P. Lovecraft, *The Dreams in the Witch-House*, in which a sorceress, assisted by a homicidal rip-off of Gef the Talking Mongoose called 'Brown Jenkin', manages to travel from an attic-room into the safety of higher dimensions to escape justice for her crimes via the exploitation of 'freakish curvatures in space'.[37]

Zöllner imbibed such ideas eagerly. From within their 4-D realm, he proposed, poltergeists were able to reach down with their ghostly hands in order to manipulate matter here in the 3-D world in a manner which only *seemed* impossible to human beings, as we ourselves were not 4-D entities, and stood in relation to them as the primitive 2-D kidnapped shape in *Flatland* did to the advanced 3-D kidnapping sphere. 'For these beings,' declared Zöllner, 'the interior of a figure of three-dimensional space, enclosed on all sides, is just as easily accessible as is to us three-dimensional beings the interior of a surface enclosed on all sides by a [2-D] line.'[38] If what looked to us like a locked chest in the shape of a 3-D cube was really a 4-D hypercube full of potential tesseracts, then maybe poltergeists could just fold the cube's fourth dimensional axis over a bit and thereby teleport away its contents in the same manner that Brown Jenkin – or Gef the Mongoose – could exploit similar 4-D folds in space-time to pass through solid walls into other dimensions?

Imagine you are a 2-D stick-man, drawn on a piece of paper, next to an equally 2-D rectangle, representing a safe. Within this safe is then placed a gold coin, but you can't get to it as you are 2-D too. You go around the top edge, the bottom edge, the left edge and the right edge, but there is no way in. Then, a 3-D person walks past the piece of paper, sees the gold coin, reaches down and picks it up. As he is 3-D, he can easily see that the safe actually has no top; it only exists on the two planes of x and y, not the vertical plane of z. If the 2-D man managed to break down one of the 2-D walls of the safe, and then found that the coin had now vanished, he would be baffled, unable even to conceive of the possibility of a 3-D entity reaching down through the vertical z axis and just pocketing the item with its 3-D hand.

When it comes to a 4-D poltergeist stealing an item from a solid 3-D box, says Zöllner, we puny 3-D humans are in the same position as the silly 2-D fellow *vis-à-vis* the 3-D theft of the coin from the 2-D safe. It might look impossible to us, but that is only because the box actually possesses another 4-D hypercube plane, which we can't see, but spooks can. So, when Hermes uses his ghost-hand to reach in through the box's secret fourth plane he can easily penetrate what only *looks* like completely solid matter to us, because we only have the ability to see the box in 3-D, when it is really 4-D. Thus, all that is required for the passing of matter-through-matter is a mere shift of perspective and the shuffling of a tesseract.[39]

Or ... was it all just a trick of a more disappointingly prosaic kind? Zöllner's descriptions of the feats performed by Slade do, by their very nature, sound just like standard stage-conjuring tricks as performed by ordinary 3-D stage magicians with only two hands to spare. Henry Slade is nowadays generally considered a notorious fraud, following his appearance on trial in a London court in 1876, during which an actual stage-magician, John Nevil Maskelyne, gave a public demonstration of how to reproduce Slade's usual acts of slate-writing via ordinary, though cunning, means of illusion. Found guilty of 'using some subtle agent, means or device ... [to] deceive or impose upon some person', Slade was sentenced to three months' hard labour, but a retrial was ordered and Slade fled the country before he could be imprisoned; presumably no mere 3-D cell could have held him anyway.[40]

Victorian Spiritualists argued that, just because some of Slade's tricks *could* have been faked, that didn't necessarily mean that they *were*; but if *real* magic looks just like *fake* magic, then how can you ever distinguish between the two? The difference between a superhuman Trickster-thief like Hermes and an all-too-human Trickster-thief as Slade was alleged to have been may only be a matter of degree. The words 'magic' and 'conjuring' are used interchangeably to refer to both the real thing and its simulation; weirdly, many stage-magicians have claimed that pretending to be psychic on-stage has led to them later developing genuine psychic powers. It has been seriously speculated that faking magic is a good way to produce real magic;[41] in which case, Henry Slade's conviction for fraud only makes him all the more reliable, doesn't it?

* * * * *

And, for the Amazing Hermes' next trick, he will endeavour to pull a rabbit straight from out of a hat … and then eviscerate it. Historically-speaking, poltergeists have enjoyed stealing into stables and frightening the horses under the guise of a now largely-forgotten supernatural entity known as the *stallspuk*, or 'stable ghost'. The classic example is the Drummer of Tedworth abusing a horse by somehow shoving 'one of his Hinder Leggs in his Mouth, and [leaving it] so fastened there, that it was difficult for several Men to get it out with a Leaver.'[42] These barnyard-botherers still appear occasionally even today, it's just that nobody now remembers the old word for them.

Particularly interesting are cases of *stallspukery* in which the molested livestock appear to have been transported right through solid barriers somehow – living matter seeping directly into dead matter via paranormal osmosis, a characteristic party-piece of the Spirit Mercurius. Harry Price culled the following account of farmyard alchemy in action from the *Daily Mail* for 28 May 1906:

> At Furnace Mill, Lamberhurst, Kent, lived Mr J. C. Playfair. One morning during this month of May he went to his stables and found all the horses had been turned the reverse way round in their stalls. Their tails were in the mangers and their heads were where their tails should have been. One of the horses was missing. Mr Playfair hunted high and low and, happening to look into the hay-room nearby, discovered the horse. How it got there is still a mystery, because a partition had to be knocked down to get it out. The doorway of the hay-room was barely wide enough for a man to enter. Other phenomena included … locked and bolted doors … found open. No-one could approach the mill unseen, and two watch-dogs were on guard [at the time].[43]

Here, not only were barriers crossed with impunity, but the usual order of things inverted and rendered topsy-turvy, with the horses' heads and tails transposed the wrong way around in their berths. Tilting the world upside-down is one of the main imaginative functions of the Trickster-figure; in his story cycles the dead become living, shit becomes food, wrong becomes right and, here, the back end of the horse suddenly becomes the front one, as in many a pantomime. The trespasses on Playfair's farm were acts of 'stealing' more in the original Homeric sense of magical, hidden actions and trickery than the modern sense of reappropriation of private property.

Skinwalker Ranch in Utah was the scene of perhaps the most remarkable of all modern *stallspuk*-type hauntings. On the cattle-breeding property of the unfortunate Tom Gorman and his family throughout the 1990s, a disturbing combination of poltergeistery, UFO sightings and encounters with grotesque animal-like beings conspired to make life unbearable. Particularly concerning was how the family's livestock began inexplicably disappearing; on one occasion, a cow's footprints came to a dead halt in the middle of a snowfield.[44] At other times, stolen cattle were later found dead, having been mutilated in a seemingly non-natural fashion with 'perfectly circular' holes cored into their anuses and their guts then sucked out bumwards without any blood being spilled.[45] It was difficult for the Gormans to hunt down the animal predators presumed to be initially responsible, as their tracks would also disappear into thin air at random places, as with the vanished cows.[46] Thus, like many a traditional Trickster, the spooks down on the farm were both skilled hunters and expert escapers in one.

The ostensibly paranormal phenomenon of 'cattle-mutilation' is most often associated with UFOs, not poltergeists, and easily explained away by critics as being simply an overexcited misinterpretation of the entirely normal feeding-habits of predators and scavengers ... those most frequently blamed being coyotes and ravens, the two most significant Trickster animals of Native American Indian lore![47] Such things do indeed sound rather like the work of Coyote and Raven. If we can trust reports, the carcasses left behind don't seem to have been used for food at all, but as playthings for someone with a sick sense of humour, with weirdly precise geometrical shapes cut into their hides, sutures filled up with sand, and organs removed and laid out on top of carcasses, as if to conspicuously say 'look, we weren't even hungry!' Suggestively, some missing cattle are reportedly found replaced inside locked pens into which they could not possibly have gained access by themselves. Stumped law-enforcement officials often complain that 'trying to catch the culprits was like chasing a ghost',[48] and so it proved on Skinwalker Ranch.

The haunted property was repeatedly buzzed by intelligent flying blue 'orbs' – small, round, baseball-sized objects filled with a glowing blue liquid. One day in July 1996, Tom Gorman released three vicious guard-dogs at one to scare it away. It flitted around the animals like a spherical wasp. Snarling and yapping, they leapt up to bite it but, each time, the orb skilfully moved just out of harm's way, guiding the dogs towards a thick copse in the distance. Having reached this cover, the animals began yelping in fear and 'mortal agony'. Tom wisely dared not enter the copse himself until the following morning. Good choice. Three large circles of brown and burnt grass lay at the centre of the trees, and in the middle of each was a 'blackish greasy mess' – the vaporised corpses of his faithful hounds, real-life scorched sacrifices to some unknown Trickster-god.[49]

The Gormans particularly feared for the health of their four Black Angus cattle, worth $100,000 each. As if reading their minds, the local Hermes archetypes greedily stole them. After frantic searching, the beasts were finally relocated ... trapped inside a small trailer, through the narrow door of which it might have been a struggle for certain obese humans to have passed successfully, never mind bulky livestock. They were trance-locked, and when the Gormans banged on the side of the trailer the animals awoke, panicked and stampeded, gaining exit the only way possible – by charging right through the trailer's metal walls.[50] The hermetic cattle-rustlers could clearly create their own doors out of nothing. There were several weird alleged sightings of what might be termed 'holes in the sky', through which blue daylight could be seen, even though on the ranch itself it was the dead of night. From such paradoxical sky-holes, UFOs would emerge, together with 'huge black humanoid forms' with 'no face' which failed to show up on camera when photographed.[51]

According to local Native Indian lore, the Gormans' property lay upon 'The Path of the Skinwalker', a corridor of cursed land leading up to a place called Dark Canyon, where such sinister entities were said to live. Skinwalkers were yet another form of Trickster-figure, shape-shifting witches who donned the hides of animals – very commonly coyotes – before magically transforming into them, like werewolves. Inverted medicine-men, they abused their knowledge of 'medicine' (that is, beneficial healing magic) to do evil, being invoked by Utah's Indians to explain the unexpected deaths of livestock. Skinwalkers are still reported from the region even today. There are several yarns involving meetings with 'a hairy man or a hairy animal in man's clothing' or Hexham Heads-esque 'humans with dog-heads smoking cigarettes', with these things somewhat confused in the Native Indian mind with other fortean entities such as Bigfoot. As one informant put it, Skinwalkers 'can take the shape of anything they want to take the shape of. Like I said, they're medicine.'[52]

It has been suggested that 'the Skinwalker legend might be a convenient way for … [Native Indians] to grasp a vast menu of otherwise inexplicable events',[53] much as I am using the figure of the Trickster in this book. When the Gormans initially occupied their ranch, though, they didn't believe in Skinwalkers, so sought more mundane explanations. From their very first day on the property, they had witnessed abnormally large (and apparently bulletproof) wolves taller than their vehicles, as well as other bizarre hybrid creatures such as 'a weird dog' with a 'head much too large for its body', and a reddish coloured hyena-type thing with a dog's head, fox's tail and 'short, stubby legs like a boar', some of which they had specifically spied attacking and biting their animals. Drawing the natural conclusion, Mrs Gorman approached the office of a local official, and asked if anything could be done about the place's wolf-infestation. The official was puzzled. The last wolf in Utah had been shot in 1929, he explained. Was Mrs Gorman sure she hadn't encountered a coyote instead?[54] In a sense, I think perhaps she had.

Another bloodthirsty *stallspuk* infested Binbrook Farm near Grimsby during 1904–05. Binbrook was the scene of many mysterious poltergeist-like movements of objects and inexplicable fires – including one that started *on the back* of a servant-girl, causing her hospitalisation. Equally as sinister was the fate of the farm's chickens. A journalist sent out to probe the situation interviewed Binbrook's owner, a Mr White, informing his readers that:

Out of 250 fowls, Mr White says he has only twenty-four left. They have all been killed in the same weird way. The skin around the neck from the head to the breast has been pulled off, and the windpipe drawn from its place and snapped. The [locked] fowl house has been watched night and day, and whenever examined four or five birds would be found dead.[55]

No creature was seen either entering or exiting the chicken-house; and no known animals are acknowledged to kill their prey in this horrible way anyhow, without even eating them. Unlike real animals, the Winnebago Trickster Wakdjunkaga *did* murder fowl in this fashion, however. In one episode from his story cycle, Wakdjunkaga lures some ducks into his lodge, persuades them to close their eyes for a special dance, and then surreptitiously wrings their necks before biting them dead.[56]

Perhaps Wakdjunkaga was really Gef the Talking Mongoose. This oddest of all poltergeists eagerly scared his adopted family of Manx farmers by proclaiming that 'I am a ghost in the form of a weasel, and I shall haunt you with weird noises and clanking chains.' A metallic sound resembling just such a clinking then rang out from thin air, before Gef produced the following dread warning: 'If you are kind to me I will bring you good luck. If you are not kind, I shall kill all your poultry. I can get them wherever you put them.'[57] At Binbrook Farm, Trickster had already proved it.

In 1969, Stan Hughes, landlord of the polt-haunted Blue Lion Inn in Flintshire, found the private menagerie on his premises under assault from a ghost; no fewer than five times the cages were discovered all open with his animals gone missing. Yet, as one account had it, 'No common thief could be the culprit for a layer of sand covers the menagerie and no signs of footprints or disturbance of its surface were found.'[58] No common thief indeed.

The most famous heist Hermes ever pulled was when, while still a mere new-born babe-in-arms, he crept from his cradle in search of meat, stole the heavenly cattle of his brother Apollo from under the eyes of his watch-dogs, then sacrificed these kine in tribute to the immortal gods (including himself), cutting them up before roasting them into greasy cinders like Tom Gorman's hounds on a makeshift altar of stone. I do not naively suggest that the myth, as described in the *Homeric Hymn*, was literally inspired by real-life ancient Greek instances of *stallspukery*; the *Hymn* has more plausibly been interpreted by Norman O. Brown as encoding a long-ago conflict between the lower-classes (represented by Hermes) and their ruling aristocracy (played by Apollo) for a fairer share of the spoils of pre-Classical Greece's pastoral riches.[59]

Nonetheless, there is an imaginative parallel to be drawn between the *Homeric Hymn* and a haunting like Skinwalker Ranch. Prior to their slaughter by Hermes, Apollo's cattle are immortal in nature, heavenly beasts, not normal ones – quite literally, sacred cows. In Brown's reading, the sacred cows which are *really* being slain in the story, though, are those surrounding the traditional over-privilege of the archaic Greek aristocracy. As Lewis Hyde puts it, 'Hermes' theft proves the boundary between his world [that of the lower-classes] and that of Apollo's [that of the aristocracy] is porous; it implies that the rules by which Apollo operates are contingent and arbitrary.'[60]

In the context of today's society, it has persuasively been argued that the golden sun god Apollo now stands not for the privileged world of the Greek nobility, but for something else entirely – the currently privileged elite of the scientific priesthood within whose jealously guarded cultural Dominant

Apollo as solar deity; in this guise, he stands in direct contrast to his brother Hermes, Master of Thieves and Lord of the Night.

events like those at Skinwalker Ranch cannot be admitted to ever take place. In this interpretation, the incredulous Gormans stand in initially for Apollo and his scientist-priests, trying desperately to prevent the slaughter of their own sacred Cartesian cows; while whatever killed and teleported the family's livestock stands in for Hermes the boundary-erasing cattle-thief. But, the *Homeric Hymn* suggests, this is a combat Hermes always wins in the end.

* * * * *

Most major thefts take place at night. So too do most major hauntings – at least in the popular imagination. In some traditional cultures, Trickster-tales, having a sacred, ritual significance, could themselves only be told after dark, when everyone in the tribe was tucked away safely in bed. If anybody so much as struck a match, the story-tellers would seal their lips, and the narrative reach an abrupt end. The flame extinguished, the legend was quickly resumed.[61] Likewise, the best ghost stories are always set and told at night, fictional or otherwise. It is a curious fact that a poltergeist often refuses to do its work during daylight hours, or even after midnight when the lights are still on. In folk tales it is evident why ghosts prefer to work the night shift – the cultural implications of high noon vs witching hour are too obvious to require listing – but why should this also be so in real life?

The Drummer of Tedworth would not 'suffer a Candle in the Room, but carry them away lighted up the Chimney, or throw them under the Bed', we are told.[62] The Irish Derrygonnelly polt of 1877 was similarly shy. Candles and lamps disappeared or were tossed out of the room by it, until finally the haunted household had to store their candles with a neighbour.[63] The chosen habit of one twentieth-century spook was to twist a bulb from its socket during the night. Detecting its pranks, the married couple of the household would jump out of bed to flip the light-switch – to no effect. The bulb had been removed and carefully placed on a nearby chair, 'still hot and unbroken'.[64] In one Portuguese haunting, knocks were heard on window panes during evening hours. A candle was lit – and, instantly, they stopped. Put out, the knocks sprang up anew. This pattern was repeated, *ad infinitum*, for quite some time.[65]

I don't see, from a purely rational viewpoint, why a poltergeist should act like this. However, adopting a more subjective and literary approach – namely, a hermeneutic one – might allow us to fumble towards the right path. The way some spooks only emerge after nightfall is suggestive of the wider fleeing from logic they in themselves embody. Light is logic's classic symbol, and 'night-time reasoning' a common way to describe the search for occult truths. Light – particularly daylight – is the symbol *par excellence* of Apollo, god of the sun. To Patrick Harpur, 'The world of "far-seeing" solar Apollo is one of light, clarity, order, formal beauty, detachment, far-sighted goals. It is easy to identify him as the god behind science.'[66] The scientific method is to look into things; and to do so, we require a good source of light. That light has since been defined, *by* science, as *being* science, to the exclusion of all other modes of seeing the world. The very term 'Enlightenment' was no accident. The pure, clear light of reason was meant to shine upon all things under the sun within the modern, materialist empire of Descartes' Dominant. Not Christ, but Apollo, is now the presiding Light of Our World. But, when it comes to examining the poltergeist, is Apollo's spotlight not the wrong intensity of Olympian illumination for us to use?

If light symbolises solar Apollo, who in turn symbolises the 'light of reason' – logic, science, that which has a definite answer to it – then night is its polar opposite, the realm of witchcraft, mysterious moon goddesses and Apollo's darkling twin, Hermes the Trickster, Hermes the Thief. Known as the 'companion of dark night' and 'furtive Hermes, the night-time chieftan', the god was particularly active during the liminal interlude of twilight.[67] Vampires

As god of journeys and transition-states, Hermes would accompany wanderers on their way.

retreat to their coffins at cock-crow, threatening shadows dissolve into more familiar, harmless shapes after a sleepless childhood night, burglars pack away their crowbars, and many polts, like Hermes, can do no other than sink into an inverted slumber come sunrise. It is another hint that the perplexing riddle they pose probably cannot ever hope to be fully solved, another means through which Hermes figuratively butchers the holy cows of shining-faced Apollo.

✳ ✳ ✳ ✳ ✳

In his guise of *Hermes psychopompos*, Hermes not only guides souls down into Hades but brings sleepers their dreams. During the just-mentioned Derrygonnelly haunting, the SPR's man on the spot Professor William Barrett tried to explain the spook's habitual candle-pilfering in terms of the focus-figure needing to be in a state of diminished, darkness-enhanced consciousness when half-asleep in bed if the ghost was to successfully manifest via her mediumship. According to Barrett: 'As in the case of dowsing, hypnosis, clairvoyance, telepathy and probably all psychical phenomena, the effect of education, the cultivation of the reasoning powers, alert consciousness, in fact, cerebral activity generally, usually diminish and ultimately inhibit the production of supernormal phenomena.'[68] Such *unheimlich* things belong to a different mental world than that of the everyday, rational mode of being we inhabit while fully awake. The supernatural's governing logic is not Apollo's clear-sighted solar brand but, rather, the illogical logic of nocturnal dreams – a world in which chairs can fly and matter pass through matter with absolute ease.

Pleasingly, in 1991 an Australian physician, Dr John Murray Johns, devised a standard 'sleepiness scale' used for measuring that borderland area between sleeping and wakefulness we all enter every night. He called it the 'Epworth Scale', after the institution where he worked, Melbourne's Epworth Hospital. But this hospital had been founded by Methodists, and was in its turn named after Epworth Parsonage, the English home of the founder of Methodism, John Wesley – a house which was, famously, haunted by a poltergeist that operated chiefly under cover of darkness, disturbing the Wesleys in their beds at night.[69] Johns could just as easily have christened it the 'Hermes Scale'.

From a hermeneutic perspective, Trickster-myths become a form of imaginative template which, when laid down over the world, can help make some sense out of it all. Parapsychologists of a more Apollonic bent could use their own myths in order to understand the poltergeist quite differently; myths such as the more hard-line brand of RSPK, which appears to me self-evidently Apollonic in its nature, seeking as it does a final, energetically-explicable solution for the poltergeist which it may not be possible to ultimately achieve. As a result, the path of Hermes appears the wiser one to pursue, even if it must be groped for in the dark. Whether true or fictional, I think poltergeist narratives are so widely told and enjoyed primarily because they tell us, in coded form, that there is more to life than just blind materialism and that no body of systematised knowledge and power has all the answers. Even the well-guarded and well-locked barns protecting the sacred materialist cows of that other shining solar deity René Descartes can sometimes be successfully raided and sacked – particularly when night falls and Hermes the Thief is in town.

IV

Keys to Meaning

It is a riddle, wrapped in a mystery, inside an enigma; but perhaps
there is a key.

Winston Churchill

Poltergeists have an undeniable obsession with locks, bolts and keys. During
a 1914 haunting in the French village of Vodable, doors were often found
double-locked by the ghost from the inside, making it impossible to regain
access to rooms without the locks being picked. Once, a visiting cousin
was found trapped inside her chamber 'as in a prison'. The relevant keys
had simply vanished. A locksmith – given good business by the spirit – was
summoned to instigate a jail-break. Once he arrived, the keys were found
'in a very obvious place' where they had clearly not been before. Things got
so bad the householders resorted to carrying the keys to each room around
with them all day long; and yet, when the sealed doors to their rooms were
opened up at night they still found bizarre assortments of objects lying there
tucked-up inside their beds, taunting them.[1]

At Calvados Castle in France, during a haunting of 1875–76, similar
stealthy pranks were played. When the occupant of the castle's most-haunted
room, a certain Abbé, left it empty he was always most careful to double-lock
the door and place the key in his pocket. It made no difference. Re-entering,
he found the place in constant disarray – a real locked-room puzzle. On one
bizarre occasion, his books had been tossed to the other end of the chamber,
'not pell-mell as out of a piece of furniture which fell, but in regular files just
as they had been on the shelves.'[2] His securely-closed window was habitually
found wide open too. One time, he actually screwed it shut. It was prised
open by the ghost anyway, and the screws placed uselessly upon the floor.
The Abbé then had the window boarded up with a piece of wood 'securely
nailed to the inner frame.' Once more, the door was locked. When it was
unlocked, the wood had been torn away and the cushions from the bedroom
couch were missing. They were found, with the piece of wood, lined up neatly
in a row on the outside window-sill.[3]

A *kobold* (a Germanic spirit who haunts houses or lives underground in
caves or mines) which haunted an Austrian maidservant called Hannie and

A *kobold* – or German fairy – in the form of a Puck-like imp-infant helps out a housemaid with her kitchen-work, as depicted here by Gustave Doré. Poltergeists sometimes continued to be labelled by their victims as *kobolds* in German-speaking lands right into the twentieth century.

her master, a Commander Kogelnick, during the 1920s also found it funny to spirit away keys. One time, this Robin Goodfellow stole the key from the cellar, leaving the household without access to its coal. It fell to the cook to go outside for more, so she went to her room to fetch her boots. However, her door was locked and the key seen flying away before several witnesses' eyes, 'too quickly for pursuit'. There followed a tedious game of hunt-the-key which, eventually, the cook won. When she unlocked the door to her room, she found her boots had now disappeared instead.[4]

During that most suspiciously ambiguous of hauntings at Borley Rectory, known inaccurately as 'The Most Haunted House in England', the following key-prank once occurred, reported Harry Price:

> As we all stood in the hall, the keys in the doors of the library and drawing-room, that opened onto the hall, *shot out simultaneously* at right angles to the doors, and fell to the floor ... I was told that this key-dropping phenomenon was common. And during the incumbency of the next rector, every key in the house vanished![5]

A January 1932 extract from the diary of one Borley occupant details an equally astonishing event:

> One night, both doors of our room were found locked. One door was locked from the inside. This showed the impossibility, therefore, of the locking having been done by a human agent ... When we returned to the Chapel we found a [relevant] key lying on the corner of the altar.[6]

A recent Turkish poltergeist, or *djinni*, possessed a similar *modus operandi*. Once, a door-key turned by itself from the inside, trapping the affected family outside. Another time, all the plates were found transported from the kitchen and laid out neatly in the yard;[7] the ghost's way of telling them to unlock the door, get some fresh air and have a picnic?

A Virginia poltergeist of 1870 was even trickier. One day, two young ladies visited the haunted house to test the extent of the spook's criminal powers. Locking all the internal and external doors, they retired to the kitchen. A few minutes later they emerged to find all doors now open and the parlour disarranged quite terribly. Oddest of all, they also found 'a strange key that would neither unlock nor lock any door in the house, sticking in the keyhole of the parlour door.'[8] This is a most subversive joke; with that marvellously irrelevant key, the spook is mocking the whole notion of keys, locks and barriers entirely, remaking them all on its own deliberately absurdist terms. It was because of Hermes' similar mastery over locks that, in ancient Greece, people's house-keys often came stamped with an image of the thieving Trickster-deity.[9] So, in a way, did this 'strange key'.

* * * * *

There are both literal keys in this world, and more metaphorical keys to meaning. With this in mind, we should ask what was the wider function of Hermes' sacred stone heap, back in the days when the Greeks still wore their sandals? Tricksterishly enough, they possessed several differing, though complementary, purposes simultaneously. Originally, these 'herms', as they were called, were simply handy piled-up cairns marking out paths and natural boundaries, but over time they acquired the shape of square-cut blocks surmounted with a carving of the god's head. These blocks were of a type termed 'ithyphallic' – they bore a representation of Hermes' erect penis. A similar stone phallus appeared on some Greek graves, a symbol of returning *psyche*, or soul; the Greeks believed in a doctrine of *metempsychosis*, a kind of reincarnation. Just as souls would return from dead corpses, like butterflies reborn from their inert-looking chrysalises (the word *psyche* meant both 'soul' and 'butterfly'), so life, as symbolised by the carved penis, could emerge from dead stone, as with lithobolia. One ancient Greek vase shamelessly represents an ithyphallic figure, possibly Hermes himself, dribbling semen, the blobs of which spontaneously form into shape of a living butterfly soul. As the Jungian Karl Kerényi put it, wherever such a magical penis is placed becomes at once '*mortis et vitai locus*, the place of life and death' – the crossroads between two worlds.[10]

You could find such herms at crossroads, atop hills or mountains, at the borderline of woods and forests, at the limit between one village's territory and the next, or at the entrance to a house; all places where it was natural for commerce between different groups to take place. Hermes became cast as both 'god of roads' and 'god of doors', as it was at such borderland zones that people from one clan, family or village met those from another clan, family or village, to exchange goods, services, money and mates ... or, whenever things went wrong, to exchange blows with a dagger, maybe. Clearly, commerce with the outside world was considered both potentially dangerous, hence the need for Hermes' magical protection in such areas, yet also potentially beneficial, hence the presence of his rock-hard hard-on.

Hermes' phallus didn't just point the way to the next convenient market-place, it also signified the potential for creative fertility which existed wherever it was that insider groups met and intermingled with outsider groups, there to engage in all the necessary forms of social intercourse which made civilisation possible. Clear and stable boundaries are necessary, but so is their penetration; if commerce is ever to occur, then men must strap on Mercury's winged sandals and travel. The Greek words for 'buy' and 'do business' were both derived from the same root-word, meaning 'beyond' or 'across'. Good fences do indeed make good neighbours, but only if they also have good gates, no matter how securely locked and barred they may ordinarily be – like a less malign version of H. P. Lovecraft's hideous Old One Yog-Sothoth, Hermes was both that gate, and the key to it, too.

As Greek civilisation progressed and flourished during the sixth century BC, herms now came to stand erect in the *agora*, or chief market-place and town-square, of Athens, designating it as Greece's main place to do business. But the herms lining the edges of the country-roads of Attica, the rural realm within which the dominant city-state sat like Ananse the African Spider-Trickster at the centre of its web, served simultaneously as milestones, linking the centre to the periphery in the Classical world's primitive equivalent of a telecommunications network, as well as acting as a physical embodiment of the region's political and military unity. Just as all roads were later to lead to Rome under the tutelary protection of Mercury, so in the Hellenic world all penises pointed Athens-wards under the erectile influence of Hermes.[11]

* * * * *

During Greece's pre-Classical early days, the centre was not quite so well-integrated with the periphery. In the ancient world, to wander aimlessly between towns like a drifter was considered a likely diagnostic sign of mental illness,[12] and the sense of potential danger when approaching a boundary-marking herm was felt acutely. As such, a primitive form of commerce known as 'silent trade' emerged, in which one party would near a herm, leave out an offering of goods, retreat to a safe distance, then return later on to find that some other, equally nervous fellow from the next village had left them something different (but hopefully useful and of roughly equivalent value) in return. Later, goods might be replaced with sums of money. This way, neither unknown trader would be tempted to stab the other in a sudden bout of suspicious terror.[13] A 1970s poltergeist from Guarulhos, Brazil, liked to make money both appear and disappear too, 'but it wasn't seen from where nor how it came'; when it stole away cash, it left behind bits of paper marked with a red cross, like paranormal IOUs.[14] Does that not too sound like a form of 'silent trade'?

Originally, it is guessed, offerings of food would be placed by cairns for Hermes then eaten by hungry passers-by, thus indicating to believers that the sacrifice had been accepted, like parents eating mince-pies left out for Santa. This free food was considered a lucky windfall of the road, a theft Hermes would have blessed, as pilfering unattended fare was exactly what *he* would have done under such circumstances. A useful social fiction then emerged: that the food, money and goods found at boundary-marking herms were not really left there by your fellow trade-seeking human beings at all, but supernatural gifts from the area's governing god. These lucky finds were deemed nothing less than *hermaions*, or 'Gifts from Hermes';[15] and there is a real parallel to be drawn between them and a regular subset of poltergeistery known collectively as JOTTs, or JOTTles.

The acronym 'JOTT' means 'Just One of Those Things', and is used to refer to the unusual appearance or disappearance of small objects such as coins, pens and (in particular) keys; when such items materialise from nowhere, 'JOTT' becomes just an alternative term for an 'apport'. Whenever you misplace your glasses and then, after many hours of searching, find them sitting in plain sight in the middle of your desk exactly where you left them, then that's one type of JOTT. Or when you stroll into the kitchen and find a £10 note lying, plain as day, in the middle of the floor, with no clue where it came from, then that's another type of JOTT – or they are to some people. Most of us fortunate enough not to live within haunted homes would ascribe such 'mysterious' occurrences to ordinary absent-mindedness. There have even been sad cases in which elderly polt-victims, subjected to repeated JOTTling, were later diagnosed as actually having Alzheimer's disease.[16]

Some JOTTs are far weirder, though. Clothes go a-wandering and then suddenly turn up hanging within a just-assembled wardrobe; you go abroad, lose your alarm clock, find a very similar, but broken, replacement version nestling inside your suitcase instead, before the original one turns up, sitting conspicuously in the middle of your hallway back at home; you drop an apple, it disappears, and then is thrown onto your plate by invisible hands in somebody else's kitchen, no longer green and fresh but unappetisingly withered. One recent collection of JOTT anecdotes, collected by the SPR's Mary Rose Barrington, features many accounts like these, which do seem rather hard to attribute to the onset of degenerative brain disease among the aged.[17]

And, as for lucky finds, how about the following? A man is off on the open road when his moped conks out, so he wheels it over into a dead-end. Turns out he needs a replacement spark-plug. Fortunately, lying there in the gutter is a nice, shiny brand-new one. The traveller accepts the proffered *hermaion* gratefully and continues on his way.[18] The actor Anthony Hopkins had an even better experience of silent trade. Cast in the Hollywood adaptation of George Feifer's novel *The Girl from Petrovka*, he thought he should read the book first, but couldn't find a copy anywhere; until, waiting for a train, he saw one lying on a nearby seat. Picking it up, he found it was fully annotated – because it was Feifer's own, personal copy! Many authors in search of a specific reference to cite have experienced something similar, when books literally fall off their shelves, opening up at the precise page needed to complete their research. Arthur Koestler, not only a famous novelist but also a paranormal obsessive, memorably dubbed this phenomenon the 'library angel', but the Jungian Hermes-worshipper Karl Kerényi sensibly preferred to label them *hermaions*.[19]

The best case of a directly spook-related library angel involved the American Episcopalian bishop James Pike, whose memoir *The Other Side* is an extended account of the poltergeistery he experienced in the wake of his son Jim's drug-induced suicide in 1966. Following Jim's death, Pike pursued research into theological topics, and found to his surprise that his son's ghost was helping him. Books Pike needed for his work would materialise unseen on nearby coffee tables, just waiting to be read. Even odder, they would have locks of hair shorn from Pike's own head, or old family postcards from happier times, affixed prominently to their pages with some unknown 'mucilaginous substance', marking out the exact chapters or passages containing the most salient references. Jim's shade, communicating via a medium, proudly took direct responsibility for such beneficial silent trades, but I think the invisible librarian working unpaid overtime here was really Hermes.[20]

Another particularly fortuitous *hermaion* occurred in the haunted Seattle home of a man named Keith Linder, where the resident poltergeist was generally of a threatening nature, but occasionally preferred to imitate a library angel. The entity enjoyed transporting household objects to new places, making a PC-tower turn up inside a kitchen cupboard, and causing new objects which Linder had never even owned to suddenly appear. Many such apports were children's playthings, like toy spiders, cars and balls, which is appropriate as similar offerings were once made up to Hermes; childhood toys were dedicated to him by little Greek boys on the cusp of growing up.[21]

Another unasked-for present was a wine encyclopaedia, which Linder found sitting on his kitchen counter one day. Not one to look a gift horse in the mouth, Linder, who had no previous interest in the subject, read through the book and, liking what he learned, became rather an oenophile, buying himself a wine-cabinet and 'a few choice bottles' to sit in it; the *hermaion* here functioned almost like one of those algorithms on web-shopping sites, which produce messages saying 'If you bought this book, you may also like …'. Admittedly, the ghost then invaded the cabinet and made Linder's bottles roll around all over the place, but at every roadside herm the god Hermes gives and also takes away. When parapsychologists visited Linder, they later found mysterious voices appearing on their tape-recorders informing them of the location of various objects they had accidentally misplaced – one was told, quite correctly, that his missing boot was hiding beneath his bed back home in England.[22]

*****

Gifts of Hermes can also be verbal in nature, as with what we now call 'Freudian Slips', where a speaker exposes their true feelings by accidentally saying something like 'I really must get around to *killing* my mother' instead of 'I really must get around to *calling*' her. For Keith Linder, Hermes revealed a hitherto-unknown taste for the pleasures of the grape. Such truths can be hidden not only from others, but also from the tongue-tripping speaker himself, leading such (un)happy accidents to once have been considered akin to spontaneous oral prophecies, gifts of knowledge provided unexpected and unasked-for, straight from the heights of Olympus (or depths of Hades).

Acts of divination operated upon the principle that the patterns cast by the dice or bones thrown by the Greek or Roman soothsayer were not actually random in nature, as they appeared to the untutored eye, but instead revealed the hidden will of the gods – particularly the will of Hermes, god of dice – and so it was with verbal slips. When Hermes causes what *appear* to be linguistic mishaps, therefore, he is really revealing what already lies alike within the will of heaven, and within the mind of the speaker.[23] Likewise, during poltergeist hauntings, the chance finding of those modern-day *hermaions* known as JOTTs can oftentimes reveal what already lies hidden away within the mind of the finder. Many apports, it could be argued, are the physical equivalent of Freudian slips.

In her book about the subject, Mary Rose Barrington cites the example of a woman scheduled to venture from her house during a fierce storm. However, she lost her car keys from their usual place on the dressing-table. She phoned her friend, with whom she had been intending to travel, to cancel the trip. Having done so, she glanced over at the dressing-table – and there were the keys, back where they always were, but temporarily were not. When told of their return, the woman's friend cautioned her that clearly 'You were not meant to go' and they postponed their journey until better weather – and less chance of catching pneumonia or skidding off-road – prevailed.[24]

Was this truly a portent of potential doom from Hermes – a gift in the form of a theft, you might say, a kind of inverted *hermaion* in shape – or more akin to a message from the subconscious self? Those who argue in favour of the RSPK hypothesis would prefer the latter rationalisation. Barrington herself cited her own experience with a JOTTling key which disappeared just before Christmas 1995, then returned some time later in deeply unlikely circumstances. According to Barrington, the 'ghost' at work here was really the hidden psychokinetic powers of her own mind:

> ... shortly before the key JOTTled, I had opened the door to what I expected to be small carol singers, but instead found myself buying liquid-soap of high price and low quality from a Good Cause. The key disappeared soon afterwards. I tried, fretfully, to use this product for two weeks, but with the dawning of the New Year I came to my senses and regarded it as a sort of receipt for giving to a Good Cause rather than as a profitable transaction and threw the useless liquid away. I learned a lesson and the key came back next morning.[25]

Having taught Barrington the true meaning of charitable gift exchange, Hermes' Ghost of Christmas Present-style work here was done and her missing key returned in yet another successful act of silent trade. Barrington really should have had a herm erected on the threshold of her property, in tribute to her celestial benefactor (if ithyphallic in nature, it might even have warded off any future unwelcome callers as a side benefit).

* * * * *

After floating through the keyhole of their Hertfordshire home in June 1991, Hermes began delivering some very enigmatic messages indeed to a married couple named Jerry and Elizabeth; objects moved, suitcases packed and unpacked themselves, photos turned back-to-front on the walls, plants uprooted spontaneously in the garden (as vegetation once did for Orpheus when playing his magic tune), letters returned from within post-boxes and, on occasion, the entire house would shake for no apparent reason. Odder yet, Jerry and Elizabeth would watch helpless while shoes filled up with water right before their eyes, or the apparitional paw of a cat poked up through their bed covers. Uniquely, the poltergeist would even complete their crosswords!

Hermes then devised some cryptic clues of his own in the shape of a veritable tidal-wave of JOTTs. Old watches and necklaces, lost by Elizabeth years beforehand, turned up in sealed jars and cake-tins, placed out like silent trade offerings on the floor. These items were described as looking 'almost as if they were presents' – which, I think, they were:

> They would be found in the house after coming home from work or after getting up in the morning [and] included: a three-tier plastic table for plants; plants for the garden; mail-order items they did not order and which were unreturnable; a camera; a set of suitcases; a fox ornament; a small green turtle ornament; coloured balls for the dog; a plastic Christmas pudding; a radio; a black jacket for Elizabeth (her size); many presents under both their pillows; and, recently, a *Flintstones* T-shirt for Jerry … [and] chocolate bars in the fridge.

As recompense for these random *hermaions*, just like an unseen Greek tradesman at a boundary-marking herm, the poltergeist took little offerings of its own in return – most commonly, cottage-cheese spirited away from the fridge, or sometimes quantities of actual cash. This latter habit became a real problem. Repeatedly, money vanished from upon Elizabeth's person, leaving her stranded travelling to or from work; once, she was fined for fare-dodging when, after boarding her train, she proved unable to pay the ticket inspector. Jerry himself had no such problems, and was forced to meet her at the station with his own full wallet after work each evening, with the pickpocket polt virtually confining her to the house without him.

What obscure message was Hermes seeking to impart? Realising the crossword-loving spook could write, Jerry tried to find out, leaving the spirit notes asking 'What can we do to appease?' The ghost tucked a reply inside one of Jerry's shoes: 'You [can] fuck off' it said. Jerry received many similarly abusive missives. 'Thoughtless bastard' read one. 'Get stuffed. You'll pay' and 'You'll learn when it's too late' read others. On vacation, Jerry opened his holiday reading book only to find the instruction 'Stay there, bastard' scribbled inside. When Jerry bought Elizabeth a poetry collection, the ghost warned 'Don't give – Elizabeth hates poetry books!' on the flyleaf. To the case's investigators, Jerry later admitted that he and his wife were having certain relationship issues, tellingly observing that the polt always 'took her side' in their arguments, and that 'the abuse I get [in its notes] is just a reflection of her language' during such tiffs.

Maybe the constant apports were paranormal peace-offerings from one spouse to another, or else hints from Elizabeth to her dozy husband about the kinds of gifts she would *rather* receive from him, like chocolate bars and clothes, as opposed to slim volumes of sensitive verse. One theory advanced was that the theft of Elizabeth's money was forcing her to stay at home with her husband more, and even travel to and from work with him, thus ensuring they spent more quality time together, giving them an opportunity to talk through their issues. Hermes' first silent theft occurred when the couple were out and about, had an argument, and Jerry decided to just drive off home – but he couldn't, because his car-keys disappeared, only to drop to the floor months later inside the spare bedroom. Hence, either the henpecked husband was trying to control his wife via RSPK, or the resentful wife was trying to control her husband via the same method, or perhaps some destructive combination of the two. Eventually, Elizabeth was diagnosed with cancer and died; and so, at precisely the same time, did the marital poltergeist.[26]

* * * * *

The *I Ching*-like divinatory art of interpreting the Freudian slips which allegedly lie hidden behind many JOTTles can sometimes be taken a bit too far, however, the chief exhibit being the books of Nandor Fodor, a likeably eccentric Hungarian parapsychologist and fanboy-like devotee of Sigmund Freud. Fodor corresponded with the Great Man himself about the topic of poltergeistery, winning some level of approval for his ideas, which were an ornate early version of the RSPK hypothesis. The story of how Fodor came to approach Freud in the first place is amusing.

In 1929, Fodor moved to London to work as a journalist for titles such as the *Daily Mail* and *Daily Mirror*, using his spare time to write a still-useful 500,000-word *Encyclopedia of Psychic Science*. This got him a position on the International Institute for Psychical Research (IPR), thereby enabling him to investigate numerous notable poltergeist hauntings of the day at first hand. One such haunting conveniently took place within the London suburb of Thornton Heath, centring upon a truly mentally disturbed individual named Mrs Forbes. Fodor concluded that this case could only really be interpreted in Freudian terms relating to issues surrounding Mrs Forbes' 'own guilt-feelings relating to sexual traumata and frustrations', and wrote up a report which proved so controversial – and, to some eyes, so obscene – that it was not published until as late as 1959.

Fodor's main problem was that the IPR, established as a rival to the SPR in 1934, had a governing board mainly staffed by 'prim, elderly ladies' who were only interested in promoting 'the spiritistic hypothesis' that poltergeists were the invisible souls of the dead, not the idea they might actually be externalised mental projections of sexual neuroses, something which 'offended the high moral tone' of their endeavours. As such, when Fodor handed in his book-length report on Thornton Heath and explained its contents, the prudish old biddies simply quarantined it away under lock and key as pure filth, without even reading it. The Spiritualist periodical *Psychic News* printed a story about this, which Fodor thought impugned his reputation by accusing him of being a paranormal pornographer so, in March 1939, he sued the newspaper for libel.

During the trial, *Psychic News*' lawyers tried to make Fodor out to be a suitable case for psychiatric treatment himself by bringing up Mrs Forbes' alleged ability to JOTTle away items from within stores via a kind of 'psychic shoplifting'. Was it true, a lawyer asked Fodor, that he had tried to test this skill by taking Mrs Forbes to the Tower of London and challenging her to make Hermes steal away the Crown Jewels from within their glass display-case? Fodor admitted he had indeed wanted to do so, and that he was 'willing to go to jail' if she succeeded. However, the old ladies of the IPR had been nervous of negative publicity, and had refused Fodor permission to carry out the experiment. Naturally, the next day every newspaper on Fleet Street was full of sensationalised accounts of this juicy titbit of psychic scandal.

Anticipating such underhand tactics, Fodor felt it might be a good idea to approach Freud himself for an endorsement. Freud was then living in London, a Jewish refugee from the Nazis, and Fodor bundled his wife out to his house, armed with a bouquet of flowers 'as a tribute from the women of England'. Over a cup of tea, Mrs Fodor told him of her husband's little problem. Distressed to hear of a disciple being persecuted for his beliefs, Freud asked to see Fodor's manuscript, by now liberated from the old ladies' clutches. He liked it, writing Fodor a helpful letter, explaining how he had possessed no prior interest in 'the stupid tricks' of any 'so-called poltergeist', but that Fodor's report had changed his mind. He had been 'richly rewarded' by its reading, concluding that 'I regard as very probable the result you come to with regard to this particular case'. Fodor now visited Freud in person and got permission to include this note of approval in his book, should it ever be published, but it turned out the Austrian had cancer of the jaw with only a few months to live, so Fodor declined to make use of the fan mail in court as 'it would have been inexcusable to drag his name' into the headlines at such a delicate time. It turned out he didn't need to. After three days Fodor won his case anyway, receiving the then-useful sum of £105 in damages.[27]

What precisely were Fodor's ideas, which won such praise from his hero? In a 1948 article printed in *The Psychiatric Quarterly*, called *The Poltergeist Psychoanalysed*, Fodor argued that we should not speak of poltergeists *per se*, but of a 'Poltergeist Psychosis', in which some traumatic childhood event, since repressed by the conscious mind of the adult, leads to the build-up of mental pressure within the individual which later breaks out from within the victim's subconscious mind and into the outside world in the form of a spook, which thereby functions as an RSPK-created secondary personality, acting out the focus-figure's psychological issues by proxy. Instead of being a 'ghost' as such, Fodor redefined a poltergeist as being 'an episodic mental disturbance of a schizophrenic character':

> In order to understand this concept, one must be familiar with the psychological state known as dissociation. This is the 'dis-association' of one part of a person's mind or personality. It may take the form of a temporary state of amnesia – in which a person will commit certain acts or take on a different personality for short periods of time and then return to the normal self with no conscious memory of what has been done. Obviously, if a person is suffering from this type of schizophrenia,

or split-personality, he may carry out destructive acts, representing his repressed desires or frustrations, without realising that he is the cause. Such switching back and forth can take place in an instant, meaning that certain acts may be completely forgotten immediately after they take place.[28]

This was then a well-accepted fact of mainstream psychiatry; what was rather less well-accepted by conventional shrinks, however, was that this same process could also take place via supernatural means. For Fodor:

> Only by historical analysis [of a patient's life story] can one reach the conclusion that, behind ... [most poltergeistery lies the repressed memory of] a sexual atrocity clamour[ing] for vengeance. My postulation is that the shock ... [a patient suffers from rape or molestation] in early childhood produces a kind of 'psychic lobotomy', by which I mean a tearing loose of her mental system, leaving it free-floating like a disembodied entity but still capable of personality development.[29]

Essentially, therefore, for Fodor polt-haunted people are playing a programme of paranormal practical jokes *on themselves* in order to work out their repressed sexual issues in a symbolic fashion, like physical, real-world dreams just waiting to be parsed for hermeneutic meaning. Viewed in this light, apports become three-dimensional cryptic crossword clues to be interpreted by the psychoanalysing parapsychologist, who divines their symbolic nature in a similar fashion to Freud parsing the contents of a patient's Hermes-sent dreams, or a soothsayer decoding the falls of his Hermes-thrown dice, bones or pebbles.

While no parapsychologists today seriously propose that all poltergeists are displaced products of paedophilia, Fodor's general hermeneutic-sexual approach has nonetheless proved influential. One modern-day poltergeist bothered its female victim by continually smashing or displacing objects which came in pairs – but it only ever destroyed or stole *one* of the pair. Why so? The conclusion of Fodor-imitating investigators was that, as the lady had endured a mastectomy six months prior to the polt appearing, the one-of-a-pair items affected really functioned as symbolic substitutes for her missing breast, to the destruction and loss of which other one-of-a-pair item she stood emotionally unreconciled.[30] Another patient went to bed only to find a ghost had transported a kitchen-knife into it. It transpired she was about to remarry, and that her previous husband had once stabbed her; a warning from some aspect of her own self to be careful in her choice of men, it was deduced.[31] To adapt Tolstoy, it seems each happy family is alike, but each haunted family is haunted in its own way.

*****

As a god of language, Hermes was also the god of metaphors, a form of inventive linguistic constructions which draw explicit connections between apparently quite different things, thereby to demonstrate their unexpected kindred; a tortoise-slow intellect, for instance, or a jelly-weak spine. It has been suggested that this is another aspect of Hermes' frequent function as an agent of Eros; his magic staff may well have been a sanitised bowdlerisation of his original magic penis, which drew unanticipated bonds between lovers, bringing them together, just like a road-marking herm linking Attica and Athens, or a metaphor connecting a wobbly dessert with a wobbly backbone. As he facilitated associations between people, Hermes was often cited as a peacemaker, but he was also a god of healing, his *kêrykeion* staff corresponding to the caduceus of Asclepius, god of medicine. The caduceus, the magic stick entwined with snakes, is still the symbol of the medical profession even today; a profession of which Fodor, as a psychoanalyst and thus a form of psychic healer and peacemaker between divided families, was also a member.[32]

According to Fodor's school of parapsychology, JOTTles and apports are metaphors too, often of an erotic nature, pointing to unresolved issues within relationships, as in the case of Jerry and Elizabeth and their many symbolic supernatural *hermaions*. As a fellow wielder of the healing caduceus, Fodor saw his job as being to interpret these physical metaphors left behind after him by *Hermes poltergeyster*, like a soothsayer interpreting patterns of tea-leaves to predict the future. The trouble is that Hermes, like many a cup of obscurely scattered tea, did not always provide clear instructions about the precise meaning of the messages and metaphors he trailed behind him, and his all-too human, all-too fallible priests could easily misinterpret the outline of their appearance.

The scholar of religion William G. Doty has argued that Hermes 'elicits metaphoric insights that startle the recipients of his ... messages into action' but he only guides them so far on this journey of self-discovery; 'he escorts one to the confrontation, but the subsequent interpretations that lead to [changed] modes of behaviour, the details of the necessary action, are not explicit.'[33] For instance, he might give Odysseus a magical herb to enable him to defeat the wicked witch Circe, but he'll let the hero work out for himself how and when to use it. With JOTTles, likewise, Hermes might show a poltergeist-focus one missing melon from a pair kept in a bowl, but he'll let her – or her amateur therapist – work out what this message means, and how to go about addressing it to facilitate healing.

Probably this approach has some basic validity. Unfortunately, so slavish was Fodor in his worship of Freud that his books often become unintentionally funny, with some of his conclusions sounding as if based more on the exaggerated pop-culture presentations of Freudianism seen in Hollywood Hitchcock movies such as *Vertigo*, *Spellbound* and *Marnie*, rather than the close perusal of Freud's actual works (which, some critics might say, were often silly enough in themselves, as illustrated by the sly old 'Sigmund *Fraud*' verbal *hermaion*). For Fodor, the poltergeist was often really an incubus in disguise, and as such he saw covert sexual metaphors lurking everywhere within a haunted house, even where they might not have really existed, like Mary Whitehouse wandering appalled through a sausage-factory. For instance, he seriously proposed that Gef the Mongoose might actually have been a living phallic symbol, psychically projected outward by the teenage daughter of the Irving household, Voirrey, to compensate for her repressed feelings of sexual frustration.[34]

The haunting which first led Fodor to develop his 'Poltergeist Psychosis' model came in December 1938, when he was called out to the 300-year-old Chelsea cottage of an obese and highly-strung movie executive named Miss Whalen, who was undergoing a severe nervous breakdown. Perhaps one of the movies Miss Whalen had made was an adaptation of H. G. Wells' *The Invisible Man*, for it was by such a being she was now haunted. For eight months, heavy, shuffling footsteps had been heard approaching her cottage, before the front-door knocker was visibly lifted and banged down twice. Then, keys would be taken from drawers and internal doors unlock themselves, while money was stolen from a cash-box. Household items would also JOTTle away, among them tins of biscuits, cups and saucers, bottles of whiskey and, most remarkably, 'a sizzling plate of eggs and bacon that vanished in a split-second at the height of the disturbance'.

Hermeneutically, what did these thefts mean? Was this invisible man symbolic of another such monster who had raped Miss Whalen as a child, thereby stealing away not only her breakfast but also her innocence, but whose visible memory had now been expunged from her conscious mind? Not quite. The sexual neurosis at play here was a little more complex, and had its roots in adult life. When he first met her, said Fodor, Miss Whalen 'looked like a ghost herself', with a pale and sickly pallor, a voice like a whisper, and whose 'obese body was constantly shaking and shivering'. As Fodor diagnosed it, 'The poltergeist had to go or she would die.' However, no exorcism was necessary: 'Only therapy was needed – and desperately at that.' It would be possible to tell once a full cure had been effected, Fodor theorised, as the stolen items would suddenly JOTTle back where they came from. 'It is possible that even the missing breakfast-plate would have found its way back to this world' by such means, although by this time the meal would surely have gone cold.

Fodor informed Miss Whalen that she was simply 'haunted by her own past', and that 'while she was successful in keeping some unhappy memories from entering into her consciousness, the bottling-up process had failed, her libido had side-slipped and walked out on her in the form of a ghost, and she had been wasting her own vitality in a vain attempt to convey a message' to herself. The phantom footsteps and knocks 'symbolised the coming of a message' – the delivery-boy being Hermes himself, winged sandals and all. If the medium could come to understand her own message, promised Fodor, 'the phenomena would automatically stop'. It might not be easy, though; the obscurely vanishing items may have represented the murky, hidden nature of the insight Hermes sought to bring to the surface. So, to help her understand what her own ghost wanted, Fodor imitated Freud directly and began analysing Miss Whalen's dreams.

His patient agreed with this diagnosis, admitting that she had already stopped the ghost's knocking antics by her own initiative, simply by writing out a snotty message and hanging it on her front-door: 'PLEASE RING THE BELL'. The subtext of this notice, of course, was really 'NO UNWELCOME CALLERS' and the poltergeist was kind enough to pay heed. This, said Fodor, was 'an astounding piece of psychological magic' which 'acted like a post-hypnotic action in reverse', proving the power to dispel the spook lay within her own mind. Reassured by Fodor's diagnosis, Miss Whalen eagerly opened up about her active dream-life, quickly realising the footsteps and rappings were 'ghostly alarm-signals to awaken her to a great personal danger'.

Essentially, the woman had been rendered sterile by an abortion or miscarriage many years earlier, something viewed as a great tragedy; rather rejected as a child herself, she had hoped to make amends by being a good mother to her own baby. Then, more recently, she had been jilted by the man she thought had loved her, which 'forced her libido into abnormal channels'. Childless and without any lover, explained Fodor, 'biologically, she felt that she was a complete failure, cut off from posterity as a ghost is cut off from the living … she went emotionally dead', and Hermes in the form of a polt was now warning her that, if she didn't snap out of the depression caused by the end of her relationship sometime soon, she'd end up physically dead too.

One of her Hermes-sent dreams concerned another Trickster-figure, Prometheus. In myth, Prometheus was punished for stealing the life-giving fire of the gods by being chained to a rock where an eagle would descend to peck out and eat his liver, which would constantly regenerate so it could be devoured over and over again, condemning the Titan to an eternity of pain. Dreams about Prometheus, claimed Fodor, often stand for 'guilt over begetting' and the fact that, in her dream, Miss Whalen was the liver-eating eagle indicated she felt herself to be a 'devouring mother' and was suffering from 'abortion guilt in which she was helplessly enmeshed'. Meanwhile, 'the rocky cleft' she saw 'fitted into a uterine fantasy'. Recognising this, Miss Whalen dreamed of a train emerging into daylight from the tunnel of her own dark guilt, a train she boarded at a junction station – presided over by Hermes god of crossrails, I'd guess – for a new life in Brighton (a 'brightened prospect', Fodor hermeneutically intuited). Another time, she dreamed of being offered some fruit – possibly a fat, juicy banana and two ripe plums – which Fodor said was 'symbolic of the scrotum' and hinted at the impending metaphorical 'return of her fertility', or will to live again.

Eventually, by facing up to her repressed psycho-sexual issues, Miss Whalen cured her poltergeist. When it left, it even returned some of her JOTTled goods, although not her plate of bacon and eggs, sadly. The key sign the demon had fled was when four of her missing cups were found hanging back on their accustomed kitchen-hooks one morning, following a significant-sounding dream in which she was challenged to build something new from a headless corpse (presumably her own) lying within a coffin, like a benign Professor Frankenstein. For Fodor, the return of the four cups was 'symbolic of the cup of sorrows which Miss Whalen had now succeeded in emptying' while four was 'the number of the square' and thus 'a constructive, integrative number', betokening her cure – a totally arbitrary interpretation. Still, the ghost was now gone for good, whatever its return-JOTTling may have meant.[35] If poltergeist hauntings are in some sense best thought of as being live-action stories – specifically, live-action psycho-dramas – then the easiest way of bringing them to a close may be simply to write out the words 'THE END' on a piece of cardboard, hang it on your door and see what happens.

The most comically elaborate attempt by Fodor to apply hermeneutics to the field of apports came during the Thornton Heath case, that same haunting whose details had so shocked the tight-corseted old crones of the IPR when they had read his report upon it. The haunting began in February 1938 and centred upon one Mrs Forbes, a hysterical personality if ever there was one, with a long history of illness, unstable behaviour and trauma.

Aged six, she thought a disembodied black arm 'like a negro's hand with big, bulging muscles' had tried to strangle her in bed; other phantom hands would clean her childhood home's windows and mirrors overnight. Aged sixteen, she began seeing her bedroom cupboard open and a faceless male apparition emerge; once, he left behind a piece of paper with 'smudgy writing, as if done in soot or charcoal' across it, which her mother burned. When seven, she was attacked by a mad dog and 'a jealous parrot' which tried to eat her eyes, and later developed recurrent kidney abscesses, needing several operations. She also split her head open on some bricks, being unable ever after to step upon such disturbing items without gaining 'the sensation of falling into a dark pit'. Aged seventeen, she made a runaway marriage, having her first baby at eighteen, and her second at twenty-one, although this died of meningitis. Aged twenty-three, she developed anthrax poisoning in her mouth and became temporarily insane, trying to stab her husband with a carving-knife and running semi-dressed into the street shouting; she only recovered after having twenty-eight infected teeth extracted. Aged twenty-four, she had a dream-vision of her father's spirit making the sign of the cross over her chest. Awakening, she found a bleeding cruciform cut there and went to hospital, where a tumour was discovered lurking beneath the stigmatic wound, necessitating a breast amputation. Aged twenty-six, she had an attack of hysterical blindness lasting six weeks; aged twenty-eight, she was so shocked at finding a dead rat in her washing that she miscarried twins. She also harboured fantasies of running away and becoming a nun.[36] And, by 1938, Mrs Forbes had also acquired her own poltergeist.

Fodor noticed that this poltergeistery was accompanied by numerous aberrant hysterical symptoms of a non-paranormal nature. Mrs Forbes heard voices, had visions and fantasies of astral projection, suffered states of blackout, anxiety and nervous exhaustion, self-mutilated, had suicidal impulses, performed acts of unconscious fakery, such as openly throwing pebbles around without even trying to hide it, seemingly sliced off her cat's toes during a trance-state, and even became so flatulent 'she appeared to be in an advanced state of pregnancy'. Taken to the IPR's labs for investigation, it was discovered Mrs Forbes was smuggling in various items – up to and including live mice and birds – within her rather cave-like vagina, pushing them out via 'strong muscular effort', then claiming them as JOTTles. This was proven both by tell-tale x-rays which showed the items located inside Mrs Forbes' abdomen, and the fact that the apports were warm, covered by 'vaginal secretion' and possessed a distinctive smell of a 'genital character'. Mrs Forbes had joked that she was 'giving birth' to her apports, and in a sense she was. Fodor diagnosed a conversion disorder; her several dead babies were being replaced by a whole legion of new, non-human ones. She didn't necessarily always know that she was performing acts of fraud, however. Fodor noted she had trained as a tightrope-walker, and that her mother had played the woman-sawed-in-half as part of a stage-magic act; was she too another woman-sawed-in-half, with her conscious and unconscious minds now totally estranged from one another?[37]

Subsequently, Mrs Forbes claimed to have been attacked in bed by a vampire, gaining two fang-like puncture-marks in the back of her neck, combined with bad dreams about entering into a dark cave containing a 'horrible smell of fungus' which lingered even after she awoke. Fodor was obsessed by the twin ideas that adults could subconsciously remember the trauma of their own births, and that many poltergeists were delayed reactions to childhood rapes; as such, he concluded the dreams about smelly caves were inherently related to the smelly apports being given birth to from Mrs Forbes' own rather malodorous fungal grotto, and that therefore when she concealed objects and animals within her vagina 'she may have been re-enacting, by repetition compulsion, the double trauma of her birth and rape [and also her miscarriages, presumably] ... Perhaps this was the reason ... [the vampire left] two puncture-marks at the back of her neck (a hint at the past), instead of over the jugular vein [on the front]'. 'Birth and death mean the same thing to me,' she once admitted. Having led a harrowing existence, Mrs Forbes really wanted 'to return into the womb to find out the meaning of life', said Fodor, a fantasy of reverse-penetration intended to compensate for the distress of once being forcibly penetrated by a child rapist.[38]

The trouble was, in order to prove this diagnosis, it had to be proved that Mrs Forbes had indeed been raped as a child – but there was no such 'credible and true' proof available. So, as with certain malcontents today, Fodor just made some up, exploiting Freudian hermeneutics to support his theory in a most twisted and arbitrary fashion. For instance, possibly the glass-cleaning polt of her childhood was actually best explained as 'the desire of a sleep-walking child to have her [sexual] purity restored, so that she could see herself in the mirror immaculate' and unsullied by semen.[39] Maybe even the cupboard from which her faceless childhood ghost had stepped to leave her indecipherable sooty messages possessed 'a symbolic genital significance', Fodor proposed.[40]

One of the most unusual aspects of poltergeistery produced by Ms Forbes, meanwhile, was that, when she went to the toilet, she was able to emit a strong scent of violets as a kind of 'psychic air-freshener', to disguise the smell: 'Her bathroom was not too sanitary. It had a bad odour. But at the bottom of the stairs there hung a curtain of violet perfume in the air. It acted as a deodoriser, it shut off the evil smell upstairs.' Might this also have been an attempt to cleanse her private zones of the polluting stigma of rape? On her wedding-night, intercourse with her new husband had been interrupted by 'a shower' of violets JOTTling down onto them from the ceiling, followed by the vile reek of rotting corpses. But why? According to Fodor, 'With a slight change in spelling, 'violet' is a [synonym] for 'violate'. Was the wedding-night an experience in violation? Did she equate the consummation of her marriage with death, and represent it as a smell of decomposition?'[41] Mrs Forbes was a virgin until her teenage elopement (discounting the hypothetical childhood rape, naturally), making naïve statements like 'I want to have three children but never get married' as a child. At school she had thought rumours about sex's existence to be 'disgusting and untrue', so her wedding-night came as quite a shock; she 'cried all night' after being 'deflowered'.[42]

Originally, however, Fodor deduced that Mrs Forbes had been more forcibly deflowered, aged five, in a graveyard. This became apparent to him when she admitted her favourite hobby was hanging around in cemeteries and 'taking an interest in gravestones', breaking pieces off and carrying them home as souvenirs. All the time, she 'felt as though I were looking for a strange grave' bearing an unknown man's name – Fodor reckoned she was seeking the grave of her rapist, to make sure he was now dead. 'I never tell my husband when I go to graveyards,' Mrs Forbes said. 'I don't know why.' Fodor did. He performed a dubious word-association test by saying the word 'rape' to his patient and seeing how she reacted. Her response? 'HORROR. DOUBT. DEATH. TREES. DARKNESS. DAMP. HORRIBLE FACE. A PAIR OF BIG GLASSES ... SOMETHING VERY COLD. A SLITHERING MOVEMENT. SOMETHING WITH SCALES ON. FLESH IS HARD. A CHURCH. A TERRIFIC LOT OF PEOPLE.' Fodor's conclusion was that, as a toddler, Mrs Forbes had been raped by man with big round glasses and a skin complaint in a churchyard, out of sight of those adults who were meant to be protecting her. The vampire who bit her in bed – together with a nocturnal incubus who 'behaved like a man and felt like a corpse' who was now also interfering with her – were the memory of this repressed event returning to haunt her, as were erotic wet-dreams she had endured about a half-man, half-alligator midget covered all over in scales.[43]

Given all this, the apports and JOTTles Mrs Forbes was in the habit of producing – both fraudulently and in a genuinely poltergeistic fashion – may have provided 'a cipher in which her tragic life story is hidden', said Fodor.[44] At one point, Mrs Forbes began being stalked by an invisible ghost-tiger which clawed her body, and which visitors could actually smell in the air. At one point, a tiger's claw fell onto the dining-table. 'Perhaps we shall get an elephant [next],' Mr Forbes joked, before a crash was heard from the hallway, where 'a huge Indian elephant's tooth, weighing over two pounds' was found. Another such tooth later JOTTled down, followed by half a shell of a tropical nut, a lump of organ-pipe coral, and two pieces of broken pottery with hand-written labels saying 'Carthage' on them, apparently pilfered from a museum.[45] What un-glad tidings did such *hermaions* come bearing? Fodor did his best to decode them:

The elephant teeth spoke of the hugeness of the man who assaulted her in proportion to the child, the tiger-claw stood for his savageness and beastliness, the pottery for breakage [of her hymen], the nutshell for the scaly feeling [of his skin and penis] and the [organ-pipe] coral for music in the church nearby ... 'organ', of course, also equates for the unconscious mind with the physical organs ... I feel inclined to think that the majority of Mrs Forbes' apports during the experimental period [in the IPR's lab] were influenced by similar unconscious motives. The ... stones with coloured veins may suggest viscera and internal organs, the petrified ammonite a serpent [i.e. penis] ... the rings and chains the bondage in which she languished, the broken and mended Roman lamps the desire to shed light on her history, the tear-vase her suffering, the pin of brooches her wounds, the lockets the womb, and the apports from her bedroom her marital associations.[46]

* * * * *

Presuming JOTTs really do carry some latent emotional meaning within them, how might a modern-day Fodor explain why by far the most commonly affected items appear to be keys (a fact Mary Rose Barrington's book recognises by carrying a large front-cover image of one – as do the covers of certain modern paperback editions of the works of Freud and Jung relating to the interpretation of dreams)?[47] One Essex spook, for example, used to take great delight in making keys vanish before depositing them on a fireside mantelpiece so hot it was used for drying clothes – and yet the keys themselves would be found 'as cold as if they had been buried in deep snow'.[48] An early 1990s haunting in Pudsey featured the detail that all the house keys vanished one day ... and then turned up again, as soon as the householders had gone to the expense of getting each lock changed.[49] Doubtless Fodor would see something sexual in this repeated motif – rigid 'keys' being inserted into yielding 'locks' and all that – but perhaps sometimes, just as with cigars, a key really is just a key, or at least not an ithyphallic penis-substitute. But what might be the key to the key's hidden meaning?

The noted ghost-investigator Maurice Grosse first became associated with the SPR, and thus with poltergeistery, following a series of meaningful-seeming coincidences attendant upon the 1976 death of his daughter in a motorbike accident, involving clocks stopping at the precise hour of her death.[50] Rather than viewing these events as psychic *hermaions*, Grosse interpreted them more literally, as evidence of his daughter's spirit trying to contact him. Many years afterwards, he told a remarkably bizarre tale of his wife losing her handbag, together with the door-keys it contained. Grosse got a new lock fitted to his front door, and put a new key for it onto his wife's key-ring. The next day, she picked her key-ring up only to find that, unbelievably, next to the new key for the new lock, was *another* new key ... for the *old* lock, which had just been removed. Another such new-old key was found on another key-ring, too. They were marked with the logo of the locksmiths Grosse had just used, but no keys for the old lock had ever been cut there, and despite seeming brand new, they bore a disused telephone number for the firm's old premises which Grosse had never visited and that had been abandoned some two years previously anyway.[51] The whole time-warped thing was a true mystery; and maybe that was the point.

Hermeneutically speaking, the ghostly manipulation of keys might best be viewed as a plea for us to allow doors of communication to remain open between life and death or between the conscious and unconscious mind, just like the commerce-facilitating herms which once criss-crossed the roads linking urban Athens and rural Attica. Patrick Harpur preferred to dub the phenomenon of JOTTs 'pixilation', whimsically attributing it to the work of pesky pixies. On the day before his mother's death, Harpur tells us, she noticed her keys had gone walkabout. Harpur's sister joked this meant 'some transition was in the offing'. It was. The next day, she died suddenly – whereupon her keys promptly reappeared (together with a missing ashtray from her car, funnily enough). Throughout her life, Mrs Harpur had been plagued by JOTTles. Ferry tickets would disappear, then pop up puckishly on top of her suitcase, or she'd lose her engagement-ring on a French beach, only to find it back home in England, sleeping safely within her jewellery box. Once, a pot of face-cream evaporated from her desk, only to re-materialise between her very fingers!

The most often afflicted items, Harpur noted, were things like tickets and keys which 'symbolise transitional states, those liminal 'in-between' times and places where the Otherworld is more likely to obtrude and paranormal events to happen.' As death represents the ultimate transitional state, speculated Harpur, it is no wonder key-related JOTTs should become associated with those who pass through the door between two worlds:

> [Any JOTT] ... opens a nagging crack in the fabric of our comfortable reality, a crack small enough to ignore or overlook if we wish ... analogous to the weak-spot on those violent, busy, invulnerable heroes [of Greek and Norse myth] ... It is a mixed blessing to be invulnerable, because it also seals you up in your own world and cuts off from commerce with the Otherworld. Thus, like the little spots of weakness on the hero – the heel or the patch on the shoulder – pixilation is a tiny fault-line symbolising the moment in the midst of our armoured surface ... when we are suddenly opened up like wounds to the possibility of death. Death, that is, of the ego and its common-sense life, and the beginning of the deeper, imaginative life of the soul.[52]

Such keys successfully unlock the door between matter and spirit whose keyhole Descartes wrongly thought he had glued shut forever – this same ineptly gummed-up keyhole really being materialism's hidden Achilles Heel.

The kind of hero with a tiny weak-spot Harpur refers to would be the Norse god Baldr the Bright, shining-faced son of the goddess Frigg, who, like Miss Whalen in Chelsea, had been suffering constant bad dreams predicting his imminent demise. So concerned did this make Frigg for Baldr's safety that she travelled the entire world extracting an oath from everything in it, whether animal, mineral or vegetable, that they would never harm him. The only thing she neglected to ask was the humble mistletoe-bush, something the Trickster Loki, jealous of the radiant youth, exploits by fashioning a small dart from the plant. The gods devise a game in which they hurl various dangerous-looking things like metal spikes at Frigg's child, only to see them keep their promise to the goddess by dropping down harmlessly just before hitting him, rather like many lithobolic pebbles. Only the seemingly harmless mistletoe-dart proves unwilling to play along; when Loki fools another god into aiming it, it pierces Baldr straight through and he falls down dead.

The story was used to explain the cycle of the seasons. Radiant Baldr is another Apollonic sun-god, and Frigg's helicopter-parenting-like desire to protect him from all possibility of harm is not only unrealistic but damaging,

The solar god Baldr the Bright could not be slain, until the Trickster Loki discovered the sole chink in his shining armour. Likewise, the poltergeist can show us the chinks in the logical armour of contemporary hardline scientific materialism.

as it prevents necessary change and growth from ever occurring. By killing the sun with the evergreen mistletoe dart, Loki not only facilitates the temporary catastrophe of winter, he also allows for the subsequent rebirth of the year. If there was no autumn or winter, then the perpetual sunshine would in the end mean no new crops to grow and no new rain to quench the summer drought, leading to ultimate disaster for all. The mistletoe, as an evergreen plant, represented the immortality of the soul via reincarnation; but a soul can only come to experience the immortality of rebirth if it is willing first to move on from its old life and die, just like the old year expiring amidst the snows of winter to be later reborn among the fresh spring shoots.[53]

JOTTs, while appearing as harmless and inconsequential as a mere sprig of mistletoe on the surface of things, possess a similar power to Loki's tricky dart. The SPR website argues that JOTTs 'may look trivial, but a small hole in a large balloon can cause a total collapse, and a discontinuity in the fabric of the environment may lead us to radical ideas about the nature of reality.'[54] To those with eyes Loki-like enough to see it, JOTTles look very much like the tiny, easily dismissed and oft-overlooked cultural darts which, in defiance of the overweening hubris of our current Apollonian Dominant, can seek out such arrogant Enlightenment gods' secretly vulnerable Achilles Heels, pierce their psychic armour and slay them.

His wicked work arranging the murder of Baldr done, the demonic Loki walks back down the path of fire and brimstone.

One of my main inspirations for this book was the US parapsychologist George P. Hansen's highly insightful 2001 text *The Trickster and the Paranormal*, where the central argument is that:

> ... the paranormal and the supernatural are fundamentally linked to destructuring, change, transition, disorder, marginality, the ephemeral, fluidity, ambiguity, and blurring of boundaries. In contrast, the phenomena are repressed or excluded with order, structure, routine, stasis, regularity, precision, rigidity and clear demarcation.[55]

And what better symbol could there be for qualities such as transition, fluidity, change and the penetration of armour-like boundaries – particularly those which exist between the worlds of matter and spirit, light and dark, conscious and unconscious, life and death – than the god-stamped Key of Hermes?

V

Borderline Personalities

> That seems to be the battle-cry of the phenomenon:
> 'Make him look like a nut!'
>
> John Keel

What kinds of people pick up a poltergeist? Surely they're not all nutty like Mrs Forbes or angry and rejected like Tina Resch? Indeed not. Many perfectly normal people end up haunted by a polt, much as many non-drinkers develop liver disease; but it would be as wrongheaded to deny the general association between poltergeists and borderline, non-standard life patterns and personalities as it would be to deny the general association between alcoholism and a wrecked liver. For one thing, *poltergeist victims have a poltergeist!* This may be a tautology, but that in itself inherently isn't normal, is it? In 1987, a guidebook was released for Anglican clergymen, giving sage advice about the kind of spook-molested individuals they might be expected to comfort:

There may be an adolescent denying his or her puberty or sexuality, or in conflict with parental beliefs; or there may be a marriage in difficulties, or a wage-earner faced with redundancy and unemployment; or a feeling of deracination where a family from an ethnic minority is finding its traditional values challenged by having to live within an alien culture ... [Victims may be undergoing] a change in lifestyle, puberty, menopause, sexual malfunction, a drastic change in personal relationship such as a death or birth in the family ... stresses between the generations in a family or at work ... There appear to be peaks at about the age of seven, and at puberty – particularly if there is an only child with uncaring parents. Retirement is another time at which the emotional stress may mount to such an extent that it discharges in the form of a poltergeist ... A move to a new home is often a cause of initiation of poltergeist activity. The move can cause great disturbance to the whole family – the father changes his job, the mother has to find a new set of shops, the children go to new schools, all of them have to find new friends in the locality. In 1968 the then-chief rehousing officer of a metropolitan authority commented that, though council housing accounted for only 32 per cent of families in the United Kingdom, 86 per cent of poltergeist cases occurred in council houses when the family had lived for less than six months in its new home ... there may be a social-class effect in that many people living in council housing may be less able to express their problems and either cope with them or obtain help in appropriate ways.[1]

It seems certain elements within the Church of England (CofE) believed more in RSPK than in unclean spirits. However, as the CofE's guide-book admitted (quoting D. Scott Rogo) 'it is obvious today's society has more disturbed families than [it has] poltergeists', so correlation clearly does not entirely imply causation.[2]

Sometimes, even the correlation itself is challenged. In 1980, researchers Alfonso Martinez Taboas and Carlos S. Alvarado published work critical of the commonly held assumption that most RSPK focus-figures were more mentally or emotionally disturbed than the average member of society; but, oddly enough, their work was studiously ignored.[3] If you wish to maintain some Nandor Fodor-like variant of the RSPK hypothesis, then you would *have* to ignore such findings, wouldn't you?

Nonetheless, for every expert, there is an equal and opposing expert, as Charles Fort is supposed to have said. In 1996, a study found that paranormal experiencers tended to have thinner mental boundaries than average, being less clear where their real lives ended and their fantasy lives began. People with thin mental boundaries are sometimes labelled 'Hermes Boys', as they possess similar characteristics to the Arch-Trickster, being, literally, 'mercurial'. Those with thin mental boundaries tend to flit from place to place and relationship to relationship; to be more likely to be bisexual; to be unreliable; to dislike schedules; to abandon tasks half-finished; to occupy jobs of a non-bureaucratic, creative or artistic nature; to be more easily hypnotised; to have more active dream lives; to think they are psychic and to have experienced childhood abuse or bouts of illness – ideal subjects for the couch of Nandor Fodor. Thin-boundary people were also more likely to be female, children or adolescents, just like poltergeist-people are popularly supposed to be. Interestingly, according to the psychologist Ernest Hartmann, who developed the whole idea in a 1991 book, such Hermes Boys also possess a greater level of mental control over their autonomic nervous systems, being able to noticeably reduce the temperature of their skin when thinking of snow, for instance; exactly the kind of person to make stigmatic wounds from invisible tiger claws rend their flesh.[4]

Many prominent psychics, mystics, polt-mediums and gurus have had bizarre and extreme sex lives, suffered alcohol problems, or been acknowledged fraudsters, even while producing ostensibly genuine phenomena. Being unusual individuals, they often fail to hold down regular long-term jobs in large, stable organisations.[5] In 1991, research was published finding that divorced, widowed and separated persons reported higher rates of encounters with paranormal phenomena of all kinds. The lower and more precarious your social status, the more likely you are to attract a spook.[6] The stress caused by poltergeistery has placed a fatal strain on many relationships;

there have even been cases in which polts have rearranged bedsheets in a suspicious manner to make it look as if one party is having an affair.[7] On the other hand, in one case a poltergeist compensated for a relationship break-up by helping out with housework until the jilted single mum in question finally got a new man to help share the domestic burden, in which case the friendly ghost manifested to a person *trapped* within a liminal position, rather than actually *causing* that liminality in the first place.[8]

George P. Hansen has called these associations 'constellational rather than causal'. 'Supernatural contact leads to disruption of relationships, but such disruption also leads to contact or involvement with the supernatural,' he has argued, a classic vicious circle.[9] 'Personality characteristics of individuals only partly explain Trickster manifestations,' he cautioned.[10] Just as a murder doesn't automatically make a ghost appear, so a disturbed adolescent doesn't automatically magic up a poltergeist, otherwise our schools would be full of levitating children.

* * * * *

It is very easy to mock poltergeist-people like the gravestone-collecting, mouse-inserting Mrs Forbes; perhaps this is why so many focus-figures (including Mrs F. herself) are given false names by investigators, to protect them from public ridicule. Many of the victims 'named' in this present book are identified by pseudonyms. The many Mrs Forbes are now better-known by their fake identities than their true ones – something else, incidentally, which makes them sound like typical con-people.

It is a most Tricksterish irony that those who are inherently more unreliable, socially marginal and fantasy-prone should be more liable to experience the paranormal as this only makes it all the easier for sceptics to dismiss their experiences in the first place. The more closely you embody the Trickster archetype, the easier it is to dismiss you as a Trickster! One prominent American debunking organisation, CSICOP (the Committee for Skeptical Inquiry, formerly known as the Committee for the Scientific Investigation of Claims of the Paranormal) has openly stated that one of its key functions is to demonstrate that paranormal beliefs are 'utterly screwball'[11] and, when it comes to poltergeistery, they don't have to try very hard. They could simply read through this present book and make notes.

Jokes are indeed irresistible. One 2003 haunting involved a spirit transporting full milk-bottles into a bathtub. When the victim told his friends, all they could ask was 'Does it put the empties on the doorstep?'[12] And you can make up your own gags about the elderly Northumberland woman who became convinced an invisible garden gnome was trying to molest her thighs in the form of a polt-like incubus, and who tried to dispel it by wearing a 'protective' woolly hat and twirling a Ken Dodd-like multi-coloured feather-duster around to re-direct malignant energy away from her home.[13] What would CSICOP make of that?

In 1936, R. S. Lambert, a (formerly) respected Oxford-educated poet, biographer, historian and founding editor of the BBC's high-brow journal *The Listener*, brought a High Court slander action against his arch-enemy

Sir Cecil Levita who had sought to get him sacked for being 'off his head' by putting it about that Lambert believed in the reality of Gef the Talking Mongoose. In 1935, Lambert had travelled to the Isle of Man with his well-connected friend Harry Price to hunt the elusive little beast, leading to the publication of a (somewhat sceptical) co-authored book, *The Haunting of Cashen's Gap*. The trial was repeatedly interrupted by public laughter at the very notion of Gef's existence, and descriptions of his many absurd actions. Naturally, Fleet Street gave the story blanket coverage; headlines such as 'BBC EDITOR DENIES THE "EVIL EYE" CHASED HIM: Says He Did NOT Believe In Mongoose That Sang In Spanish' successfully conveyed Lambert's courtroom denial of lunacy while at the same time implicitly libelling him as *non-compos mentis*. Questions were raised about Gef and the governance of the BBC in the House of Commons; PM Stanley Baldwin named a Commission to investigate. So embarrassing was this relentless campaign of public ridicule that the Beeb actually passed a specific rule banning presenters – particularly comedians – from using the phrase 'Talking Mongoose' in any broadcasts, lest it give further ammunition to the Corporation's critics. Lambert won £7,500 in damages, but lost his dignity.[14] Even high-status individuals are instantly rendered the lowest of the low when they publicly admit to an association with spooks.

The typical victim of poltergeistery – or the *perceived* typical victim, anyway – is highly liminal in nature, with conventional society's ribbing of them functioning very effectively to keep them that way. Be honest, if *you* heard a Talking Mongoose singing in Spanish, would *you* really want people knowing about it? Even the often credulous Spiritualist Press of the 1930s mocked Gef as being a load of old cobblers, printing cartoons implying his alleged witnesses or investigators such as R. S. Lambert were gaga, and labelling the case 'purely a psychological one'.[15]

The word 'liminal' is key to this book's analysis. It comes from the Greek *limen*, meaning the space under the front-door frame or the threshold of the house – a space from beneath which Gef himself sometimes spoke.[16] A liminal area is a boundary or a transitional space, like crossroads or doorways, precisely the kinds of places presided over by Hermes; as the gods of border-crossing, Tricksters are gods of liminality.[17] A liminal person is not at the centre of society, but operates at its margins – like Lord Byron (who also claimed his own ancestral home was haunted, incidentally) or Mrs Forbes, they are mad, bad and dangerous to know.

It is appropriate that poltergeist focuses tend to be liminal in nature, as ghosts in a wider sense are inherently liminal in nature themselves, too. A ghost is the very personification of the notion of the 'borderline', made ... well, not made flesh, precisely, as that would not be liminal enough, but something more like ectoplasm, halfway between the solid and the ethereal. Are ghosts real, or fake? Are they living or dead? Like Dickens' Yuletide phantoms, do they hail from past, future, or present? Are they visible or invisible, solid or ungraspable? Are they fact or are they fiction? Human or non-human? Devils or angels? Scary or funny? Or ... are they all of these things at once, hovering eerily upon every frontier possible?[18]

Traditionally, poltergeists – or polter-fairies – also lived within the most liminal, dark and spooky areas of the home, those which were hardly at the heart of the building, like attics, garrets, cellars, junk-rooms, cess-pits and storage-spaces.[19] Such spirits were also said to live inside the walls, as with 'Knocky Boh', an obscure Yorkshire goblin who spent his nights rapping behind wainscots.[20] Gef the Mongoose was, as usual, a key example. As well as inhabiting the unseen space behind the Irving household's wainscoting like Knocky Boh, he had a special 'Sanctum' where he liked to sleep, dance and take exercise by pushing around a heavy wooden chair several times his own size. This was a boarded-off area at the top of some stairs, where the Irvings would leave their hungry little Hermes offerings of food – or 'chukko', as he called such tasty treats – to eat.[21]

Yet Gef did not inhabit a liminal zone only physically, but also imaginatively. Gef's recent biographer Christopher Josiffe summed up the weird entity's borderline status expertly:

> Gef occupies a liminal space between fraud, psychological disturbance or pathology ... and the supernatural. Gef is the shaded area in the centre of a Venn diagram consisting of all these possibilities. The elusive Gef is only to be found in the gaps. He lurks – just out of view – behind the hedges in the fields, emerging through a gap in the hedge [the name of the haunted farmhouse, 'Cashen's Gap', meant 'the gap in the gorse'] ... he hides behind the matchboarding in the farmhouse; he enters through the cracks in the walls, the meeting place between the interior and the exterior of the house ... Attempts to define or fix Gef, as a poltergeist, hoax or projection of the Irving's mind, are doomed to failure. One cannot pin Gef down. He doesn't want to be trapped, or put in a bottle [like a genie].[22]

Nor do any poltergeists. The more talented polt-focuses have often been tested within parapsychology labs, but, while sometimes managing to produce mild psi phenomena to the satisfaction of investigators, never have they been able to make anything as sensational as Gef appear within one. Possibly this is because the tasks they are asked to perform are so damn boring. Consider the following description:

> REGs [Random Event Generators] were hooked up to computer monitors that allowed participants to view their digital output ... The viewer would see a graph with two axes, a vertical axis counting 'bits' and horizontal axis for 'trials'. Participants would be asked to perform one of three tasks: 1) will the REG to produce *more* bits of 1 or 0 than it would randomly (for example, 52 1s vs 48 0s or 43 1s vs 57 0s); 2) focus their minds on influencing the output of the REG toward *lower* values than the baseline; or 3) try not to fall asleep.[23]

I may have made up that final task. Unsurprisingly, one common finding of parapsychology that even hard-line sceptics might have no problem believing is that the more boring the task, the greater the failure-rate. Given this, why not ask participants to try and do more interesting things, like make poltergeistic 4-D ghost-hands tie knots in solid string? Possibly because, when Johann Zöllner tried that out 150 years ago, nobody believed him, and his test-subject Henry Slade ended up being prosecuted in court as a fraudster.

Anyway, the ghosts could choose not to participate. Sensational beings like Gef may deign to manifest intermittently to a few select people within a remote Manx farmhouse, far away from prying mainstream eyes, but never within the shiny, well-equipped laboratories of a CERN. George P. Hansen terms these spontaneous and uncontrolled phenomena occurring in the field as taking place under 'unbounded conditions'. These, he says, are a real turn-off for those who work in established fields of experimental science:

> These unbounded situations are overlooked or avoided by most researchers, especially by those in laboratories, or with tenured academic positions, or with established reputations in respectable areas. Unbounded phenomena are messy; gathering reliable information is difficult, and Trickster manifestations are acute. These factors conspire to discourage scientific investigation, despite the intriguing results.[24]

Scientists can't control unbounded phenomena as they can chemicals in test-tubes, so they tend simply to ignore them. Polt-people can't control their wild talents completely to order either. Instead, they seem more like flaky, inconsistent sportsmen, who one game can be man-of-the-match, the next totally anonymous; and yet, just because a footballer misses a penalty in one game, people don't refuse to believe he scored a hat-trick the previous week. Poltergeistery is non-repeatable to order in the lab, just like hat-tricks on a football field.[25]

In any case, most organisations devoted to hunting ghosts or studying psi are poorly funded, unstable, low-status and liminal in themselves, with high turnovers of short-term staff. Psychical research may once have had a Victorian and Edwardian 'Golden Age' when Nobel Prize-winners, prominent philosophers and even Prime Ministers got involved, but that era has now long passed. Amusingly, some researchers have even guessed that the more liminal and poorly-funded a lab, and the more uncertain its future and lower-calibre its staff, the better results it will produce ... but if this is so, then the fact that better-funded, higher-status labs would prove unable to replicate their findings would simply be taken by most people as meaning that the more liminal lab's findings were faulty in the first place, due to its poorly funded, lower position![26] George P. Hansen put it like this:

> Those who believe that parapsychology's academic acceptance can be gained by presentation of evidence and rational discussion are simply naïve. The problem is far deeper than ideology or belief. The evidence is ubiquitous that the phenomena inherently become marginalised. As a consequence, direct investigation of them can only be effectively conducted in the margins.[27]

Liminal people, investigating liminal phenomena, produced by liminal persons under liminal circumstances within liminal arenas; and parapsychologists are *surprised* that mainstream authorities don't believe ghosts exist? Any field of science which even begins to hint at accepting the reality of paranormal phenomena immediately becomes redefined as being fringe in nature.

Surely, like Groucho Marx, respectability-chasing parapsychologists would never join any club that would sink so low as to have *them* as a member?

* * * * *

As god of crossroads and borderlands, Hermes is the god of psychological transition states, the key one of which is surely adolescence, the 'crossroads of life' when a child slowly becomes an adult. The very concept of liminality was originally devised by anthropologists studying tribal rites of passage undergone by adolescents in primitive cultures; those young people undergoing initiation-rituals into adulthood were deemed to be metaphorically like ghosts as they too were temporarily neither one thing nor the other.[28] Poltergeists have become associated in the popular mind these days with teenage girls and, while this is hardly a universal rule, there is a persistent claimed correlation between polts and female teen focus-figures.[29] Indeed, certain hauntings have seen phenomena directly correlate with the onset of such mediums' menstrual cycles, leading some to conclude that special psychic energies are produced when a girl enters puberty.[30] Surprisingly, there are clear historical analogues for this idea. The anthropological writer Sir J. G. Frazer gave a good account of several primitive menstruation-related taboos in his book *The Golden Bough*:

> ... the touch of a menstruous woman turned wine to vinegar, blighted crops, killed seedlings, blasted gardens, brought down the fruit from trees, dimmed mirrors, blunted razors, rusted iron and brass ... killed bees ... caused mares to miscarry ... in various parts of Europe it is still believed that if a woman in her courses enters a brewery the beer will turn sour; if she touches beer, wine, vinegar, or milk, it will go bad; if she makes jam, it will not keep; if she mounts a mare, it will miscarry; if she touches buds, they will wither; if she climbs a cherry tree, it will die. In Brunswick, people think that if a menstruous woman assists at the killing of a pig, the pork will putrefy. In the Greek island of Calymnos a woman at such times may not go to the well to draw water, nor cross a running stream, nor enter the sea. Her presence in a boat is said to raise storms.[31]

As such, girls and women had to be kept away from the tribe during their monthly bloodshed; 'enveloped in her hammock and slung up to the roof' in South America, or 'raised above the ground in a dark and narrow cage' in New Ireland. By being shut off from close contact with the earth below or the sun above, the menstruating female can pollute and destroy neither with the emission of her evil liminal fluids: 'she is rendered harmless by being, in electrical language, insulated.'[32] Frazer explains the reasons for the taboo thus:

> ... the girl is viewed as charged with a powerful force which, if not kept within bounds, may prove destructive both to herself and to all with whom she comes in contact. To repress this force within the limits necessary for the safety of all concerned is the object of the taboos in question. The same

explanation applies to the observance of the same rules by divine kings and priests. The uncleanness, as it is called, of girls at puberty and the sanctity of holy men do not, to the primitive mind, differ materially from each other. They are only different manifestations of the same mysterious energy which, like energy in general, is in itself neither good nor bad, but becomes beneficent or maleficent according to its application.[33]

Those who say that periods produce poltergeists are saying essentially the same thing as Frazer's pre-modern tribesmen, are they not?

So, during her time of the month, a newly menstruating girl might be big trouble, as is well known. This is the stereotype; but how true is it? The idea of pubescent RSPK is now fairly well known (albeit not under that name), largely through its representation in Hollywood horror movies such as *Carrie*, based upon the 1974 Stephen King novel of the same name, in which a bullied pubertal schoolgirl gains revenge on her teen tormentors via psychokinetic means. King himself was influenced by the writings of Charles Fort, who in his 1932 book *Wild Talents* had humorously written about the potential for what he termed 'poltergeist-girls' being employed by the military to set enemy troops on fire or drown them with deluges of teleported water using only the powers of their minds:

> Girls at the front – and they are discussing their usual not very profound subjects. The alarm – the enemy is advancing. Command to the poltergeist girls to concentrate – and under their chairs they stick their wads of chewing-gum. A regiment bursts into flames, and the soldiers are torches. Horses snort smoke from the combustion of their entrails. Reinforcements are smashed under cliffs that are teleported from the Rocky Mountains. The snatch of Niagara Falls – it pours upon the battlefield. The little poltergeist girls reach for their wads of chewing-gum.[34]

Even better, joked Fort, such period-powered poltergeist-people could be encouraged to develop completely world-destroying powers, the very threat of whose use would banish war from the globe forever: 'Really, the Christian thing to do would be to develop the uses of the new magic [of poltergeistery] so that in the future a war could not even be contemplated.'[35] In this fantasy, focus-figures become like walking RSPK-ready nuclear-bombs; inadvertently, Fort had independently hit upon the Cold War-era doctrine of 'Mutually Assured Destruction' about thirty years too early!

The *Carrie* influence has helped create a stereotype that poltergeist-focuses are overwhelmingly teenage girls, although actual figures show gender distribution is rather more even. A combination of *Carrie*, Fort and the scepticism of Frank Podmore has led to this stock image being developed.[36] When a focus-figure who perfectly fits in with this nexus appears in real life, she can then be exploited for all she is worth in order to reinforce the picture even further among the general public – for a variety of different motives. Re-enter here the tragic figure of Tina Resch.

In tabloid-speak, Tina was the real-life *Carrie*. William G. Roll wanted to use her story to bolster his case for the existence of RSPK. But CSICOP's army of latter-day Frank Podmores wanted to use it to bolster their own case for poltergeists really being caused by delinquent teen prankery. Resch had been characterised all her young life as a 'weirdo … freak … outsider', culminating in an attempt to slit her own wrists just before she turned sixteen.[37] She might have been better off succeeding. Tina's life was almost parodically liminal. Horribly bullied at school, she received no bucket of pig's blood over her head on prom-night, but she was tied up, pushed off the school bus and had her clothes torn off in the playground. Her teachers labelled her 'an easy target' and did nothing. They would hold her inept schoolwork up in class as excellent examples to other children of what not to do before deriding her uncombed hair, and failed to hide the fact Resch was on Ritalin for her ADHD, leading to further bullying. Her only friend then died in a car-crash.

Resch was home-schooled for a while, but her adoptive parents were cruel, Dickensian figures who administered harsh discipline and beatings, put all her toys in bin bags in the attic, forced her to wear old-fashioned clothing from previous decades, denied her sugar and gave strict instructions for her to sit in the corridor and be excluded from school parties in case she was given any cake. Worse, her step-brother began sexually molesting her and when she blabbed, Tina herself was treated as the guilty party, as well as being labelled a liar. Suffering psychological problems, she feared nocturnal attack from vampires and had hallucinatory chats with her dead best friend; desperately needing someone to talk to, all she could manage was a figment of her own imagination.[38] The obvious solution was to move out; but she was too young to legally do so. Roll compared her home to a prison, and theorised that the RSPK incidents were symbolic of her desire to cross the liminal threshold into the escape of adulthood. When sent to bed too early, her polt messed about with her bedside alarm-clock, changing the display to a bed-time more appropriate for a girl her age, it turned channels from TV cartoons being watched by her younger step-siblings towards something less childish, it defied her bullying stepfather's wishes in such a way as to make him look like an idiot, and it smashed a bottle of beer to express Tina's annoyance at being under-age for alcohol.[39]

If Tina's extreme liminality made her great material from an RSPK-fan's perspective, it was the same for CSICOP. Investigating policemen literally just wrote the word 'Mental' on her file and walked away.[40] When reporters later rolled up, CSICOP dispatched media magician James 'The Amazing' Randi to debunk by making jokes about not believing in polts because he didn't believe in Santa Claus either, and to pull a $10,000 cheque from his cape and offer it to the Resches if they could make an object fly before his very eyes in a non-fake manner (but, of course, if Tina ever *did* do so, he would just repeat that objects couldn't fly so it *must* have been faked by definition, and so hold onto his cash that way …). Randi predicted the Resches would not let him into their home and, by insulting them, ensured he would be proved correct – thereby also 'proving' the whole thing was a total scam.[41] Under pressure to perform before cameras, Tina made a very weak attempt to knock over a lamp after being instructed by her adoptive mother to get rid of impatient journalists who had been camped out there for nearly eight hours, and now Randi was here to push her even further into liminality with his satirical ways.[42] An innocent teenage girl, ridiculed in the national Press by a prominent media magician ... we're back at Swanton Novers Rectory again, aren't we?

One way for a young girl to escape a besieged, unhappy home is to take up with a man and get pregnant; Resch picked up quite a few unsuitable heels down the years, one of whom later admitted sodomising and beating her toddler, who later died. Resch herself said she wasn't directly involved, but was sentenced to life imprisonment in 1992, allegedly scapegoated by local officials seeking re-election by appearing tough on crime. As a liminal, low-status person with a horrific life story who had already been ridiculed in the press, Tina was easy to paint as a dangerous, disreputable individual. It was even revealed in court that she had starred in an amateur porn-film. The media, predictably, played up the whole poltergeistery angle to discredit her further; she became the 'Telekinetic Mom' who went 'from celebrity to cellblock'. Advised to make a plea-bargain, Resch pleaded guilty to murder, even though she maintained in actuality that her only crime had been stupidity in not taking her toddler to hospital quickly enough when she found it 'banged up' from her partner's brutality (he said the child had fallen).[43] Most people just read the headlines, though, so once more the social message is hammered home loud and clear: stay away from poltergeist-girls, they're hazardous, delusional lunatics who kill their own babies.

*****

The clichéd image we now have of a poltergeist-focus is of a lower-class female teenage serving maid from the late Victorian or early Edwardian eras, as at Swanton Novers. Being neither adult nor child, these low-class, low-status females trapped within a man's world were yet more classically liminal figures. From a sceptical perspective, the historian Owen Davies has reasonably speculated that this 1800s and 1900s alleged epidemic of teen poltergeistery was simply a social 'manifestation of emotional problems created by the servant–employer relationship':

> One recognises the insecurities and frustrations that must have been a common experience for young servants ... They were removed from their families and familiar environments at a formative age, and had to live with strangers and negotiate the inequalities and sexual politics between masters and servants ... [Such a maidservant] found expression for her emotional state through a form of displacement activity that enabled the release of pent-up frustration through vandalism, while at the same time attracting the attention she obviously craved ... poltergeist activity can be read as a way in which adolescents can and did transform the supernatural into domestic power, radically altering the dynamics of household relationships.[44]

However, as Davies admits, sceptics like him 'share common ground' with those who would prefer to use these same psychological factors to provide motives not for human fakery, but for the emission of RSPK forces. Hating their jobs, the eruption of poltergeistery may have provided scope for revenge against hated employers. A polt-like *lutin* causing 'extraordinary disorders' at the house of a wealthy Italian merchant in Bologna in 1579 pinched and slapped the harsh mistress of its servant-girl medium, before throwing cold water over her in bed.[45] In a house in the Greek village of Mavrovo in 1924, vinegar, sugar, jam and olive-oil spilled themselves across the kitchen floor and glassware and windows spontaneously shattered. The head of the household was a strict and violent-tempered man, from whom events were initially concealed; when he found out, he exploded, furiously blaming the housemaid Dimitra and his children, punishing them cruelly. Eventually he was forced to recant, as chairs floated onto tables, bread removed itself from ovens, curtains gained triangular rips, heated stones poured from thin air and cooking pots overturned, making hot meals impossible. If Dimitra was indeed responsible, she certainly got her own back on her bullying, patriarchal – and now doubtless rather hungry – master.[46]

Alternatively, a maid's attendant poltergeist could act as a simple supernatural cry for help. In 1887, a Londoner named Hugh Dixon engaged a fourteen-year-old girl, Mary, to act as servant in his home, causing bells to paranormally ring by themselves. Dixon realised this was Mary's first paid employment and that she was suffering from nerves at entering into the adult world, falling into hysterical trances and reciting entire church sermons word-for-word. Rather than sacking her, Dixon showed understanding of her liminal distress, helped ease Mary into her new role, and the phenomena subsided soon enough.[47]

These ghosts could sometimes be helpful, cleaning up so servant-girls wouldn't have to. One 1980s poltergeist operating in a Californian holiday resort performed numerous useful tasks, folding towels and washcloths over neatly, making beds and leaving guests out complementary bars of soap, thus saving the real maids a bit of trouble.[48] When acting like this, polts were traditionally dubbed brownies, a form of helpful household fairy. At other times, however, they could deliberately dirty up the home, making more work for their focus-figures to perform. At such times they were traditionally deemed boggarts, a malicious breed of household familiar.

Poltergeists may begin as brownies, but transform spitefully into boggarts when riled, a parallel with Frazer's findings about the occult potential of periods being used for good or ill depending on who was making use of them and why. One modern-day case centred upon an English couple named the Boltons, who were implausibly informed by their new home's former occupants that there were brownies living at the bottom of the garden. Sure enough, when the Boltons were at work, their clothes would be washed and dried for them, and the shed tidied. One day, however, Mrs Bolton lost her temper with her elvish helpers and the brownies shape-shifted into boggarts, smearing jam into her carpet, knocking over her furniture, ruining her food with soap-powder and putting plugs in sinks before turning taps on. Eventually, the Boltons moved out.[49]

By muddying the place up rather than keeping it clean, poltergeist-maids, whether consciously or otherwise, inverted their usual social role, a key function of the Trickster. The fact that many of these girls quickly got sacked also had the happy effect of freeing them from boring drudgery, at least temporarily. By making them unemployed – and possibly unemployable – it also heightened their liminality.

*****

Nowadays the low-status jobs which low-status young girls go into straight out of school and quickly hope to get sacked from are often no less mind-numbing, unrewarding and ill-paid than being a maidservant once was. The classic example is that of the poltergeist which appeared in law offices in the Bavarian town of Rosenheim in 1967, when a nineteen-year-old female secretary, Annemarie Schneider, made pictures rotate on walls, light-bulbs and fuses explode, photocopiers malfunction and light-fittings swing as she walked beneath them, many such pranks being caught clearly on film for German TV. Innumerable phonecalls, as many as fifty in quick succession, more than could be physically dialled by human hands within the short time they were made, were put in to the local speaking-clock; evidently Annemarie couldn't wait for home-time. Whenever Schneider was absent, the office was quiet, but whenever she came back she would give co-workers electric shocks. According to investigating parapsychologist Hans Bender, Annemarie was insecure, hated her work and her boss, and had emotional problems stemming from a broken-off engagement, sometimes suffering hysterical paralysis in her limbs. Finally the tearful girl was forced to leave the office for good, having caused 15,000 Deutschmarks' worth of damage. Boggart phenomena tailed off when she got married in 1969 and escaped the liminal zone of late-adolescence more fully.[50]

A rough British equivalent of the Rosenheim polt occurred in 1970, on the Yorkshire premises of Air Heating Ltd, where broken telephones repeatedly had to be replaced after being thrown to the floor. Work became impossible, due to filing cabinets falling over and paper whizzing around. Poltergeistery greatly decreased when one unnamed female employee left the firm – evidently, like Annemarie Schneider, she had been rather bored at work.[51] D. Scott Rogo has called such modern-day workplace spooks 'Electronic Poltergeists', which 'often go undiagnosed' due to the rather prosaic and easily-dismissed way in which they manifest, namely by 'causing machinery and equipment to malfunction inexplicably or to behave oddly'. In 1978, Rogo investigated one such Electronic Polt in a Hollywood plastics factory, where phones would go 'haywire' and 'weird wailing noises' be heard over the tannoy system in the presence of one particular disgruntled female employee.[52] As stable, routine and non-liminal workplaces, you can see why poltergeist-girls might have trouble fitting in at offices and factories. Just like parapsychology labs, these places are extremely mind-numbing environments, inherently unsuited for the employ of thin-boundary figures like a Tina Resch. No wonder so many paranormally gifted people have trouble holding down a steady job. Bosses must hate them as much as their pet ghosts hate their bosses.

*****

An alternative tactic would be for a polt to continually act up in such a fashion that it becomes impossible for you to even take up any new job-offers in the first place. This was the method employed by one of the most entertaining poltergeists of all time, christened 'Donald', who appeared in the Battersea home of fifteen-year-old Shirley Hitchings in 1956, as revealed in a fascinating 2013 book co-authored by Shirley herself, *The Poltergeist Prince of London*. Events began in late January when that classic *hermaion* of Hermes, an unknown key, was discovered atop Shirley's bed. It was tried in every lock in the house, but would not fit; instead, it would fit the lock of Shirley's heart alone, like Cinderella's glass slipper. Abandoned on a table overnight, it apported back onto Shirley's bed the very next day.[53]

Despite just turning fifteen, Shirley still slept in her parents' bedroom with the door locked, on account of her dangerous old childhood habit of sleepwalking.[54] A teenager would clearly resent that, and Nandor Fodor would have no hesitation in saying the Key of Hermes was asking Shirley's parents to unlock their restrictive cage and let her free. When a polt later appeared on the scene and slapped her dad in the face with a glove, it would not be hard to view this as Shirley's mind rebelling against parental authority.[55] When Shirley argued with dad, the spook threw a milk-bottle at him, or threatened – via rapped-out messages and written notes – to 'BOP [him] ONE RIGHT ON THE NOSE', this being the entity's 'DUTY AS A GENTLEMAN'.[56] Following a spell squatting in the attic, the ghost was given the spare-room as its own, which it swept out and decorated, a brownie inhabiting its traditional junk-room. It even hung up a 'Knock Before Entering' sign on the attic-door.[57] This was precisely the kind of personal privacy young Shirley must have longed for. Once Donald was given the spare-room, his mistress was allowed to move her own bed in with him.[58]

The daring ghost could say what Shirley could not. When she argued with her grandmother, Donald threatened to 'TIP HER OUT OF BED' for 'DISOBEYMENT', calling her a 'SILLY OLD COW ... SILLY OLD BUGGER ... OLD BATTLE-AXE ... FACE LIKE NOSE OVERGROWN BEETROOT ... SHIT-PAN ... MONKEY-CHOPS ... BUM-FLUFF ... SHIT YOU SHIT ... SILLY OLD COURPS ... NUT-CASE'.[59] Shirley admitted to rather liking the spook, treating him as 'a joke, rather than a nuisance', which is unsurprising, as he shared several characteristics with herself; Donald's misspelled notes revealed it was clearly dyslexic, it liked sweets, and possessed a surprising interest in '50s rock 'n' roll sensation Tommy Steele.[60] With momentary honesty, the ghost once admitted 'I AM SHIRLEY' and promised 'I AM HERE TO GUARD YOU FOR EVER GIRLY'.[61] Donald even tried to bully the girl's parents into paying for her to have a new haircut and make-over, complaining her current non-trendy style was 'LIKE A SHABY DOGS TAILS' and saying he wanted her 'TO LOOK BEAOUTIFUL'.[62]

However, like many a liminal adolescent, the ghost was unsure whether or not it really wanted to grow up after all, and performed many overtly childish acts. When Shirley's pet hamster died, Donald held an infantile mock-funeral, covering its corpse in a black cloth, with candle and cross placed over it to stand vigil.[63] At Christmas, Donald was as excited as Shirley was, putting up paper streamers, sticking cotton wool 'in vast quantity' onto 'every available surface', and writing 'JOYEUX NOEL' on a mirror. It sent out Christmas cards, and made its own very short Christmas list: 'I WANT TRAIN!' It got one, too. In return, Donald apported the family presents, including necklaces, handkerchiefs and bottles of perfume. Sometimes, it would JOTTle free items into the Hitchings' bags when they went shopping. It then demanded it be given 'A CAT FOR CHRISTMAS – A BLACK ONE', but when it didn't get one, Donald threw a wobbler in his characteristic cod-Franglais: 'JE WANT A CAT – VOUS PROMISE – IF VOUS DO NOT GET IT FOR ME JE WILL CRY ET CRY AND CRY AND NO LIKE VOUS.'[64]

The tension between whether Shirley was to be allowed to cross the limen into adulthood was seen when Donald stole some money, saying he would only return it if it was used to buy Shirley a new pet. 'WILL YOU SAVE LIFE OF AN ANIMAL?' Donald asked. 'THERE IS ONE ALL ALONE WAITING FOR YOU' in a Wandsworth pet-shop, he promised, and he 'LOOKS SO SAD'. This animal, a hamster, must be bought immediately and christened 'Pinky', it was ordered. Shirley objected she would rather spend the stolen cash on face-powder, not hamsters. Donald got angry. 'YOU DO NOT WANT MAKE-UP – IT SPOILS FACE ... I WILL LOVE PINKY'. Yes, but teenage girls love make-up more ...[65]

Donald was particularly disturbed by the idea that Shirley might get a job – and thereby grow out of him, following successful entrance into adulthood. Or then again, maybe Shirley herself, being a creative individual with an interest in the arts, didn't want the lacklustre job her parents had lined up in a London department-store. Shirley wanted to design dresses, not sell them, and disruptive spirit-raps followed her along on the bus and into the store. An occupational doctor heard these raps too and gave Shirley a fortnight's leave. Donald was trying to get her sacked, just like Annemarie Schneider's boggart at Rosenheim; by mid-March Shirley was co-operatively handing in her resignation at the management's specific request.[66]

A distinct pattern became established. Another position being secured for Shirley in a bank, Donald threatened to tear up all her clothes then stole her keys so she would have to call in absent. 'I VERY BIG ANGRY' he said, in the comical manner of *The Beano*'s Little Plum, 'I WARN, IF THINK OF GOING TO WORK MONDAY I BREAK EVERY BIT OF BANK UP'. If Shirley disobeyed, he set things on fire, emptied slop-buckets over her underwear, hid her work-clothes, threw a hot kettle, knife and scissors around, put 'something hairy' in her bed to tear her sheets, hid her ticket-money, drew crosses on walls, untidied rooms, and threatened to pull Shirley's hair, cause a car-crash and set off a nuclear explosion. Shirley never did manage to start work at the bank.[67] Other employment offers were sabotaged by mud from flower-pots being smeared over Shirley's work-clothes, and more keys being stolen.[68] When Shirley's friends then teased her about being unemployed, Donald flew into a violent rage, wrecking the house and gouging the eyes out of her dolls, bashing their heads in and shredding their clothes.[69] Was it time to put away such childish things after all?

If Shirley did want to dump her dolls forever, there was now a problem; her case had attracted the newspapers who, as with Tina Resch, did their best to unjustly make her sound insane. Donald claimed either to be the ghost of

Shirley's childhood playmate-cum-boyfriend of that same name, or to have come to 'PLAY CUPID', reuniting the childhood sweethearts in the flesh, and thereby 'MAKE A LINK OF HAPPYNESS OF TWO PEOPLE'. 'I COME TO MAKE LOVE BETWEEN SHIRLEY AND DONALD', said the polt, which journalists found hilarious. Quotes from a ghost to effect that 'I LOVE GIRLY – I GOT A SECRET FOR YOU – DONALD ... LOVES YOU [but] HE'S NOT AWARE' made great copy.[70]

Problems arose when Shirley brought back a real boyfriend one day, a teddy-boy who was quickly frightened off by having a bowl of nuts thrown at his head after expressing the opinion that, if Donald dared appear, 'I reckon I could do him'. 'IF VOUS LET THEAT COMMON PERSON COME INTO MON HOUSE [again]', warned Donald, he had 'ALL FURNITURE PILLED UP ALL READY IN UPSTAIRS BEDROOM – ALL JE HAVE TO DO EST SET ALIGHT TO LA CURTAINS'.[71] The *South London Advertiser* sent a female reporter to ask Donald to marry her, thus freeing the teen from the spook's attentions. When he refused, she accused him of being gay! He got his own back by saying she was just too old; Donald liked them a bit more young and liminal. The Press generally ran with a jokey 'ghostly love-story' angle, even though the haunting was no such thing.[72] Donald did try to set Shirley up with a dishy male reporter, but as he was presumably not interested in dating children, nothing came of it. The polt threatened to 'POKE' and 'SUFFOCATE' the man for this rejection, but never did.[73]

Donald refused to perform for the BBC on film, so some papers pursued the alternative angle that it was all an attention-seeking scam.[74] The *Weekend Mail* went with the wilfully absurd headline 'SPOOK WAS IN GIRL'S BIG TOE!', claiming Shirley possessed a deformed right foot, allowing her to crack her toe-joints to make it appear Donald was rapping answers out. Donald's raps had already been described as coming from 'a demented Fred Astaire', so the accusation made sense ... if you ignored all the notes the ghost wrote, the objects it threw, the money it stole and the fires it set.[75] Furthermore, when some visitors left the Hitchings household, they were followed away by Donald's raps on their bus home.[76] Donald himself dismissed the *Mail*'s accusation, tying Shirley's big toe up with string in bed one night as if to lampoon the reporters' idea.[77] Nonetheless, most people don't think like this, and Shirley's fringe, liminal position in society was reinforced; who is going to want to employ a crazy hoaxer who makes fake ghost-lovers come out of her freaky feet?

Eventually, Shirley found tolerant employers willing to take her on as a clerical assistant. They had apparently not read about her or her haunted toe in the newspapers, and she kept quiet about Donald, hoping he wouldn't follow her into the office this time. Shirley enjoyed the work, got on well with her colleagues, and Donald did indeed stay away. She held down the job for years, and Donald began slowly to fade away, like old ink. 'MY [Shirley] HAS STARTED WORK, AND AS I GO WITH HER, MY DAY IS FULL [so] I CANNOT TAP OR MOVE THINGS', he complained, with his/ her attention now fully occupied by everyday clerical tasks, and less with facilitating amusing poltergeistery. 'JE DO NOT WANT TO GO TO WORK ON A COLD, COLD MORNING' Donald complained, 'JE AM SO TIRED'.

But tiring Donald out with the workaday routine was precisely what Shirley had to do to dispel him – it was exorcism via tedium, not *Te Deum*.[78]

When Shirley got a serious boyfriend named Derek, settled down and got married, Donald departed for good, but not before leaving them some wise, parental-style advice: 'DON'T ARGUE, CHILDREN ... BE GOOD CHILDREN – VOUS BOTH GOT A LOT TO LEARN – TAKE THE ROUGH WITH THE SOOMTH ... STAY HAPPY ET STAY SMILING – JE LIKE VOUS BOTH – DON'. Donald correctly informed Shirley she was pregnant, and instructed Derek to build a doll's house, but Derek told Donald where to go. Donald had advised the new husband 'DO NOT LET [Shirley] GET ALL HER OWN WAY', and it appears this was some advice Derek took, in a way. An amazing *twelve years* after first appearing, Donald finally flew away back into the Never-Never Land realm of eternal childhood, alongside Peter Pan.[79] The liminal threshold separating adolescence from adulthood had finally been successfully negotiated; but surely there must be an easier way for a girl to grow up than to battle her personal demon for twelve years? Once upon a time, there was indeed ...

Another typical boring day at work for a housemaid; it's enough to make a girl unleash a poltergeist from her pants just to liven things up a little. (Nilfisk-Advance under CC 3.0)

VI

Shamans Without the Shamanism

The only difference between myself and a madman is that I am not mad!

Salvador Dalí

These days, there are no viable career-paths open to poltergeist-girls which make any good use of their amazing alleged powers. But at certain times in human history, focus-figures' inherent liminality could, ironically, have found itself embraced as a central and highly-valued facet of mainstream society. In 1936, Nandor Fodor investigated one of his first-ever cases, an outbreak of paranormal bell-ringing at Yorkshire's Aldborough Manor. The spook was being partly emitted by a maidservant named Joan, 'a beautiful creature of sixteen' with 'something very odd about her psychological make-up'. Having an abnormal affinity with animals, birds were constantly flying into the house and perching on Joan's shoulders unafraid, and mice running up into her cupped hands.[1]

Joan was dismissed, but had she lived a few thousand years earlier, she would surely have been acclaimed as a shaman, that breed of archaic mystics and tribal priests who were also supposed to be able to produce supernatural phenomena and communicate with animals; one traditional sign of possessing a vocational shamanic calling was to have a bird land on you during childhood, just like Joan had. As has been argued by the American religious scholar Jeffrey J. Kripal, 'What the modern [paranormal person] lacks is any adequate cultural framework or mythology for making sense of his or her experiences ... We lack a paradigm ... and so these events can only appear bizarre, anomalous or even just crazy.'[2]

Once, Joan would have been the village priestess; by 1936, she was taking her place in the queue down at the local labour-exchange. Charles Fort jokingly suggested a possible career for such girls in the incipient PMT-powered WMD-wing of the US military, but then atom-bombs came along, so that avenue was cruelly closed forever too. During the late-Victorian era a brief window of employment opportunity did arise with the widespread Spiritualism craze, however, when it was possible for liminal shamnesses to gain attention, praise and money for their gifts. The spirit-mediums of this age produced similar phenomena within the séance-room as could be encountered in the more unbounded conditions of a haunted house, albeit in a more directed way. Indeed, many Victorian spirit-mediums first became aware of their gifts after being plagued by polts during their youth.

* * * * *

The classic example is the Italian peasant woman Eusapia Palladino, possibly the most remarkable spirit-medium in modern history, at whose séances an incredible array of alleged poltergeistery occurred. Furniture would levitate, as would Eusapia, solid spirit-hands (complete with attached forearms) materialise, sometimes from within Eusapia's dress, and allow themselves to be shaken, anomalous lights, flames, clouds and mists fly around, pistol shots ring out from thin air, bearded ghostly faces kiss onlookers, musical instruments play by themselves, objects apport, then JOTTle away again, palpable apparitions appear, and objects dance as if 'moved by the breath of invisible gnomes', even when the medium was tied up or held down. Chairs would increase or decrease their weight at Eusapia's command, marks appear on blank pieces of paper, electric sparks shoot up, and imprints of spectral hands and faces be made in clay. Eusapia herself could purportedly alter her height by 10 cm at will, while taking on 'strange forms, so that it was sometimes difficult to say how many arms or legs she really had'. Most peculiarly, Eusapia conjured up bemusing organic shapes termed 'plasmasts', formed of living black cobwebs, these ersatz protean beasties ranging from 'black things like small heads at the end of stalk-like bodies' to 'shadowy things like faces with large features' to 'curious black long knobbly things with cauliflowers at the end of them'.

A good account of Palladino's liminal life appears in the psychical researcher E. J. Dingwall's book *Very Peculiar People*, and she was certainly one of those. Illiterate, crude, 'very ignorant' and, despite her rather stout appearance, highly sexualised, she made quite a contrast to the educated elites who eventually deigned to investigate her; imagine if the sit-com character Mrs Brown could fly and drop phantom limbs from her genitals and you get the general idea. Eusapia was very coarse indeed, having 'a most primitive morality', and had orgasms in the séance-room. Enjoying sex so much that 'she thought of little else', she would hiccup and yawn excessively, go into a crimson-faced trance, and when the sitting was over jump into the arms of her male investigators, 'signify[ing] her desire for more intimate contacts'. Having her first child aged sixteen, Eusapia claimed to have an 'invisible lover' – presumably an incubus – and, being dubbed the 'Queen of the [Séance-Room] Cabinet', it was said by her critics that the only real spell she could cast was an erotic one which made her previously hard-headed male investigators into gullible hard-trousered sex-slaves. Amusingly, her attendant poltergeists shared Eusapia's bad character; they (or Eusapia herself) would pickpocket sitters' wallets and watches from within the darkened séance-room! Her spirit-helpers once apported a parcelled present onto a séance-table as compensation. Opened, it was found to contain a dead rat. These polts, it was aptly said, were in need of 'a deal of educational development'; evidently, the sitters were not aware of the natural character-traits of the Trickster.

Born into dire poverty in the hillside village of Minervino Murge, where peasants 'eked out a miserable existence from the barren soil', Eusapia's mother died shortly after giving birth, and her father paid for her to be raised by a neighbour. When he was later murdered by brigands, the unwanted child was quickly abandoned, aged only twelve. The country folk parcelled her off to Naples, where some middle-class dupes were found, looking for a little girl to adopt. They took Eusapia on, but attempts to make her behave like a good little lady were unsuccessful; she resisted bathing, combing her hair or learning to read and write, and was soon palmed off temporarily to another family. There, intrigued by the raging Spiritualist craze, the family tried holding séances of their own, and Eusapia proved to be an excellent poltergeist-medium. The temporary living arrangement became a more permanent one – just so long as the kid kept making chairs dance.

Also in Naples was a Mr Damiani, a one-time sceptic who had been converted to belief after, he said, a lady friend had her 'almost horizontal' teeth set right by a ghost-dentist in her sleep one night. Discovering Eusapia, Damiani introduced her to his fellow Spiritualists, and the liminal young tearaway found herself suddenly acclaimed rather than rejected by society. Then her ghosts started pickpocketing and apporting dead rats, however, so she was sent away to begin a new career as a maidservant, to keep her out of trouble. Guess what happened. Bringing her boggarts along with her, Eusapia's employment was abruptly terminated when china smashed itself before her master's appalled eyes. Eusapia fell back on the kindness of strangers once more, even though she was now seeing apparitions, being followed by spirit-raps, and having her bedclothes torn off her at night.

In 1888, one Spiritualist, Dr Ercole Chiaia, had the idea of writing an open letter to Cesare Lombroso, the world-famous criminologist and materialist cynic, challenging him to investigate Eusapia. Once he saw her levitating and giving birth to cobweb-creatures, Chiaia said, Lombroso would soon change his mind. Eventually, in 1891 Lombroso accepted the mission ... and found, much to his amazement, that Eusapia Palladino could indeed fly, at least to his own satisfaction. Lombroso witnessed many wonders, even a living wardrobe which advanced towards him 'like a huge pachyderm ... [trying] to attack us', leading him to specifically compare Eusapia to a tribal shamaness. Once word of Lombroso's apparent conversion got out, other eminent men of science flooded to see the poltergeist-lady for themselves, some of whom came away blissfully convinced, others of whom fled her erotic embrace laughing.

The trouble was that, during her séances, Eusapia would indisputably cheat – often quite openly, both consciously and unconsciously. Lombroso himself catalogued her many deceptions; lifting up 'flying' tables with her hands or knees, touching people then saying a ghost did it, or secretly picking flowers to throw around the séance-room as makeshift 'apports'. But she frequently made zero attempt to hide any of this. 'Hold me tight or I'll cheat!' she once shouted. Was this just an elaborate double-bluff, allowing her champions to argue that, with such a criminal, liminal character, you had to take the rough with the smooth, and the real with the fake, or was something far weirder going on? Invited to Cambridge to be investigated by the SPR

A Goldes shaman-priest, complete with sacred costume and regalia; but what comforting ritual paraphernalia does a contemporary poltergeist-focus have to fall back on?

in 1895, she constantly faked phenomena, leading the organisation to conclude she was nothing but a low-class swindler. Given free hospitality in the Dons' neat-lawned gardens, she even cheated at croquet; she just couldn't help herself. But, in her defence, some sitters would make silent mental commands like 'make that chair float, Eusapia', and these would be instantly obeyed. Her defenders used this fact to argue that sceptical observers were unsportingly exploiting this marvel to say 'cheat now, Eusapia', thus making her appear deceitful when she was actually demonstrating amazing powers of telepathy.

Either way, Eusapia now embarked on public tours of Europe and America, being alternately fawned over and condemned by prominent men of science; not bad for a liminal little peasant girl from the backwoods of Italy. As for Cesare Lombroso himself, the opposite happened. His brand of criminology – which held, essentially, that you could spot a wrong 'un just by looking at the shape of his or her face, hands, feet or extra limbs – is now rightly condemned as a form of abject quackery. Analysing Eusapia in light of his own pseudo-science, Lombroso concluded that she was a borderline lunatic slut-criminal, possessing 'morbid [mental] characteristics which sometimes extend to hysterical insanity', such as having strange phobias and fits of violent anger which involved beating people up, and suffering hallucinations of being haunted by her own ghost and a pair of disembodied eyes which stared at her from behind hedges. During séances, she would emit excessive amounts of bodily fluids – 'sweat, tears, even the menstrual secretions' – *il professore* further noted. When condemning his teachings, modern-day critics rarely fail to raise his embarrassing relation to Eusapia Palladino and the world of poltergeistery, thereby discrediting him further by association; by openly consorting with the liminal, the once celebrated Cesare Lombroso ultimately ended up becoming rather a liminal, outlaw figure himself.[3]

* * * * *

Employment prospects for poltergeist-focuses during prehistoric times must have been even greater than during Eusapia's Spiritualist heyday. Recall the case of Swanton Novers Rectory, in which gallons of water were seen to pour from walls in the presence (and sometimes absence) of a teenage maid, Mabel Louisa Phillipo. Parched desert tribesmen might have worshipped her as a rain-making goddess, not slapped her around and tried to frame her for hoaxing. Phillipo was not unique. During one 1990s Polish case, a little boy was continually rained upon from ceilings – it even fell from the roof of a bus he was travelling on![4] In an Italian haunting of 1903, a little girl could make hats and beds fill up with water, jets of which would 'deluge' her household, together with other liquids such as milk, wine and coffee; the drinks were very much on her.[5]

But imagine if you could *deliberately* control such abilities – back in caveman times, you would have had it made. Supposedly, Don Decker, the so-called 'Rain Man', could indeed do so. In 1983, liminal Don, then twenty-one years old and serving time in a US prison for receiving stolen property, was granted temporary release to attend the funeral of his grandfather. This proved disturbing to Don as, unbeknownst to everyone else, this man had been abusing him since he was seven years old. Estranged from his parents, Don was staying with friends when he saw the possibly symbolic ghost of 'an evil old man wearing a crown' reflected in a window, before a series of cuts suddenly appeared on his arms. Soon, Don was entering trances and levitating, being thrown against walls as invisible claws scratched marks upon his neck, while internal rain oozed from walls and ceilings; police saw droplets hover in mid-air then head towards them horizontally. Back in his cell, Don could have a shower any time he liked, just by willing it; the prison warden was fully satisfied Decker really could do this. In 2012, Don fell foul of the law again, accused of an act of arson for purposes of insurance fraud.[6]

Possibly Don Decker set the fire by accident, as other poltergeist-people appear able to act as human fire-lighters; he could have established the ultimate protection racket, threatening to combust premises if you didn't pay him, but acting as a handy mobile human sprinkler-system if you did. In 1959, a case known as the 'Voodoo Fires of Alabama' occurred, in which conflagrations erupted around the new home of the Tuck family, seventeen in one day alone. Mr Tuck's solution was cuckoo. Thinking himself afflicted by a voodoo spell, the man piled his family's 'cursed' property outside and, to dispel the black magic, burned it all, the rough equivalent of flamethrower-wielding US marines destroying a Vietnamese village in order to save it. Police blamed the Tucks' nine-year-old son Calvin Jr, from whom they extracted a Swanton Novers-like 'confession' that he had lit the blazes himself with matches, hoping to spook his family into moving back to their much-missed old home. The local fire-marshal disagreed, arguing some burned items were meant to be non-combustible, that many fires started high up on ceilings, and that the colour of the flames was inconsistent with match-lit fires, more resembling chemical blazes. Still, it was easiest to libel Calvin Jr as a delinquent, wasn't it? At least they didn't tie him to a stake and tell him to concentrate really hard on Joan of Arc.[7]

A similar case occurred in Macomb, Illinois, in 1948, when brown spots began appearing on wallpaper, followed by flames reaching 450 degrees Fahrenheit, in the presence of a young girl named Wanet McNeill. Wanet was unhappy at having to live with her father rather than her mother after a divorce, and was perhaps inadvertently trying to say so via RSPK. Yet again, an impossible pseudo-confession was wrung out of little Wanet and that was the end of the matter.[8] If only the US military had been informed, they may have been able to recruit her into their ranks to burn up their opponents on the battlefield. A traditional sign of shamanism was possessing mastery over fire, perhaps being able to handle hot coals; non-fatal exposure to fire, it was said, transforms a person into pure spirit, like fire transforms wood into smoke.[9] So, when during one 2012 Turkish poltergeist haunting a three-year-old boy was found with his blanket ablaze within metre-high flames but his flesh and clothes both remained miraculously unsinged, ancient peoples might have said he had become marked as a future smoke-bodied shaman, not an unfortunate target of a devilish fire-*djinni*.[10]

*****

What were shamans, precisely? It is actually a composite-term, meaning 's/he who knows', used initially to describe Tungus holy men from Siberia, but now a generic word describing witch doctors, wise men and mystics, both male and female, from pre-modern cultures globally. Sometimes described as 'walkers between worlds', shamans are paradoxically both liminal to their societies and central to them simultaneously, living on the margins in some way, but being respected, honoured and consulted by everyone, even high-status folk. Natural healers and magicians, they are said to possess many psi powers; in hunter-gatherer societies, they may use clairvoyance or their natural control over animals to facilitate successful hunting expeditions. They also speak with or control ghosts, often totemistic spirit-animals who act as their companions and helpers. Able to pass over into the realm of the dead, possibly in trance states or under the influence of hallucinogens, they may take on the role of soul-guides to the recently deceased, like *Hermes psychopompos*, helping them cross the narrow bridge into the Otherworld. Having powers of magical flight – or levitation – they are often chosen for their path in life as children or adolescents, when they undergo holy illnesses, psychological problems, or hauntings from spirits, gods or demons.[11]

Shamans are rather like Hermes enfleshed, or poltergeist-focuses given a proper direction in life. Essentially, they attain the contradictory status of permanent central liminality, or sacred outsiderhood, inhabiting both the interior of the social circle and its margin simultaneously. The anthropologist Victor Turner defined them as having a 'statusless status', which, like the court-jester of old, gave them an inherent right to criticise and disrupt the usual social structures of power in a way which, if performed by any ordinary pleb, would get them beheaded by kings, high-priests or chieftains. By retreating into wildernesses and deserts in search of visions, or living outside or on the edge of their villages, shamans deliberately subvert boundaries by wandering beyond them; they are human bridges, connecting the worlds of flesh and spirit, Heaven and Earth.[12]

One way in which they bridge these realms is sexually. Like hermaphroditic Hermes him/herself, many shamans seem gay or bisexual, cross-dressing and leading non-standard sex lives, up to and including tupping ghosts – as do many poltergeist-focuses and spirit-mediums.[13] Their frequently bizarre sexuality only renders such folk even more liminal, making them easy to taunt. One prominent US psychic, Prudence Calabrese, even offered lessons to clients on how to psychically taste former US President Bill Clinton's penis! (Judging by Slick Willie's own prior reputation, it might have been easier simply to ask him.) According to George P. Hansen, 'Ms Calabrese is a wonderful exemplar for Trickster theory ... Her public visibility makes her especially effective in tainting the field [as ridiculous] and assuring its continued marginality.'[14] Indeed so. These 'perverted' and 'taboo' associations make the paranormal seem doubly perverted and taboo itself.

Another case of shamanic supernatural sexuality laced throughout with the distinct taint of logical perversion was reported by the Jungian analyst Mary Williams. Around 1950, Williams began sessions with a thirty-two-year-old schizophrenic named Roger. Roger was an extremely promiscuous man although, strangely, unable to achieve full orgasm. Attending a séance with one of his many girlfriends one day, he felt invisible fingers pulling his hair, accompanied by cold blasts of air, raps and object-movements, leading to mental problems. Poltergeistery now trailed him wherever he went. Knocks rapped out, doors opened and shut, and he felt himself groped by unseen 4-D perv-hands, as witnessed by Williams herself. The ghost would play up particularly badly every time Roger visited his girlfriend, even tormenting her in his absence. In bed, Roger would be held down by hands unseen and forced to have his face tickled. Finally, the haunting came to a halt when the entity pressed up against him one night and seemed to be 'merging' with him. At this point the ever-eager Roger promptly rogered it, orgasming fully for the first time in his life, probably making his succubus gush some ectoplasmic fluids of her own, too. The poltergeist never returned and, at last, Roger was cured; he could ejaculate normally, and his therapy sessions were deemed complete.[15] Bear this notion of the self-induced, spirit-facilitated 'supernatural cure' in mind as you read on.

* * * * *

In 1951, the pioneering scholar of religion Mircea Eliade produced a lengthy study of the typology of shamanism, called *Shamanism: Archaic Techniques of Ecstasy*, finding many other features of the shaman which are recognisable in the contemporary figure of the poltergeist-focus. Most strikingly, they are associated with lithobolia; gods can indicate who they want to become a shaman by making stones fall on them from the sky, with such items sometimes considered as solidified celestial light, or portions broken off from the vault of Heaven, linking above with below. By swallowing rocks containing shiny crystalline quartz, the shaman symbolically filled himself up with heavenly light, thereby acquiring supernatural powers such as levitation. Older shamans would produce pebbles from within their bodies and hurl them at youths, thereby hailing them their successors; they could also retrieve them from within sick patients' bodies, probably via sleight of hand, relabelling them demonic infestations which had to be excised to ensure a cure. During shamanic séances, objects would float, disembodied voices be heard, tents shake, and stones shower down. One shamaness' feats were described thus: '[she] rubbed a small stone and a quantity of pebbles dropped from her fingers and piled up in her drum. At the end of the experiment the pebbles formed a sizable heap.'[16]

While some shamans are hereditary – remember, 'shamanism' is a general term, encompassing innumerable different traditions – many are only revealed by the actions or attentions of ghosts. From adolescence onwards, they may become epileptic, hysterical or mentally disturbed, self-mutilating with knives and displaying the same extreme behaviour-patterns later demonstrated by Tina Resch or Mrs Forbes, having visions, hearing voices or suffering lapses in consciousness which, to the primitive mind, can only be explained by demonic possession. Sometimes they will fight or wrestle with these devils, trying to resist their calling as unasked-for and disturbing.[17] Some studies have suggested a link between schizophrenia and shamanism, just as many polt-focuses have obvious split-personalities.[18] Other potential shamans might be supernaturally tormented in their beds at night, causing them to become 'nervous and dreamy'; another standard trope of poltergeistery.[19] In 1726, for instance, a fourteen-year-old Norwegian boy from Vaagen was bothered by an invisible entity which whispered Danish and Latin into his ear, pulled him out of his bed, and poured water over him during the night.[20] The Victorian folklorist Andrew Lang also pointed out similarities between the strange whirring, wing-like noises heard during shamanic séances and the same sounds heard in the presence of Western poltergeist-mediums in their beds.[21]

The point of this whole polt-induced mental sickness was rather like the point of a grub going into a temporary coma within its chrysalis; it was what is sometimes termed a 'beneficial sickness' which led to the childhood caterpillar becoming an adult butterfly in shape of a shaman. The 'evil' spirits who first torment him later *cure* him, gifting him special knowledge, status or abilities; the boggarts turn out to be brownies, after all. As Eliade put it, 'the shaman is not only a sick man; he is, above all, a sick man who has been cured, who has succeeded in curing himself.'[22] In a way, isn't that just what Nandor Fodor was trying to say too? And isn't that just what happened to Roger, when he cured his erectile problems by summoning up an invisible ghost?

This 'beneficial illness' was sometimes more physical in nature, described in terms of a ritual dismemberment of the body by ghosts. The point of this was to remove the future shaman's weak human bones, and replace them with stronger iron ones. What does not kill the shaman only makes him or her stronger: 'The candidate's limbs are removed and disjointed with an iron hook; the bones are cleaned, the flesh scraped, the body fluids thrown away, and the eyes torn from their sockets. After this operation all the bones are gathered up and fastened with iron.'[23] Recall the case of 'Rain Man' Don Decker; he was physically attacked by an evil ghost that scratched his body with invisible claws, and then he developed special powers. Later on, once his rain-making abilities had been recognised, his prison warder called a sympathetic priest to bless him, who ended up befriending Don and eliciting a confession about the great wrong his grandfather had done to him as a child. This dark secret finally revealed, all body-rending poltergeistery stopped, Decker was cured and found some mental peace; a classic shamanic narrative of psychic healing, disguised as a ghost story.[24]

Consider also Eugenio Rossi, a nine-year-old Sardinian boy who in 1972 was admitted to hospital with a liver complaint, only to find puddles of water seeping up through the ward floor around him for no reason. Moved from room to room, the impossi-puddles followed him.[25] And think also of Jennie Bramwell, a sickly orphan girl rescued from a Toronto orphanage in 1891 who reputedly fell even more sick soon afterwards, before going into trances and setting fire to any object she then pointed at, even her own clothing.[26] Once upon a time, bouts of tell-tale childhood illness, followed by sensational events like these, and Eugenio and Jennie would have been recognised as shamans on the spot. Shorn of the healing social narrative-structure once provided by shamanism, however, these tragic kids' life-stories become truncated, their ordeals meaningless and incomplete.

The idea of a 'beneficial sickness', or 'creative illness', was first advanced by the psychoanalyst Henri Ellenberger in 1964, and later adapted by the anthropologist Larry Peters as a possible explanation for the epidemic of adolescent depression and teenage delinquency we see in the modern world. Youths who self-harm by cutting themselves, or starve themselves with anorexia, are unconsciously recapitulating the techniques used by shamanic initiates during their path towards self-transformation, said Peters; it's just that, in the archaic world, there was an acknowledged and valued social status waiting for such people on the other side of their trial. Now all they get is hospitalisation and prescription drugs.[27] At Battersea, Shirley Hitchings was once sent away for medical assessment, receiving a clean bill of mental health; she showed 'no sign of any neuropathic condition'. But once exposed as having a haunted big toe in the newspapers, the police threatened to have her taken away and forcibly fostered if she didn't 'voluntarily' attend the Maudsley Psychiatric Hospital, where she was given large, blue sedative-pills to take – pills which, when Donald saw them, he admirably dissolved in a big bowl of water before Shirley could swallow any.[28] As a kind of 'natural cure' himself, Donald was much better than any pharmacological palliative.

In his 1909 book *The Rites of Passage*, the anthropologist Arnold van Gennep coined the very term 'liminal' in order to describe the way that ancient societies used to devise elaborate rituals or ordeals which people at

Henri Ellenberger, originator of the quasi-shamanic theory of 'beneficial sickness' or 'creative illness'. Is a poltergeist best considered as another symptom of such a disorder?

borderline states of life, such as adolescence, had to participate in prior to coming out the other end as a fully-fledged adult/warrior/bride-to-be. In such rites, the initiates become rather like ghosts as they 'die' to their old life, and are then 'reborn' into their new one. Associated with darkness and the dead, they become temporarily 'invisible' to society, like poltergeists, perhaps being temporarily banished or locked away until their trial is complete.[29] In Native American vision-quests, youths were exiled into the wilds to seek communication with a totem-spirit who would agree to become their tutelary deity, granting powers to succeed in warfare, hunting, love, magic or shamanism.[30]

Such initiates were adolescents and young people of all kinds, not poltergeist-focuses. But, when such mediums *did* pop up in your local village, it was known what to do with them. An acknowledged social 'script' could be acted out, allowing them to become a shaman. Today, such scripts have been burned or forgotten. Operating within a social environment that lends them zero credence, and now actively condemns them as dangerous marginal nutters like Tina Resch, might not some of those who would once have gone on to become shamans become instead gross Tricksterish *parodies* of shamans, producing little truly beneficial phenomena, but merely childish vandalistic nonsense? Might, in short, the very structure of modern society have forced our potential brownies to become so many boggarts? Instead of spirit-*helpers*, most focus-figures now have spirit-*hinderers*; Gef the Mongoose certainly comes across as being a direct parody of a totemistic animal-spirit.

* * * * *

Today, contemporary anthropologists, shackled by the doctrinaire PC mindset currently destroying Western academia, often downplay or even cover up the more disreputable aspects of traditional shamanism, such as shamans' associations with schizophrenia and hyper-sexuality, hoping to unrealistically portray other cultures in a wholly positive light. This is only to ignore what has been called shamanism's 'inherent incompatibility with Western rationality'.[31] However, the Trickster-figure has openly been linked with the shaman by many other anthropologists, scholars and commentators from less PC-haunted eras, such as C. G. Jung and Paul Radin.[32] As the Trickster is utterly antithetical to the currently prevailing and oppressively strait-laced mainstream Western mindset of culturally totalitarian 'illiberal liberalism', it is no wonder more modern academics no longer understand him or his mercurial messengers, whether they be shamans, poltergeists, spirit-mediums or focus-figures.

An interesting example of this reductive process at work can be seen in a 1993 essay by the US Professor of Religion and Philosophy Mac Linscott Ricketts, *The Shaman and the Trickster*, which argues that the Trickster-figure is a mythological parody of the shaman, with sceptical tribesmen, who sensibly do not really believe in shamans' powers to contact gods or perform acts of magic, making their holy-men look stupid by inventing ludicrous stories about them in disguise. There are many tales in which the Trickster learns to fly from some birds, but ends up, like Icarus, over-reaching himself and falling farcically back to ground. This would be a parody of the shaman's false claims to possess powers of levitation, says Ricketts, which he gains by donning a feathered bird-costume and beak-mask, dancing around and flapping his arms like wings. Meanwhile, when the Trickster demonstrates skills of ventriloquism, this is a sceptical skit exposing how it is that shamans really produce disembodied, polt-like spirit-voices during their séances; just like how some cynics have sometimes accused the teenage daughter of the Irving household of ventriloquising Gef's squeaky voice. There are even parodic Trickster tales in which shamans' tutelary helpers are not totemistic spirit-animals, but talking turds! These shamans' pet ghosts are, quite literally, talking crap, as are the lying shamans themselves. Shamans' costumes, masks and dances are ridiculed in such Trickster yarns, says Ricketts, their message being 'why should a human want to imitate the form and comportment of an animal? See how silly the Trickster is when he tries to fit a "beak" to his face and tries to fly with the geese!'[33]

Essentially, Ricketts is praising *Scooby Doo* again; just as the ghosts in that show are all really men in masks, so the shaman, too, is really just a costumed con man, so why not yank his rubber mask off like Scooby and the gang do every week, and expose him? Ricketts argues that, as a satiriser of fraudulent religious authorities, 'Unlike the shaman, the priest and the devotee of supernaturalistic religion, the Trickster looks to no [supernatural] 'power' outside himself, but sets out to subdue the world by his wits and his wit', as when throwing his voice and pretending it is ghosts speaking to gain status, like a fraudulent medium. Within such a story, spooks become 'powers not to be worshipped, but ignored ... or in the last analysis mocked'. As Ricketts sees him, 'the Trickster is a symbolic embodiment of the attitude today represented by the humanist', atheistic liberal humanism being a creed I would guess most academics these days would proudly subscribe to.[34]

There is something to this argument – the Trickster does sometimes parody the shaman, as Ricketts rightly perceives – but to claim this made the tales' inventors into prototype Richard Dawkinses seems a bit much. George P. Hansen argues that Ricketts' role as a high-status academic means he occupies a privileged social role which unconsciously 'leads him to a completely rationalistic interpretation' of the Trickster-figure which is exaggerated, and rather misses the point of his overall true meaning, something which 'reflects [Ricketts'] societal position, which shapes his understanding of the world'. The Trickster embodies many competing meanings concurrently, and Hansen suggests that 'scholars who share more in common with the Trickster', who are more marginal and liminal, are more likely to 'show more insight' about this than higher-status tenured academics like Ricketts do.[35] For example, I can get away with writing a Trickster-related book implying the paranormal might be real, because I'm a total nobody – but if Ricketts did it, there would be likely consequences for his career. Having no career to speak of myself, however, I am liberated to speculate wildly! It's the intellectual equivalent of the tramp's freedom of the road ...

Ricketts' attitude stands as the direct academic equivalent of Frank Podmore's attempts to dismiss all poltergeist-girls as naughty young hoaxers. When Podmore found an example of a teenage servant-girl throwing a brick and used it to dismiss an entire case as a hoax, unmasking the miscreant as all-too-human, he too failed to recognise the confusing way that the traditional shaman-figure, as a Trickster, patrolled that hazy liminal borderland between the genuine and the fake. Ancient people were well aware, as Ricketts correctly argues, that shamans faked much of their phenomena; but they appear, most confusingly, to have done this partly because poltergeists don't always operate obediently on-cue, and in order somehow to then induce genuine phenomena in the fake phenomena's wake as Eusapia Palladino and Henry Slade supposedly did.[36]

* * * * *

Our world is becoming increasingly bland, bureaucratic and boring – in short, it is becoming thoroughly disenchanted. 'Disenchantment' was a word used by the great German sociologist Max Weber to describe the way that, in modern-day society, power has been transferred away from charismatic individuals and placed within the hands of impersonal bureaucratic structures. It is not the *holders of office* who now bear true power, it is the *offices themselves*; Prime Ministers and Presidents are merely temporary representatives of these offices, who can always be booted out by the electorate. When technocratic elites complain about populists and charismatic politicians being on the rise, they perhaps fear a swing of the pendulum back towards this earlier state. Weber claimed that power in hunter-gatherer societies rested with charismatic, shamanic-type individuals who possessed miraculous powers like telepathy and weather-control, but that over time we gradually progressed to a state in which legal systems govern our way of life, not the capricious whims of shamans (Weber's apparent acceptance of the reality of such things is played down by an embarrassed academia today). Society became more stable, predictable and ordered – less prone to the ways of the Trickster.[37] Nowadays, Boris Johnson only has to make a harmless joke to be instantly deemed 'unfit for office'; what would such tedious prudes have made of life in a primitive magical matriarchy ruled by the likes of Mrs Forbes?

Today, the possibility of the *Führerprinzip* (or 'leader principle') has been ruthlessly excised from Western politics, supposedly forever; but back when there was an *actual* dictatorial *Führer* in the world to be scared of, there was a bizarre attempt made to label the highly charismatic Adolf Hitler as being a poltergeist-medium himself. In 1941, a war-time British newspaper article appeared implying the Nazis were basically a bunch of Hitler-conjured poltergeists, claiming there were:

> … extraordinarily significant points of resemblance between the records of poltergeist haunting and the Nazi movement. Both are manifested in a subconscious desire for power … both suck, like vampires, the energies of adolescents; both issue in noise, destruction, fire and terror … Hitler speaks best in a state of semi-trance … Whether the uprush of unconscious energy generated through him and sucking into itself the psycho-physical forces of German youth is merely the outcome of an unformulated group-desire for

power, or whether, like some poltergeist hauntings, it would seem to have another source, is an open question.[38]

The polt-obsessed writer Sacheverell Sitwell whimsically said that he could 'readily believe' that, if he 'felt so inclined' Adolf could easily 'displace objects and move them about in oblique and curving flight ... rap out equivocal answers ... or cause lighted matches to drop down from the ceiling.'[39] Maybe that's how he burned down the Reichstag?

Hitler may not actually have been a fascist focus-figure, but among all the many genuine demons he unleashed onto the world, one was State-funded parapsychology. Prior to the Nazis' rise to power, Hans Bender – in later life the investigator of the Rosenheim poltergeist, and a tenured professor at the Freiberg Institut, but then a mere doctoral student – was pessimistic about the prospect of gaining any public cash to investigate spooks. The liberal Weimar Republic was simply unwilling to recognise such things as being potentially real, he lamented. The Nazis, however, stuffed with previously fringe weirdos and open fans of the occult like Heinrich Himmler, proved more accommodating. Recognising their love of pseudo-science, Bender coined the still-used term 'border science' to describe parapsychology, couching it within an 'epistemology of science' in order to appeal to fascist authorities in hock to much racial border science of their own. For example, why not just relabel astrology as 'cosmobiology', as that sounds much more technical? This plan worked. Joining the SA in 1933, the year Hitler became Chancellor, Bender's career took off, gaining a 'significant endowment' of Reich-tainted money in 1942 to set up his own lab, the Paracelsus Institute for Border Science. In the post-war world Bender became a media-friendly *Spukprofessor*, but his entire rise from liminality to centrality was only facilitated by extreme social chaos. Bender's media promotion of the Rosenheim case in 1969 led to a 10 per cent increase in belief in the reality of poltergeists among the Bavarian public; but if Germany had remained disenchanted, Brownshirt Bender would never have been on TV in the first place.[40]

* * * * *

George P. Hansen has hypothesised that mainstream hostility to the reality of the paranormal is not simply down to the materialist philosophy of our current Dominant, but is far more fundamental, being nothing less than 'a consequence of the structure of society'. Our five-day week and nine-to-five lives are more routine now, more governed by the dull drone of economics than by *Führerprinzip*-style charisma. If the Trickster thrives in chaos, then he may be less able to manifest within a modern-day disenchanted society than within an archaic, enchanted one where shamans and charismatic dictators still rule – recall how Shirley Hitchings finally disposed of Donald.[41] The collapse of the Weimar Republic was characterised as a time when 'the materialisation of the extraordinary found wide acceptance', both in parapsychology and in politics.[42] As such, it might be in our interests to keep poltergeist-people liminal and thoroughly ridiculed, as to do so would reduce their power. After all, if society becomes re-enchanted via increasing belief in the paranormal's reality, then one day Tina Resch might be released from prison and become our Queen Carrie I.

One person who apparently believes this to be possible is Jason Reza Jorjani, once teacher of a course in Science, Technology and Society at the New Jersey Institute of Technology, whose 2016 book *Prometheus and Atlas* is an interesting examination of the reasons behind the liminality of the paranormal in Western society, which contains a peculiar mixture of both great insight and great strangeness. Jorjani was aware of something called the 'psi inhibitor effect', in which the presence of sceptics in a parapsychology lab puts psychics off their game, leading to poorer test results. He felt that this phenomenon might apply on a wider societal scale, meaning that, if everyone started believing in such things then huge-scale paranormal events of the kind normally only seen in Hollywood might begin breaking out all over the place, causing social panic and total chaos, like at the end of *Ghostbusters*. As 'mainstream scientific recognition of the paranormal could in itself amplify manifestations of it', who knew where this could lead?[43]

According to Jorjani, René Descartes might have been motivated to try and separate mind completely from matter because he himself had endured a paranormal experience and it scared him, while another key architect of the current prevailing Dominant, Immanuel Kant, considered the supernatural to be both real and a kind of practical terrorism against the stable world-order, so he recommended mocking it in public 'whether it may be justified or not' to prevent it gaining more traction. 'If it was once found necessary at times to burn' people like poltergeist-mediums as witches, Kant argued, 'it will now suffice simply to purge them' via laughter, instant dismissal and putting them in mental homes, even if they are sane and telling the truth, in order to prevent 'disorder in civil life'.[44] That's liberal humanist progress for you.

What would such civilizational disorder look like? Jorjani claims the liminal nature of ghosts will undermine the very structure of Western politics. Other paranormal phenomena will have legal implications, too; if you are reincarnated as a child and then approach your former husband Humbert Humbert as a twelve-year-old Lolita, will this really still count as paedophilia if you died aged seventy, and are therefore really eighty-two and thus technically not under-age? And what if a psychic scanned the future and stole next year's big inventions from Apple and Microsoft? How would they enforce copyright laws on things they had not yet created? Would our entire economy not collapse? Jorjani thinks it might, and whether you agree with him or not, I think you'd at least have to commend him on the originality of his thinking.[45]

This is obviously a total disgrace. Whether Jorjani be right or wrong in what he's saying, how can a man teaching at a mainstream Western university these days be allowed to have *interesting* and *entertaining* ideas? Simple. He can't. Suspended from his post, accused of harbouring Far-Right sympathies and outlandish fantasies about psychic Nazi supermen straight out of Castle Wolfenstein (which he denies), the increasingly liminal Jorjani can today be found online making some very odd speculations about the true nature of UFOs. I really enjoyed Jorjani's book, but he doesn't seem to realise that, if what he is saying is true, then the text's very publication would in fact tend to undermine belief in the reality of the paranormal, because so many of its arguments sound comical, at least to those whose minds have successfully been made all Cartesian – it concludes with an extended account of a man who could supposedly bring down airliners by firing telekinetic lightning at them like Raiden in *Mortal Kombat*. Such paradoxes are the very *métier* of the Trickster. Getting too close to him and his liminal ways can ruin both your career and your life.

* * * * *

Possibly the nexus between all these things is again more constellational or analogical than causal. The parapsychologist William G. Braud proposed the idea of 'labile systems', in which he noted it was easier for a psychic to influence something that was inherently 'labile' in its nature – that is, already prone to change – than it was to influence something rigid. For instance, psychokinetically dimming a candle-flame may be easier than making a light-bulb fail.[46] Liminal, labile times of life-transition like the adolescence of so many poltergeist-mediums, liminal, labile processes such as flickering candle-flames, and liminal, labile periods of history involving rapid and chaotic social change, like Nazi Germany, seem to correlate somehow with upsurges in the occurrence of paranormal phenomena, we are told. Anthropologists have demonstrated how the paranormal is both associated with, and allegedly acts as a facilitator of, social change; for instance, the reported miracles of Christ led to the founding of a whole new religion which eventually conquered the entire ancient world.[47]

However, such social changes, like all crossroads haunted by Hermes, can be either positive or negative in nature; they can unleash benign brownies like Christ, or malign boggarts like Hitler. As such, possibly it is wise to keep these things hedged off, liminal and taboo via mockery and laughter after all, as Kant cynically recommended. If poltergeists and psi really are real, then potentially they might be very dangerous. Perhaps, in a typical Tricksterish irony, when spooks appear in deliberately ridiculous and positively unbelievable shapes like dog-headed men, living, medium-born cobweb-children or talking animals with human hands, they are actually trying to protect us from belief in themselves? Long may the liminal remain liminal. There is an old saying, 'Hermes is the midwife of Dionysus', the Greek god of wine and orgiastic excess, whose priestesses got drunk and tore their innocent victims limb from limb in grape-fuelled frenzy with their bare nails and teeth. When you invite a god of the margins too far into the centre of things, there must come a point in the end at which things fall apart and that same centre cannot hold.

VII

Traps of Logic

We have to remember that what we observe is not Nature herself, but
Nature exposed to our method of questioning.

Werner Heisenberg

In a disenchanted world, there is little place left for the Trickster. Even
our comedians are now becoming right-on propagandists more than they
are actual jesters; attending many of their tiresome gigs is more akin to
going to listen to a political lecture with lashings of gratuitous swearing
included than anything else these days. Fortunately, many modern ghosts
are rather funnier. Sigmund Freud defined the typical joke as working via
the breaching of taboo, as with a joke about sex. But the taboo poltergeists
break most radically is that of logic, namely that of a causative variety.
Why must we seek definite mechanisms and causes for everything? It
is surely because the concept of causality is the underlying basis of our
current scientific Dominant. We take it for granted that, when C occurs,
something else (A acting upon B) must have caused it, via means of
comprehensible energetic transfer. When a poltergeist appears, however,
we cannot attribute causality quite so clearly. Here is a fascinating case
in point ...

In 1967 an Indian CID Inspector, Guru Sharan Lal Srivastava, had a
house built in Lucknow. During construction, one of the builders was
lynched in a half-constructed room. As a later report justifiably put it,
'Whether this had anything to do with subsequent events is unknown.'
First, stones fell in the courtyard. Then, fires erupted, objects flew and
smashed, taps turned on and off, a ceremonial sword stabbed furniture,
and the Inspector's children were transported about the house while asleep.
One son, Shasti, showed signs of being possessed. Another child endured
visions of hooded snakes slithering around the place. Going to and from
college, Shasti was repeatedly accosted by an old man who either gave him
sweets or scolded him for being late before vanishing into thin air near a
certain tree. The poltergeistery climaxed in July 1975 when the Inspector's
wife, Shanti, spontaneously combusted. 'The evil spirit is burning me!' she
cried. The flames were quenched with water, but she died in hospital that

same night. The fire-demon finally disappeared in 1976, after a visiting pair of traditional exorcists from Uttar Pradesh succeeded where many had failed before them by banishing the ghost for good.[1]

* * * * *

Where to find causal explanations in such an elaborate case? The most obvious place to begin is with the hanged man. However, if his lynching did cause the poltergeist to manifest, then this cannot be the *whole* explanation. I'll not test it out just now, but I'm reasonably certain that, if I killed a man, his spirit wouldn't just automatically return to torment me. Every time there's a murder, there isn't a ghost. Anyway, the whole hypothesis that the dead man's spirit was responsible is, in itself, problematic. Why would he transport sleeping kids around in the middle of the night? What would be his purpose? And why kill poor, innocent Shanti? If he wanted revenge, why not burn whoever had actually murdered him? But here, we seek to attribute motives to the dead and must of necessity draw a blank.

Further ambiguities proliferate. Take the vision of the snakes. Did the spook cause that, directly? Or did the child, in a state of apprehension, independently begin hallucinating of his own accord? Was the other child, Shasti, really possessed by an evil spirit, or just driven to mental imbalance through fear, an imbalance which expressed itself in a time-honoured and culturally-sanctioned way? Did such fits then cause some strange RSPK-like energy to be released by him? Perhaps Shasti subconsciously disliked his mother and grill-cooked her by proxy, thereby relieving himself of any conscious guilt in the matter. And who was that old man following Shasti to college each day? Was he the astral projection of a malicious native *fakir*? Or might he have been the temporary disguise of a local devil? Is this why the exorcists were able to banish the ghoul, by using their holy powers to dispel evil? Or did their rites act as a psychological placebo, causing the RSPK-addled Shasti to believe that, such ceremonies being completed, they must surely have worked? Then again, with his mother dead, perhaps Shasti's subconscious realised it had gone too far, and so brought matters to a quick close. Or was it nothing but lies and trickery? The fatal fire could have been a tragic accident, misinterpreted amid the panic. Some would say the childhood 'visionaries' were mentally ill, or guess it was all an elaborate murder plot to rid the Inspector of an unwanted wife. Maybe the reader-hungry newspaper where the reports first appeared made up every last detail? In short, however you want to interpret the haunting, you can pick and choose (or even invent) your evidence to allow you to do so.

* * * * *

Byzantine hauntings like Inspector Srivastava's have a multiplicity of potential causes lurking implicit within them – and, when potential causality appears everywhere, the very notion of causality itself becomes essentially meaningless. In such cases, I'd prefer to say that the events are somehow acausal. They just happened. I don't know why, *you* don't know why, even if you're Harry Price himself. According to Mary Rose Barrington, chronicler of JOTTs:

> ... paranormal events do not occur in an ascertainable sequence and in that sense are acausal. Indeed, if a cause is found, the event is not paranormal ... To demand an explanation [for a paranormal event] comparable to a scientific explanation of a causal, sequential event, or to deplore its absence, is to make a serious category error.[2]

Yes, indeed! Poltergeists continually tease us with apparent clues to their true nature which ultimately prove to be nothing more than comic dead-ends, like Tony Hancock's library book detective story with the final chapter removed in *The Missing Page*. We should be prepared to admit that, like the Trickster, poltergeists are at root unknowable, that they constantly lie to us – or make us lie to ourselves – and to laugh at this fact. If we do not, our minds can easily play tricks upon us.

* * * * *

Here is a good example of just such a trap of false logic set up for theorists to fall into. In his 1931 book *Lo!* Charles Fort talks of the Charleston earthquake of 31 August 1886, and of the showers of hot stones which rained from the sky during aftershocks, upon 4 September. At 2.30 a. m. stones fell from the heavens just outside the Charleston *News and Courier* building, bouncing into the newspaper offices through open windows, being found 'warm' to the touch. At 7.30 a.m. more fell: 'It was a strictly localised repetition, as if one persisting current of force.' At 1.30 p. m. 'again stones fell, and these were seen, coming straight down from a point overhead.'[3]

But was this even a poltergeist at all? The American psychical researcher Hereward Carrington thought so. In *The March of the Poltergeist*, his heroically over-ambitious 1949 attempt to chronologically list every known poltergeist case in existence up to the point of publication, Carrington definitely classifies the events as such:

> Showers of hot stones reported, some in the press room of the newspaper. Some of these were seen to fall from a point overhead; they fell over an area of 75 feet, and more than a gallon of them were picked up. Never explained.[4]

Carrington presumably considered Charleston to be a case of poltergeistery because it sounds like a large-scale variant of lithobolia. Fort, however, being something of a Trickster himself, half-jokingly conceived of poltergeists and mysterious falls from the sky as being different shapes of manifestation of some kind of essentially inanimate – and possibly senile – teleportive force. In June 1884, Fort tells us, in a field near Trenton, New York State, two farm-workers experienced repeated bouts of lithobolia, with stones 'falling from a point overhead' over the course of two days.[5] As Fort, wearing his Cosmic Jester's hat, memorably put it:

It could be that, in reading what most persons think are foolish little yarns of falling stones, we are, visionarily, in the presence of cosmic constructiveness – or that once upon a time this whole Earth was built up by streams of rocks, teleported from other parts of an existence. The crash of falling islands – the humps of piling continents – and then the cosmic humour of it all – or utmost speculariy functioning, then declining, and surviving only as a vestige – or that the force that once heaped the peaks of the Rocky Mountains now slings pebbles at a couple of farmers near Trenton, NY.[6]

In his works, Fort details numerous instances of strange falls from the sky occurring during, before, or after earthquakes. He then implies that there *might* be some kind of causal relation between the two classes of event though, as ever, he states nothing for definite. Some readers would laugh at this idea, saying that the apparent correlation between lithobolic stone-showers and earthquakes is simply 'mere coincidence'. Maybe so; but what, Fort asks, *is* coincidence? Just a convenient label? Once you start invoking it, you open yourself up to the Tricksterish counter-argument that maybe reliably observed processes like chemical reactions, though apparently repeatable in nature, are really just frequent coincidences too; that hydrogen and oxygen don't *really* make water, they just *seem* to do so because, every time they are added together, by complete chance, water appears on the scene. Perhaps the way that 'offsprings so often appear after marriage' is only a coincidence too, and all babies are really just spontaneous births, but nobody has ever noticed because, by incredible coincidence, no child has

Hereward Carrington and Charles Fort, who held differing views upon the strange stone-showers which followed hot on the heels of the Charleston Earthquake.

ever been born to someone who has not had sex before. Likewise, a hard-line believer in RSPK might dismiss the occasional appearance of ghosts around murder-scenes as mere coincidence; but a hard-line Spiritualist might dismiss the occasional appearance of ghosts around focus-figures as mere coincidence too. 'It is either that our data are not of coincidences, or that everything's a coincidence,' Fort proposes, confusingly – by which I mean confusingly on purpose.[7] Maybe every ghost is an orange ghost?

* * * * *

How to address the problems of causality and coincidence when it comes to cases like that of the Charleston stone-showers? Instead of proposing some complex mechanical theory, whether involving poltergeists, senile teleportive forces or otherwise, perhaps we may better invoke the notion of acausality. This term's most famous use was by Freud's one-time disciple C. G. Jung in his 1952 monograph *Synchronicity: An Acausal Connecting Principle*.

What Jung meant by synchronicity can be simplified by the term 'meaningful coincidence'. An amusing example of just such a cosmic *hermaion* in action was given by the French astronomer and psychical researcher Camille Flammarion in his book *The Unknown*. When still a schoolboy in Orléans, the writer Émile Deschamps was one day obliged to share a table with a certain Monsieur de Fortgibu. While visiting England, de Fortgibu had acquired a taste for plum-pudding, a dish barely known in France. He insisted Deschamps try some. This rare delicacy never again passed Deschamps' lips until, ten years later, he unexpectedly spied another such morsel in a Paris restaurant. However, the food was reserved. If he wanted any, Deschamps would have to beg a slice from the customer who had already bought it. This stranger soon arrived – it was that very same Monsieur de Fortgibu. Many years afterwards, Deschamps was served a third plum-pudding during a friend's dinner-party. He laughed, joking the only thing missing now was Monsieur de Fortgibu. At that very moment the door opened, and in he walked! Now elderly and senile, the poor old fellow had got the wrong door, being invited to dinner himself at a different apartment nearby. Three times in his life did Deschamps eat plum-pudding; and three times did he meet Monsieur de Fortgibu.[8]

Such stories, while amusing, appear initially meaningless. It seems as stupid to say that eating plum-pudding *caused* Monsieur de Fortgibu to appear, as such, as it would be to say that the Charleston earthquake *caused* stones to rain from the sky a few days later. But to Jung, the fact that no discernible natural laws could be discovered to account for such Hermes-sent coincidences did not mean they should simply be dismissed. Jung was familiar with twentieth-century discoveries in sub-atomic physics. With his 'uncertainty principle', the physicist Werner Heisenberg had shown the precise location and the exact speed of any given sub-atomic particle in existence could not both be calculated simultaneously. The 'non-locality principle', meanwhile, held that twinned particles could act upon one another instantaneously, without having to take any amount of intervening space into account. Thus, certain aspects of the sub-atomic world appeared independent of both space and time, and therefore were not terribly receptive to methods of human measurement. As Jung argued:

> Natural laws are *statistical* truths, which … are completely valid only when dealing with macrophysical quantities [a cup, say]. In the realm of very small quantities [the individual atoms *in* that cup] prediction becomes uncertain, if not impossible, because very small quantities no longer behave in accordance with the known natural laws. The philosophical principle that underlies our conception of natural law is *causality*. But if the connection between cause and effect turns out to be only statistically valid and only relatively true, then the causal principle is only of relative use for explaining natural processes … This is as much as to say that the connection of events may in certain circumstances be other than causal, and requires another principle of explanation.[9]

But how can a cause be considered something 'other than causal'?

Causality, in everyday common-sense terms, is conceived of as involving energetic processes. If you kick a ball, then it will move, as you have transferred kinetic energy from your foot to the ball. We feel safe in saying the kick caused the ball to move, as a) repeated observation seems to prove the fact and b) there is a clear theoretical framework available to explain the process. Jung, however, knew of the now-famous experiments in telepathy performed by the parapsychologist J. B. Rhine at North Carolina's Duke University in the 1930s. These involved subjects guessing – or telepathically perceiving, if you prefer – the designs on sets of so-called 'Zener cards'. These small white cards, marked with simple symbols such as crosses, circles and wavy lines, were looked at and concentrated on by another experimenter, the hope being that the psychic being tested would read the viewer's mind and thereby prove the reality of ESP, or 'Extra-Sensory Perception'.

The validity of these tests has since been questioned, but Jung accepted them. Particularly interesting were Rhine's attempts to determine whether the distance between the card-viewing experimenter and the card-guessing telepath had any meaningful effect upon the percentage of correct guesses made. Apparently not. Whether the participants were in the same room, separate rooms, or even 250 miles away, had no perceptible influence; accuracy did not decline the further the two participants sat from one another. Time was no factor either, as during some tests Rhine had his putative psychics *predict* in which order the randomly machine-shuffled cards would be picked up, rather than just trying to read the card-viewer's mind, and found that, again, the rate of positive results was not negatively affected.[10] Other ingenious experiments later performed by the parapsychologists Helmut Schmidt and Karlis Osis also seemed to confirm that psychic powers remained unaffected by the complexity of the experimental task being undertaken.[11]

To Jung, this was highly significant. If ESP was unaffected by both space and time, then it seemed impossible to continue thinking about psychic powers in terms of the transmission of some kind of waves, like 'mental radio' signals being beamed out from person to person, or (as with RSPK) from person to object. Waves are nothing more than an expression of energy;

and, if waves are not involved in psychic processes, then neither can energy itself, in the eyes of Jung. When it comes to paranormal or synchronistic events, therefore:

> We must give up at the outset all explanations in terms of energy, which amounts to saying that events of this kind cannot be considered from the point of view of causality, for causality presupposes the existence of space and time in so far as all observations are ultimately based upon bodies in motion.[12]

So the term 'acausal' does in fact refer to a form of causality; but some new, non-energetic kind, which, 'as all observations are based ultimately upon bodies in motion', we cannot hope ever to perceive, measure or, presumably, understand. The term 'acausal' is thus somewhat misleading – but it sounds more scientific somehow than the word 'magic', so Jung calls it this. I am also a little embarrassed by the word 'magic'. If somebody asked me to explain how I thought poltergeists made showers of hot stones fall from thin air and I replied 'magic!' they would think I was either joking or insane. If I replied that I felt that lithobolic materialisations of stones were triggered by an acausal connecting principle which expresses itself purely via non-energetic and therefore non-observable processes, however, then they might presume I actually had some idea of what I was talking about.

Therefore, when I use the term 'acausality' in this book, what I mean is not that there is, in an absolute sense, no reason for a thing happening. What I mean instead is that there is no *discernible* or *comprehensible* reason for a thing happening. Like Jung I don't believe poltergeists are necessarily an energetic process – be that the energy of focus-emitted RSPK or the kinetic energy transferred to a pebble by the hand of an invisible dead person immediately prior to throwing it. Thus, the analysis of poltergeistery in terms of the search for understandable causes for it is, in my opinion, a rather futile one. If you pursue such a mirage excessively you might be fooled into making such misguided assertions as that earthquakes cause time-delayed stone-showers or plum-puddings attract Frenchmen.

*****

The comic aspect of acausality is of its very essence. We tell people about amazing coincidences we have experienced, as a form of entertainment. Recall an old episode of the classic British sit-com *Father Ted*, wherein the titular priest keeps on running into the exact same annoying woman in a lift, at traffic-lights and elsewhere, causing much awkward embarrassment, until eventually he returns home to find her sitting on the couch in his living-room. It's the precise same joke as the universe told us about Monsieur de Fortgibu. If anything, the fictional example is less extreme than the real-life one. 'There is a view ... that there has never been a coincidence', wrote Fort in his book *Wild Talents*, thereby deliberately contradicting some of his earlier statements about the matter.[13] Indeed not; laughter proves it.

To Jung, if synchronistic and paranormal events were indeed acausal in nature and thus, as Rhine implied, operated somehow outside the normal boundaries of space–time, then within them the original unity of all things, both material and mental, before the act of physical creation of the universe first took place stood revealed, a state Jung termed the *pleroma*. As this fact can only be recognised, not explained, *meaning* and *connection*, not energetic causality, therefore govern all synchronistic phenomena, just as Nandor Fodor felt such subjective qualities governed the precise nature of apports and JOTTles.

By revealing certain apparently meaningful connections between certain apparently unconnected phenomena – plum-puddings and Frenchmen, lithobolia and earthquakes, murder-scenes and poltergeists – the universe thereby implies to us the original interconnectedness of all things, or what Fort termed 'Continuity'. In a sudden flash of laughter, this recognition may take place within us. It seems funny, when we think about it, that Monsieur de Fortgibu and plum-puddings were once one and the same thing. By subverting categories in such a fashion, coincidence is yet another profoundly Tricksterish, liminal, barrier-dismantling conceit.[14]

If we are sensible, we will laugh along with the outrageous coincidences planned out for us within the Cosmic Joker's intentionally unlikely scripts, not seek dubiously to explain how it is such ridiculous plot-devices might actually work. Remember the satirical American journalist H. L. Mencken's wise old advice that dissecting jokes is a bit like dissecting frogs; it doesn't tell us much worth knowing, and in the end the frog dies of it. Oddly enough, Mencken himself hated Charles Fort, calling him 'a quack of the most obvious sort' who was 'enormously ignorant of elementary science'; apparently, he didn't realise most of Fort's wilfully ridiculous pseudo-theories were themselves intended as jokes.[15] When Fort wrote calculated absurdities like 'I think we're all bugs and mice, and are only different expressions of an all-inclusive cheese'[16] and 'We shall pick up an existence by its frogs',[17] Mencken took him at his word and, in so doing, unnecessarily killed off a fair few harmless amphibians himself; interpreting their messages too literally is always a grave mistake to make when dealing with Tricksters.

In the words of one assessment, Fort's pseudo-theories were 'simply rhetorical devices; a counterpart to dogmatic pedagogy. By deliberately deriving absurd examples [i.e. devising absurd theories] from the same data as 'official' explanations, he could demonstrate the weakness of some arguments.'[18] Fort's pseudo-theories actually function more like Zen *koans* than they do genuine theories about how the world works. Should we consider the various theories advanced for the existence of poltergeistery as functioning (albeit inadvertently, from their champions' perspectives) in a similar fashion? Was William G. Roll an unconscious Charles Fort?

* * * * *

Poltergeists might profitably be considered as an inherently synchronistic phenomenon in and of themselves. Maybe even their repeated occurrence around a focus-figure is a kind of coincidental non-energetic synchronicity after all, like the repeated occurrence of plum-puddings around Monsieur de Fortgibu. Recall the ancient Greek legend of Proteus, the shape-shifting Old Man of the Sea. He was yet another Trickster-figure; try and cast your net over him, and he'd quickly transform into something else and swim away from you. Proteus was also symbolic of something far wider. According to Plotinus, the greatest of Neoplatonist philosophers: 'The Cosmos is like a net which takes all its life, as far as it ever stretches, from being wet in the water. It is at the mercy of the sea which spreads out, taking the net with it just so far as it will go.'[19]

Plotinus' sea – of which Proteus is a personification – is the old Neoplatonist idea of the world-soul or *anima mundi*; or, if you are a Jungian, the collective unconscious, perhaps. This ancient school of mystical philosophers also felt, like Jung, that there was once a kind of *pleroma*, called 'The One'. It was all things at once, simultaneously. You might wish to call it God. Pouring out from this, at some later rung down the Great Chain of Being, was a world of potentially separate ideas and things, called the *anima mundi*. Here it was that 'The One' slowly began to split into, potentially, 'The Many', and here the Forms abided. These Forms were non-physical 'guiding templates' for distinct classes of things possessing a later solid, individual existence within the physical world. There would be a Form of Man, for example, in which all actual men would participate, making them human by giving them a head, a body, two arms and two legs. While the collective Form lying behind man is stable, however, his particular expression in the flesh is not. All individual existing men are different; they have different heights, facial features and skin colours, and yet the Form of Man stands behind each of these temporary earthly versions of itself, making them broadly recognisable as being of the same family. This *anima mundi* where the Forms reside in their infinite potential is that same sea of which Plotinus speaks. It is the realm of collective, common soul, not individual personality.

If the sea in Plotinus' metaphor is the world-soul, then the net is the world of visible embodied individual Forms; it shifts constantly its shape with the motion of the ever-moving waves beneath it. So does the poltergeist. Whatever way the wind blows the waves, he alters his shape – but not his essential underlying Form – to fit it. Within medieval Europe, he appeared as a demonic agent of witchcraft; in the Arabian Peninsula even to this day as the *djinn*; in the modern, materialist West, as RSPK phenomena manifesting repeatedly around a focus-figure. But, in the end, the poltergeist is very probably none of these things. If you take him too literally, as Mencken took Fort, then you will only end up mistaking the net for the sea, or an existence for its frogs.

*****

Protean poltergeists refuse point-blank to be pinned down. A celebrated seventeenth-century French ghost known as the 'Devil of Mascon' took particular delight in the company of a local likely lad named Michael Repay, much prone to 'ludicrous misadventures' and vain boasts. One time, Michael bragged to a friend on his way to church that he was going to spread a net out for this Devil and catch him. Being independent of space and time in a way J. B. Rhine might well have recognised, the polt overheard this promise. 'Wilt thou now spread thy net to catch me?' it asked the boy mockingly, knowing full well Michael could not.[20]

Proteus cannot be netted for close personal study while he keeps on shifting his forms; and the Devil of Mascon claimed, at various points, to be both an angel and a demon. Logically, what are we to make of such cases? Logically, very little. The poltergeist belongs not to the realm of causal logic, but to that of *aporia*, or unsolvable paradox; the term, another Greek one, means something like 'impassable barrier' or 'blocked passageway', being the opposite of a pore, through which things can easily seep.[21] This is a particularly Tricksterish paradox, but being able to slip through the pores of any net, the poltergeist also acts in a way to sew that same net up behind him, subverting its purposes and rendering it useless. It is as if Hermes had floated through a keyhole in misty form, then suddenly transformed himself into strong glue and blocked that very same hole up in his wake, just like Descartes wished to do when dogmatically insisting upon the rigidly dualistic separation of mind and matter. Hermes can not only unlock doors, he can also firmly bolt them.

Proteus, the 'Old Man of the Sea' from Greek myth, who would shift his shape, thereby making him impossible to catch, just like many a Trickster – especially the poltergeist. (Rijksmuseum)

VIII

Our Minds Playing Tricks on Us

Truth is denied to the constipated.
Alleged 1954 message from an alien to a
French UFO Contactee

The Trickster was in a certain sense actually real – for he was primitive man. Early man must have been far more animalistic than his modern equivalent. He will have had to hunt, seek shelter and face the possibility of a violent death on a daily basis; he will have washed in rivers, defecated outdoors and copulated free of shame. This is why the Trickster is so often depicted as being a human–animal hybrid, or else a fully-fledged bodily beast with human-like mental characteristics, with many Trickster tales demonstrating a preoccupation with the most obviously animalistic functions of man, those of shit and of sex. The Trickster is a personified metaphor for the incomplete development of human consciousness during our species' early days upon this planet. When Prometheus stole the blazing fire from heaven and used it to give life to humanity, this was perhaps a mythological metaphor for mankind's first realisation of his inner-soul, of the sudden blooming of self-consciousness within the previously inert clay of his animal flesh.

The particular shift of consciousness Trickster represents most clearly is that which changed early man from the hunted into the hunter, as in the tale of the Norse mischief-maker Loki and the invention of the fishnet. Such a yarn is a personification of a mental process, a transformation of one of mankind's greatest intellectual leaps into an entertaining, narrative-based form. The story goes that Loki had again angered the other gods of the Aesir, and so entered hiding in the mountains. Seeking distraction, Loki shape-shifts into a salmon to swim and leap across the alpine rivers. Trying to anticipate how the gods may try to ensnare him while occupying his fun-yet-vulnerable fish-form, Loki fashions the first fishnet from linen string – an ingenious food-catching device in which he is, characteristically, then later caught up himself by accident.[1] A living oxymoron, Loki here embodies both Roadrunner and Wile E. Coyote in one.

Like Loki the net-inventing, net-caught Trickster, early man will have had to show great cunning – when pursued by fierce predators that were faster and more powerful, he will have had little choice – and yet, naturally, he will have also fallen prey to his own simultaneous great stupidity. Who could have foreseen that the berries of this plant would be poisonous while those from another were simply tasty? Consider an episode from the Winnebago Indian Trickster story cycle wherein Wakdjunkaga, their version of the archetype (his name meant 'The Tricky One') encounters a talking plant-bulb, chanting 'He who chews me, he will defecate; he who chews me, he will defecate!' Wakdjunkaga, never having witnessed such a thing before, treats the bulb as an amusing novelty and swallows it, arrogant in his assumption it will surely not affect *him*, the great Trickster. Yet it does affect him, and before long he is forced to climb a tall tree to escape the ever-growing pile of excrement and Wakdjunkaga, blinded and covered in shit, is almost drowned in his own filth.[2] A less fairy-tale-like version of this same basic narrative must have afflicted early man quite frequently.

No longer being so close to our animal-origins, within our disenchanted world, we don't today act much like the Trickster. And yet, more civilised though we now are, the Trickster archetype, this anarchic, incomplete and self-contradictory consciousness, is still contained somewhere deep down within us – or, in Jungian terms, within the collective unconscious or *anima mundi* of our race. We are just, on a normal day-to-day basis, buttoning him up. And, without an effective safety valve, such things can have a habit of returning tenfold to haunt us …

* * * * *

Today, the poltergeist is frequently defined by parapsychologists as being a kind of externalised consciousness, broken off from the internal mind of its focus – if, indeed, consciousness is the correct word. A series of dissociated mental processes is a more apt description. When you hear of a ghost that spoke from out of an unplugged CD-player to wish a woman 'Happy Birthday' and then immediately pushed her down the stairs, fracturing her ankle,[3] it is hard to know if this was meant as a cruel joke or simply an expression of a profoundly schizophrenic character.

Like the Trickster, the poltergeist is rarely a well-rounded and coherent personality. Some are playful one minute and malevolent the next, another case of being concurrently both Roadrunner and Wile E. Coyote. Consider the powerful South Shields poltergeist of 2005–06. When the polt's chief victims, a couple named Marianne and Marc, were sitting watching TV their Digibox constantly flashed up unasked-for reminders that certain appropriately-titled programmes – such as *House of Horrors* and *Most Haunted* – were about to start. Upon checking listings magazines, none of these shows were even scheduled for broadcast.[4] These were only harmless puns. Less amusing was the time the polt kidnapped Marianne's young son Robert from his bedroom. Frantically, the couple tore apart the house looking for him, with no success. Terrified, they tried again in all the places they knew perfectly well they had already checked. One such place was a bedroom closet – within which Robert was now found, sound asleep and wrapped in a blanket, having become a human JOTTle.[5]

Such was the spirit's incoherence that it once repented of its Tricksterism and actually apologised for the inconvenience it had caused. A thump was heard in a cupboard after Marianne had pleaded with the ghost to leave them alone. Its door shot open to reveal one of Robert's doodle-boards inside, bearing a written message: 'I AM SORRY.'[6] At other times, the uninvited visitor had less sympathy, laughing out loud at the terror it caused: 'This was not normal laughter, no matter how joyous it may have sounded superficially. There was a malign, sickening quality to it that ... [was] particularly disturbing.'[7] So obviously inconsistent were the poltergeist's actions that some commentators have suggested there might have been more than one entity involved here, and you can certainly see why.

* * * * *

Jung, in a piece entitled *On the Psychology of the Trickster-Figure*, had this to say about the similarities between the fractured personalities of both poltergeists and Tricksters:

> Since [in the Jungian view] all mythical figures correspond to inner psychic experiences and originally sprang from them, it is not surprising to find certain phenomena in the field of parapsychology which remind us of the Trickster. These are the phenomena connected with poltergeists ... The malicious tricks played by the poltergeist are as well-known as the low level of his intelligence and the fatuity of his 'communications'.[8]

I think the phrase 'low level of his intelligence' is misplaced. It is not that the poltergeist is dim-witted, it is more that his intelligence is somehow incomplete, as with Loki's inseparably intelligent-and-stupid invention of the fishnet in which he was later caught. There is an idea in certain branches of anthropology that the mindset of primitive man later personified in the figure of Trickster was not one in which any conscious thinking could be done but, as Jung puts it, one in which 'thoughts *appear*. The primitive cannot assert that he thinks; it is rather that "something thinks in him".'[9]

Consciousness, in the sense of self-awareness of oneself as a completely autonomous mental unit, with the capacity to direct one's thoughts and thus develop a direct appreciation of one's own personality, cannot have developed overnight. Instead, in the opinion of some, notably the maverick American psychologist Julian Jaynes, it may have seemed to ancient man that certain disembodied ideas were being projected, somehow, inside of his own head. This leads to the possible idea of two separate incomplete consciousnesses once having subjectively existed to ancient man; that of the man himself, and that of a god or spirit that was perceived as interacting with him from without (even if there was nothing there, in reality). Neither consciousness can have been fully complete, at least not initially – otherwise the individual man would either have been a fully aware and self-conscious individual, or subject to a form of total mental 'possession' by an ostensibly external entity. Dismissing both propositions as being unlikely, we are left with a pair of Trickster consciousnesses – that is, incomplete personalities – which must, to primitive man, have seemed as if they had their seat both inside and outside of his own head simultaneously.

* * * * *

According to the anthropologist Mary Douglas, the pastoral Dinka people of the Sudan do not:

> ... distinguish the self as an independent source of action and of reaction ... The self acted upon by emotions they portray by external powers, spiritual beings who cause misfortune of various kinds. So in an effort to do justice to the complex reality of the self's interaction with itself the Dinka universe is peopled with dangerous extensions to the self.[10]

These supposed 'external powers', in different places and in different times, have been conceived of as being creatures as diverse as gods, demons, Tricksters and the spirits of dead ancestors, just like poltergeists have been. Even in more advanced civilisations like that of pre-Classical Greece, the tendency to attribute one's motives and emotions to such 'extensions of the self' appears, to judge from poems like *The Iliad*, to have persisted. According to the historian R. B. Onians:

> In Homer one is struck by the fact that his heroes with all their magnificent vitality and activity feel themselves at every turn not free agents but passive instruments or victims of other powers ... a man felt that he could not help his own emotions. An idea, an emotion, an impulse came to him; he acted and presently rejoiced or lamented. Some god had inspired him or blinded him.[11]

If such ancient people were indeed partially 'possessed', then it was not by any genuine spirits or gods but by aspects of their own personalities over which they felt they had no control, and which they therefore simply did not recognise as being 'them'. The whole modern-day idea of poltergeist possession could be considered a kind of atavism, a harking back to the days when early mankind felt he had no real control over, or responsibility for, his actions. Reading contemporary haunting accounts, it is clear some part of the victim enjoys acting out fantasies that their everyday personalities are not usually sanctioned to articulate. Maybe possession is just the internalised expression of the poltergeist and the poltergeist the externalised expression of possession-states?

* * * * *

One suggestive haunting of 1960–61 centred upon an eleven-year-old girl named Virginia Campbell, who was forced to move to the small Scottish town of Sauchie with her mother while her father remained back home in Ireland to sell the family farm. Staying with relatives, Virginia had to share a bed with a younger girl, called Margaret. Virginia's upbringing had been an isolated one, with only her parents and a much-loved dog called Toby for company. This shy and pliant child was perturbed by her sudden change in circumstances, but did not seek to express her frustration with deliberate paroxysms of misbehaviour. Instead, according to the standard reading of the case, her distress expressed itself via the medium of poltergeistery.

When Virginia began suffering fits at night, writhing around on her compulsorily shared bed and speaking in an uninhibited way, a local doctor, William Logan, was called out. Logan happened to bring his pet dog along, an animal which reminded Virginia of her own lamented Toby. The presence of Logan's pet inadvertently 'triggered off a series of suppressed emotions in the child,' realised the medic. He later found Virginia:

> ... with her eyes shut, talking in a loud (and, for her, unnatural) voice. She kept reiterating that her dog Toby was 'the best in the world' and demanded that her dog ... be brought to her immediately. During this episode she threw herself around the bed and disarranged the bedclothes considerably. She appeared to be able to hear questions put to her and some of her replies indicated that any inhibitory control normally exercised by her higher centres appeared to be absent, almost as if she had been hypnotised and thoughts normally repressed were spilling out.[12]

Another, more external expression of these same feelings was recorded by a different visitor, one Reverend Lund. Witnessing the alarm caused by the spook, Lund suggested Margaret should get into bed with Virginia and the pair calm down and go to sleep. As soon as he said this, however, 'violent knocking broke out from the bed-head'. Furthermore, 'When Margaret got into bed with Virginia the knocking became very impressive indeed, as if ferociously resentful of Margaret's proximity.' Lund therefore proposed Margaret should sleep in a different bed, and all knocking ceased.[13]

It does not take Sigmund Freud (nor even Nandor Fodor) to interpret this. Think how shy, submissive little Virginia must have felt about being compelled to share a bed with a virtual stranger. Could she openly rebel against the situation, though? She was not the type and, even if she had been, her parents would hardly have moved them all back to Ireland just because she missed her old dog. Virginia had no viable outlet for her emotions, but they still needed to find expression somehow – and so unconscious tantrums of both a hysterical and a poltergeistic nature occurred. D. Scott Rogo summed up this variant of the RSPK theory thus:

> I'm sure that all parents have seen how their child will run to his room when scolded and slam the door; rip up pictures of adults out of magazines; or write all over the walls ... He is displacing and acting out his frustrations, since he cannot directly strike back at his parents ... who have punished him. But when too much anxiety-provoking feelings and emotion are repressed into the subconscious, something is bound to give ... At its simplest level, this is what causes the poltergeist. The poltergeist throws things, pounds

on walls, breaks things, and annoys persons in the household. These are all things that the child or immature person does when frustrated.[14]

* * * * *

But what might happen if, rather than a focus-figure's pent-up RSPK energies being endlessly repressed, they were instead openly engaged with in a positive fashion? If a poltergeist's personality is inherently incoherent, containing any number of opposing potentialities present within it, like Loki the malign/benign, intelligent idiot, then might spooks be encouraged to get along with their human playmates rather than flying into wild rages? In the Victorian Spiritualist séance room, less destructive polt-like manifestations were reportedly produced by sitters engaging in Music-Hall-type sing-songs, as melody and jokes helped create a relaxed psychic atmosphere conducive to the subsequent appearance of friendly ghosts. At one séance attended by the great Victorian scientist Sir William Crookes, when *He's A Jolly Good Fellow* was sung, the lyrics were musically augmented by 'a sort of anvil accompaniment on chairs and tables', not angrily hurled objects or blows from invisible hands.[15]

A 1960 paper by the parapsychologist K. J. Batcheldor claimed that, by copying such methods, a group of modern experimenters working under his supervision had managed to make a table rap and tap-dance about in a similarly jovial fashion.[16] Inspired, Iris M. Owen and her own Toronto séance group followed parallel plans when conjuring up their 'fake ghost' Philip:

> When a particularly good joke was told, there would be a series of loud raps, giving a kind of rolling effect, almost as if the table were laughing. During the singing of the group's favourite songs, in which all members joined, loud raps beating in time to the music would be heard.[17]

In 1974, Owen held a Christmas party, during which someone asked 'Is there anybody there?' A loud knock on a table answered in the affirmative. 'Are you Father Christmas?' it was then enquired, in jest. Through raps, the polt replied that it was indeed, and subsequent questions about reindeer, presents and the climate at the North Pole were all answered in perfect character. As Owen observed, 'This episode was a perfect example of the child-like approach to the phenomena that we recommend.'[18]

Another modern séance group, meeting in the Norfolk village of Scole during the 1990s, received instructions from discarnate intelligences advising them to play cassette tapes of joyful music during their meetings as 'mournful music lowered the vibrations while jolly music raised them.'[19] Accordingly, a recording of the TV comedy duo Morecambe and Wise singing their signature tune, *Bring Me Sunshine*, was played, during which the noise of invisible clockwork false teeth chattering in mid-air was heard – one of Eric Morecambe's favourite jokes! The sitters could only conclude the spirits had a sense of humour.[20]

Another agreeably irreverent investigator was Charles Cathcart, an ex-Indiana Congressman who felt that the prevailing craze for Spiritualism then raging across nineteenth-century America was just so much nonsense. Aiming to demonstrate so to his children, he staged a parodic séance in which he commanded the spirit of Balaam's talking ass from the Bible to trot out from within that Great Stable in the Sky. No sooner had Cathcart made his deliberately preposterous bid to make drop down the dead donkey, however, than his makeshift Ouija board actually began to move about of its own accord, followed by the table upon which it sat. Soon, Cathcart's sons were making furniture fly at the merest touch of their fingertips. Finding this funny, Cathcart jokingly asked the ghost to rap three times if it was the Devil. It did so.

Ashamed, Cathcart said he doubted the polt was really Satan. 'Now old fellow,' he said. 'If you think as I do that it's a shame for two old fools like you and I to be talking nonsense before the children, just give the table a parting salute, and run off with it.' Immediately, the table bolted. It was not the Devil.[21] The spirit – now calling itself 'King', and no donkey at all – stuck around and became a beloved playmate of the smallest child, Henry, tossing him about the room 'like a feather', levitating him up as high as the ceiling. 'Go to it, old King! I'm not a bit afraid; take me again; take me again!' Henry is meant to have shouted, with evident delight.[22] I wonder if the phenomena would have taken on this agreeable form if Cathcart had persisted in addressing the spook by the name of Beelzebub, however? Perhaps not.

* * * * *

A further variant on such theories was proposed by the scientist G. E. Browne to Harry Price in relation to the fêted 1920s Romanian poltergeist-girl Eleonore Zugun. Zugun caused a British media sensation when scratches and teeth-marks repeatedly appeared stigmata-like all over her body, supposedly inflicted by an invisible entity calling itself 'Dracu' – the Romanian term for the Devil. Browne proposed this biting was merely an expression of antagonism by Zugun's secondary subconscious personality towards her primary, everyday conscious one. This Dracu, he said:

> ... bites when it is particularly displeased with the primary, waiting until in a moment of distraction it can get command of the body and its functioning ... It bites *when it is bored*. I will engage that when Zugun is kept amused there is no biting, no scratching; for then the secondary is also amused, which it loves most of all. Similarly, when the secondary enjoys the play of the primary, *especially motion of any kind*, ball-playing, running about, motion games – then you may look for objects being thrown about and perhaps even more elaborate telekinesis.[23]

Price said his own experiences with Eleonore 'fully confirm this theory'. The biting usually took place when Zugun was in a state described as 'quiescent'. However, when she was occupied playing, harmless JOTT-like apports and object-movements seemed more likely to occur, just as Browne had predicted.

At one point, she was given a handsome black clockwork cat to mess with, a beast 'with eyes that spat fire, if not brimstone; a fit plaything for Dracu'. When she saw the toy, Zugun's eyes 'sparkled as much as the cat's'. Price looked on with amusement as the child gleefully wound up the mechanical feline and let it speed across the floor in his lab when, all of a sudden, a small L-shaped piece of metal fell onto Zugun's head from thin air. It was a stick-on letter from the notice-board four flights downstairs, which had mysteriously JOTTled itself into the room – but vicious vampiric biting was there none.[24] When Eleonore played nicely, so did her poltergeist.

One school of RSPK-related thought, therefore, holds that what is needed for many a focus-figure is some kind of emotional release valve for their repressed psychic energies. If this is not provided, then, just like Dracu, these very same forces will come back to bite you and your potential brownie will become a boggart. The classic mythological example is again that of the Trickster Loki, punished by his fellow gods for his senseless murder of Baldr the Bright by being bound underground with ropes fashioned from the guts of his own children. A monstrous snake was then positioned so as to drip venom onto his face for all eternity; as a grudging nod to mercy, Loki's wife Sigyn was allowed to hold out a dish to catch the poison. However, it was periodically necessary for Sigyn to empty the bowl when full, which led to the snake's acidic fluid dropping into the eyes of the tethered god. Loki's resultant painful writhes were so powerful they shook the entire planet from within, causing earthquakes.[25] Such large-scale disasters may have been avoided had Loki not been bound up so tightly – and a Freudian interpretation arises so obvious as to be unnecessary to even need articulating here.

While I am suspicious of the idea that RSPK and Freudian-style interpretations can be used to explain away the poltergeist in any overall universal sense, I would nonetheless recognise these theories' symbolic power. Imaginatively, poltergeists – just like Loki's earthquakes – do represent a Tricksterishly powerful shaking up of the natural order of things. That this shaking up is most frequently destructive in its nature may be partly a function of our own prevailing Dominant's determined programme of irrationally over-rationalistic cultural repression of things it simply cannot explain; in short, hard-line materialism's futile aim of disenchanting the irredeemably enchanted.

IX

Loki Unbound

Anyone who isn't confused doesn't really understand the situation.
                                                Edward R. Murrow

In the modern West, with our irredeemably bland and banal, utterly disenchanted, mainstream public culture of political correctness and smug humourless piety, Loki is as tightly bound as ever. This is not to imply that outright anarchy is desirable, but there is surely a need for some kind of occasional psychic outlet for our fellow-citizens' more Tricksterish traits. Such a socially sanctioned pressure valve was once provided in the shape of the medieval Feast of Fools, or *festum stultorum*, an annual event reminiscent in spirit of the ancient Roman Saturnalias, wherein the usually sacrosanct realm of the Catholic Church was subjected to a tirade of profanities from which it was kept thoroughly sheltered throughout the rest of the year. People would dress up in grotesque and obscene costumes, eat meat from the altar where the sacred Mass was usually performed, shout obscenities, hop around, play dice and fart loudly in church, burn old festering shoe-leather or excrement instead of incense and elect a *fatuorum papum* or 'Fools' Pope'. Even the clergy would ride through town in carts filled with dung, eating sausages and hurling turds at the crowds. Jung called such occasions 'a veritable witches' Sabbath', and it is hard to disagree.[1]

Regrettably, such events no longer occur today, beyond such comparatively tame vestigial half-survivals as the Italian and Spanish *carnivales*. Another such withered ceremony is the German tradition of the *polterabend*. This took place on the night before a wedding, when noisy tricks were pulled outside the bride's home by friends. While in Berlin, Harry Price once witnessed such an occasion for himself. Forty youths were gathered smashing bottles and 'perfectly good' china plates outside a flat. Before long, the youngsters would run inside, bang and break some pots and pans and get thoroughly drunk. This whole *charivari* was entirely sanctioned by German law, just so long as they cleared up all the mess left behind in the street afterwards.[2]

Price was informed that this *polterabend* was symbolic of the breaking of the bride's home-ties 'and other things' – presumably her hymen. The night before their wedding was a tense one for many young virgin-brides;

With typical cunning
stupidity, Loki wields
the net in which he will
himself later be caught.

the *polterabend* was intended to make it less so. The word may be a contraction of an older phrase, *poltergeistabend*, or 'evening of the noisy ghost', with the cracking of crockery originally intended as a magical prophylactic to prevent the newly-weds from being bothered by any real plate-smashing evil spirits.[3] I don't think the practice still occurs nowadays, though, thanks to the contemporary development of public-order offences. Another relevant German word is *polterzimmer*, which Price defined as 'a room set aside for children, where they can make a noise, smash their toys, and work off their animal spirits.'[4] This is probably derived from the original term *polterkammer*, meaning a 'junk-room' or, literally, 'room of the noisy din', wherein German household spirits were traditionally said to reside.[5] We now have Ritalin to deal with this kind of rumbustious childhood behaviour instead, and call it an advance.

In German culture, a distinct linguistic relationship was therefore specifically once drawn between the figure of the poltergeist and the idea of releasing tension. There is certainly a metaphorical connection, if not necessarily always an actual definable causal one, present between these two concepts. While it is not literally the case that, just because the *polterabend* and *festum stultorum* are no more, Loki has been unbound to wander the earth once more in the form of the poltergeist, there is nonetheless much that the poltergeist does which can be viewed, symbolically, as being a rising up or rebellion against repression and those figures of authority who attempt to enforce it. Perhaps he is himself a kind of imaginative safety valve, within whose ever-popular stories the possibility of revolt against the prevailing order of things is entertainingly encoded.

Nowadays, the mutiny he leads is directed primarily against our ruling Dominant of scientism. Formerly, however, priests were in effect our scientists – our interpreters of the world, our figures of unimpeachable if-I-say-so-then-it-is-so – and, back when poltergeists were still largely viewed as being demons and invisible devils, representatives of the Catholic Church filled the role of such beings' basic enemy. According to the medieval Welsh chronicler Giraldus Cambrensis, in 1184 a 'foul spirit' in Pembrokeshire channelled the equally obscene spirit of the Feast of Fools quite directly and threw pieces of smelly shit at the clergymen sent out to exorcise it, before ripping their holy vestments to shreds with unseen claws in an uproarious act of explicit Tricksterish insurgence.[6]

The holy rite of exorcism sometimes works, and sometimes doesn't; but both would be interesting results in a way. The esteemed polt-investigator Guy Lyon Playfair tells the tale of a boarding house in São Paulo where, on the night of 7 July 1972, a poltergeist announced its arrival by shouting out the immortal words 'Luisa, there's a hand on your bed!' There wasn't, as it happens, but the arrival of the voice was just as disturbing, as were the actions of a pan of milk which went floating through the air. Following a sleepless night, a Catholic priest was sent for and holy water procured. The priest duly came and blessed the house. It was no good; as he walked down the stairs to leave, a bottle flung itself at him, smashing against the front door. He never returned. As if to rub it in, the holy water then levitated and deliberately spilled itself over one of the building's tenants in her bed, soaking her.[7]

An even more forceful response to an attempted exorcism can be found in the Bromley Garden Centre poltergeist of 1973, as detailed in an obscure privately published booklet, *The Persecution of Mr Tony Elms*. This Mr Elms belonged to a non-conformist religious group, and took it into his head to perform an impromptu exorcism upon his suburban workplace after a spook appeared there – rather unsuccessfully, it has to be said. As Elms went into a haunted supply shed wielding a crucifix, a big bag of Goodwin's Peat shot over and hit the door-frame, while a tap on a container of liquid-fertiliser turned itself on, spilling its contents. Elms was then greeted by a demonic scream as the door slammed shut, shaking the entire shed. As he went around blessing objects, images of crosses, fashioned from cane-rods and lines of fertiliser, spontaneously formed all around him, while a price board developed a matching cruciform shape made from drawing-pins. On the counter a portrait of Christ executed itself 'with perfect detail' from more fertiliser-powder. Elms kept calm and carried on – whereupon his shoe was pulled from his foot, his wallet stolen from his pockets and his pound notes scattered all about, one being shoved down the back of an onlooker's collar.[8] As 'terrific noises' rang out, it seemed the shed might collapse, with the 'substantial' iron door swinging open under impact of invisible blows. The shed now looked 'as if it had been hit by a bomb', with items ripped from shelves and flowerpots 'in constant motion'. The sounds were so loud they were heard by local residents, who gave the place a wide berth at night.[9]

Here we can see the would-be exorcist being expertly humiliated, with the cross-wielding Mr Elms robbed of both his dignity and his authority. Most interesting was the spontaneous production of religious iconography which occurred in direct response to the ritual. As one SPR man noted, these phenomena seemed intended 'As if to mock poor Elms, the would-be exorcist'[10] but in actual fact they were mocking something far larger – the entire notion of the spiritual efficacy of the Christian Church itself. By irreverently reproducing the image of the cross, the poltergeist simultaneously ridicules the idea of the symbol's power; if an apparent 'evil spirit' can wield the chief symbol of Christ so easily, then it openly taunts the uselessness of both the religion and its holy images, like an atheist vampire spitting on a crucifix.

*****

An amusing case of similar ilk concerned the so-called 'Black Monk of Pontefract', a quite remarkable ghost, occasionally glimpsed in the form of a dark figure dressed in a cowl, which infested the North Yorkshire home of the Pritchard family during the late 1960s. One other unwanted visitor here was a sceptical aunt, Maude Peerce, described as being 'of an evangelical disposition'. Like a latter-day Frank Podmore, she declared her opinion that the 'ghost' was simply the Pritchard kids playing tricks. No sooner had she expressed this view than the fridge door swung open and a jug floated out to upturn itself directly over the woman's head, drenching her in fresh, cold milk. Still irrationally maintaining it was all childish tomfoolery, Aunt Maude decided to stay the night. Upon retiring to bed, all in the same room, the Pritchards were bothered by flying lamps, dancing light-bulbs, and a pair of 'hands' floating over the top of the bedroom door. Closer inspection revealed these to be Aunt Maude's fur gloves, apparently being worn by a pair of invisible mitts placed 6 feet apart. When one glove clenched itself into a fist and shook itself threateningly in her direction, Maude burst into a loud rendition of *Onward Christian Soldiers*. Far from dispelling the spook, the gloves responded by conducting her singing in perfect beat with the woman's warbling, as if to mock her. Even Mrs Pritchard admitted that she 'had to smile' at this action.[11]

An unsuccessful exorcism later took place in the Pritchard home. Vic Kelly, a relative who lived nearby, went around saying prayers, scattering holy water in each room. Once he had finished, Vic was asked how long before they would know if it had worked. Instantly, a gigantic crash was heard from upstairs. 'Never mind. It didn't,' said Mrs Pritchard. Then, streams of water began trickling down the walls, an entirely new development.[12] Again here, we have the upturned ceremonial distortion, with Vic's holy water finding its parodic counterpart in the mysterious watery oozings. A similar thing happened to one Andrew Smith, who tried to sue the vendors of his new house in Upper Mayfield, Derbyshire, in 1998 on account of its being haunted. Whenever exorcisms were performed there, the walls would 'stream with water' but, ten minutes later, appear 'bone dry.'[13] Back at Pontefract, other parodies of Christian symbolism ensued – on Easter Sunday inverted crosses were stencilled onto the doors and walls in gold paint. A crucifix then jumped onto the back of the Pritchards' teenage daughter Diane and stuck to it pseudo-magnetically, while pictures of Jesus dropped from walls. When the crucifix finally fell from Diane's back, a cross-shaped red mark lingered between her shoulder blades for three days.[14]

So what great authority did eventually banish the Black Monk, then? A bishop? The Pope? A visit from the Turin Shroud? No – it was some garlic. A friend of Joe Pritchard, the man of the house, had just been on holiday to rural Scotland. He told Joe the crofters he met there had a tradition of hanging cloves of garlic above their doors and windows to keep unclean spirits out. Joe sent his son to the supermarket to buy some fresh cloves. They were dotted around the house and, quickly, the Monk vanished.[15] How? Why? What exactly is the causal mechanism at work here? I cannot for the life of me see one. Instead, I would prefer to think of this exorcism as being an essentially acausal or synchronistic phenomenon. The only alternative would be to presume the Monk was actually Dracula. Most poltergeist infestations fade away at random like this, in much the same way they often spring up. The births and deaths of spooks alike frequently make little sense.

*****

Recall the São Paulo boarding-house spook of 1972 which chased away an exorcising priest by throwing a bottle at him. More successful was a young man from a local *candomblé* (a Brazilian spirit-cult) centre who placed candles and glasses of rum at strategic points around the residence. The man explained the troublesome entity was not in fact a poltergeist, but an *exu morcego*, a kind of pagan spirit who lived in the shadows, probably 'a former criminal who had nothing better to do'. Whatever the accuracy of this diagnosis, the cure proved effective, as the spook obediently departed. The exorcist said he lured the spirit outside by promising him a drink of beer and the sacrifice of a nice, fresh goat. Then he carted him off to the *candomblé* centre, there to treat him with love and kindness, so placing the invisible criminal safely on the path to spiritual reform.[16]

How might this have worked? One guess would be that perhaps the ghost's focus-figure was mentally calmed by something in the *candomblé* ritual which she did not find to be present in the unsuccessful Catholic one; perhaps she was a member of the cult herself, and so, subconsciously, believed the ceremony was bound to succeed, and thus it did. The process of 'exorcism by placebo' is not unknown. Investigating a Norfolk poltergeist of 1967, the SPR's Tony Cornell wanted to help out, but he was a man of science, not a priest. So, he decided to play-act. Collecting some 'mysterious-looking odds and ends' from his car, Cornell went into a bedroom, saying ominously 'Whatever happens while I am in there, no matter what you hear, you must not come in.' Closing the door, he promptly pulled out a cigarette before emerging fifteen minutes later, having taken his jacket off and loosened his tie so it appeared he had been involved in a violent battle of wills. Dramatically, he stated to the impressed householders that the poltergeist would not come back – and, lo and behold, it didn't ... for the next three months, anyway.[17]

Here, it does seem tempting to say that maybe the ghost skedaddled (for a while) simply because Cornell was trusted as being a representative of modern scientific authority by the haunted family, and so in this way he dispelled both their fears and their own self-created spook with it. However the non-process worked, Cornell was not averse to repeating it. He successfully extinguished another polt by wandering around a haunted kitchen casting a mixture of soil and bleach onto the floor as part of some wholly imaginary magical ritual. Entirely invented it may have been, but the nonsensical procedure still worked.[18]

*****

During a 1970s haunting in Guarulhos, Brazil, a local eccentric described as having 'more than a touch of Don Quixote about him' arrived on the scene and decided, with typical dunderheadedness, to exorcise the invisible entity by stabbing it with an invisible (that is to say, totally imaginary) sword. As with Tony Cornell, this quixotic windmill-tilting succeeded. For two whole months afterwards, the spirit stayed away.[19] And yet, at other times, stabbing at spooks with a *real* sword has failed most miserably. During the Woodstock case with which we opened this book, a servant was so rash as to draw his weapon upon the ghost, but 'he had scarce got it out when he perceived another invisible [being] had hold of it too, and at length prevailing struck him … with the pommel, [so] that he fell down for dead.'[20] A German poltergeist of 1713 also showed no fear towards the brandishing of a sword. When the spook-afflicted Dr Gerstmann tried slashing around at the air blindly with a blade, the demon sneakily filled the sword's scabbard entirely up with soil so it could not be replaced following the unsuccessful exorcism. This sword itself was later found broken into little pieces and thrown into a corner, in an act of open contempt.[21]

An even more unsuccessful attempt at human-on-ghost violence occurred during a 1600s Scottish case in which a 'merry' maidservant decided to stand up to a bothersome polt by throwing half a cannon ball at it. This maid took the cannon ball to bed with her one night and, being awoken by the entity's usual disruptive noises, jumped up and threw it down onto the precise spot the sounds were coming from in an attempt to dash the spirit's brains in forever. Before the ball could reach its target, however, it simply JOTTled away into thin air! Even worse, when the maid's employer found out what she had done, he sacked her on the spot for 'talking to it'.[22]

*****

There are clear discrepancies between what works to banish a poltergeist in one case, and what fails miserably in another. Professor William Barrett gives a rather picturesque description of the successful religious dismissal of a spook haunting a remote Irish farmhouse in 1877:

It was a weird scene … The noises were at first so great we could hardly hear what was read [from the Bible] then as the solemn words of prayer were uttered they subsided, and when the Lord's Prayer was joined in by all, a profound stillness fell on the whole cottage. The farmer rose from his knees with tears streaming from his eyes, gratefully grasped our hands, and we left for our long midnight drive back to Enniskillen.[23]

Another religious exorcism proved rather less successful at France's Calvados Castle. Here, a 'Father H. L.' was dispatched by the local bishop and, from the moment he arrived, 'a sudden and absolute calm set in. Nothing happened either by day or by night.' He stayed for a fortnight, performed a religious ceremony, and then left – and, as soon as he did so, the ghost returned, as noisy as ever.[24] If the service of exorcism works for good in one case but only transiently in another, then surely there can't be anything inherent in the holy words spoken that makes the devils go away (or not). This again implies the connection between the two events may be somewhat less than causal. Compare the New Age notion that magically-charged crystals might possess the power to dispel polts. During one haunting, a ghost wholly disproved this theory by simply stealing all the hippie crystals left out to ward it off with. During another haunting, however, a ghost was successfully dispelled by the exact same means.[25] What are we to make of such total, Tricksterish inconsistency?

What else can act occasionally to exorcise a poltergeist for no apparent reason? Sometimes just turning all your electrical appliances off from the standby position overnight can do the trick. The malicious South Shields poltergeist was investigated by intrepid ghost-hunting duo Michael J. Hallowell and Darren W. Ritson, who detailed many tricks the ghost liked to play with electronic devices; batteries continually drained dead inexplicably, electronic toys spoke by themselves and, as we have seen, strange things happened to the household Digibox. This aspect of the case interested one Stephen Swales, a Druid who also lectured in Information Technology at a nearby university.

Combining his two unlikely disciplines, Swales had a pet theory about polts feeding off a combination of human fear and the National Grid in order to manifest themselves. As such, he asked a series of questions: do the family leave their TVs on standby overnight? Have they recently bought any new hi-fis or DVD players? Did they live near to a mobile phone mast? The answer to all these queries proved to be 'yes'. When Hallowell asked the woman of the household about her TVs and videos, she replied: 'Do you know, that's strange. We bought those things at almost exactly the same time as we started having the trouble. In fact, I think it was the same week.'[26]

Swales advised the family to stop leaving their goods on standby, thus to 'starve' the electric vampire of its source of electromagnetic energy. Maybe he got this idea from MAPIT, a well-regarded Manchester-based paranormal investigation society, who recommend that in an ideal world all haunted houses should be vacated for a period of seven to eight months with the electricity turned off at the mains, a procedure they claim proves effective at robbing polts of their regular energetic food-supply.[27] Swales' method apparently worked, with the hungry ghost soon wasting away. As a result, Darren W. Ritson once proposed an experiment as comic as it was ingenious. Following a Westminster-led Green advertising campaign aimed at encouraging citizens to turn their appliances off from standby mode to save electricity, Ritson advised conducting statistical research to see if, together with rates of greenhouse-gas emissions, the rates of poltergeist infestations across the country had also reduced in a parallel fashion! Never before has the phrase 'correlation does not necessarily imply causation' been so ably illustrated.[28]

The idea of the poltergeist as an electrically-fuelled phenomenon is as unsatisfactory, as a broad and all-encompassing theory, as is the idea of attack by evil spirits; polts have been appearing for a lot longer than there have been three-pin plug-sockets within the nation's homes. Phone masts are of even more recent vintage. It is utterly ridiculous to claim that poltergeists can be dispelled simply by pulling one's plugs out overnight – except, of course, in this particular case where, for no apparent reason, the method *did* happen to work! It all seems utterly acausal and synchronistic to me; or, then again, maybe the polt was merely trying somehow to mock the modern religion of scientism?

However things may have stood during previous epistemic reigns, nowadays the scientist is far more the Trickster's natural enemy than the priest is. At least some priests actually deign to still believe in him, after all. We might, as such, expect the poltergeist steadfastly to refuse to disappear in the face of the more materialistic exorcisms of this new representative of the prevailing social Dominant too. That, however, would be far too obvious a trick for such a cunning arch-Trickster to play. Instead, the poltergeist now flees not only in response to the faked scientific authority of a man from the SPR, but also as a result of TV switches being flicked. For good measure, he also chooses to sometimes evaporate in the face of Catholic exorcisms, cloves of garlic, stabs from an imaginary sword and the promise of a nice dose of rum and a tasty tot of goat's blood. This is far more confusing than simply refusing stubbornly to leave in the face of any authority at all.

To a typical representative of the current scientific Dominant, the poltergeist's consistently Tricksterish inconsistency only makes him all the more damned, as it means he cannot very usefully be theorised about. He is, in each specific instance of his appearance, apparently governed by quite different and quite separate laws; and science tends to recognise only universal and consistent ones, like those of gravity and elasticity. The *festum stultorum* is still alive and well after all, then; but it is not only Catholic priests who now find themselves being ruthlessly mocked during the course of the street-party. The disenchanting morning of Enlightenment has not yet fully broken upon the saturnalian midnight of the *polterabend*.

X

The World Turned Upside-Down

Paradox has been defined as 'Truth standing on her head to get attention.'
G. K. Chesterton

Today, we consider the Trickster something from mankind's past, but this is true only in the sense that nobody believes in Robin Goodfellow anymore. According to Jung, the Trickster archetype:

> ... does not crop up only in its mythical form but appears just as naively and authentically in the unsuspecting modern man – whenever, in fact, he feels himself at the mercy of annoying 'accidents' which thwart his will and his actions with apparently malicious intent. He then speaks of 'hoodoos' and 'jinxes' or of the 'mischievousness of the object'. Here the Trickster is represented by counter-tendencies in the unconscious, and in certain cases by a sort of second personality, of a puerile and inferior character, not unlike the personalities who announce themselves at Spiritualistic séances and cause all those ineffably childish phenomena so typical of poltergeists.[1]

Such concepts as fate, luck or chance, or our emotional engagement with the malfunctioning item of lifeless equipment that we beg to 'please work' represent, to Jung, a watered-down contemporary resurfacing of the Trickster archetype, temporarily embodied as inhabiting an inanimate object or concept. Such an undeveloped psyche, being projected outwards by man, seems naturally incomplete. The 'personality' of bad luck residing within one of Jung's 'mischievous objects' has only the one quality to it – that of imparting bad luck. These personifications of the Trickster are, as Jung indicates, very 'inferior' in nature. Their undeveloped quality parallels that of the small child; and the 'ineffably childish' nature of the poltergeist has often been noted. However, there is one positive quality to be valued in such an undeveloped psyche; that of potential creativity.

The physical world is like a sandbox for the poltergeist to play in – chairs and other furniture are placed atop of one another like children's play bricks, and small objects hidden, thrown, moved about and reordered. The world is thus constantly being remade by the poltergeist, just as it is by the Trickster and his chief allies, synchronicity, chance and coincidence.

* * * * *

Most characteristically in terms of creative reordering of things, the Trickster allows for the liminal crossing of borders. The following breaching of the wall between matter and spirit was truly spectacular. It involved Janet Harper, the teenage focus at the centre of the famous Enfield poltergeist manifestations of 1977–78, who claimed once to have been transported bodily through her bedroom wall into the council house next door by the ghost, now the most celebrated polt in post-war British history. The teenager's neighbour, Peggy Nottingham, immediately sought evidence of the miracle. On the floor by her bed, she found a book. It was called (surely significantly) *Fun and Games for Children*. Peggy had seen it only a few moments beforehand, sitting safely on the mantelpiece in Janet's room next door. Apparently, it had come right through the wall, just like Janet herself.[2]

Here, the representative barriers of the physical world – the walls of the haunted house itself – had been breached as easily as if they were thin air. Perhaps they *were* thin air momentarily, who knows? When asked by the SPR's man on the scene, Guy Lyon Playfair, how it felt to 'go through a wall' Janet replied that it 'Just felt like I went through, like through the air. You just go through. You don't feel anything.' Janet also claimed the bedroom had been 'all white, and there were no doors or windows' when she seeped into

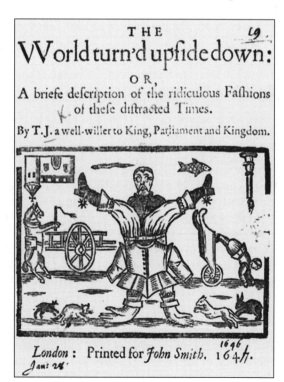

A seventeenth-century woodcut perfectly (if accidentally) illustrates the imaginative function of the poltergeist.

THE 19.
World turn'd upside down:
OR,
A briefe description of the ridiculous Fashions of these distracted Times.

By T.J. a well-willer to King, Parliament and Kingdom.

London : Printed for *John Smith*. 1644/7.

163

it like Hermes through a 4-D keyhole; it sounds like one of the hypercubes or tesseracts once spoken of by Johann Zöllner.[3] Janet's transportation came about as the result of a dare issued by one David Robertson, also of the SPR, who asked the entity to 'make a solid object pass through solid matter'.[4] Like an attention-seeking child eager to show-off, the clever polt accepted this challenge – and passed with flying colours. As an encore, the spirit made a large red cushion appear on the roof outside in response to another of Robertson's requests. 'ALL RIGHT, DAVID BOY; I'LL MAKE IT DISAPPEAR' it snarled, with evident relish.[5]

Like the Trickster, the poltergeist phenomenon represents the creative impulse and the reordering of our usually physics-governed world; at Enfield, even solids could not be trusted to act like solids. In 1894, a house upon the Dorset estate of Lord Portman became haunted. A little girl saw a muddy boot soar through the air and kick itself against the back door, leaving a dirty stain. The gamekeeper, Newman, was having none of this, putting his foot down on the prone item and saying out loud 'I defy anything to move this boot.' Instantly, it shot back up into the air, kicked him in the head and knocked his hat off![6] The noncompliant polt defied the laws of physics even more openly than it did the gamekeeper's commands, as Newman later testified to the SPR:

> I saw, coming from behind the door, a quantity of little shells. They came round the door from a height of about five feet, one at a time at intervals varying from half a minute to a minute. They came very slowly and when they hit me I could hardly feel them. With the shells two thimbles came so slowly that in the ordinary way they would have dropped long before they hit me. Both thimbles struck my hat. Some missed my head and went past and fell down slanting-wise ... Those that struck me just fell straight down.[7]

Compare this description of a TV which levitated during a 1974 haunting in Bridgeport, Connecticut:

> The TV began to float off its resting place and hung in mid-air. The [investigating police] officer went close to the TV to look around it and see what was holding it up. He found nothing. He backed away, and watched as the TV started to swing to the left and right, very precisely, like a pendulum. It started slowly, and gradually sped up for a time. Then it slowed down, paused a moment, turned 45 degrees and set itself back down in the same spot.[8]

Here, as inanimate objects do not simply levitate, but fly unnaturally slowly around corners and through doors as if alive, we see the laws of physics not just being broken, but thoroughly shattered.

* * * * *

An interesting utilisation of the poltergeist as a symbol of the complete reordering of the world in a political sense can be found in a booklet entitled *Anomalous Phenomena of the Interregnum*, a short anthology of pamphlets taken from the time. The curious interlude of the Interregnum – that post-Civil War space between the execution of Charles I in 1649 and the Restoration of his son Charles II to the throne in 1661 – was hardly the most stable period in England's history. As such, the collected pamphlets fulfil a propagandistic function, being a coded comment upon the topsy-turvy, *Kali Yuga* nature of the times. The prodigious contents are deeply unbelievable – it's all monstrous births and ponds full of water turning into ponds full of blood – but the phenomenal world in these tales is clearly supposed to reflect, in an allegorical sense, the then-present disorder in the human one. The manifestation of the supernatural was a traditional symptom of a disordered world. According to the French historian Claude Lecouteux, historically-speaking:

> ... poltergeist phenomena have been interpreted as the sign of a disagreement. By throwing stones, ashes or filth, by turning houses upside-down, our invisible neighbours ... let us know a taboo has been violated, that an unspoken agreement has been broken ... They avenge themselves in their own distinct style, and their deeds and gestures smack of the symbolism of disorder ... Because they transgress all laws of physics, paranormal phenomena ... [have traditionally been understood as being] messages. To restore order we must know how to decipher them and discover what prompted the wrath of our invisible neighbours.[9]

It is within such light that we should interpret the following deeply stupid narrative entitled *Horrid and Strange News from Ireland*, written by a certain Henry Lovel (Gent.) and purporting to be a true account of what had happened to him at Ballimarter Castle in Munster, 'to the amazement of all the Beholders', shortly beforehand.[10] The story begins stereotypically enough, with dogs running for shelter under beds and candles being blown out by mysterious winds, before a large phantom cat appears. Mr Lovel then has his bedclothes dragged away by invisible hands, and before long lithobolic stones are being thrown and tables are dancing of their own accord. The English language didn't have the word 'poltergeist' back then, however, so these are depicted as the actions of a 'Divell'. Hearing a strange noise while in bed, Lovel presumes it is just his companion being 'broken winded', but then looks up only to see 'the shape of a man, and he pissed in my face; said I to my friend here is a rogue pisies [pisser]; he would have said something to me but the Spirit pist in his mouth: you unmannerly Rascall said I, this is the entertainment you give to Gentlemen? This is the roguest trick that ever I did see.' Another spirit dressed in white then appears and begins masturbating under his shirt: 'he made such a tunable noise [with his 'instrument'] that I could not but help laugh at his roguery. How now sirra said I, are you good at that sport?'[11]

This onanistic 'Divell', while evidently fictional, still performs an interesting imaginative role; that of a Trickster. I cannot speak definitively for the motives of 'Mr Lovel' (possibly he wrote simply to entertain) but it is tempting to paint the Irish ghost's actions as some coded comment upon the outbreak of Civil War. The piece was first published in 1643, the year after that terrible conflict began, when the entire kingdom was indeed knocked upside-down and radically reordered.

Alternatively, it could all be a satirical scatological broadside against seventeenth-century English colonialism. According to A. R. G. Owen, the inhabitants of Ballimarter Castle at this time were a garrison of government (that is to say, English-backed) soldiers. They were lampooned in the text, Owen implies, for propagandistic purposes, with ghosts being pressed into service as insurgent irregulars, 'Irish warfare being terrifyingly unconventional'. The poltergeist-Trickster could be a joyous personification of the downtrodden natives rising up against their masters; in 1641, a major Catholic rebellion, known as that of the 'Wild Irish', had just taken place. The tale makes the Protestant English look stupid, implies that even the supernatural realm (and so by implication God) is against them and depicts a gratifyingly inverted world in which the current military masters of Ireland find themselves lying in a new and less exalted place right down at the bottom of the pile while their former Fenian slaves gleefully trample – and piss and wank – all over them.

Owen mentions another haunted Irish castle from the period, that belonging to Lord Castleconnell in Limerick. Here, phantom footsteps were reputedly heard, along with unearthly screams and 'curious musique'. Priests sent out to exorcise the place suffered ghostly beatings and were allegedly teleported away against their will. Considering this is said to have taken place in 1640, not long before the 'Wild Irish' rebellion of 1641, Owen interprets some of the phenomena as genuinely having been experienced in actuality, but that it all 'doubtless started as crude jokes played by the Irish to take a rise out of their Anglo-Irish masters.'[12] Whatever the true original intention of such highly dubious narratives, the literary significance of the poltergeist trope is already, even before this class of paranormal entity has even acquired a specific English name, quite clear; that of Tricksterish agent of imaginative chaos.

Or am I just being naïve? The poltergeist may be *symbolically* creative, but in real, everyday terms, it is highly destructive. It makes a mess and it smashes things up – one thing polts particularly like to smash being taboos. At Enfield, the ghost began speaking through the mouth of its focus-figure, Janet, delighting

Some baby-bayonetting atrocities allegedly committed during the rebellion of the 'Wild Irish' – during which the native Catholics apparently had masturbating poltergeists, as well as God, on their side.

in saying embarrassing things, as when asking the ever-relevant question 'WHY DO GIRLS HAVE PERIODS?'[13] Three of the spook's earliest utterances were 'FUCK OFF', 'BUGGER OFF' and 'SHIT'. Janet's reaction to such puerilities sounded equal parts shocked and impressed: 'Did you hear what he said? He said 'S-H-I-T'?' Evidently, just as with Shirley Jekyll and Donald Hyde at Battersea, the polt in the house could say what the young girl couldn't.[14]

Scatological taboos were later broken more physically. Mrs Harper found Janet coming out of the bathroom one day 'with a strange expression on her face'. Upon entering the bathroom, her mother found out why. There were bits of sloppy schoolgirl turd everywhere: 'When I looked ... part of the excreta was in the sink, and the other part ... in the flannel. I can't say I saw her do it, because the door was shut, but I just got that feeling that she did it and afterwards realised there was something there, and she sort of didn't know what to do about it.'[15]

Mrs Harper's guess is that Janet performed this act of deviant defecation unconsciously. While the poltergeist usually spoke *through* Janet, it generally claimed to be a dead old man named Bill Hobbs, and so the true identity of the dirty-protestor here was unclear. Was Janet *made* to do this by the spook, somehow? Did she do it herself, of her own accord? Or did the polt itself manage the motion somehow? It is deeply unclear; why do children perform mischievous acts anyway? We are faced once again with the mysterious interaction of two separate, incomplete consciousnesses – that of the literal child, Janet, and that of her mischievous infantile twin, the poltergeist. The exchanges of Janet with Bill are like a 'conversation with the self', of the kind *Batman*'s Two-Face enjoys. Maybe it was Janet who really wanted to know why girls had periods, not Bill. She was an adolescent girl herself at the time; possibly she was too embarrassed to ask an adult openly about the scary changes occurring within her liminal, pubescent body. Did Bill's voice provide a safe medium through which she could voice such impolite, taboo queries? Possibly; but why did she then shit in a sink? What conceivable purpose could that have served? Surprisingly, it is possible to view this as also being in some sense a creative act.

It is an anthropological commonplace that dirt is a socially-created construct. Yes, most people would consider mud and faeces to be dirty, but often we declare things to be subjectively filthy and then exclude them, depending upon which social groups we belong to. For instance, orthodox Jews do not eat pork because it is regarded as unclean. By this definition, dirt is simply a form of socially agreed-upon disorder. To introduce dirt into a place is therefore not only to make something messy; it is, yet again, to redefine boundaries and thereby remake the world.

The fable of the Trickster Japanese storm-god Susa-Nö-o, brother of the sun goddess Amaterasu, provides a neatly subversive illustration of the theme. Amaterasu is sitting in her divine Hall of the Sun, waiting to taste the first fruits of the harvest. Her Hall is clean, orderly and sun-lit, representing an eternal and unchanging summer. When the chaotic mischief-maker Susa-Nö-o enters, however, he immediately begins flinging his faeces right throughout the sacred space like a drunken reveller at the *festum stultorum*. Disgusted, the bright-shining personification of the solar lamp jumps from her throne and retreats into a cave where she sulks while darkness engulfs the entire land;

winter has finally arrived and Trickster has killed the summer sun. This *sounds* destructive – but is it?

The story is a Japanese variant of Baldr's murder by Loki with the mistletoe-dart. Its moral is that a world of pleasant but ultimately turgid stability has been altered by the scatologically inclined storm-god so as to incorporate its own rebirth; for if summer does not end, then how would further crops grow without a new spring? How would life ever go on? Susa-Nö-o does not fling *filth* throughout the Sun-Palace, but *fertiliser*. Amaterasu subsequently returns from her cave of repose, and the whole natural cycle of the seasons is thereby instituted for the benefit of all.[16] If even the best soil needs fertiliser, then it may also be that the human imagination in some sense needs poltergeists and other such destabilising, liminal personifications of the supernatural – those items dismissed as being mere waste-products, mere worthless dung, by the prevailing Dominant of scientism – in order to help 'refertilise' certain aspects of our own civilisation.

According to the anthropologist Mary Douglas, the so-called 'renewal-rites' of many primitive cultures have traditionally made ritual use of impurities or pollutions – whether actual physical substances like shit or merely conceptually 'unclean' ideas and classifications – in order to lure Amaterasu back out of her cave and so bring about the continual annual rebirth of the seasons and their own societies. For Douglas:

> ... a garden is not a tapestry; if all the weeds are removed, the soil is impoverished ... The special kind of treatment which some religions accord to anomalies and abominations to make them powerful for good is like turning weeds and lawn-cuttings into compost.[17]

Might the poltergeist not also be just such a 'beneficial weed', whose complete removal from the neatly-trimmed garden of our world would leave its imaginative soil seeming all the poorer?

* * * * *

If this all seems rather a grand parallel to be drawing with a teenage girl shitting in a sink, then I would probably be prepared to concede the point. And yet in a sense the poltergeist really *does* remake and refertilise our world. It acts to dismantle the surface realities of the existence around us, even of physics itself, and thereby allows us instead a glimpse of something strange beyond – something magical, something fascinating, something inherently 'Other'. In this way, the poltergeist is indeed the close twin of Susa-Nö-o, refertilising the quotidian, prosaic façade of a nondescript North London council-house into becoming the magical gateway to another world.

This is not to say that it would be pleasant to experience a poltergeist in your own home. Regenerative chaos, like the fecund ash that spews forth from a volcano or follows after forest-fires, is often necessary and yet generally best perceived from a safe distance. So are Tricksters and poltergeists. Nobody wants to wake up to find any turds floating in their own sink.

XI

Identity Crisis

Why is this lying bastard lying to me?

Louis Heren

Poltergeists, like life-forms in general, often evolve. A typical polt haunting – if there is such a thing – generally begins with bangs, scratches and rappings, and, if it does not simply fade away, can end up with messages being written on walls or the sound of a distinct disembodied voice being heard. Yet at all times the incomplete mental nature of the phenomenon is obvious for all to see.

The Enfield poltergeist's vocalisations began as simple barks from an invisible dog, before a raspy human voice later identified itself through the teenage Janet's mouth as being a former tenant of the haunted home who, the spook (accurately) claimed, 'WENT BLIND, AND ... HAD A HAEMORRHAGE, AND ... FELL ASLEEP AND ... DIED ON A CHAIR IN THE CORNER DOWNSTAIRS'.[1] 'MY NAME IS BILL HOBBS AND I COME FROM DURANT'S PARK [the local cemetery] AND I AM SEVENTY-TWO YEARS OLD AND I HAVE COME HERE TO SEE MY FAMILY BUT THEY ARE NOT HERE NOW' it added. When asked how it felt to die, Bill's angry response was 'I DIDN'T DIE', despite just saying that he lived in the graveyard. A confused old ghost, then; especially as, in the middle of these two utterances, the supposedly vulnerable dead pensioner told one bystander, 'YOU FUCKING OLD BITCH, SHUT UP, I WANT SOME JAZZ MUSIC. NOW GO AND GET ME SOME, ELSE I'LL GO BARMY.' Such overt dissociation was described as sounding 'just as if two people were fighting to use the same telephone, one grabbing the mouthpiece from the other.'[2] The spook also identified itself upon untraceable terms as someone called Joe Watson who had a pet dog named 'Gober the Ghost', thus explaining the initial barking. The polt said it took sixty-eight dogs around with it everywhere it went, 'TO PROTECT ME FROM PRAYERS', although this rather undermined its other claim that these same hounds were gifts 'FROM THE HOLY SPIRIT'. It also once cut up bits of electrical-tape and stuck them to a door, spelling out the dread words 'I AM FRED'. Another time, it boasted there were 'TEN' of it in the house. Bill was surely more honest when later whining that 'I DON'T KNOW WHO I AM' and '[I] DON'T KNOW WHAT I'M TALKING ABOUT.'[3]

Perhaps the reason Bill didn't know who he was is because, at first, he wasn't anything much at all. When confronted with a poltergeist, the natural human reaction is to anthropomorphise. The logical, culturally-conditioned presumption of the haunted family was that the thing in their house was a disembodied dead person – and so, naturally, 'Bill Hobbs' claimed to have 'COME FROM DURANT'S PARK', this being the closest convenient source of dead souls. However, as far as we know, the throaty manifestation of Bill's shade had little relationship to the personality of the real man when alive. Was Bill really highly interested in why girls have periods or in causing teenagers to shit in sinks while he was still made of flesh, for example? If so, then he must have been a thoroughly odd person and have had his name placed upon some kind of register.

*****

An astonishing watery poltergeist affected a house in Rochdale in the early 1990s.[4] The Swanton Novers-like disturbances in the home of the Gardner family involved wet patches forming on the ceiling in a way which defied the laws of physics; liquid 'would start dripping in one place then shoot from corner to corner', with the edges of these ceiling-puddles being unnaturally well-defined, or 'jagged like broken glass'. Once, 'thousands of tiny droplets suddenly and instantaneously' covered a door, while some water curved intelligently around obstacles. So much fluid dripped from the ceiling that it was essentially raining inside the house, with its occupants needing umbrellas in the kitchen. Incredibly, some of this rain fell *upwards*! Other poltergeistery included a flying hairdryer hitting someone on the head and a small statue JOTTling about. This statue was of Themis, Greek goddess of Eternal Law and Justice, mother of Prometheus and sometimes depicted as a natural opponent of Hermes.[5] Evidently Themis' Eternal Laws of physics were not *that* eternal after all, at least not in 1990s Rochdale, where Hermes slipped through the keyhole from Olympus one day and made it rain upside-down and inside-out.

Later, other things more suggestive of the presence of an actual ghostly human personality occurred; the smell of liquorice-tinged cigarette smoke invaded a bedroom, simultaneously with a loud coughing. The deceased former husband of the house, Geoffrey, had been fond of smoking cigarettes rolled in liquorice-papers, something which had hardly helped his chronic asthma. Voices then emanated from within an old clock radio, although it had no batteries. These were throaty, unclear and surrounded by static, like the kind of thing you hear over taxi radios – and, during life, Geoffrey had been a taxi driver. The obvious conclusion to draw was that Geoffrey had returned from the dead. But why? By all accounts he was not the nicest of men, but nor was he the type of person who enjoyed causing random flash-flooding incidents and throwing hairdryers. Is it not likely that, when confronted with poltergeist phenomena, the Gardners, knowing Geoffrey had died of a heart-attack in the haunted house, automatically would have considered him as being the most likely culprit? This thought having occurred, the spook may then simply have adopted his 'personality' – or a superficial impersonation of it – as a sort of convenient term of reference.

In the opinion of Nandor Fodor, 'it is not the spirits of the dead that mould the thoughts of the living, but the thoughts of the living that shape the ideational content of "supernatural" manifestations.'[6] A visitor to the family home during the Pontefract haunting once opined that a good way of telling whether the Black Monk really was a poltergeist would be if it ripped up any photographs. Polts were very fond of doing this, he affirmed. As the visitor left, a crash came from the living-room; a wedding portrait had been thrown to the floor and slashed from end to end.[7] The poltergeist was patently eager to confirm that, yes, it *really was* a poltergeist – and yet, in all my reading, I have seen no particular evidence that spooks have any special fondness for shredding photos. It is not unknown, but is hardly *the* main poltergeist signature-mark. Once again, a ghost had Tricksterishly agreed to act in the manner its observers had expected of it.

*****

It would be useful here to examine poltergeist narratives from other cultures, where departed human souls are not always given the automatic credit for causing such occurrences in the popular mind. A 1921 outbreak of lithobolia in the Indian city of Madras was blamed by one of its witnesses, a female mystic known only as 'The Mother', upon 'three little entities of the vital'. These lithobolic imps she described as being 'small entities which have no strength and just enough consciousness confined to one action.' The Mother determined they had been conjured up by a local cook-cum-sorcerer named Vatel, to annoy his enemies. Using her psychic powers, the woman actually saw, and then dispelled, these three 'entities of the vital', so she said:

> They were frightened, they were terribly frightened! I said: 'But why do you fling stones like that? What does it mean, this bad joke?' They replied: 'We are compelled, we are compelled ... It is not our fault. We have been ordered to do it ... Don't you want to keep us? We shall do all that you ask' ... 'But what can you do?' 'We know how to throw stones' ... 'That doesn't interest me at all ... could you perchance bring me flowers? Can you bring me some roses?' Then they looked at each other in great dismay and answered: 'No. We are not made for that. We don't know how to do it.' I said: 'I don't need you, go away, and take care never to come back for otherwise it will be disastrous!' They ran away and never came back ... it is enough to put purely one drop of the true pure light ... the supreme light of construction ... upon them [and then] they dissolve as though there had been nothing at all there ... it is so alien to their nature that they disappear.

Following these entities' exorcism, their conjuror, Vatel, was supposedly admitted to hospital, the force of his spells having been turned back upon him.[8] No Westerner would ever 'see' a poltergeist as being down to creatures like these, however. 'Entities of the vital' are just not part of our culture.

Such incidents have been aptly described as 'personalised experiences occurring within a shared cultural framework.'[9] Some researchers, speaking of small children's encounters with apparitions of the Virgin Mary, have asked why it should be that the Mary met at Lourdes in 1858 or Fatima in 1917 was apparently not the same Virgin Mary met on a hill outside Mexico City in 1531. When the Queen of Heaven appeared there, it was in the shape of a 'wonderfully beautiful' glowing fourteen-year-old Mexican girl with brown skin, black hair and brown eyes – but no European child has ever witnessed Mary going Mexican.[10] The writer Hilary Evans explained this curiosity by guessing such apparitions 'manifest in stereotypes, but stereotypes with variations: as standard models, but customised' for the individuals who encounter them.[11]

Likewise, phenomena like lithobolia and JOTTling might represent manifestations only of the basic, impersonal typological 'stereotype' of the poltergeist. The subsequent more baroque details – such as the scent of flavoured tobacco-smoke, or the visionary appearance of 'entities of the vital' – would then correspond to the individually customised aspects of different children's visions of the Virgin Mary. It is possible such things are entirely subjective; in the Rochdale and Madras cases, maybe the genuine poltergeist-stereotype was encountered in reality and then subconsciously manufactured visual and olfactory hallucinations stepped in to help the witnesses comprehend the phenomena in terms culturally acceptable to them. Or maybe, in the words of the SPR's Alan Gauld and Tony Cornell, the interaction of polts with their victims could lead to them 'building up a whole framework of beliefs about the phenomena. The phenomena in turn accommodate themselves to the beliefs, and the beliefs may be supported by shared visions and hallucinations.'[12] The whole process could be a two-way street, a kind of paranormal *folie à deux*.

Many modern people do not accept the existence of paranormal phenomena at all, however. What happens when a poltergeist attacks them? One such case concerned three families from the Washington State town of Fircrest, who in 2007 thought the sudden appearance of uncatchable 'people' screaming and banging on the walls of their houses indicated they were being pursued not by noisy ghosts, but by super-elusive stalkers with unfathomable motives. Perhaps as a result of this perception, this is exactly what the spooks then became. Texts appeared on victims' phones, to the effect that 'They tell us that they see us and know everything we're doing', including what food they were eating and what colour shirts they had on. Voice-messages with sandpaper-throated tones began threatening shootings at local schools. 'I'm warning you ... Don't send [your children] to school. If you do, say goodbye,' one said. Police proved these messages were, quite impossibly, coming from the families' own phones, even when switched off, with huge near-$1,000 bills being run up for no reason. One girl's ringtone spontaneously changed itself to an Enfield-like rough voice saying 'Answer your phone'. The cops could do nothing. One family was sent voice-mail recordings of interviews they had just had with an investigating detective, as if the polt was mocking the officer's total lack of powers of arrest over it.[13]

* * * * *

Poltergeists often act to confirm prevailing social and intellectual mores. This can be seen in a 1526 case from Lyons, wherein an eighteen-year-old nun, Anthoinette de Grolée, was apparently haunted by the spirit of another nun named Alis de Telieux, who had died two years earlier. One night, Anthoinette felt something lift her veil and kiss her. A few days later, odd tapping sounds came from beneath her feet. Having formerly been a close friend of Alis, Anthoinette presumed the ghost was her. The dead nun had been ejected from the nunnery some years beforehand for bad behaviour and then buried outside the convent against her dying wishes, so Anthoinette guessed Alis would have good reason to return, to redress the wrong of her burial.

Accordingly, Alis' bones were disinterred but as they were being carried back into the nunnery in a wooden box, violent rapping sounds rang out across the building. The Bishop of Lyons was summoned, and communications began via a variant of the time-honoured 'one knock for yes, two knocks for no' method. The answers to forty-one questions asked of the poltergeist were recorded; half referred to the once controversial Catholic doctrine of purgatory, then coming under assault from the new Protestantism springing up across Europe. Unsurprisingly, given who was questioning her, the dead nun's answers all backed up the official viewpoint of the Church of Rome. Alis confirmed that purgatory was real and that she was currently suffering there, reassuring her eager audience that fasting, alms, prayer and pilgrimage would all speed her path to Heaven. Happily, she also verified that the Vatican's Holy Days had been correctly appointed, as her punishments were temporarily suspended on Good Friday and All-Souls' Day, as well as during the various Feasts of the Virgin Mary. When Alis later disappeared, she said it was due to her final release from purgatory into paradise – an event once more attended by incredible bangs and raps.[14]

It is highly unlikely similar messages would be delivered by a polt today; to most modern people, such arcane doctrinal issues would be irrelevant. At the time, however, Alis the ghost-nun fulfilled a handy Counter-Reformational role on behalf of the Catholic Church. The history of such an ideologically-sensitive case could easily have been doctored; according to its original chronicler, he only bothered to record it to serve as good propagandistic testimony, not for its own inherent value as a ghost story. But, if Alis really was a genuine poltergeist, then it is easy to see how she took on the desired role assigned to her by her Catholic observers. By appearing as a soul from purgatory, 'Alis' not only provided those around her with further grounds for belief in their own under-siege doctrines during troubled times, but also, thereby, *with simultaneous grounds for belief in herself!* There is a definite cyclical relationship at work here, between believers and that which apparently wishes to be believed in.

* * * * *

Talking of his experiences with the common mediumistic practice of automatic writing, C. G. Jung recalled how initially all that tends to come through in such sessions are squiggles and 'senseless jumbles of letters'.

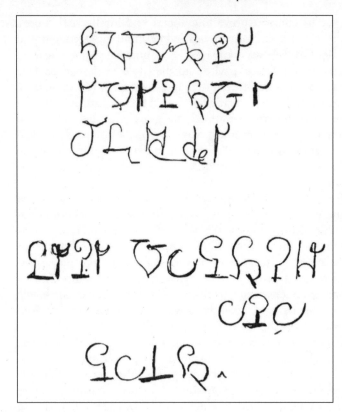

Examples of automatic writing, supposedly done in a 'Martian' language; do such practices allow for the creation of false secondary personalities, and are such phenomena also encountered during many poltergeist hauntings?

Eventually, through practice a few coherent words and sentence-fragments may then appear, allegedly from 'Beyond'. Jung felt that these actually came from within the medium's unconscious mind – although the mediums generally presumed, quite naturally, that they originated from some disembodied spirit. The question 'who is speaking?' then tends to be asked, and this enquiry thereafter 'acts as a suggestion for synthesising the [medium's] unconscious personality … Some name or other presents itself, usually one charged with emotion, [like that of a dead relative] and the automatic splitting of the personality is accomplished.'[15]

In other words, you can inadvertently turn random motor-actions produced by the unconscious mind into the fake simulacrum of a coherent 'ghostly' personality, apparently existing apart and separate from the medium's waking intellect, simply by treating them as if that is what they really are. Jung cited the transcripts of one automatic writer, who sat down with a pad and pencil to ask the unseen world some questions one day. His hand soon provided him with intelligent answers, although he himself was not conscious of his own brain formulating them. Here is one early set:

Who are you? – *Clelia*.
Are you a woman? – *Yes*.
Have you lived on earth? – *No*.
Will you come to life? – *Yes*.
When? – *In six years*.

These sound like the words of an as-yet unborn spirit milling around up there in the *anima mundi* waiting for her own personal moment of fleshly incarnation, perhaps. However, during a subsequent session the following answers were then received:

> Am I the one who asks the questions? – *Yes*.
> Is Clelia there? – *No*.
> Who is here then? – *Nobody*.
> Does Clelia exist at all? – *No*.
> Then with whom was I speaking yesterday? – *Nobody*.[16]

Jung explains, 'One can see from these extracts how the unconscious personality builds itself up: it owes its existence simply to suggestive questions which strike an answering chord in the medium's own disposition.'[17] If we were to apply this same idea to the Enfield case, then Janet must have had a certain element of the Tricksterish Bill Hobbs lying deep within her somewhere originally, in order for him later to be able to manifest himself through her own mouth – as, perhaps, all young girls do. It must be said, though, that Bill himself would dispute this whole idea most vociferously. When it was once put to him that he was, in fact, nothing more than an externalised RSPK aspect of Janet's brain, Bill's response was admirably clear. 'FUCK OFF,' the ghost growled. 'COURSE I'M NOT!'[18]

* * * * *

Most poltergeist voices build themselves up from small beginnings, like a song slowly emerging from an ill-tuned radio-set, as in the following description:

> The *bloonk* [noise] came again ... but it kept going this time. And ... it slowly transformed into a human tone. It sounded like it was backwards and stretched out, like that backwards masking on records in the '60s and '70s ... It was trying to form words, but it never did. The [abortive] voice sounded ... kind of ... aquatic.[19]

The joyously silly tale of Gef the Talking Mongoose is very important here. Gef first appeared on 14 September 1931, when members of the Irving family heard an odd growling within the attic of their isolated farmhouse on the Isle of Man. Concluding an animal must have got in, they listened closely to figure out what kind of creature it could be. As they did so, the Irvings started to think they were actually listening to a voice and not an animal at all – and, this thought having occurred to them, it then came true. Gradually, words became mixed up in the snarling, just like the Enfield polt's own voice began as a dog's bark. Gradually, it was realised the words from the attic were exactly the same as those being uttered by the family down below; the voice was directly copying the Irvings' own chatter, like an infant learning to talk! Eventually, the family's two initial assumptions about the spook – firstly that it was an animal, and secondly that it was a mumbling human intruder – coalesced into the composite form of a talking mongoose called Gef, who, he informed his shocked listeners, had been born in Delhi, India, on Monday 7 June 1852 (there is actually an old Indian tradition it is possible for humans to reincarnate in the shape of a mongoose).[20] Before long, Gef was entertaining his adopted family with songs, poetry-recitals and practical jokes. One day, he solemnly announced he was dying from poison only to later burst out laughing, telling the distraught Irvings that he had, in fact, been joking all along. As their reaction to this fake news implies, the family actually became friends with the mongoose in their attic; they found his Tricksterish presence entertaining.[21] Gef doesn't really conform to most of the usual polt-stereotypes; he stayed around for years and seems to have generally been quite pleasant, even highly likeable. He also allegedly developed some kind of palpable, material form. On one occasion the wife of the household, Margaret Irving, supposedly stroked his fur like a tame pet. This made Gef jump, however, and he accidentally cut Margaret's finger with his sharp teeth. The fuzzy Manx Trickster urged her to go and dress the wound.[22]

Surely Gef's absurd adopted mask was an obvious case of ghostly identity fraud, but what I find most interesting are the abortive and highly Trickster-like attempts he made to prove the reality of his presence. For example, there were the hairs supposedly belonging to the creature he left out upon the mantelpiece for the Irvings to take away as evidence – and which, upon testing, proved to have come from the family dog. The one identity Gef straddled most expertly of all was that between real and inexplicable occurrence and blatant and laughable fakery upon the Irving family's behalf. Consider the prints Gef allegedly left behind him one day. Casts were sent to the Natural History Museum in London for analysis, and the results were extremely confusing. There were three sets, each produced by a different animal. One set belonged to a dog. The second were from a North American raccoon (sadly not a North American coyote), a creature not frequently observed on the Isle of Man. The third set of prints was of indeterminate origin, but, said the Museum, definitely did not come from a mongoose.[23] Here, the plot merely thickens – what *was* Gef, then? Just a pathetic human hoax? Or was he somehow more than one 'animal' at once, like many a classical Trickster? And where did that immigrant raccoon come from? The conundrum just gets deeper and deeper. These tracks lead us on not right into the lair of mystery beast, as you might initially expect, but instead much farther away from it than we ever were.

Something comparable occurred during a 1590s haunting in the village of North Aston, where an Edward Lee and a maid, Joan Measey, became perhaps the first people ever to try and observe poltergeist phenomena under controlled conditions. Disturbed by the bolsters being removed from a bed, Lee drew a chalk-circle around them to test if they would be moved once more. Then he and Measey left the room – but, returning, found the circle wiped away. Repeating the trial, upon re-entering the room Lee and Measey found their new chalk-marks perfectly intact. However, a paw-print, apparently from a bear-cub, was found imprinted on a floorboard to one side of the chalking and, on the other side, was the scratch of a hawk's talons.[24] Edward Lee was looking for evidence of object-movements; and, instead, he got animal-prints, of several different shapes, just like Gef left behind him. It was almost as if the poltergeist was deliberately trying to confuse him ...

There is a direct mythological parallel for all this: that of Hermes and his theft of Apollo's sacred cattle. The *Homeric Hymn* informs us that Hermes magically reversed these animals' hooves, tied myrtle and tamarisk-leaves to the soles of his sandals, and then walked backwards across a sandy beach with the stolen livestock, leaving behind deliberately perplexing footprints to obscure the path of his escape.[25] Hermes did well to leave some evidence of his passage behind for Apollo to find rather than none at all, with such confusingly contrived tracks, so akin to those of Gef, disguising far more than they revealed. According to Lewis Hyde, with such misleading prints Hermes:

> ... confuses polarity. It is as if, lost in the woods, you took out a compass and the needle spun aimlessly instead of pointing north. You could not then get oriented or find a path; you could not proceed. In this way, confounded polarity makes the world unpassable and is a kind of *aporia* [unsolvable paradox] ... When Apollo comes upon the tracks that Hermes and the cattle leave, he is stopped in his own tracks, unable to move.[26]

With that memorable phrase, 'confounded polarity', Hyde seems inadvertently to have hit upon an excellent description of the poltergeist – if something's polarity is confounded, then it is neither one thing nor the other, not North, South, East nor West. The poltergeist is far more like the centre of the compass, where all points converge, than it is any individual direction in and of itself; not unlike Gef's paw-prints, which were neither just mongoose, dog, nor raccoon, but, rather, an inextricable tamarisk tangle of disparate and apparently incompatible elements. So are poltergeists. They are not 'just' dead people, RSPK, fairies, nor demons, elementals or entities of the vital. From examining the contradictory evidential tracks they leave behind them, nobody knows precisely what they are ... other than massive Tricksters.

In legend, Apollo is credited with the ability to infallibly read signs and portents – to see immediately what it means when a bird drops dead from the sky, using this knowledge to predict future events. Apollo, it has been said, is a skilled reader or *de*coder, but Hermes is an equally skilled writer or *en*coder, whose messages are often impossible even for his knowledgeable brother to properly decipher.[27] The Apollonic mindset of our current Dominant of scientism, just like its presiding solar god, also claims to be able to 'read' everything in Creation, in the sense of being able to explain and account for it all. But can it really? Not when it comes to the poltergeist. If we look for definite answers in relation to polts then, just like Apollo when faced with Hermes' incomprehensible tracks, we are left with no option but to pause befuddled for a moment and to admit that, if we're being honest with ourselves, we really don't know in which direction to turn next in search of an answer.

XII

Motives Unknown

The hand is the cutting edge of the mind.

Jacob Bronowski

The myth cycles relating to the Winnebago Indian Trickster Wakdjunkaga begin with a being essentially undifferentiated from Nature, with no coherent conception of his own self – who believes, for instance, that his penis and his anus are independent entities parasitic upon his body, their various natural actions being caused not by him, but by outside agencies – and end with Trickster coming around to a sense of basic self-awareness of himself as a more complete psychic entity. Early on in his career, Wakdjunkaga kills a buffalo with his right arm, something his left arm immediately protests about, grabbing the right and attempting to stop it from skinning the beast. The right arm fights back, they quarrel, and the left arm is left bleeding profusely from wounds inflicted upon it by the knife-wielding right limb, leaving Trickster suddenly in great pain and wailing out loud, 'Oh, oh! Why did I do this? Why have I done this? I have made myself suffer!'[1]

During a later entry in the story cycle, Wakdjunkaga places his anus on guard over some food that is then stolen by foxes. To punish his errant organ, he shoves a burning stick up the mouth of this supposedly separate posterior, leading Wakdjunkaga to exclaim 'Ouch! Ouch! This is too much! I have made my skin smart. Is it not for such things that they call me Trickster?' After this, Trickster finds solace in eating some tasty burning blobs of fat he finds trailing across the floor – only to realise they are his own intestines, which, due to the trauma of his arsehole being burnt, have plopped right out of his body. Again, Wakdjunkaga laments: 'My, my! Correctly, indeed, am I named Foolish One, Trickster! By their calling me thus, they have at last actually turned me into a Foolish One, a Trickster!'[2]

Here, finally, Wakdjunkaga has begun to know himself; for the first time, he is able to refer to himself by name, and even to accept the accuracy of this moniker and thus evaluate his own actions. He has learned to accept that his bowels are a part of him, and so starts to emerge from the fog of an undifferentiated consciousness and into some kind of semi-coherent personality – that of 'the Foolish One'. This act of naming is rendered especially significant by the fact that, in traditional Winnebago society, a new-born child actually had no legal existence until he had been given a name.[3] Until he was named, Trickster too did not really exist – or did not really exist *as* Trickster. Beforehand, he was just a bundle of incoherent physical actions linked together purely by the words of the storyteller. Poltergeists, too, often chart this rough path of mental development. Perhaps naming them 'Bill Hobbs' or 'Gef' somehow helps drag them into more complete being, too?

Recalling Mr Irving's testimony, the haunting of Gef the Talking Mongoose initially began with animal-noises emanating from the loft. Then, however:

> Something happened which made us speechless with marvel and apprehension: the animal was making gurgling sounds like a baby when it begins to talk. It was something like DOMADOMABLUMBLUMBLUM ... I repeated the noises of various animals: *vow-vow* – dog, *meow* – cat. Back came the same sound and the human word [for the relevant animal] ... in a shrill and high-pitched voice, issuing from a very small throat ... in a few weeks' time 'he' spoke fluently, using all our words and lots of others. There was incessant questioning and a prodigious thirst for knowledge. 'One more question, Jim,' the voice used to plead, 'then I will let you get to sleep!' ... 'For years,' he said, 'I understood all that people said, but I could not speak until you taught me.'[4]

The comparison with a babbling baby is very apt. When we are really, really young, I'm not sure we have personalities as such. Do you know any snobbish babies, for instance, or any hopelessly romantic ones? When very small, we have not yet begun to construct what we might call the 'narrative of ourselves', that body of personal qualities, likes and dislikes, interests and habits that, when we are older, makes us *us*. As babies we are undifferentiated from Nature itself, mere collections of unconscious biological processes, just like Wakdjunkaga was once imagined as being.

One way in which we later begin to anchor our identity in the world is by learning language. Most significantly, we learn our own names; that label which means 'I'. We also start to learn the names for all of the separate objects, people, animals and things that surround us, and thereby grow to sense that we are different from them. I am *me*, and not *that*, is one of the small child's most useful lessons. The baby's learning of language thus allows him to acquire more complex knowledge about the world. Regard this statement about Gef made by Nandor Fodor: 'It appears that he picks up his words by listening to people. On returning home, he asks Irving what they mean. 'Jim, what is 'countenance?' What is 'loco'? What is a 'nun'?"[5]

According to Jung (who noted how often shape-shifting poltergeists pop up in the guise of animals)[6] the Trickster-figure of old represented a kind of 'divine–animal' consciousness who initially fails to fully appreciate the sense of Cartesian Dualism inherent between the concepts of the self and the world. The Trickster's beast-like mind only later progresses towards the more differentiated mental level of a human being by virtue of his possessing 'considerable eagerness to learn', just like that possessed by Gef.[7] If Gef was really a comical externalised psychic creation of Mr Irving, as has been suggested by the likes of Nandor Fodor, then this would indeed represent

Cashen's Gap, the isolated Manx farmhouse where both Mr Irving – and Gef the Talking Mongoose – made their home. Given such bleak and remote surroundings, is it any wonder Irving's subconscious powers of creativity felt the need to liven things up about the place via paranormal means?

a blurring of the consciousness between animal and man of the kind Jung showed was highly typical of the Trickster; if part of Gef's mind lived within Irving's head, then it follows part of Irving's mind must have lived within Gef's head, too. Jung cites a legend about Wakdjunkaga – he gets his head jammed within the skull of an elk, followed by him lodging a hawk's head up his own anus. The two peculiarly inverted insertions represent the insertion of animal consciousness within a human body, Jung suggests, and *vice versa*.[8] So does the legend of Gef.

* * * * *

I'm sure we all know small children who are full of Gef's brand of endless questioning. We must have been full of it ourselves at some point too. When we start making such enquiries, it is clear we wish finally to know about things other than our own immediate physical needs and desires. As a child establishes a new interest in trains or dinosaurs, rather than just food and drink, it is a sign of them drawing away from being mere eating, sleeping and defecating machines and becoming instead something more truly conscious. By the time we have reached this question-asking stage (the 'heuristic stage', as it is called by linguists) we are well on our way towards becoming differentiated from an unformed new-born infant mind that has just been 'dropped down' into this world, so to speak, apparently from nowhere.

Gef, just like a little human baby, followed this precise path. After mastering spoken language, most people then progress towards the decoding of written language, that classic skill of Apollo. The written word provides a permanent record of people's thoughts, allows for the transference of knowledge from generation to generation, and provides a separate 'space' for man to think within. It aids the process of man becoming a consciously cogitating being, rather than merely a slave to his own animal appetites, as a tiny baby (or a fully-grown Trickster) is. It allows him to get as far away from being an anus-denying, Wakdjunkaga-like 'undifferentiated being' as possible. And Gef also learned to read. How? In the usual fashion: he *went to school*! In Fodor's incredible account:

> There is a peephole in the kitchen ceiling which gives Gef a direct view to Irving's newspaper when he is reading it … Irving tested him by putting his finger on certain words [in the paper]. Gef read them correctly or, if Irving covered a picture, answered with an association … Where did Gef learn reading? By his own statement, he had been visiting a school nearby, crouching on the window sill and also in a tree. Helped by an abnormal eyesight and a remarkably keen hearing, he was a free and unsuspected pupil and picked up an education extraordinarily fast.[9]

Sadly, Gef didn't then learn to write, but quite a few poltergeists have. The noted English psychic-healer Matthew Manning gave a detailed account of just such a pencil-wielding polt which haunted his own Cambridge adolescence. Before the ghost, calling itself Robert Webbe, began signing its name and daubing messages like 'Matthew Beware' on the walls, it produced childish scrawl and vague circles of the kind children make when first learning to pick up a crayon to develop their motor skills.[10] Linguists (after Dr Kathy Barclay) term this the 'scribbling' stage. Then, the spook made recognisable signs on the walls – for instance, something rather like the astrological symbol for Leo – before moving on to fully-fledged words and sentence fragments. This corresponds well with Barclay's second and third stages of children's writing development, the 'mock handwriting' and 'mock letters' stages, wherein letter-like symbols and shapes are produced by the infant before they start marking out full, accurate letters of the alphabet as a prelude to spelling out full actual words.

It would appear that the poltergeist, just like mankind himself as depicted allegorically in ancient Trickster-tales, emerges into some kind of vaguely coherent personality from within an original state of complete undifferentiation. By that term 'undifferentiation', what I mean is the initial lack of coherent, world-separating identity that is present both in a baby, just after its birth, and in the poltergeist, during the early period after its first appearance. The poltergeist, whenever it develops basic sentience, seems to tell in dramatically shortened form the story of mankind himself. Through the difficult process of differentiation into actuality from out of a state only of potential being, both men and spooks come to know themselves. If the

Trickster is the mythological representation of this historical and biological process, then the poltergeist could frequently be viewed (either literally or figuratively) as being an actual recreation of it out in the world at large.

*****

It has sometimes been suggested that consciousness, in a form separate from its biological vessels, is inherent within the universe around us, a variant of the old *anima mundi* idea. The pioneering Victorian-era psychologist and American SPR member William James postulated that we inhabited a universe full of diffused 'soul-stuff'. This was once described as being:

> ... like a vast reservoir of consciousness ever trying to force itself through matter, the walls of the reservoir. Through the microscopic body of an amoeba there has percolated a very minute drop from the reservoir. As evolution advances, the walls of the reservoir become more and more porous, and little by little the drop increases to a tiny rivulet. Through the higher animals, the tiny rivulet flows as a brook. Through man ... the brook flows as a deep and broad river.[11]

The SPR's Sir William Barrett considered this same matter in specific relation to the poltergeist, back in 1911. Asking why a focus-figure should apparently be so often necessary for a spook to manifest, he recalled certain features attending the formation of crystals:

> In inorganic Nature we find in the behaviour of saturated solutions of salts a state of unstable equilibrium such that a particle of solid matter dropped into the quiescent liquid will suddenly create a molecular disturbance which spreads throughout the solution, causing solid crystals to appear and aggregate ... Here we see the effect of a *nucleus* upon a previously quiescent state of things ... We may term a ... [focus-figure] the *nucleus* ... We ourselves and the whole world may be but nucleated cells in a vaster living organism, of which we can form no conception.[12]

The RSPK-promoter A. R. G. Owen's later interpretation of this passage was as follows:

> There is an undifferentiated psychic substratum to things. Occasionally an irregularity in the substratum, constituted by an unusual psychic state in a person, acts as a point of 'condensation'. As a result of this process of condensation, differentiation takes place in the psychic substratum and shows itself as an entity with some psychic life of its own. On this theory the 'poltergeist' is a psychic reality, is not coterminous with the personality of the medium and has a psychic life of its own ... [Alternatively] we might imagine that an unusual personality-state allows the augmentation of the [focus-figure's] normal personality as the result of fusion with it of previously undifferentiated psychic elements available in the 'substratum', if the latter be supposed to exist.[13]

D. Scott Rogo dubbed this the '*Forbidden Planet* Hypothesis', after Hollywood's 1950s sci-fi rewrite of *The Tempest*, in which humans stranded on an alien planet accidentally utilise the ancient technology of a dead ET civilisation to unleash a hideous 'Monster from the Id' (which, curiously, looks not unlike some of the bizarre animals sighted at Skinwalker Ranch) out upon the world from within the confines of their own subconscious minds, or ids, to use a Freudian technical term.[14] In this view, Fodor-friendly entities like Gef the Mongoose are equally 'Monsters from the Id', fusions of our subconscious minds with an external undifferentiated 'mind-field' lurking unseen all around us. Those familiar with that other popular Hollywood movie *Ghostbusters* might wish to rename this same scenario the 'Stay-Puft Marshmallow Man Hypothesis'.

These are fascinating ideas. However, like all over-arching explanations for poltergeistery, the theory has massive flaws. It is far from certain that James' 'soul-stuff' (or *anima mundi*, if you prefer) actually exists. Furthermore, not *all* poltergeist cases have a focus; some appear location-based, not person-centred. Maybe Barrett's proposal could be the best explanation for many poltergeist outbreaks. Perhaps there are others, however, wherein the 'soul-stuff' somehow spontaneously accumulates around *its own* nucleus, not that of a focus-figure, and some kind of temporary, fluid, and non-pre-existent pseudo-personality appears to haunt a person or place – in which case, we may as well say that demons are effectively real. Nobody really knows where the consciousness of either mankind or the poltergeist originates, in truth.

* * * * *

Parapsychologist and psychoanalyst Nandor Fodor, no doubt examining something of supernatural import.

To Trickster and to primitive man, shit happens – rather like his turds, his actions just seem to come to him, delivered unexpectedly free of charge from external sources, another form of *hermaion*. When Wakdjunkaga kills the buffalo, his right hand fights his left; he doesn't really know what he is doing, or why. Modern, differentiated man is not like this. We are usually reasonably aware of both our actions and our motives. Interestingly, though, not all poltergeist-people always are. Tales of focus-figures committing Eusapia Palladino-like acts of fakery are legion; the most interesting cases being those wherein the fakers are not actually *conscious* of their fraud. During the Thornton Heath haunting, the disturbed medium Mrs Forbes produced the following (presumably fraudulent) phenomenon in front of Nandor Fodor, after boasting she was able to perform acts of 'psychic shoplifting' by magically JOTTling items out of stores and into her own hands. In Fodor's account:

> Once, early in the day, I noticed that her right hand was getting restless while the left, next to me, was lying quietly in her lap. I thought that something might happen and watched from the corner of my eye. For a second or two I saw her right hand disappear, then it was back over her right knee and I saw something blue. I took her hand and found on the index finger a cheap ring with a large artificial blue stone ... Mrs Forbes said ... the ring was not known to her.[15]

While this was surely just sleight-of-hand, Mrs Forbes might not have been actually lying about this fake apport as such. Fodor gives many examples of this crazy, liminal lady entering trance-states and performing various strange actions without her explicit knowledge of the fact, like a non-sleeping sleepwalker. In the instance above, it seems the same thing was happening – and aptly, just like the Winnebago Trickster of old, her left hand appeared literally not to know what her right one was doing! Her right hand is described by Fodor as 'getting restless', as if she was unable to control its tricky, stage-conjuror-style actions – Mrs F was, indeed, the daughter of a magician's assistant. To Mrs Forbes, sometimes events like this 'just happened', without her ever knowing that she was the one responsible for performing them. The spirit she was truly channelling here was not really a JOTTling polter-thief, but that of Wakdjunkaga killing the buffalo.

XIII

Poltergeist Art

Where do I get my ideas from? If I knew, I'd go there.

Tom Stoppard

Artists' best ideas, so they tell us, frequently just suddenly 'come to them', unbidden and unexpected. Bad art often has too much of the artist's conscious mind visible there within it. The fable of Wakdjunkaga slaughtering the buffalo with the one arm (the right) and trying to stop himself with the other (the left) echoes this. It has been said of the two halves of the human brain that 'the left is a scientist, the right is an artist'; the left brain seems to deal with logic and language, and the right with things like musical and artistic ability. Imagine there are two people living inside your head. Your conscious mind lives in the left side of the brain. On the right side is a slightly mad stranger, the unconscious, trying to break in. He is spontaneous, irrational and inventive. He may also be somewhat dangerous; if allowed to take up permanent residency within your skull, then you will seem quite insane, like loopy Mrs Forbes. This is not to imply he should be kept locked out of sight in Loki's chains forever, though. It can be beneficial to allow this odd stranger out for visits from time to time, thereby to unleash the imaginative impulse. Consider Wakdjunkaga; his right arm commits a brutal act of violence, but it is necessary, creative violence. Without the right arm's intervention, the other arm would have been left to starve without any meat. Likewise, without the right-brain unconscious' intervention, poets and artists might be left to starve in creative and poetic sterility.

* * * * *

Nandor Fodor viewed Gef the Talking Mongoose in a similar light, seeing Mr Irving, unusually, as being the adult focus-figure responsible for conjuring this particular ghost, not his teenage daughter Voirrey. Gef often pleaded with Irving to the effect of 'Jim, let me go, let me go', to which he would reply 'I am not keeping you, be off. Where are you going anyway?' Gef's answer was deemed significant: 'Back to the underground. Vanished.'[1] 'I never die,' Gef further explained, he simply returned to 'the Land of Mist'.[2]

185

Fodor interpreted this misty Freudian 'underground' as being Irving's unconscious. The eventual disappearance of Gef from our plane of existence coincided roughly with the onset of Mr Irving's final fatal bout of anaemia in 1944–45, during which time he was rendered bed-bound, helpless and rambling.[3] As his own mind faded away, so did Gef's.

Fodor found that, before he wound up living on the Isle of Man in 'the cabined and confined life of a sheep and goat-farmer in a God-forsaken spot where he was constantly struggling against physical starvation', Irving had been a commercial traveller with wide horizons. Now he had failed in life, but could not bear to admit the fact, even to himself. Thus, Irving began to suffer 'mental starvation' alongside his physical hunger. However, 'There was no way to relieve this by conscious means, so his unconscious took care of the job and produced the strange hybrid of Gef.' To outsiders, Gef's squeaks would often appear unclear. As such, it was mainly Irving who interpreted the spook's speech, explained Fodor, adding that nothing could have lent him 'a better chance to express the contents of his unconscious in a creative manner … than this role of official interpreter of Gef.'[4]

Essentially, Fodor proposed that Mr Irving was a kind of accidental artist, or script-writer. The creation of a fictional character like Gef is an artistic act. It seems Irving was effectively devising his own unconscious play via a form of three-dimensional automatic writing, with himself in one of the two leading roles, forming up a formidable comedy double act with his antic mongoose chum, like a ventriloquist whose promethean wooden dummy suddenly comes to life. Stuck on a remote outpost with only farm animals and his immediate family for company, the frustrated fellow had no available outlet for his latent creativity. Perhaps if Irving had taken up painting or writing verse in his spare time, Gef would never have appeared. But Mr Irving did not – and so Gef burst free from his lair in 'the underground', every bit as hungry for some Tricksterish sensation as Loki unbound must once have been under similar circumstances.

*****

Do poltergeists themselves ever create any actual artworks, it may be asked? Some spooks certainly enjoy constructing elaborate tableaux. In 1850, the family of Reverend Eliakim Phelps of Stratford, Connecticut, returned home from church to find a polt had been busy. Furniture was strewn about and eleven life-like figures, fashioned from items of clothing stuffed with pillows, were arranged to depict a parodic scene of worship. All but one appeared female. Some had their foreheads placed so as to be nearly touching the floor; others kneeled before Bibles, opened at passages relating to the topic of spirits. In the middle of the group was the incongruous figure of a dwarf, 'grotesquely dressed' and above them hung a figure *suspended in mid-air*, as though flying![5] Another time, a makeshift 'corpse' was found lying in a bed, formed from a nightgown and chemise with their arms folded across the breast and stockings for legs, ready for its coffin; to complete the scene of mock mourning, black crêpe was tied to the knocker of the back-door and mirrors covered over with sheets and table-cloths.[6]

The strikingly similar activities of the 1695 Scottish Ringcroft poltergeist were recorded by the haunted farmstead's local Minister, Alexander Telfair:

> On Saturday, the Family being all without-doors, the Children coming in saw something like a Person sitting by the Fire, with a Blanket about it; which frightened all of them but the youngest, who being about Ten Years of Age, chid the rest for being afraid, telling them, that if they bless'd themselves they needed not fear; and, perceiving the Blanket to be his own, blesses himself, and saying, Be what it will it hath nothing to do with my Blanket, he runs and pulls the Blanket away, but found nothing under it save a four-footed stool turn'd upside down.[7]

More makeshift mannequins appeared during an 1865 haunting in the French town of Fives; a 'curious figure' was found traced on a bed with hats, and, on the stairs, three men's overcoats left stretched out with a hat surmounting each where the wearer's head might go.[8] A Glasgow poltergeist of 1974–75 once arranged some bedclothes in the shape of a body, with a polystyrene wig-holder bust for a head.[9] Another polt once laid out a shirt with a badminton racket stuffed through the neck-hole, which then had a baseball cap perched on top of it.[10] One Dallas poltergeist was more sinister in its resourcefulness. Besides scrawling out notes filled with bogus messages about the end of time and eternal judgement, it also liked to leave chicken-skeletons posed into human-like sitting positions beneath a mulberry tree in the garden.[11]

During a 1722 haunting at Sandfeld, Germany, noises were heard, objects thrown, and an appalling stench perceived within the living-room, so a servant took the household's children away into the kitchen. He kept peeking into the affected room at intervals, as strange noises continued to occur. To his amazement, he found a picnic scene was slowly being assembled. Each time he popped his head around the door, more and more objects had been set up. A cloth was spread out across the floor and dishes filled with food laid out ready for two doll-like picnickers, cleverly sculpted from empty clothes.[12] Likewise, during a Scottish case from 1635, the haunted family would hear:

> ... all the locks in the house ... to fly open; yea, their clothes, which were at night locked up into trunks and chests, they found in the morning, all hanging about the walls. Once they found their best linen taken out, the table covered with it, napkins as if they had been used, yea, and liquor in their cups as if company had been there at meat.[13]

A South African poltergeist of 1869, which haunted the home of a farmer by performing lithobolia inside locked rooms, also made good use of his crops by positioning them to resemble a traditional rural wagon-team; the spook was a dab-hand at 'arranging oranges and pumpkins in a double-row, with a large head of Indian corn attached to them by a chain of straw'. The double-row of pumpkins or oranges were the usual double-row of oxen, attached to the corn-cob representing the wagon itself, with the straw being the rope-chain linking them all up. The farmer considered this less a work of art, and more a symbolic warning to leave the infested farm to live elsewhere.[14]

We also have accounts of polt-produced pictures. During a case of 1862, the children of a Swiss lawyer and politician named Melchior Joller discovered, in front of the family's grindstone, 'as if poured on', a small white picture the size of a coin and 'so like a death's head in the smallest detail that an engraver could not have bettered it.' They could not work out from what substance this image had been formed and it soon grew black and faded away.[15] A religiously-flavoured poltergeist affecting a sick child called Mary Jobson in Sunderland in 1840 was less macabre in its subject-matter. A voice told Mary to 'Look up, and you shall see the sun and moon on the ceiling!' whereupon bright images of these celestial bodies, fashioned in green, yellow and orange paint, appeared. These were permanent, resisting attempts to whitewash over them.[16]

The most famous such case was that of the 'Faces of Belmez', a small village in southern Spain.[17] Here, remarkable facial portraits first appeared on the afternoon of 23 August 1971 in the kitchen of a local woman named Maria Gomez. She saw a dark smudge on the floor near her cooker, and thought it was damp rising through the cement. Over the next few days, the smudge transformed into a clear representation of a face, complete with unbearably melancholic expression. The stain was concreted over. Two weeks later, a new face appeared in almost the same spot. This time the floor was dug up; a mass of human bones were found. The house, it turned out, was built on top of several old cemeteries. Soon, dozens of faces were appearing, both male and female. Some lasted barely long enough to be photographed, others were semi-permanent. When chiselled out and taken away for analysis, they tended to dry out and disappear but, when water was poured on them,

A rather unclear example of one of the Faces of Belmez; much better ones do exist, but sadly not all images of the dead are entirely copyright-free.

would return. Most were anguished in expression, and some even visibly aged as you looked at them, running through a whole lifetime in a matter of hours.

A neighbour soon claimed that objects were moving around, pictures falling off walls and mysterious bangs being heard in his own house. When a parapsychologist set up shop in the haunted kitchen, melodramatic phrases, such as 'Hell begins here', 'Mammaaaa', 'Do you like my company?' and 'I was once ... YOU' were captured on his tape-recorder. Various theories were advanced to account for the phenomena, but, *quelle surprise*, none provided an ultimate solution. Maybe the point of these pictures lay *in* the pictures; not in how they were made. According to one description of the Belmez portraits, they were 'evidently much troubled ... It was as if the faces were trying to communicate some great tragic secret.' And what was this 'great tragic secret'? Probably no more than what the Mona Lisa was smiling at.

* * * * *

The word 'art' is derived from the ancient Greek word for joint, *árthron*. From this Greek root, we get two Latin words, *ars* and *artus*. The latter means a bodily joint or hinge; the former denotes skill, craft and practical creativity.[18] But hinges and joints can either hinder or facilitate access. A door has hinges. It lets people in or out, and allows for change, it is the border-marker of the *limen*. But doors can also be closed, locked and bolted. The Trickster-poltergeist-artist trinity represents the more open hinges, not the restrictive ones. They open the door and allow there to be intercourse between two realms, like Hermes the Thief, picker of locks. Perhaps the brain of the artist is one whose door betwixt and between the two competing cerebral hemispheres is hinged more loosely.

If art is a kind of hinge, then what is it that is passing through this liminal door? Poems, paintings and other works of art do not (except in a certain figurative sense, as with a landscape picture) represent something that pre-exists themselves. The best art is, rather, a kind of spontaneous outburst from the generative power of the imagination, wherein it essentially creates itself. Likewise, it seems possible that poltergeists do not represent the temporary embodying of any entity that in some way pre-exists its own appearance, either – rather, it often appears as if the poltergeist, like the artwork, essentially generates itself. No 'form' of any specific poem pre-existed it; probably no coherent 'form' of the Enfield poltergeist preceded itself, either. Both may be represented metaphorically, therefore, as being the bursting forth of *potential* creation (call it *anima mundi* or the subconscious, if you like) into *actual* creation, a thing that is embodied only in itself.

* * * * *

Acts of profound artistic creation have occasionally been precipitated by poltergeist phenomena, as if both had the same ultimate source, or were somehow aspects of one another. Georgie Hyde-Lees, wife of the great Irish poet W. B. Yeats, purported to be a medium, able to communicate with spirits via automatic writing. During such occult experiments, certain polt-like events occurred. When Yeats asked 'the spirits' what they wanted, they replied through Georgie's hand simply that 'we have come to give you metaphors for poetry'.[19] Yeats gratefully made use of them.

Hermes also delivered C. G. Jung *hermaions* of literary inspiration via the medium of ghosts. One visitor to his home, struck by the peculiar atmosphere, talked of the great man's 'exteriorised libido' and how when he had 'an important idea that was not yet quite conscious' the furniture and woodwork 'creaked and snapped' of its own accord.[20] In 1916, Jung was at a creative dead-end, feeling 'an urge to give shape to something'. Jung intuited that the dead wanted him to write – but write what? As he wrestled with the dilemma, poltergeistery exploded. One of his daughters saw a white figure passing through her room; another had her blanket snatched away by invisible hands; the doorbell rang repeatedly, its mechanism actually seen pressing in by itself. At this point, Jung:

> ... knew that something had to happen. The whole house was filled as if there were a crowd present, crammed full of spirits. They were packed deep right up to the door, and the air was so thick it was barely possible to breathe. As for myself, I was all a-quiver with the question: 'For God's sake, what in the world is this?' Then they cried out in chorus, 'We have come back from Jerusalem where we found not what we sought' ... [This became the first line of *The Seven Sermons of the Dead*, Jung's next book] Then it began to flow out of me, and in the course of three evenings the thing was written. As soon as I took up the pen, the whole ghastly assemblage evaporated. The room quieted and the atmosphere cleared. The haunting was over.[21]

These spirits invading Jung's home were less poltergeists, more Muses.

*****

In 1960 Nandor Fodor met a brooding and lonely seventeen-year-old boy from Baltimore named Ted Pauls, in whose presence bottles would burst, windows shatter and pictures fall from walls. Ted, like Mr Irving, was too intelligent for his limited surroundings. He had recently dropped out of high school, not because he was dim, but because he found the intellectual level of the lessons far too low for his liking. Ted was a reasonably talented wannabe sci-fi writer, with no legitimate outlet for his skills. Fodor thought his propensity for writing endless space stories represented a desire to escape the reality of impending adulthood by returning to the dark, interstellar safety of the womb; he needed to become more outgoing. Fodor advised Pauls' family to read his tales and praise them. Then, he went on TV and deliberately lied to the world that he had discovered 'a near literary genius'. Suddenly, Pauls was transformed in the eyes of his family and peers from a weird, introverted geek, obsessed with spaceships and aliens, into someone destined for great things. The plan worked; the more Ted wrote, the happier and more sociable he became, with the haunting ending for good soon after.[22]

Fodor's thinking was coloured by his earlier experiences at Thornton Heath. Mrs Forbes took part in séances, becoming convinced her 'spirit-guide' was an artist. One day, she brought two drawings to show Fodor. They were produced one morning when Mrs Forbes was suddenly overcome by a strong feeling that she simply must abandon her housework, sit down and draw. It took a ringing telephone to snap her from her reverie; after which, she said, she could sketch no more. According to Fodor, this was a positive development, as 'Mrs Forbes was gaining confidence from the belief that a discarnate artist might guide her hand, and it seemed possible she might secure a constructive outlet for her creative tendencies.'[23] She didn't really pursue this route, however, and so the extreme poltergeistery continued – the exact opposite of what happened with Ted Pauls.

According to the beliefs of ancient Rome, each person was born with a familiar or tutelary spirit, known as his *genius* (or *daemon*, in Greek). The ideal path was to cultivate this 'guardian angel', by making it sacrifices. Nurtured correctly, the *genius* would repay its human twin by making him become more 'genial' – more potent creatively, spiritually and intellectually. By developing your *genius* properly, when you died it would transform into a helpful household spirit called a *lar*, to aid in the protection of your descendants. Neglected, repressed, ignored or abused during a man's lifetime, however, his *genius* would become a malevolent, poltergeist-like *larva* or *lemur* after his death, an evil spirit that liked to molest the living, another example of the old brownie-boggart dichotomy.[24] This is an excellent metaphor for the sacrifice, in terms of labour and effort, which all great artists and writers must put into their art – but in cases like that of Ted Pauls, the age-old metaphor seemed to explode into a state of actual reality.

* * * * *

In 1944, the Jungian psychologist John Layard proposed that a poltergeist should be viewed by its victim more as a *cure* than an *illness*, rather akin to the state of 'beneficial sickness' often endured by shamans prior to them being called to take up their accepted role in archaic societies, or the periods of mental-breakdown-like 'creative illness' undergone by many literary and artistic figures in more recent times, from C. G. Jung to August Strindberg, prior to them producing their best work.[25]

The case of Matthew Manning is supportive of Layard's idea. Now best-known as a successful shamanic-style psychic healer, Matthew's original brush with the paranormal came in the shape of childhood encounters with a poltergeist around his family home. At length, Manning's polt followed him to boarding school too. This was serious; he didn't want to get expelled. Fortunately, he found a method of controlling the spook – automatic writing. Writing a class essay, he suddenly found his hand 'taken over' by some strange force, and began scribbling gibberish. Experimenting in his dorm at night, Matthew was soon producing intelligible, though silly, messages. One read: 'John has got my spoons. Take them from him before he loses them. They are dear to me and they must not be lost. David Fraser, 1971.'[26] Others were in foreign languages; all were produced in handwriting quite different from Matthew's own. Whenever he produced them, however, all poltergeistery would temporarily cease, often for days on end.[27] According to Manning: 'if it looked as though disturbances were imminent, I would sit down and write ... It appeared that the energy I used for writing had previously been used for causing poltergeist disturbances.'[28]

Later in life, Manning preferred producing automatic drawings, ostensibly channelling the tutelary *genius* of dead artists like Picasso and Dürer into his body and then churning out (highly convincing) works in their style, something which had a similarly prophylactic effect upon his polt. A clear equivalency is suggested here between the production of the ghostly phenomena and the production of the automatic writing and drawing; they seem merely different expressions of the same thing. When this creative energy finds a natural outlet for itself, then it may produce creative works. When it does not find its own natural outlet, then it may express itself destructively, as the poltergeist. As for what this 'creative energy' in itself actually is, though ... well, that must remain as much a mystery as is the *genius* of a Shakespeare or a Leonardo.

*****

The controversial theoriser Stan Gooch also saw poltergeists as being the result of excessive mental repression of powerful imaginative energies. Gooch argued the suppression of naturally creative paranormal acts in a psychically-gifted child by their nervous or disapproving parents could engender an unhealthy mental state with dangerous repercussions for that same child in later life. He warned that the over-strict parental discipline of infant visionaries or ghost-seers could lead to the occurrence of 'unpleasant and uncontrolled paranormal events' of a poltergeistic variety when the child reached adolescence and began to emit puberty-powered RSPK energies.[29] Imagine an aspect of a child's personality being hacked off, locked away and then going rotten, cut off from fresh air and sunlight. If the paranormal aspect of the child's creativity had not been so foolishly suppressed in the first place, then it would never have descended into this dire state and simply gone away of its own accord, or even transformed into something actively beneficial and brownie-like, such as Matthew Manning's later ability for faith-healing. Excessive repression, however, leads to the eventual unleashing of something more boggart-like, rancid and eager for revenge, like Loki unbound.

Gooch noticed that, when producing his polt-repellent sketches, Manning often started his drawing in the middle of the paper before it then began to spread out anticlockwise. Anticlockwise is the natural motion for left-handed people to make when drawing, even though Manning was right-handed.[30] The left hand is controlled by the right-side of the brain; the creative centre. Therefore, the production of automatic art by Manning was an expression of the creative, artistic aspect of the right-side of his brain, given a useful and appropriate route through into the material world outside. The poltergeist is thus for Gooch that very same expression of right-brain creativity but in another less pleasant form, uncontrolled and malignantly destructive – a *lar* become a *lemur*, you might say. The *lares* were gods of the domestic hearth as well as post-death offshoots of a man's personal creative *genius*, but so, in certain traditions, was Hermes. Ancient Greek homes might contain *lar*-like statues of Hermes-as-Hermaphrodite within them, handed down from generation to generation as embodiments of the inexhaustible cosmic life-force, symbolised by the union between man and woman, which guaranteed the future of the family line. Such statues presided over the innermost sanctums of the home, the bedrooms and bridal chamber, and also the hearth, symbol of the united family unit, from whose ashes the Trickster-god would sometimes leap like a fairy to frighten maidens. Hermes here inhabiting the centres of the home rather than his usual liminal zones may seem counterintuitive, but is typical of the deity's paradoxical nature.

Hermes also presided over the front door into the house, thus facilitating both exits to the periphery, the world outside, and entrances to the centre, the family home. In this guise of door-god, he is known as *Hermes stropheus*, this '*stropheus*' being the socket within which the door-hinge pivots. Thus, he was also 'Hermes the Hinge', that through which both good and baleful influences could be either admitted into or barred from the home.[31] Substitute the word 'unconscious' for the word 'home' here, and you have a good analogy for what the poltergeist is in Stan Gooch's estimation. If the hinge through which unconscious content passes through into our world in the form of art, imagination and creativity is allowed to grow too rusty and stiff, then Hermes will have his revenge, the door begin to creak, and the home over which he presides lose its familiar calm and become an unquiet one.

* * * * *

Ask the general public what their perception of the stereotypical artist, poet or 'creative-type' is, and they will probably respond with a lot of generalities about eccentricity, oddness or unusual ways. These are clichés – for every Salvador Dalí, no doubt there is also an equal and opposing Jane Austen – but they do have some basis in reality. In 1927, the prank-loving French Dadaist Marcel Duchamp had a trick-door installed in his Paris studio, which swung on its hinges in such a way that, when it opened up a passage to one room, it automatically blocked up the passage to another. He meant this as a joke; a palpable visual defiance of the common-sense old French proverb 'a door must be either open or shut'. Not in Duchamp's Schrödinger's Cat-like world; there, a door can be both open and shut simultaneously, like a lock to Hermes, or a sealed container to a 4-D poltergeist. Duchamp's prank reminds me of the joke about the man who tossed a coin and found it landed neither heads nor tails, but on a third side – the *inside*. Duchamp's reason for undermining logical polarities in this way was equally as comic as artistic; he liked to 'open up a corridor of humour' in his life with such boundary-subverting art, he said.[32]

The humourless Apollonian world-view that our scientism-worshipping Dominant of Cartesian Dualism enforces today is based fundamentally upon the norms of Aristotelian logic, a black-and-white (or red-and-yellow) world of dichotomies or binary oppositions in which something is considered to be either 'A' or 'not-A' – a door being 'open' (A) or 'not open' (not-A), for instance. Normally, you can't have a door which is both open and closed at once, a principle known as the 'Law of the Excluded Middle'.[33] But, in the grey-orange worlds of art, the paranormal, Tricksterism and humour alike, it seems you actually *can* have such a door! When JOTTling Janet passed

193

French Dadaist subversive
Marcel Duchamp, owner of
a very strange door indeed.

through a brick wall into the house next door at Enfield, she proved it, the door of solid matter standing open for her even while being shut. In 1888, at a schoolhouse in Madras, India, spooky bricks were falling down from thin air. A clergyman advised marking one with a white cross and leaving it in the centre of the room to scare off the demon. Immediately, the polt then apported another brick, of exactly the same size, down on top of the first one, balanced precisely on top of it. It bore a black cross, the white cross' logical binary opposite, A and not-A simultaneously.[34] Had this happened a century later, I would have said it was the ghost of Marcel Duchamp.

Artists are often seen as being a kind of Trickster (and Trickster as the first artist). Think of Picasso's incomparable dictum, 'Art is a lie which tells the truth.' That was worthy of Hermes himself! Artists' brains are assumed to work differently than those of the rest of us, and their personalities to be less differentiated in some way, in order to allow ideas of great *genius* to come in to them from elsewhere, perhaps through one of those special trick doors which, in defiance of Aristotle and his heirs, is both A and not-A at the same time. If the poltergeist is also potentially an artist, with a form of radically undifferentiated personality, then we would naturally expect it to be an eccentric Trickster. We might also expect it to be in some sense funny, to 'open up a corridor of humour', just like Duchamp's door. When we read of some of the odder incidents in the lives of the artists, we are apt to smile. It is normal to laugh at the ways of men like Duchamp. It should also be normal to laugh – if only from a distance – at the ways of the poltergeist. Let us now see precisely why.

PART TWO

High Spirits: A Catalogue of Poltergeist Tricks and Humour

The world is indeed comic, but the joke is on mankind.
H. P. Lovecraft

Any fool can play tragedy, but comedy, sir, is a damned serious business.
David Garrick

The fate of all explanation is to close one door only to have
another fly wide open.
Charles Fort

Virtually everything the poltergeist does can be viewed as being amusing or humorous in one sense or another. We are all aware of what makes humour; bizarre and unexpected conjunctions, flirting with taboos, the subversion or complete inversion of pre-existing rules, assumptions and attitudes. Viewed like this, even a banality like a spook smashing a plate on the floor can be considered an expression of the humorous. So can a floating cup, or a series of impossible rappings. They are expressions of humour, because they *shouldn't happen*. They shock us into laughter (perhaps mocking laughter, for sceptics) by their open transgression of the known rules of the universe. I shall try in the pages that follow to provide you with some instances of ghostly wit that are rather more entertaining and imaginative than mere flying crockery. Fortunately, we are not short of examples.

I

Practical Jokes

The heart of fools is in the house of mirth.
Ecclesiastes 7:3-4

As a child, I once hung a pair of my father's dirty underpants from the window for the whole street to see, hoping to embarrass him. It amused me at the time. While researching this book, I was pleased to find that the actions of a 1974 Birmingham spook traced a direct parallel with my own childish game. According to the man of the haunted household, the polt in question:

> ... loves to have fun with my underwear. He throws them downstairs, and if I don't pick them up he creates chaos in the kitchen. Once I had a bath and asked my wife to get my pants, but she couldn't find them. The next morning I was astonished to see them hanging on a branch at the top of a tree.[1]

This is really extremely childish; it also might not seem entirely credible. And yet, there are innumerable equally infantile poltergeist pranks on record. The Enfield poltergeist once kicked someone up the bum in the bathroom, which is even more reminiscent of the *modus operandi* of mischievous schoolboys than hiding underwear is.[2] A 1949 spirit haunting a London shoe shop was just as naughty; it repeatedly dyed brown shoes black, poured liquid into others, and stole footwear to hide outside.[3] I am deliberately citing instances which sound as if committed by invisible *Beano* characters. A Turkish ghost of 2012 enjoyed putting salt in a sugar bowl and filling a drinking water bottle up with vinegar; so did Dennis the Menace.[4]

At Skinwalker Ranch, it is said the Gorman family 'got so used to finding the salt in the pepper shaker and vice-versa that they would always shake a small amount onto their hand as a test prior to putting it on their food.'[5] Confusing opposites is just the kind of thing you might expect Hermes to find amusing. The Skinwalker Menace also hid boxes of cereal in ovens and freezers and stole towels from bathrooms when people were showering. Once it had all been carefully stored away, the family's weekly shopping would later be found all carefully unpacked again on the kitchen table. This was specifically described by investigators as being 'Trickster-like phenomena'.[6] Indeed it was.

Another Tricksterish speciality is that perennial childhood favourite, knock-and-run. In 1996, pensioners living in Riverside Close in Cuckney, Nottinghamshire, were continually awoken by ringing doorbells and tapping on their windows. A huff and a puff, and a few moments later the elderly were at their doors – only to find no one anywhere to be seen. No mystery there; except that some incidents occurred during snow falls, and no tracks were visible where the tracks of any mischievous children should, by rights, have really been.[7]

Remarkably similar tricks were played upon the Curé d'Ars, a nineteenth-century French clergyman of highly liminal personality, who thought he was being stalked by Satan. The haunting began with loud blows upon his front door, 'as if someone were trying to break it open with a great club.' He asked who it was, but answer came there none. This continued for several nights. Fearing robbers, the Curé asked 'two courageous men' to sleep in his house for protection. Hearing the din themselves, they blamed not burglars, but devils. According to the Curé:

> I was soon convinced of this myself; for one winter's night, when a quantity of snow had fallen, I heard three tremendous blows in the middle of the night. I sprang hastily from my bed, and ran downstairs into the court[yard], thinking this time I should catch the evil-doers ... But to my great astonishment I saw nothing, I heard nothing, and what is more, I saw not a trace of footprints upon the snow. I had no longer a doubt that it was the Devil who wanted to terrify me.[8]

Sometime during the 1800s, at a haunted parsonage in France's Languedoc region, 'a great hammer blow' was struck on the front door by an uncatchable jester every evening without fail, at some point between ten and midnight. The irritated servant, Antoine, stood prepared just inside the door one night, clutching a thorny stick in one hand and the latch by the other, ready to throw open the portal and administer a good thrashing. Hours passed; no knock. Eventually, overcome by sleep, Antoine began wearily to descend the staircase to his bed – at which point, no prizes for guessing, the knock returned, loud as ever, upon the door whose watch he had just abandoned. Furious, he raced back upstairs and straight outside. Puck was not there to meet him.[9]

At Homem Christo's haunted Portuguese villa, the ghost – which we met at the very start of this book comically trapping a guest's head beneath a falling window-pane – was even more badly behaved. As soon as the lights had been extinguished one night, several 'big blows' were heard on the back door. Christo ran downstairs and waited for more; as soon as they came, he opened the door. Nobody there. Venturing outside, the door banged shut behind him and locked by itself. His wife had to let him in. Blaming practical jokers, the hot-headed Christo produced a revolver and stood on the stairs *ready to kill them*. While his matches held their flame during this eerie vigil, there was silence. As soon as they went out, doors shook and bursts of laughter echoed throughout the whole building. Spooked, Christo summoned policemen. Some waited inside, another kept watch outside. The ones inside heard knocking; they opened the door and asked who had done it. The officer stationed outside had seen nothing, he said. He had heard nothing, either – even though it was upon the outside of the door right next to him that the knocks had apparently been rapped.[10] This was surely another trick-door, fetched straight from the studio of Marcel Duchamp!

A related form of trickery was once frequently encountered in the shape of paranormal bell-ringing; the bells concerned being those which Lords of the Manor would use to summon their lackeys in days of old. The classic study is *Bealing Bells* by Major Edward Moor. At Moor's mansion in Great Bealings, Suffolk, for a period of fifty-four days during 1834, bells rang, rang and rang again, with no discernible cause.[11] The victims of such annoyances often find they quickly grow boring rather than scary, and so attempt to silence the bells by fair means or foul – to little avail. During one French haunting, the polt's victims stopped up the unquiet bells' clappers with paper. A good solution … until the ghost quickly caused the paper to fall out and the ringing to recommence.[12] At Borley Rectory, the bell-wires themselves were cut, to stymie the ghost's schemes; but still these same bells jingled.[13] During one 1867 haunting, the wires were actually physically removed from the pestered household's ever-pealing bells; and yet still, impossibly, they continued to clang.[14]

* * * * *

A ghost at The Grenadier pub in Knightsbridge, London, did what I always did when I was seven and it was bath-time – it pulled the plug out when the tub was full.[15] One further tool of the Trickster-trade I had as a child was a fake five-pound note on a fibre-glass string. Place it on the floor, hide in the bushes, and when someone bends down to pick it up – yoink! Run away laughing. A poltergeist residing in a haunted Silesian castle during 1806 also liked to play this game. A visitor named Hahn was awoken one night by the ghost throwing tobacco at him. When he stooped down to pick it up seeking free smokes, it flew away. This whole process being repeated several times, Hahn got bored and threw a heavy stick in his unseen tormentor's direction instead. The same spook later drained poor Hahn's shaving-bowl of water just when he had got it to the right temperature, not unlike the bath-hating pub-ghost of Knightsbridge.[16] The Victorian folklorist Andrew Lang recounts the similar tale of a Frenchman disturbed by food continually shooting off his table and his wineglass fleeing away from his hand as he went to drink from it, almost as if attached to more hidden strings.[17]

During the Scottish Sauchie haunting, the poltergeist removed the stoppers from hot-water bottles, soaking the bed of the little girls involved. The entity also stole from a store of hidden sweets in the haunted house, piecemeal, over the course of a few days – or, at least, that's what the children said …[18] The 1914 French poltergeist of Vodable was just as impishly annoying. It used to hide the hats of visitors before they left; much time was wasted before they were found pointlessly secreted away behind furniture.[19] There are none of these tricks I didn't try as a child myself. I'm sure the reader is the same.

Some poltergeists are somewhat more daring than was my childhood self, however. A 1930 French polt enjoyed draining cups of their coffee just before they were about to be served to eager visitors, for which I would have received a severe parental scolding.[20] The Bromley Garden Centre poltergeist similarly delighted in instantaneously draining mugs of their tea and replacing it with foul-tasting fertiliser. I would have got a clip round the ear for doing that. It threw beakers at people too, and upturned a wastepaper basket onto someone's head so it looked like he was wearing an oversized fez. Bed with no supper for that – and grounded. It also stole £40 worth of holiday-money.[21] For *that*, I would have been kicked out of the house.

* * * * *

Most poltergeists come across as being terminally bored and lacking in inspiration in their tomfoolery. Or perhaps their increasingly pointless behaviour just reflects certain unfortunate trends in modern society? According to the historian R. C. Finucane, a typical modern ghost would 'take more liberties' with its victims than a Victorian one would, citing as an instance of this sad moral decline the recent case of a young woman, sunbathing in her bikini one day, who found an invisible entity chucking small mud-balls into her exposed cleavage. The missiles had no apparent source, but were thrown 'unerringly' into their target.[22] A UFO-Contactee called Martha Anderson experienced similarly breast-centric phenomena after her meetings with 'spacemen', with an unseen polt-like force twanging her bra open as she laid face-down on her bed at night.[23]

Why would ghosts do this kind of thing? When asked this very question, the Enfield poltergeist once replied with nothing more profound than the phrase 'I LIKE ANNOYING YOU.'[24] There must be many a schoolteacher who, when handing out detentions, has been told by the little sods in question that they 'didn't know' why they had misbehaved either. Is there really much difference between the poltergeist and the bored and errant schoolchild in these cases? Maybe Frank Podmore had a point after all.

II

Vandalism

Another fine mess!

Oliver Hardy

The terminally bored often resort to vandalism; but how bored, exactly, must the following ghosts have been? A house in Etchingham, Sussex, in 2005 – a newly-whitewashed wall. Then, a newly-whitewashed wall filled up with purple crayon marks. We are told a spirit was responsible.[1] In 1892 a family return to their haunted Chicago home only to find there had been 'an orgy of curtains'. Not only torn curtains, but also drawers ransacked; nothing taken, but watches and jewellery pulled out and smashed pointlessly.[2] The Canvey Island poltergeist of 1709 did almost nothing but break windows, albeit with a certain artistry. Once, a 'great knock' was heard followed by a sound of cracking glass from the parlour. Inside, three panes were found broken by a tile, but a tile which was hanging 'in such a strange Geometrick Manner, betwixt the broken Lead and Glass' that the author of a contemporary pamphlet was moved to venture that a veritable 'artist' must have been responsible.[3] It was much the same at a haunted house in Marcinelle, Belgium, in 1913, where the spook's curiously symmetrical window-demolition was described thus:

> I have seen a stone arriving in the middle of a large window-pane, and then came others in a spiral round the first point of impact, so that the whole of the glass was broken up methodically. I even saw, in another window, a projectile caught in the fragments of glass of the first hole it made, and subsequently ejected by another passing through the same point.[4]

The Daventry poltergeist of 1658 sounds just as annoying, and nowhere near as concerned with aesthetics. It dismantled a spinning-wheel, smashed objects and then threw the fragments at witnesses. Most typically, it ruined food and drink. Milk was spilled, a barrel of beer mixed with sand, cheese crumbled into useless atoms, bread thrown onto the floor and dirtied and salt 'mingled most perfectly with bran'. Large quantities of wheat were strewn about, and chickpeas stored in the barn thrown all over. Even a visiting baker had the crumbs from his basket jump into someone's lap.[5] The wastage of food on a farm during the 1600s was a rather more serious matter than a polt sprinkling cornflakes in a kitchen would be nowadays; imps placing peat in porridge or dumping dung in cooking-pots were once a cause of genuine woe.[6] Another instance of spinning-wheels being broken comes from the haunting of Frances and Elizabeth Dixon in Newry, Northern Ireland, from 1776 to 1785. Their yarn was also cut up, which was awkward because spinning cloth was the sisters' only livelihood.[7] Sometimes poltergeist vandalism appears deliberately directed against those objects the loss of which will cause their owners the most financial loss or frustration.

A ghost troubling a home in the Hertfordshire village of Burton in 1669 is supposed to have hidden loaves of bread in hard-to-find places, set piles of peas, pulses and grain on fire, thrown cheese, hops and meat around and, most disturbingly, caused all the flesh to disappear from a roast pig, leaving only clean bones behind.[8] A demon infesting the house of a weaver named Gilbert Campbell in Glenluce, Scotland, in 1654, reduced his family down to near-starvation by hiding away their food and cutting up their thread 'as if with a pair of scissors'. Eventually, the Campbells had to subsist on bread and water, as the spook graduated from concealing their meat in holes and under beds to JOTTling it away altogether.[9] An 1135 polt who hid seed-pellets, cinders and bitter suet inside dishes, as well as knotting up thread meant for weaving until it 'resembled the famous inextricable labyrinth',[10] and a brownie (surely a boggart?) who in 1615 mixed scraps of metal and pieces of shot inside meals,[11] sound positively benign by comparison. A 2010 Malaysian *djinni* which enjoyed dumping huge quantities of salt and rotten fish-heads into cooking-pots, while strewing food-scraps across clean beds, shows such things still occur.[12]

Modern poltergeist-vandals now have a wider variety of household goods to ruin than just food and thread; the above-mentioned Malaysian genie also enjoyed transporting clothes inside a refrigerator. One 1970s pub-polt in St Albans made a speciality out of puncturing people's car-tyres,[13] while a 1950s spook in a Whitechapel dressmaking factory preferred to pour vases of water over the proprietors' income-tax forms rather than more predictably slicing up their clothing.[14] Other items typically targeted, such as furniture, are more-or-less constant. The following account of a bedside dressing-table being demolished is from the 1950s, but could just as easily have hailed from the 1750s:

> [The ghost] started by removing one wing and the mirror with a resounding crash. Next, the two large single drawers were removed and thrown across the room, just missing the heads of [the witnesses] ... The remaining wing crashed to the floor, the fronts of the two double-drawers ... were bashed inwards. The joints in the woodwork began to give way and panels from the back were ripped off, all to the accompaniment of furious and rapid banging.[15]

The simplest form of ghostly vandalism is the smashing of breakables. When, at a haunted house on Russian Hill overlooking San Francisco Bay in 1856, the home's owner rashly challenged the spook – by way of a 'scientific exercise' – to break whatever it could lay its hands on, fifty dollars' worth of china and glassware was pitched at his feet, shattering into unrecognisable shards.[16] That was very much his own fault. A block of flats in Hamilton, New Zealand, was subjected to a 'torrent' of milk, beer, pop and coffee bottles being smashed against it for three consecutive days in 1974. Police could find no culprits, despite being present for four non-stop hours of projectile-hurling one night. Maori elders blamed irate 'forest spirits' for the crimes.[17] Less exotically, in 1969 the Parr family of Manchester suffered the attentions of an invisible midnight assailant who flung bricks, stones and milk bottles at the back of their council house. Windows were broken – and yet police could do nothing.[18]

A 1900 Turin poltergeist investigated by Eusapia Palladino's friend Cesare Lombroso was simply very thorough. It didn't just smash bottles in a haunted wine-cellar, it broke their fragments down into smaller fragments, *ad infinitum*, until all that was left was a pile of glass-dust.[19] Equally as methodical was a 1970s polt infesting a Glasgow tenement flat. The tenants awoke to find their window-panes smashed and every last piece of china, crockery and glassware in the place crushed down into atoms of coloured sand.[20] A cat-like animal ghost haunting Killakee House, County Dublin, during the 1960s and '70s may have had OCD; a medieval oak chair was discovered systematically dismantled, joint by joint, with the brass tacks that had once held its tapestry in place lined up on the floor next to it in neat little rows.[21]

The poltergeist expert Guy Lyon Playfair visited a slum near the Brazilian town of Carapicuíba, where a row of six houses had been subjected to three

When hurling around stones, it is only natural that poltergeists should sometimes smash things up, as in this image illustrating the lithobolic vandalism of a Paris poltergeist of 1846.

weeks of bombardment during September 1974. When he arrived, he found a large concrete block had just fallen, shattering roof-tiles. There was a pile of such blocks lying on the ground – Playfair asked the largest child he could find to see how far she could throw it. She couldn't even lift it. Within ten minutes, Playfair witnessed 'a hail' of stones and bricks falling from 'a cloudless blue sky'.[22] There is a quite amazing account of a house on Paris' Rue des Grès being almost entirely destroyed by a poltergeist in 1849. Large-scale demolition work was taking place nearby; perhaps the scene provided the ghost with its inspiration? The demolition site certainly furnished the ghost with its main projectiles. Torn-up paving stones, parts of torn-down walls, even entire mouldings from destroyed buildings were hurled at the house, piercing its walls, smashing its windows, and reducing its doors to splinters.[23] Did a naughty teenager toss those around too, Mr Podmore?

* * * * *

Innumerable acts of paranormal arson also occur. Possibly the most dramatic happened during 1870–71 within the home of a Russian official named Shchapoff. Phenomena began with the noise of invisible dancing and strange sounds emanating from within a chimney. Then, 'a small ball of light the size of a plate' was seen, and objects flew around. Shchapoff and his wife temporarily fled, but when they returned a neighbour named Portnoff declared that in their absence he had seen an 'apparition of bright meteors' flitting outside their sitting-room: 'There were several of them, varying in size from a large apple to a walnut. Their shape was round, their colour deep red or bluish pink; they were not quite transparent, but rather dull … the globes were trying to get in at the window.' Items of clothing and furniture around the neighbouring homes now began bursting into flames, with Portnoff burning his hands trying to beat out fires. Worse, the polt actually set Mrs Shchapoff alight; she went into the hallway one day only to encounter 'a hellish roaring' as the floor shook, followed by 'a bluish spark' shooting up to engulf her. Hearing her wail, Portnoff found his neighbour standing within 'a literal pillar of fire'. Uncannily, the woman herself was entirely unharmed by the strange blue flame; only her dress was scorched to cinders.[24] Another potential fire-shaman, perhaps?

As the figure of the poltergeist to some extent grew from out of the ancient *lar*-like figure of the household hearth-spirit, and angry hearth-spirits were, according to old legend, said to burn down their owners' houses when displeased with their actions, perhaps we should not be too surprised by the repeated recurrence of this hellish motif.[25] Amazingly, there was even a case wherein an insurance company was prepared to pay out compensation to somebody who said a poltergeist had fire-damaged their home! Harry Price rescued this soot-blackened 1942 newspaper report from the archives:

Mansion Fires Mystery. An insurance company has paid £400 for damage alleged to have been done by a poltergeist or mischievous spirit … In a mansion in Fife, twenty rooms had been set on fire, furniture had been heaped in the drawing-room, and ewers of water left in the bedroom were emptied over the bed immediately the room was vacated. Faced with a claim for £400 fire-damage, the insurance company had investigated the matter. It was certain the fire had not been started by the occupants, and that it had not been caused accidentally. So the claim was paid.[26]

Apparently, the original claim put in was for £800, so it seems the insurance men were hedging their bets with this one. The haunted mansion in question was Pitmilly House, home of the Jeffrey family. Pitmilly's fiery phenomena lasted for around thirty years (not a misprint), the first sign that something was wrong being the sudden appearance of a lump of coal in the middle of the Jeffreys' dining-table one day in 1936 – their hearthside *lar* must have become a *lemur*. It wasn't until around 1940 that the spook really entered its stride, with innumerable objects flying around or JOTTling, and paintings turning backwards on walls. Most characteristically, curtains, carpets, beds, clothes and sheets were all scorched or burned to cinders. Piles of flaming coals were found sitting on furniture. Hats were torn from heads and thrown into fireplaces. When Captain John Arthur Jeffrey, the family patriarch, saw a conflagration 'like the spirits of wine' moving across his bedroom carpet he tried to beat it out with a pillow – only to find that the fairy in fiery form reacted intelligently, dodging out of his way. Equally as odd, these living flames were cold, and left no scorch-marks behind whatsoever. Once, as John's wife walked across a room, small infernos appeared behind her on the floor with every step she took, like burning footprints of the Devil.

The events relating to the insurance claim took place on 7 March 1940, when no fewer than seventeen separate blazes broke out, requiring the attendance of the fire-brigade. Eventually Pitmilly House was turned into a hotel, but guests would find alcohol vanishing from bottles, clothes being flung onto floors, and apparitions wandering around. Flaming phantoms continued to appear; one guest saw a line of fire, 30 yards long, run down an entire corridor before just as suddenly vanishing, leaving behind no damage. The building was finally demolished in 1967; the only surprise was that it hadn't burned to the ground decades earlier.[27]

*****

The ruination of clothes is also common – in rural France, finding pieces of cloth, cut as though with scissors, lying around the home was once considered a sure sign of the dead revealing their presence.[28] The most remarkable such narrative concerned the 'Wizard Clip' of West Virginia, a nineteenth-century ghost which earned its nickname from its habit of destroying clothes in a very peculiar manner.[29] Whether in plain view, locked away in drawers or even still on the wearer's back, strange crescent moon-shaped holes appeared in garments, sometimes accompanied by the sound of invisible scissors at work! Crescent moons and scissors are now used as municipal logos on the district's street-signs, such is the fame of the occurrences locally.

One visitor to the haunted house took precautions, taking her new black silk cap off and placing it within her pocket to escape the ghost's attentions – but, when she later stepped outside, found it in ribbons anyway. Shoes were sliced into spirals, as though by an expert orange-peeler; boots which appeared whole would collapse into long strips as soon as touched. The edges of such cuts were unnaturally straight, as if done by laser. Another case was of a haunted house in Perthshire where, in 1718, a woman had her underwear cut into strips ... while still wearing it.[30] A spirit haunting the house of a tanner near Cambridge in 1802 was known for similar perversions. According to one account, the house became something of a tourist attraction: 'eighteen or twenty of the neighbours, who went in to examine, were served by the spirit just the same way – multitudes of people flocked from all quarters to have their clothes spoilt, and all went away satisfied and in rags.'[31]

* * * * *

Yet another type of poltergeist-vandal is the 'phantom sniper'. During the late summer of 1985, strange things were afoot at a villa on the French Riviera, belonging to the Oliveros family. As well as fires and lithobolia, the Oliveros' veranda windows were being smashed, seemingly by shots from a concealed gun. Bizarrely, no bullets could anywhere be found, despite repeated professional searches by police. According to contemporary reports, 'there were no signs of bullets or even bits of plastic, wax, fragments of lead of the smallest calibre ... nothing.' The 'progressive destruction' only halted when every pane was broken. As is usually the way, the family's adoptive son was ultimately blamed for causing all the trouble – but if so, then how? I'd like the police to actually tell us that, just for once.[32]

The mysterious 'Phantom Wall-Smasher' of Peckham was equally elusive. The first victim of this unusual vandal had just finished tidying his garden one evening during July 1977 and, stepping into his house for a moment, returned to find he now had no wall. By the end of September, twenty-five other nearby garden-walls had been either partially broken or utterly destroyed. Residents kept watch for the invisible criminal – a thankless task. Two informed police that, after glancing away from their windows for 'no more than a few seconds', they turned back around to see the dust settling around big piles of broken bricks. The ghost gained a tabloid nickname – 'Harvey Wallbanger' – and a spurious 'explanation'; an out-of-work bricklayer, it was asserted, was going around making easy repair-work for himself by sneakily ruining walls.[33] That's as bad a 'rationalisation' as ever I've heard. Hermes never did like walls, did he?

* * * * *

The psychologist and American SPR man William James once proposed that acts of vandalism by humans and acts of vandalism by poltergeists were essentially two differing modes of expression of the same basic thing.[34] Maybe so. In 1965, a spook invaded – like the proverbial bull – a china-shop in Bavaria. Glasses, vases, tasteful ceramic *objet d'art*; nothing was safe from the poltergeist that followed around a disturbed fifteen-year-old apprentice named Heiner. One of Heiner's jobs was to collect empty bottles, which he became known for breaking – whether by accident or deliberately, through tedium, is not entirely clear. Heiner resented his dull work and, as a result of his repeated bottle-smashing, was dispatched to a psychiatrist to discover what was wrong with him – whereupon the definitely *paranormal* breakages began.[35]

Perhaps it takes a writer of imaginative fiction to really tease out what might have been happening here. Angela Carter, in her short story *The Fall River Axe-Murders*, details the mundane and frustrating home life of Lizzie Borden, the infamous real-life American parent-killer. Then, she talks about a vandalistic intruder to the Borden household who 'pissed and shat on the cover of the Bordens' bed, knocked the clutter of this and that on the dresser to the floor, smashing everything, swept into Old Borden's dressing room there to maliciously assault ... [his] coat ... retired to the kitchen, smashed the flour-crock and the treacle-crock, and then scrawled an obscenity or two on the parlour window with the cake of soap that lived beside the scullery sink.'

There are no prizes for guessing that the perpetrator of these vile acts was no intruder at all but, rather, the pathologically bored Lizzie Borden herself, acting quite unconsciously: 'What a mess! Lizzie started with vague surprise ... What was she doing, clad in only her corset in the middle of the living-room? How had she got there? ... She did not know. She did not remember. All that happened was: all at once here she is, in the parlour, with a cake of soap in her hand.' Borden's stepmother has her own suspicions about who had really caused all this mess, though: 'The possibility of a poltergeist occurs to Mrs Borden, although she does not know the word; she knows, however, that her younger stepdaughter is a strange one and could make the plates jump out of sheer spite if she wanted to.'[36]

Carter has picked up on the RSPK-related idea that jaded adolescents can somehow externalise their frustration at their own *ennui* in the shape of a destructive poltergeist. Related back to Heiner's haunting, his intentional bored bottle-breakages and his unintentional paranormal ones can be seen as two sides of the same coin; namely, attempts by the terminally fed-up lad to destroy (and thereby remake) the unsatisfactorily limiting world which surrounded and trapped him. It was the same with Carter's fictionalised Lizzie Borden, in terms of motive if not execution. One is human vandalism, the other superhuman; but the end result of both is exactly the same – a Tricksterishly broken world.

III

Slapstick

In comedy there are only two main parts: he who slaps and
he who gets slapped.

Georges Feydeau

What's the 'purest' form of humour? Is it that which most crosses
boundaries and transcends nationality? If so, then the type which fits this
description best is slapstick. Humour that relies more upon pratfalls and
comic violence than complex and sophisticated verbal wordplay, or the
more shaded nuances of characterisation, can be understood by anyone,
whatever their language or level of intelligence. As such, poltergeists
everywhere have been quite fond of it down the years. What is the very
essence of slapstick? It is the image of a man getting hit in the face with a
big, wooden plank; the hinged plank which slaps back in on itself, making
a loud noise so that its impact sounds more violent than it really is, is
where the whole genre derives its name. Harry Price, in his *Poltergeist
Over England*, gives just such a case from Romania, in which a plank shot
from the corner of a room and slapped against a young man's head in a
fashion that would have made Charlie Chaplin proud; Price even provides
an illustrative cartoon for his readers to smile at.[1]

William G. Roll gives an uncharacteristically comic account of a series
of droll assaults perpetrated by a Sicilian poltergeist of 1890. When a
young woman visited the haunted house, she 'clasped her fan tightly in her
hands wedged between her knees and defied the spirits to take it away' –
but 'in a flash the fan was torn away and smashed on her head.' Another
time, a policeman locked his club in a drawer and challenged the ghost
to get it; the drawer shot open, the club flew out and started bashing him
on the bonce. A priestly exorcist was treated likewise; his Bible jumped
from his hands and beat him up.[2] If you were going to pen a comedy script
about Spiritualism, then this is *exactly* the kind of stupid scene you would
include.

The ghost of a young RAF pilot haunting a home near Croydon Airport
in 1979 is alleged to have repeatedly twanged the bra-straps of the woman
of the house during an exorcism; just what would happen if they ever

207

made a *Carry On Haunting*.[3] Also distinctly filmic in quality is the case of the one-legged man, James Clay, who in October 1901 stood outside his house in Harrisonville, Ohio, shouting that the weird lithobolic showers the place was experiencing were not the actions of ghosts but, rather, those of mischievous boys. As soon as Clay said this, a veritable 'boulder' from nowhere struck away his crutch and broke it, presumably causing him to fall over.[4] I'd also really like to have seen the occasion during a 1695 Scottish haunting in which three men quietly saying their prayers were suddenly assaulted by an unseen ghost swinging a dead polecat against their heads.[5]

Within an unquiet carpenter's workshop at Swanland near Hull in 1849 we can envisage the following amusing scene taking place, as recorded for us by a Mr Bristow, then apprenticed there:

> I was working at the bench next the wall, where I could see the movements of my two companions ... Suddenly one of them turned round and called out: 'You had better keep those blocks of wood and stick to work, mates!' We asked him to explain, and he said: 'You know quite well what I mean; one of you hit me with this piece of wood', and he showed us a piece of wood about an inch square. We both protested that we had not thrown it ... The incident was being forgotten, when, some minutes afterwards, the other companion turned round like the first, and shouted at me: 'It is you, this time, who threw this piece of wood at me!' and he showed me a piece the size of a matchbox. There were two of them accusing me now, and my denials counted for nothing, so that I laughed and added: 'Since I did not do it, I suppose that if someone was aiming at you it is now my turn.' I had hardly said this when a piece hit me on the hip.[6]

I suppose, if I had the power to hurl things about invisibly, I might try and start fights among people too. It's the kind of thing I'd probably find amusing. Several other ghosts could potentially have pursued a career on the silver-screen alongside Fatty Arbuckle and Harold Lloyd. Such was a South African poltergeist dubbed 'Old Griet', which haunted the farm of a 'Mr K' sometime prior to 1912. Given what transpired there, I suspect this 'Mr K' may actually have been Buster Keaton:

> It began in this way: One night my brother-in-law was awakened by someone pulling hard at his big toe. He thought it was his wife and asked her why she had played such a silly joke on him. When she declared that someone had pulled her toe as well, they lit the candle and searched the house, but found nothing. But hardly had they gone back to bed and blown out the candle than they both felt someone touching them [again]. The rest of the night they kept a candle burning ... If there was a jug of water [placed upon Old Griet's favourite table], it would be thrown over us ... If it was a cold night, Old Griet would not allow us to tuck ourselves in [to bed]. The blankets were either pulled off us or they were rolled up from our feet to our heads ... And woe betide him who move or spoke [during such ordeals] for then Old

Griet would beat him with a quince-twig ... Sometimes, after ... all was quiet once more and we had fallen asleep, the bed would suddenly turn turtle [flip upside-down] and Old Griet would lie on it heavy as lead. When we crept out, our heads would be pressed to the floor ... Women covered their faces, for Old Griet slapped them ... with an [invisible] object like a boxing-glove ... Stones were thrown at us ... The ghost ... had a man's shape. It walked bent forward, taking long strides, and had big feet. It wore a large broad-brimmed hat and its clothes were in rags ... One evening ... Old Griet came boldly up to the tree in which the fowls were perched and pushed them off with a stick ... [we shot at the ghost, but this] did not interrupt the game with the fowls, and had no effect whatsoever.[7]

That would all make quite a movie. In fact, right from slapstick cinema's very first days, images of ghosts were explicitly exploited for comic purposes. As early as 1900, a minute-long short called *Uncle Josh in a Spooky Hotel* appeared, in which an apparition slaps a man as he talks to his landlord, then becomes invisible. Thinking it must have been his landlord who thwacked him, the tenant punches his landlord back and they get into a fight.[8] The film was produced by none other than Thomas Edison, but its scriptwriter must surely have been one Mr Bristow from Swanland.

I well remember the enjoyment I gained at school from pulling the chair from beneath a friend just as he was about to sit on it. The famous Bell Witch, about whom a lot more later, once performed this very same slapstick act upon one of the sons of the affected household, Drew Bell:

Drew leaned his chair back against the bureau, which set against the wall, placing his feet on the rounds. Instantly, the bureau was snatched from behind him and Drew tumbled down on the floor. The Witch told him to get up, that he ought to have better sense than to lean against the bureau.[9]

That's just what my mum used to tell me. At Homem Christo's Portuguese villa, likewise, an investigating policeman once went to sit down on a bench – only to find it snatched away by the ghost 'so suddenly' that he fell flat on his arse.[10]

The Bell Witch also enjoyed tying together the shoelaces of its main victim, Betsy Bell, as well as pulling her hair and tangling it up in labyrinthine knots.[11] The bitten and scratched Eleonore Zugun, too, had her hair pulled by her attendant poltergeist Dracu – who also liked to fill her shoes with water.[12] Leaving sharp pins on chairs for people to prick their bums is another commonplace of slapstick – and Harry Price says this happened at Borley Rectory. He assures us that the points were all facing upwards.[13] Price also informs us of a ghost haunting a mill in Westmorland in 1887, which mostly affected a place known as the 'wheel room'. Here, it piled up all the boxes, parcels and cases stored away within so that they leaned up against the inside of the door. If the house's occupant had not taken the precaution of looking through the window prior to entering, then this entire precarious arrangement would have toppled down comically on top of him.[14]

* * * * *

The upending of buckets onto people's heads is another slapstick stereotype. The arrival of a cook at a house in Malvern in 1942 triggered a cavalcade of just such events, including the Pythonesque scenario of 'a huge bucket of coal ris[ing] in the air and pursu[ing] the cook across the kitchen, eventually emptying its contents over her shoulders before falling to the ground.' Similar scenes were later repeated with a full swill-tub and a large strainer packed with old tea-leaves. Eventually, the cook was asked to leave.[15]

An American poltergeist of 1879 also enjoyed flinging fluids. During meals, milk, tea, coffee and hot soup were thrown into diners' faces, while their spoons suddenly twisted out of shape or broke in their hands – 'painful scalds and burns' were inflicted by the malicious dinner-table ghost.[16] Foolishly, a female neighbour of a haunted Aberdeenshire crofter named James Wiley decided one night in 1825 to engage the spirit in a tug-of-war with Wylie's bedclothes. She held them down with all her might, and challenged the spook to whip them away. Instead, it picked up a pail of water and threw it over her head.[17] A French polt of 1615 once broke a flask full of rosewater with a stone – but, before the liquid could fall to the floor, it was cheekily carried up into the air and splashed down over the lady of the house, to drench her. The puckish prankster, thought to be a fairy by its victims, also forcibly blacked-up someone's face with a tin of polish; not terribly PC.[18]

Another thoroughly slapstick spirit was the Naples poltergeist of 1696–97, which haunted a young Hieronymite novice named Carlo Maria Vulcano. On one occasion, it is said Carlo and his uncle knelt before the altar after Mass only to find the polt had stitched their cassocks below the knees to the altar-cloth. When they arose, they dragged the cloth with them, upsetting the altar – much to the amusement of all present. Even ordinary members of the Italian public were not safe. When people came into church hoping to see some of the amazing supernatural spectacles which had become so commonplace during ceremonies, the entity bound their legs to balusters so that, when they turned around to leave, they fell flat on their faces.[19] The *festum stultorum* had been successfully reborn!

* * * * *

Slapstick is generally characterised as being a largely innocent form of humour. No swearing, no sex, no risqué references. Early silent comedies can seem quite safe, even quaint, to modern tastes. Perhaps the worst you'll get is a quick flash of someone's bloomers – something which poltergeists, too, have engineered from time to time. The Canadian Amherst poltergeist once unbuttoned a small boy's clothes and tore them off, for example,[20] little Virginia Campbell's pyjama bottoms were pulled down and her nightdress lifted by invisible hands at Sauchie,[21] there is the case of a man who had his buttons suddenly vanish from his shirt on the driveway of his haunted home one day, letting it all hang out,[22] and the maid-servant Emma Davies at Wem once had all the stitches from her apron undone followed by the buttons on her dress being wrenched away, exposing her knickers to all,[23] but none of these events, if captured on film, would really merit an '18' certificate.

Many palates nowadays prefer their humour to be more near the bone, even actively offensive in its nature. So do many poltergeists. As a tester for how you may react to the next section, see what you think of the following image. A young girl is being raped, apparently by an invisible entity. Her boyfriend, naturally, is outraged. Trying to save her, he strikes out at the filthy fiend with a chair – but it is incorporeal, so the chair passes straight through the ghost and the would-be saviour ends up whacking his panicking lover with the heavy item of furniture.[24] Supposedly, this actually happened. It definitely has an element of slapstick to it; but, somehow, I can't quite see the Three Stooges or the Marx Brothers being willing to participate in the scene.

The Bell Witch liked to tie the shoelaces of its victim, Betsy Bell, together, like an invisible Beano character.

IV

Sick Jokes

All in the best possible taste!

Kenny Everett

Poltergeists, just like people, can sometimes exhibit a rather warped sense of what is funny. The 1998 Humpty Doo poltergeist of Australia took great delight in taunting a dead man's friends about the horrible, fiery nature of his demise in a car-crash earlier that year.[1] What began as a simple case of lithobolia developed a more sinister tone when messages scrawled on walls, or spelled out with Scrabble tiles and piles of pebbles, started using words like 'FIRE', 'SKIN', 'CAR', 'HELP' and 'TROY', the latter being the (misspelled) name of the friend who had perished. The ghost's victims, perhaps perceptively, thought the polt had picked up on their grief about Trouy's death, and was simply impersonating his spirit falsely as a rather tasteless prank. Furious, the housemates performed their own impromptu exorcism, walking through the house shouting out such un-priestly things as 'You're not Trouy, you piss-weak bastard. Why don't you just FUCK OFF!' whereupon all references to the dead man immediately ceased.

An equally insensitive Irish spirit of 1916 was reported to police by a distraught farmer. It was, he said, 'wrecking my house' and, worst of all, had 'flung a bottle of ink' over his youngest child as he lay dying in his bed. As the youth's health declined, the disturbances grew stronger; the day prior to his demise, butter was stolen from the kitchen churn and thrown against the ceiling 'ten feet high.'[2] Harry Price tells us of similarly disrespectful disturbances affecting the family of a Mrs Ethel Wilkinson, who lived as tenants in an old mansion at Walton-on-Thames between 1894 and 1911. This house was owned by a 'Mrs X'. When this woman died, 'a merry peal of bells' rang out at the local church during her funeral. Calling upon the Wilkinsons later, the woman's sons revealed that 'No human hand had pulled the ropes'. The sons were easily believed. Once before, the Wilkinsons had been awoken in the night by that exact same 'merry peal' on the church-bells; it turned out Mrs X had been taken ill that very hour.[3] Something in the house didn't like her...

The most well-known case of a poltergeist delighting in a death is that of the Bell Witch, the entity behind a notorious Tennessee haunting beginning in 1817. This spook supposedly killed the head of the household it plagued, John Bell, via poisoning; in place of his usual medicine, it JOTTled up a smoky vial of liquid which he accidentally drank from, killing him, so the legend goes (and it is indeed merely a legend; early accounts just say the spirit apported a 'vial of poison' down the chimney and *threatened* to kill Bell by pouring it into the family cooking-pot, rather than *actually* doing so[4]). When a single drop of this liquid was subsequently given to a cat for testing, the animal died in mere seconds. Poor old Bell, for whom the Witch had a pathological hatred, couldn't even enjoy his funeral in peace. No sooner had his grave had been filled with earth than the Witch began bawdily singing, from out of thin-air:

Row me up some brandy, O,
Row row, row row,
Row me up some brandy, O,
Row me up some more.[5]

It seemed the Witch wished to convene an impromptu toast, in celebration; some equally sick human souls acted the same when Mrs Thatcher died.

*****

Some taboos poltergeists break are so taboo that they are very rarely even mentioned. How many of us know about the delicate issue of racism among ghosts, for example? The Bell Witch, we are told, once uttered the following choice phrase during its reign of terror – 'I despise to smell a nigger, the scent makes me sick'[6] – yet I've seen precious little reference to the fact, even in specialist literature. The murder it supposedly committed, fine – but its use of racist language? Taboo, even to most supernaturalists. The Witch was an inveterate racist, actively colluding in the punishment of the Bell family's slaves. A young black houseboy called Harry had the sleep-disrupting duty of lighting the Bells' fires for them before daybreak. However, he began getting up late, and the Witch vowed to teach him a lesson. When John Bell was scolding the lad for his failings, the Witch interrupted his criticisms with the phrase 'Hold on old Jack ... I will attend to this nigger!' With that, she seized him invisibly by the scruff of the neck and 'flailed him unmercifully.' Harry was never late again.[7]

The Witch constantly asserted that black people smelled; she point-blank refused to haunt the Bells' slave-cabins because of the alleged stench. This led to the mother of the household, Lucy, having a rather unusual idea. She got an eighteen-year-old slave-girl, Anky – 'a real Negro, so to speak, exuberant with that pungent aromatic' – to hide under her bed to scare the spook away as a kind of human skunk. Lucy's plan didn't work; as soon as the Witch manifested, it discerned the nature of the trick instantly. 'There is a damn nigger in the house; it's Ank; I smell her under the bed and she's got to get out,' the polt shouted. A sound 'like that of a man clearing his throat, hawking and spitting vehemently' came from beneath the bed and Anky shot out, 'like a log starting down a hill', with her head and face 'literally covered' with a horrible foam-like white spittle, before running away wailing. As she did so, the Witch openly expressed its disgust: 'Lord Jesus I won't get over that smell in a month!'[8]

Another prejudiced polt haunted a house on Russian Hill overlooking San Francisco Bay in 1856. Here, the white inhabitants were not harmed (rather, disembodied hands cured their toothache by stroking them[9]) but the domestic servant – a 'poor darky' – was dragged out of bed and dashed down into the floor outside his room one night. When the white folk went to investigate, the servant was found to have a 'severe contusion of the eye' and a 'violent bump on the cheek.' His master seemed to find this all rather amusing, professing 'much sympathy for his poor servant, but yet more merriment at the remembrance of his ludicrous adventures' and jokingly regaling his guests with jolly anecdotes about the fellow having once 'been hurled through a French window in presence of the whole family' and boasting that 'it was quite a common occurrence to see him thrown hither and thither with the facility of an india-rubber ball'.[10] He doesn't sound too sympathetic to me. We should note these stories hail from the pre-Civil War slave-owning period and reflect then-prevailing social attitudes; maybe the tales weren't terribly taboo then, but they certainly are now.

*****

One major purpose of the poltergeist, imaginatively speaking, may well be to break taboo; its occasional sick humour could be a coded expression of this. But what is the point of them doing so? The anthropologist Laura Makarius showed how many primitive societies believed that magical and occult power could be gained from the deliberate breaking of taboo. In such societies, she says:

> ... forbidden acts are committed for the same basic reasons for which they are forbidden. That is why they express themselves only if they are [first] suppressed ... The deliberate violation of taboo constitutes one of the deepest contradictions of primitive life. Its purpose is the obtainment of magical power.[11]

The lack of popular reporting of the Bell Witch's racism now begins to make a kind of sense; by virtue of it, a taboo (that against racism) is upheld. Thereby, whenever such a taboo actually is transgressed, the act seems more powerful – more Tricksterish. When we read that the Enfield poltergeist was a rabid anti-Semite, like so many living in North London, we may therefore recoil from its anti-Jewish utterances even more.[12] We do, however, definitely *react* to it all; and it may be that, in doing so, we help lend the poltergeist even more power, whether literally or in an imaginative sense, I leave it to you to decide.

The sacred Trickster clowns of many cultures would often perform sick, taboo-busting acts in public in order to enhance their magical powers. (Mike Fisher under CC 2.0)

The explicit breaking of taboo is one of the main sources of human comedy. It cracks the usual mould in life, and releases often extreme reactions, whether of shock, disgust or laughter. In *The Trickster and the Paranormal*, George P. Hansen discusses the Pueblo Indians of New Mexico and the outrageous public ceremonies of their clowns, a breed of Tricksterish magic-workers who masturbated and sodomised each other in front of the whole tribe. These taboo-busting actions, supposedly, increased their capacity to later perform miracles. They are also, to my eyes, quite funny. According to Hansen, 'I find it great fun to playfully recount these examples and observe the reactions to them.'[13] It does not take too much imagination to work out what the average reaction would be; some will laugh, but many others will be disgusted. According to Hansen, however, 'The connection between the scatological and the magical should not be overlooked.'[14] Indeed not; as such, the following section shall be fairly graphic.

V

Toilet Humour

When a society has to resort to the lavatory for its humour,
the writing is on the wall.

Alan Bennett

Nowadays, scatological matters are generally considered highly inappropriate subjects for polite conversation, but things were not always thus. According to George P. Hansen:

> In times past, and in other cultures, clowns, buffoons, and other Tricksters were recognised and given their due, sometimes even places of honour. In the modern world, they are mere shadows of their former selves. They are now forced to be more socially respectable, more restrained; today many of their activities are suppressed. We no longer comprehend their messages.[1]

Ritual clowns once ate their own shit as part of their obscene public ceremonies so the rest of us wouldn't have to, the idea being that society would be cleansed and made holy again by their deliberate acts of coprophagic filth. However, Hansen is correct; our modern, mainstream comedy 'heroes', the most visible forms of Trickster in this current media age, tend to be somewhat sanitised, breaking real taboos only verbally, if at all. Occasionally, little-known amateurs at open-mike events will bravely conjure up the spirit of Dada, as did, according to comedian Stewart Lee, a performer he once saw who 'squatted naked over a plate of chips and then shat on it',[2] but it is noticeable that Lee himself did not perform such an act when he later got his own TV show.

It is now left to the poltergeist to reacquaint the sacred with the profane, which may be why so many have played tricks involving faecal matter. We have already mentioned Janet shitting in the sink at Enfield – but the spirit there also wrote the word 'SHIT' *in* shit, on the bathroom wall.[3] Faeces was further found smeared behind taps, floating in bathwater and squiggled across tiles, 'just like someone scribbling'.[4] One of the first signs of the Canadian Dagg poltergeist of 1899 was 'a long streak of filth' spread across the floor of the haunted house 'from back to front', after which turds unappetisingly materialised in food and beds.[5] During a 1935 haunting in Madras, India, human waste began plopping next to the plates of people eating their meals – very off-putting.[6] The Sandfeld poltergeist of 1722 screamed the words 'Your health!' then swilled a tankard full of crap into the house.[7] A Russian fairy-spook dwelling inside an oven, from which it threw cow manure at a visiting priest, was similarly unhygienic.[8]

A Lutheran theologian named Professor Schuppart was plagued by poltergeistery between 1703 and 1708, with swords and knives being lobbed at him and his wife, and stones and pieces of shit materialising inside his pupils' satchels.[9] A case from Dortmund during 1713 centred almost exclusively around shite, large quantities of waste frequently being transported into the unclean house from the garden's 'necessarium'; for variety, sometimes objects were thrown from the building into the cesspit instead.[10] When it finally left, the spook mockingly announced its departure by crying 'The end, the end today of mischief and stench!'[11]

There are pissing polts, too. In 1996 a Roz Wolseley-Charles told *Fortean Times* magazine (a long-running British publication devoted to continuing the fine work of Charles Fort) about her haunted house where 'odd happenings abound', none odder than the pools of piss that kept on appearing in covered pans and casserole dishes, or flooding out her cooker. The urine was professionally determined to come from 'a carnivorous animal', probably 'a badger or large hedgehog'.[12] There were also piss puddles at Enfield. An 'unusually large and foul-smelling' one was bottled and sent off for analysis. It came from a cat.[13] In certain cultures, toilets are considered stereotypical dwelling places of evil spirits; in the Islamic world, it is traditional to say a protective blessing to rid a toilet of any lurking invisible *djinn* when entering the bathroom.[14]

*****

We can easily see the scatological element here – but where is the sacred part? Well, I'm not about to go all poetic over skid-marks being found in a North London bathroom or turds in a schoolboy's satchel, but there is a certain magic to be found in such accounts, isn't there, in the marvellous implausibility of it all? As with many dung-related Trickster legends, the shit is in some sense fertiliser, and the result of its spreading a world creatively reborn. When in one North American legend the Chippewa Trickster Wenebojo transforms pickings from his anus into tasty lumps of tobacco – a substance which, for the Chippewa, possessed a sacred ritual function – he magically turns his own dirty bum-stuff into holy items.[15] To the academic William J. Hynes, Tricksters 'find the lewd in the sacred and the sacred in the lewd, and [so grow] new life from both.'[16]

An old Yoruba saying holds that the Trickster Eshu 'turns shit into treasure'. How so? There is a sense in which such Trickster-gods once acted as an imaginative laxative for any over-fossilised society trapped within a state of excessive stasis. In his analysis of Eshu, the Trickster-expert Robert D. Pelton argues that in repressive societies where 'order becomes a prison', it is as if 'the passages of life are clogged' just as surely as with chronic constipation. Eventually, the pressure for necessary change will build until such a point that 'as the myths say, all becomes as fluid as water, as destructive as fire, and violence

The Chippewa Trickster Wenebojo/ Manobozo, who would pick brown bits from his bum and transform them into tasty tobacco.

shatters peace' in a disastrously explosive bout of civilizational diarrhoea. By keeping society's imaginative anal passage permanently well-lubricated, says Pelton, a Trickster like Eshu seeks instead 'to open these passages of life by transforming them into *limina*', or border-crossing outlets, which is a 'way of turning ordure into order' in the shape of a new, more modified way of looking at the world that allows more gradual, beneficial change to occur.[17]

When the baby Hermes is picked up by Apollo in the *Homeric Hymn* and accused of stealing his cattle, Hermes' initial response is to fart and dribble shit all down his brother's toga; take *that*, hard-line Apollonic outlook! For Pelton, the Trickster's 'scatological bent' is presented in myth as being this kind of raucous joke, as jokes, being inherently illogical in nature, imply that in this life anything is possible – even, ultimately, a whole new way of living. Pelton sums it up thus:

> For the pre-modern mind ... human life is seen to be so porous, so vulnerable to forces that will dissolve it, like so much food turned into faeces, that only carefully maintained social structures can arrest and control this wasting process. However, these structures too become clogged with waste, and thus the Trickster lays hold of them and shakes the stuffing [i.e. the impacted shit] out of them. He celebrates life's porosity, revealing its open-endedness to be hilarious [thereby showing that] anything is *possible*; even faeces can be turned into treasure.[18]

A tale is told about the Tibetan Trickster Uncle Tompa, who becomes the malicious advisor to a Buddhist king. Shitting onto a pile of white lime, Tompa pushes his turd around with a stick until it turns as white as the clouds. Then, he writes a message to the king on it, and drops it onto him through a skylight. Awaking to find the mysterious white turd on his lap, the illiterate king calls for Uncle Tompa to read out what it says. Tompa tells his boss it is a pile of holy 'Miracle Shit', and recites his own misleading message: 'WOODEN-HANDLED AND WHITE-BOTTOMED, THAT IS THE SHIT FROM HEAVEN. HE IS THE LUCKIEST RULER WHEN IT DROPS ON

HIS LAP!' Uncle Tompa advises the king he must eat a lump of the foul turd to gain its full blessing. Awe-struck, the duped monarch smears Uncle Tompa's white-frosted chocolate all over his head, swallows a big chunk, then sets the rest up on an altar to be worshipped as a sacred relic – proof that, in Trickster-legends, dung is often only one short step away from holiness.[19]

The now largely ignored link between the scatological and the divine is illustrated in the thirteenth-century life-story of Blessed Christina of Stommeln. Each saint has their own cross to bear; in Christina's case, it was made of ordure. Peter of Dacia, a Swedish Dominican, recorded her case, noting that for weeks on end the Devil taunted her with poltergeistic 'deluges of indescribable filth' from thin air, splattering anyone who tried to visit, including Peter himself. When an attempt was made to exorcise Satan, a violent bang blew out candles and drenched the exorcist in shit; the most explosive fart on record. Sulphurous phenomena followed Christina to church, with a dirty brown rain cascading onto disgusted onlookers. Once, as she sat praying, a 'filthy, stinking bag' landed at Christina's feet. Opening it, she found a fine collection of reeking turds … together with a stolen prayer-book, miraculously unblemished.[20]

One of the Devil's favourite polt-like tricks to play upon that saintly nineteenth-century Frenchman the Curé d'Ars was to cover his favourite pictures of the Virgin Mary and St Philomena with what is euphemistically termed 'mud and filth' until their features 'were no longer distinguishable.'[21] Similar blasphemies occurred during an Indian haunting of 1920, during which a polt repeatedly smeared cow-dung and ashes over protective crosses which had been daubed across the infested house's walls by the spook's Christian victim, as if to mock his wayward choice of religion in the land of Hinduism (where, of course, cows and their dung are considered literally sacred).[22]

Martin Luther, the Protestant reformer and another *polter geyster* victim, had chronic constipation, coming to believe that a devil (he saw poltergeists and devils as one and the same thing[23]) was living up his arsehole and stopping stools emerging. Whenever he successfully managed to have a dump he celebrated a

Precisely the kind of filthy demon you might expect to have spent its days tormenting Blessed Christina of Stommeln.

small victory for God over the forces of evil, writing in a fabulously unhinged way that Satan should 'Wipe your mouth on *that* and take a hearty bite!'[24] He even believed it was possible to exorcise evil spirits simply by farting on them, although he didn't recommend the procedure as it could prove 'dangerous'.[25]

The impurities of faeces and the purities of God were once happily reconciled in the story of one of history's more obscure and scatological saints. In the sixth century, Saint Simeon Salus travelled to the Syrian city of Emesa where he became a 'Holy Fool', simulating madness in public. He found a dead dog abandoned on a dung-heap which he tied to his belt and dragged along after him as a free pet. Like Jesus, he consorted openly with prostitutes and, quite unlike Jesus, shat publicly in the marketplace and deliberately ate large quantities of beans so as to cause himself massive flatulence. Once, he invaded a church and extinguished all the candles before commandeering the pulpit and throwing nuts at women. Salus simulated a Trickster-like form of scatological madness expertly; yet he also possessed powers of clairvoyance and telepathy and could painlessly handle hot coals and magically multiply food, or so the Holy Church would have us believe.[26]

Nityananda of Ganeshpuri, a twentieth-century Indian mystic, was known for producing miraculous healing, possessing the gift of prophecy, and being able to control the weather. He also used to wait for sacred cows to shit near him, grab dollops of dung in his hands, and eat it like chocolate ice-cream. Once, he smeared cow-pat all over his body, offering more to his horrified followers as a kind of 'sweet'.[27] A century beforehand, Sri Ramakrishna, a Hindu holy-man, transgressed social rules by dressing hermaphrodite-like as a woman, worshipping his own genitals as gods, and using his hair as a mop to clean floors with. He identified himself so excessively with the monkey-god Hanuman, swinging through trees and subsisting on a simian diet, that, so the legend goes, his coccyx inexplicably grew until he was left proudly possessing a small pink tail![28]

The significance here lies in terms of what anthropologists term 'binary oppositions', or direct opposites – 'As' and 'not-As', in Aristotelian terms – and their absolute subversion, as with Marcel Duchamp's impossible open-and-shut door. In these tales, shit becomes food, man dresses as woman, human becomes monkey. Likewise with the poltergeist, the dead live, gravity becomes anti-gravity and physical barriers like walls become open doorways for the entrance of paranormally-hurled turds. The impossible becomes Tricksterishly possible. Consider one recent British haunting in which phantom smells were repeatedly detected; scents perceived by the man of the household to be of perfume, but by his female partner to be of dog-shit.[29] 'A' and 'not-A' again concurrently, I think you'll find.

*****

Another particularly striking transgressor of binary oppositions was an eighteenth-century French Jansenist mystic known as the 'Eater of Ordure' who, after publicly eating shit, was apparently able to vomit up fresh milk in its stead.[30] Are shit and food just two variegated expressions of the same thing? Ultimately, yes; all food is shit waiting to happen. I recall an old *Private Eye* cartoon, in which a doctor tells his patient: 'It's bad news … Your stool samples show an excessive amount of sugar-content. But, on the plus-side, they taste delicious!' If you laugh at that, then you are laughing, like Trickster, at the demolition of the boundary between binary opposites, of the shitty, liminal revenge of the excluded middle.

Distinct from pure victims like Christina of Stommeln, people like Salus, Ramakrishna and the Eater of Ordure are depicted in the stories told about them to have been able to direct paranormal phenomena rather than being their passive sufferers. Their deliberate taboo transgression allowed them, somehow, to control such phenomena to a certain degree – whether in reality or simply in myth, I make no comment. As Laura Makarius noted in relation to primitive magicians, sometimes loss of control can ironically be seen as being the *creator* of control, as when occultists perform taboo-transgressive acts, often sexual in nature, as part of their rituals. Presumably, the relationship is an acausal one; transgression of sexual and scatological barriers purportedly producing, by some inexplicable relation of sympathy, something else that transgresses *logical* barriers. I am not actually suggesting here that defecating in the street and then eating it will allow you to gain control over the supernatural (although please feel free to experiment!), merely pointing out some possible imaginative interpretations of some very strange – and perhaps very tall – tales.

* * * * *

These narratives are undoubtedly laughable, but this should not automatically disqualify them from serious discussion; and yet it generally does. Few if any parapsychologists have ever made a detailed study of such embarrassing matters, presumably because they *are* so embarrassing. And yet if they happened, they happened; they deserve our attention just as much as anything else. However, if you wish to establish the poltergeist as being a definitely real phenomenon (as many writers on the topic undoubtedly do) then, like William G. Roll, you will naturally play down the more outré elements of the subject and concentrate instead upon less overtly implausible things, like the psychokinetic movement of small objects. Tell a sceptic about a ghost that shat itself and see what their reaction is; collect a ghost-turd and try and present it to someone as such and await your rapid collection by the men in white (or brown) coats.

Gef the Talking Mongoose once went to great pains to demonstrate he was not in fact a polt but a real flesh-and-blood animal. When Nandor Fodor sent Gef a publication entitled *Bulletin of Poltergeists* to read, he replied sniffily, 'I am not like one of those.' Referring to another investigator then present on the spot, Gef huffed 'I want to show Captain Macdonald that I am an animal.' To do so, he 'performed one of his natural functions' and showed it to the man. I'm sure he was delighted; Plop Goes the Weasel.[31] Another time, Gef ejected something from his other end after deviating from his usual diet of biscuits, chocolate and bacon. According to Mr Irving: 'Once he cried: 'Jim, Jim, I am sick.' We heard him vomiting. In the morning, under our bed, we found half-digested carrots. We had no carrots in the house.'[32] Neither Gef's vomit nor his shit was preserved for posterity, though. Half-digested carrots and animal-stools are not even remotely conclusive evidence for the reality of ghosts. In fact, they are *comically* not so.

* * * * *

And so, we brush these things aside. But should we? Consider the unlikely story of Carlotta Moran who, it is alleged, was raped by a poltergeist throughout the 1970s. Carlotta was raised by a pair of borderline Puritans who taught her nothing of sexual relations, or the female menstrual cycle; when she had her first period she was nonplussed. Ashamed, Carlotta buried her blood-stained knickers in the garden each month. Such an extreme denial of bodily functions was, claimed the writer Stan Gooch, central to her subsequent claims of supernatural rape. Eventually, the rapist stopped being invisible. It was 7 feet tall, green, Chinese and very muscular, with large veins popping out of its neck. According to Gooch, this demon was a horrific personification of Carlotta's repressed sexuality: '[the incubus] was in fact a sort of giant penis, the swollen veins in the neck very much recalling the erect male organ ... the sexual symbolism of Carlotta's vision, as well as its actual behaviour, implicates sexuality as a major force – perhaps *the* major force – in paranormal phenomena.'[33]

To Gooch, the denial of bodily functions – sex and menstruation – and their symbolic power can lead to nothing less than a penile green nightmare appearing. But why is scatology such a powerful taboo in the first place? According to Mary Douglas, in her classic work *Purity and Danger*, it is because among primitive peoples the human body is often a metaphor for what she calls a 'bounded system', like society itself. The body's boundaries can come to represent the boundaries of any given society; and bodily fluids, which break these liminal boundaries, are thus viewed as potentially dangerous.[34] Just so long as the body's boundaries are kept intact then, just like with the borders of a state, people are safe; but such barriers, once breached, are transformed instantly from a form of protection into major sources of risk, like holes in the Great Wall of China. Says Douglas, 'all margins are dangerous; if they are pulled this way or that the shape of fundamental experience is altered.' Substances like blood, urine and faeces, which seep out from bodily boundaries, therefore become powerful symbols of the potentially dangerous reordering of society itself.[35]

However, sometimes borders can be deliberately broken only to subsequently be remade again, different in form, yet stronger than ever, as when Eshu makes turds become treasure. This is what the Trickster teaches us, and the inherent imaginative power to be found in the breaking of scatological taboo is why those human Tricksters, holy ritual clowns, existed too; as Laura Makarius said, taboo, if *acknowledged* rather than repressed, is made less hazardous. The ritualised breaking of taboo can thus act as a form of 'safe release', as when public sodomy or turd-chomping was once supposed to produce magic; but the refusal to acknowledge it at all seems in equal parts dangerous and dull. Scatology, the ancient tribes recognised, is one of the most powerful and potentially regenerative sources of all magic, and the poltergeist reminds us of this fact through some of his more disgusting tricks – symbolically, anyway. I fully admit that, viewed up-close in a poltergeist victim's own unclean home, Susa-Nö-o's fertiliser would just look like a load of old shit.

VI

Absurdity of Location

Geography is everywhere these days.

G. V. Desani

Poltergeists often spring up in situations and locations which appear designed to provoke little more than laughter; sometimes, *simply by existing in a certain way*, polts can act to undermine belief in their occurrence even more than by not occurring at all, rather a neat little paradox. Let us remain with our recent theme to illustrate this fact, and examine the surprisingly common motif of haunted toilets. One such unquiet loo belonged to the Goodyear family of Leeds, who lived, punningly, in a place called Leek Street. Despite repeated investigations by plumbers in 1974, nothing could be found physically wrong with the thing and yet it kept on re-flushing itself repeatedly of its own volition, eventually flooding the entire house, ruining carpets. A ghost was blamed.[1]

That same year the Raine Engineering Co. Ltd, of Gateshead, also found one of their lavatories flushing spontaneously. Grown men were afraid to go for a wee in broad daylight while the firm's cleaner, a Mrs Elizabeth Liddle (whose name, given her profession, sounds like a form of rhyming slang), claimed to have had an uncanny experience in the cubicles one morning: 'I heard an awful scream like a boy falling to his death – it was so eerie I couldn't sleep for nights.' The firm's boss, James Morgan, was unimpressed: 'This is awful – the whole thing is ridiculous. If these people are Spiritualists they should do it in their own time, not in the work's time. We have enough problems as it is.'[2]

A poltergeist infesting the King's Arms pub in Croydon in 1980 also liked to linger in the lavatories, which were often found unnaturally ice cold. Once, a stream of water shot out of a urinal, flooding the floor. Due to the urinal's specific construction, this should have been impossible. Again, plumbers could find nothing wrong.[3] Pubs have a particular propensity for this sort of thing, perhaps simply because they have so many toilets. At Yorkshire's Low Valley Arms pub in 2006, police were called to investigate the sighting of the ghost of 'an elderly woman with silvery grey hair, dressed in a white gown' with half her face missing, 'from cheekbone to jaw'. While officers were examining the premises, they were shocked to witness the toilets repeatedly flushing themselves: 'The handle was going up and down of its own accord, and the bowl filling and overflowing.'[4]

Such reports reach us from across the globe. In 1997, a woman in Nishan, India, was taken to hospital suffering from shock after claiming that a poltergeist – or perhaps a bowl-haunting *djinni* – had slapped her arse as she sat down to urinate in a public lavatory. Citizens were so alarmed that armed guards had to be placed outside the convenience.[5] In 2001, Buddhist monks were summoned to exorcise the *South China Morning Post*'s new offices in Hong Kong. Invisible spirits had taken up residence inside the women's toilets and begun breathing heavily at them as they performed their natural functions. It is hard not to laugh at the remark made by one of the monks: 'There is a strong sense of the spirits of the nether world inside. There is simply an absence of life in that room, like a vacuum.' So oppressive – or smelly – was the cubicles' atmosphere that one of the spooks hiding there apparently 'called out for help' to the lead exorcist.[6]

Another uncanny convenience was owned by an eighty-three-year-old lady named Emily Sparks, who in 2019 was forced to sleep in a Southend Travelodge on the grounds that a poltergeist haunting her home was somehow 'leeching off' her vital energy by stealing her hair and repeatedly

Ghosts haunt toilets with surprising frequency, as proved in this 1948 advert from *The Ladies' Home Journal.*

flushing her toilet after dark. The Travelodge was expensive, said Sparks, but also safe as the ghost 'couldn't work the toilet there'. The spook could certainly work the toilet at Sparks' home; it was its 'party piece'. The appliance would flush by itself for as long as three solid hours, keeping Sparks from her sleep, and would even spontaneously flush while Sparks was sat on it. In the end, Emily took to tying the toilet-handle in place overnight.[7] Some toilet-hauntings sound more sinister than comic. At South Shields, the family's bowl once filled itself up with a red liquid that appeared to be blood. Before it could be captured on film or scooped up for analysis, however, the chain flushed itself, and all trace of the blood – or whatever it may have been – was gone, to be replaced only with fresh, clear water.[8]

The most wonderfully ludicrous haunted toilet was found in the Bavarian dental surgery of the appropriately named Dr Karl Bachseitz in 1982. A rather abrupt disembodied voice began emanating initially from a spittoon in the consulting room, telling one female patient to 'Shut your mouth!' when she leant over it, and a second to 'Open your mouth wider, stupid!' When another female patient visited the dentist's toilet and sat on it, a voice boomed out from the bowl, shouting 'Move your behind, I can't see a thing!' Inevitably, it was this aspect of the case that subsequent newspaper articles focused on, one reporting the affair under the quite brilliant headline 'A Voice of Unknown Extraction'.[9]

* * * * *

The English ghost-hunter Andrew Green, in his 1973 classic *Our Haunted Kingdom*, is often held responsible for popularising the (true) idea that ghosts don't just haunt old mansions and castles but also walk abroad in less romantic locales, such as council homes and warehouses – as the paperback edition's back-cover blurb asks, 'You might expect to hear of ghosts haunting churchyards, stately homes and abbeys, but how about ghostly goings-on in a caravan? A bingo hall? A trendy boutique? Offices of the Marriage Guidance Council?'[10] A haunted caravan certainly sounds comical, but consider the unpleasant account of Jim and Susan Barker, whose mid-1950s holiday in just such a vehicle was disrupted by disembodied voices, shit and dirt being dumped over their beds, and ten gallons' worth of pig's blood pouring down through the ceiling.[11]

There is no inherent reason why caravans, supermarkets and bingo halls should not be haunted; but, when we read about a spook inhabiting the comically prosaic locale of the Tetley Tea factory in County Durham, it is hard to take it entirely seriously, particularly when the manifestations are said to include such PR-friendly events as the leaving of half-drunk cuppas in the staff kitchen and the spontaneous malfunctioning of teabag-making machines.[12] A tale of a haunted ASDA supermarket in Crawley also sounds silly, but there appear to be numerous witnesses, both staff and customers, who have experienced moving groceries, howling noises and sudden temperature-drops, as well as flickering lights and apparitions. Tell someone about flying vegetables in ASDA, however, and see how seriously they take it. Most of the stories in this chapter have their ultimate origins in tabloid newspapers and it is not too hard to guess why this might be.

The locations of some hauntings are simply ironic. In 1917–18 a British man named R. P. Jacques was busily building himself a bomb-shelter for protection against possible German zeppelin raids. It was never tested against German bombs – but it certainly provided no protection from assaults by lithobolia. Stones were thrown at Jacques whenever he was inside the supposedly safe location; he would actually have been more out of harm's way simply by standing around on the lawn above and waving his fists openly at the passing Hun.[13]

* * * * *

Other poltergeist locations are just embarrassing. In 2002, the 'Pillow Talk' sex-store in Kent became haunted by an invisible ghost. According to Alan Butler, the owner, the store used to be a brothel and the ghosts of the dead whores were causing much poltergeistic annoyance: 'Knickers and bras are removed from pegs and left littering the floor … French-maid outfits are found lying over the back of chairs and hanging from door handles.'[14]

Another haunted brothel was in Canberra, Australia, the workplace of a prostitute known to clients as 'Caressa' – we met her at the start of this book, being pestered by supernatural potatoes. Caressa was an early-bloomer, sexually-speaking. Aged nine, she began performing certain unspeakable acts upon the family dog and, by the time she was old enough, eagerly pursued a career in the sex industry. When she went off to work at the brothel, business was disrupted as her fellow-hookers repeatedly broke off relations with their clients to see objects floating around and mysteriously JOTTling in her

The kind of evocative location you would more typically expect a ghost to inhabit.

presence; the ghost's perverted tricks were preventing the girls from turning their own. Sometimes, the spook even played games of noughts and crosses with Caressa on her mirror, using lipstick. Eventually, she was forced to set up shop on her own.[15]

Interestingly, one slang term for a brothel is a 'knocking shop' – the (disputed) supposed etymology for this comes from the idea that some Victorian prostitutes operated falsely under the guise of spirit-mediums in order to account for the constant influx of strange males into their homes, who were then passed off as only wanting to hear some spirit-raps. In fact, the whore and her client would be 'knocking one another up' in another sense; in 1859, a Maidstone servant-girl named Harriet King confessed to simulating poltergeistery around her place of employment as a distraction intended to facilitate the smuggling of male clients into her room for her side-career as a hired whore.[16] Surely 'The Knocking Shop' is the name Liz Fleming should have chosen for her own polt-infested establishment?

There is no real reason why ghosts *shouldn't* haunt toilets, brothels and sex-shops, of course; indeed, that arch-Trickster the Spirit Mercurius was supposed to haunt dungheaps and sewers, and was often depicted engaged in pornographic poses like the *Kama Sutra*-type 'menus of service' that used to appear in old Roman brothels.[17] It's just that, by doing so, polts provide yet more fodder for those who wish to claim, volubly, that they don't exist. Actually, this is quite an illogical attitude; sex-shops and toilets are just as 'scientific' places as abandoned castles and graveyards. All contain electrons; gravity works in them all. I wouldn't like to use a toilet where it didn't. But, in this facetious comment we have the root of the whole problem: humour. I think there is an entire school of poltergeist humour based around the notion of ghosts deliberately undermining their own plausibility. Time and again, ridiculous evidence appears, apparently reliable evidence disappears and, overall, we are left with abortive investigations which sceptics would simply snort at.

The alchemical trickster Mercurius, who would sometimes live in dungheaps.

VII

Hide-and-Seek

Where there is mystery, there is power.

Charles de Gaulle

Poltergeists do not like to be seen – after all, they *are* invisible. When Sydney's *Channel 7 News* sent a team of reporters to the haunted house at Humpty Doo in 1998 they saw many objects flying around but were unable to capture any on film, with cameramen always facing the wrong way at the crucial moment. So, they left the house empty, locking five running cameras inside. These recorded precisely zilch until the 'battery out' alarms triggered. Then, as one man took in new batteries, the rest of the crew, out drinking on the patio, would hear loud noises as objects were thrown around inside with nothing there to catch it all. Written messages – 'NO CAMERAS', 'NO TV' and 'PIG CAMERA' – appeared on walls and floors to taunt them, with barely any usable footage retrieved from the whole futile exercise.[1]

Similar camera-shyness was encountered in a Seattle home known as the 'Bothell Hell House', where much extreme poltergeistery erupted during the mid-2010s. Parapsychologists' video-cameras would be turned around to face uselessly at walls, or simply disappear entirely, never to be seen again. Voices were caught on-tape, however, saying things like 'This is the spirits. Turn off [the cameras]', 'It's a camera. I think it's a camera', 'Night-cam' and 'Image-recording device'. Once, a female voice said 'There's nothing to be proved,' and there certainly wasn't. An alarm was triggered by invisible footsteps running past it, as if something had been drawn to the device by curiosity; having triggered the trap this once, however, the ghost never repeated its error. As one investigator said, it was 'almost as though the entity had learned what would happen when it passed through the beams and didn't want to make that mistake again', rather like a coyote – or indeed Coyote – learning how to avoid a hunter's future traps.[2] A TV crew called in to probe the case exploited their lack of usable footage as a platform to accuse the man at the centre of events, Keith Linder, of hoaxing, leading to such public ridicule that his lover left him, a classic example of a poltergeist's behaviour reinforcing the liminal status of its victims.[3]

228

When Graham Morris, a *Daily Mirror* photographer, visited the Enfield poltergeist, he was hit by a paranormally-thrown piece of Lego. He thought he had captured this on camera, but upon examination of the negative the Lego was nowhere to be seen: 'It must have been somewhere in the 10 per cent of the room not covered by his wide-angled lens.'[4] Devices commonly malfunction suspiciously at the critical moment; one investigator found batteries in her tape-recorder had been mysteriously switched back-to-front by a spook, meaning she couldn't get the loud bangs it made on tape.[5] As always, the Enfield poltergeist went one further. When a substantial quantity of video equipment was brought into the house, it angrily roared 'GET THAT SHIT OUT OF HERE' repeatedly.[6]

It is not hard to deduce what a sceptic's response would be to all this – 'Oh, how terribly convenient.' I agree – it *is* convenient. It is very convenient indeed for persons who wish airily to dismiss such matters. What would such sceptics make of the account of the photographer Fred Shannon, who found the only way to capture a telephone which kept on flying around during the Tina Resch haunting was to point his camera down, gaze away from Tina and snap a picture whenever he caught a flash of sudden movement? Sometimes he would get a shot of the phone as it flew past the telekinetic teen, but often he would be too late and it would already have fallen to the floor.[7] Photos of telephones lying on floors are not, however, evidence of anything.

Poltergeists sometimes have distinctly violent reactions to recording equipment. Recall the case of Carlotta Moran, who was being raped by a giant green Chinese ghost-penis. It is said two parapsychologists decided to build a replica of Carlotta's bedroom inside their university lab, install her in it and attempt to trap the entity there with liquid helium. When the ghost appeared, it purportedly smashed up all of their equipment, including the cameras. Allegedly, several university personnel actually glimpsed the phallic incubus at work, but what little film could be salvaged from the event showed absolutely nothing.[8]

The Trickster at Skinwalker Ranch possessed an equally violent-yet-elusive quality. When a team of parascientists set up a series of enclosures containing guard-dogs to act as natural 'biosensors', they found Hermes was outsmarting them. Compound doors would open of their own accord leaving the dogs free to escape, in spite of all the padlocks and wires used to secure them, and the dogs would often get loose 'by unknown means'.[9] When CCTV was installed, the situation worsened. Cameras were set up overlooking a pasture-field, mounted 15 feet high on telegraph poles, their wiring secured with industrial-strength duct tape and PVC tubing. Nonetheless, one morning this arrangement was found totally destroyed. The duct tape had been elaborately unwound from its tubing, whereupon the wires had been unceremoniously yanked from three of the surveillance cameras, all at 8.30 p. m. the previous night. Fortunately, another undamaged camera had been pointing directly at the other three throughout this same time period – at last, whatever was lurking on the Gormans' ranch and killing their cattle would be revealed! Sadly not. The relevant footage showed … nothing. You could see the red lights on the bottom of the ruined cameras suddenly lose power at 8.30 p. m., and yet, in spite of the wiring clearly having been sabotaged, the footage didn't show anything whatsoever dismantling it.[10]

It is an amusing fact that the American SPR once developed an expensive-sounding 'mobile unit' for poltergeist investigation, a kind of real-life ECTO-1 from *Ghostbusters* – but they hardly used it, because they were afraid that, if they ever took it out to visit the scene of a real poltergeist infestation, the ghost might smash all their expensive recording-equipment up![11] Given events at Skinwalker Ranch, perhaps they were right to keep their vehicle locked safely in its garage.

*****

Another notorious aspect of poltergeist-shyness is how the items which fly around or materialise suddenly are very rarely seen actually *initiating* such actions. I could find relatively few counter-examples, although three were very interesting. Firstly, during the Eleonore Zugun case, apports were seen by the investigator Countess Zoë Wassilko-Serecki appearing initially as 'dark grey shadows', or 'holes in the world', one of which 'glided down slowly in front of the window and not straight but zig-zag [fashion]'. Upon closer examination, these proved to be ordinary household objects, which faded into more solid being from their temporary shadowy form. According to the Countess, she 'had always the impression' that such apports were 'only again submitted to the normal laws of the physical world' when each was 'perfectly itself again'.[12] The second case occurred during a 1955–57 poltergeist infestation at Mayanup, Australia, when one witness observed how a flying stone 'took shape' in the sky above her, a sight she compared to 'a kaleidoscope: a few jerks this way and that and it was there'.[13] Thirdly, during the Indian Poona affair, one victim successfully managed to train her eyes to see the JOTTling of coins from nowhere:

> On several occasions in broad daylight we ... saw coins fall among us from above ... At first we could not always see the coins in mid-air, but merely saw them fall, being startled by the contact of the coin with the floor. Soon, however, we were able to observe more closely, and actually saw the money appear in mid-air.[14]

More typically such processes remain stubbornly unobservable. Apparitions themselves are often described as being seen only 'if you relaxed your eyes' or tried to catch them 'in your peripheral vision'.[15] In horror fiction, ghosts are stereotypically spied liminally through the corner of one's eyes, and so it is with poltergeistery in general. One classic case was that of the haunted carpenter's shop near Hull where, as we saw earlier, pieces of wood began flying around of their own accord during 1849. A non-witness on the spot wrote to the SPR describing the polt's coyness:

> Nobody ever saw a missile at the time it started. One would have said that they could not be perceived until they had travelled at least six inches from their starting-point ... the missiles only moved when nobody was looking

and when they were least expected. Now and again one of us would watch a piece of wood closely for a good number of minutes and the piece would not budge; but if the observer stopped looking at it, this same piece would jump on us.[16]

Another good non-eye-witness report came from Thornton Heath, where one investigator talked of wineglasses suddenly shattering in highly elusive fashion:

Mrs Forbes ... was holding her glass by the stem ... when there was a loud noise which can only be described as a 'ping', and the next noise half a second later was the glass breaking in the air three feet over my head ... I at once ... handed her an exactly similar glass to the first ... I watched it intently and exactly ten minutes later there was another 'ping' quite as loud as the first and this was followed by the glass breaking on the floor at our feet. Although I know I never took my eyes off her hand and the glass, I also know I did not see it go. The first indication I had was the noise in the first place. It would seem as though it went so quickly it deceived the eye.[17]

Nandor Fodor, beset by similar frustrations, positioned a mirror on Mrs Forbes' stove so he could keep sneaky watch through it upon the kitchen table, where he had placed glasses as bait. Fifteen minutes later, a milk bottle smashed down on the stove from above – falling deliberately *behind* the mirror, so its trajectory could not properly be seen.[18] According to Fodor, the smashing of the milk bottle 'seemed to suggest that the placing of the mirror on the gas stove had been taken for a challenge. It restricted the poltergeist's field of invisibility, but it did not diminish its activities.'[19] In other words, it played hide-and-seek with him.

Another excellent account of a shy spook comes from Harry Price, who spoke of his attempts to observe Eleonore Zúgun's vampiric Dracu at work thus:

... during my investigation ... I saw a cushion on a chair *begin* to move, then it appeared to hesitate, and then it slipped quietly to the floor. It was just as though the cushion knew I was looking at it and decided not to make a real flight ... In the room was a bookcase with open shelves filled with books. Time after time ... we would stare at them for ten minutes, hoping to see them move ... the moment we took our eyes off them, the books were again disarranged.[20]

Weirdest of all was the eerie, skull-like face once fashioned by the Bromley Garden Centre poltergeist from two different colours of fertiliser. The outline was formed from white sulphite, and the details – eyes, mouth and hollow nose – picked out in brown Maxicrop. Investigator Pauline Runnalls described how the image dissolved whenever she averted her gaze:

During our stay the whole object gradually disintegrated: at first very slowly, beginning with the left eye, the Maxicrop appearing to run out of the corner and down the face. Then the same eye started to fill in with sulphate. The other features started to run and were very slowly filled up with material. Hollows appeared in the cheeks, and the material was gradually changing from one position to another. Although the face was being observed almost constantly by myself or others, *no actual movement* of material was seen.[21]

Such spooks remind me once more of magicians – and poltergeists have occasionally been induced to perform actual Paul Daniels-style magic tricks from time to time. A spook infesting an office in the City of London during 1901 would repeatedly get a French penny to appear inside a bottle of oil, whose neck was too narrow to take it; a standard conjuring-trick. Interestingly, when the noted poltergeist-scholar Father Herbert Thurston consulted a magician, he told him how the trick could be performed – adding that, for reasons the Magic Circle would not allow me to divulge here, French pennies were ideally suited to it.[22] The Australian Mayanup poltergeist also performed coin tricks for guests' entertainment. Before dinner, the head of one of the haunted families, Mr Dickson, would regularly mark a few florins and put them aside. Then, he would tell his fellow-diners to look beneath their plates to check there was nothing there. Come the end of the meal, guests would be asked to lift their plates again, there to find JOTTled the very same marked coins.[23]

Cynics would suggest the 'magic' here was really performed by Mr Dickson himself; but how? Conjurors operate most commonly via sleight-of-hand – they distract your attention from observation of the actual dextrous trick being performed, thus to make their act *look* like magic. Do poltergeists do something similar? Consider the case of one Commander Kogelnick, who challenged a spook to throw a small iron box off a shelf and then stood there watching it, very intently, for five full minutes, before – bang! A porcelain cup from further down the same shelf smashed to smithereens on the floor. Kogelnick did not actually witness this event, however, as his attention had been expertly diverted around towards the decoy iron box instead.[24] Like illusionists, poltergeists decline to have their tricks observed too closely, in the actual performance; that would spoil the glamour. Maybe seeing it all too clearly would reveal the mysterious mechanism present behind them; or, even more intriguingly, the possible acausal *lack* of any mechanism.

A particularly unusual series of events were witnessed – or otherwise – by Matthew Manning in his haunted childhood home. The polt enjoyed vandalising Matthew's bedroom with graffiti; over 500 names, ostensibly of long-dead locals, appeared on the walls and ceiling, apparently written using a pencil whose tip was becoming ever blunter. Such graphological vandalism only ever appeared when the room was empty. Two sharpened pencils were therefore left on the bed in a crossed position, so it could be determined whether or not they were being used directly for signing the names. Apparently not – their positions remained exactly the same the next time the Mannings entered. However, there were yet more names on the walls, and the pencils' tips had indeed been further blunted. But how were the spooks writing if they weren't physically wielding the pencils? According to Matthew, 'It appeared that the graphite was being transferred directly from the pencil tips to the walls.'[25] Would people even be *able* to see such a process at work? Possibly certain acausal events, by virtue of their having no discernible physical or energetic mechanisms behind them, never can be witnessed by the eyes of either humans or cameras.

*****

Good old Nandor Fodor preferred other explanations for spooky shyness. If, said Fodor, a poltergeist is merely an external manifestation of repressed elements of a person's subconscious mind, then perhaps the avoidance of direct observation is just another 'part of the [Freudian] repression mechanism'. As polts are generally anti-social and destructive it is 'only by a failure of repression' upon behalf of the focus-figure that such 'attitudes [can] see the light of day'. As such, 'Concentration on the part of the observers and self-consciousness on the part of the poltergeist-subject results in increased self-control' and the disturbances momentarily cease.[26] Fodor tried to apply this theory to Gef the Mongoose who, he noted, often disliked being seen, scolding Mr Irving 'Damn you, take off your eyes, I cannot bear it!' or saying 'You're looking, stop looking! Take off your eyes, you bastard!'[27] Hoping to cure this pathological timidity, Fodor vowed to take some clear, close-up photographs of the beast. But Gef had other ideas, lamented Fodor:

> I bought a kitchen scale … and trained … [a] camera on it, with a flashlight so fixed that Gef, if he could be persuaded to mount the pan of the scale, could take his own photograph, also showing his weight … Gef's first question was 'What is Fodor up to?' When it was explained to him, he answered: 'It is a trap.'[28]

Gef later exploded the flash when the room was too light, thus ruining the entire roll of film. In addition to escaping from acts of clear photography – and thereby of precise definition – Gef was also able to evade some literal physical traps that had been sprung to capture him, most notably that of John Cowley, a motor-mechanic who attached a contact-plate to the bottom of the Number 81 Bus to electrocute him. Gef was supposedly hitching free rides along the bottom of local transport to eavesdrop on passengers' private conversations. He had also stolen a bus conductor's sandwiches. Hearing this, Mr Irving warned Gef a trap had been laid for him on a bus, but he knew not which one. Gef did. 'Oh, I know all about it,' he replied calmly. 'It is under Bus 81.'[29] Gef once refused to come out and allow himself to be seen and touched when one potentially suspicious Spiritualist came to call. 'No damn fear. You'll put me in a bottle,' he reasoned, the traditional means of ensnaring and corking up a *djinni*.[30] According to Mr Irving, Gef 'has a great dread of being kept prisoner, as he says so.'[31]

The Drummer of Tedworth was similarly elusive. Joseph Glanvill, who went along to probe the story, saw movement within a linen bag. He thought it a mouse and, catching it up with one hand, drew its body down to his other waiting hand, ready to catch it. When he got the bulge down to the bag's opening, there was nothing there; another potential explanation had literally

Three alleged photographs of Gef the Talking Mongoose; some might be criticised as being too clear, others as not being clear enough.

slipped right through an investigator's fingers.[32] The Little Burton poltergeist of 1677 once manifested as a disembodied hand. Two teenage girls felt it in bed with them, bound it within their sheets and beat it with bed-staves 'until it were as soft as Wool', before weighing it down with a large stone. The next morning, when one went for a faggot of flaming furze to burn the trapped spook, the stone threw itself away and the hand was gone, leaving only a small pool of water behind.[33] More extreme was what happened to the owner of the haunted house on Russian Hill when he made an effort to grab a nearby apparition – it exploded! As the figure 'melted out' instantly, 'Every piece of furniture ... was thrown or rolled out of its place, several panes of glass were broken as if by an explosion, and cushions were dashed with blinding dust and force into the faces of everyone in the library.'[34]

* * * * *

We can usefully recall those many legends in which Tricksters like Hermes, Loki, Proteus and Coyote escape from traps or, more daringly, subvert their rules so they become no traps at all, but simply toys to be played with. Coyotes are obviously also real flesh-and-blood creatures as well as magical mythological ones, and anecdotes about such beasts' native Trickster-like cunning in the face of traps still persist, even to this day, among hunters in the American West. Wolves, mink, foxes and skunks quite frequently die in traps, or eat poisoned animal carcasses laced with strychnine; but coyotes? Hardly ever. They prefer to dig up or turn over traps, then piss and shit all over them. For the naturalist François Leydet, 'it is difficult to escape the conclusion that coyotes ... have a sense of humour' and are mocking their hunters by thus transforming their snares into toilets.[35]

Equally relevant (especially given Gef's one-time boast that 'I am a ghost in the form of a weasel'[36]) is the Zulu Trickster-figure Thlókunyana, who appeared either as a small man 'the size of a weasel' or as an actual human-brained weasel with red fur and a black-tipped tail. To the Zulus, this weasel-Trickster and his real-life animal counterpart were 'cleverer than all others', because, whenever an ambush was set for a wildcat, the weasel would come along and steal the bait for itself. According to Zulu lore, if a hunter did ever manage

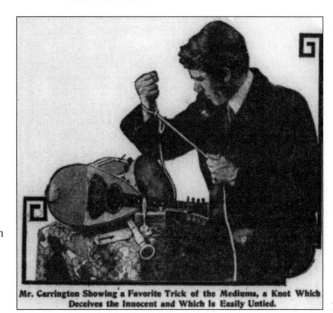

Psychical researcher Hereward Carrington demonstrates his powers of sleight-of-hand. Do some poltergeists operate similarly?

Mr. Carrington Showing a Favorite Trick of the Mediums, a Knot Which Deceives the Innocent and Which Is Easily Untied.

to ensnare a weasel somehow, then its magic 'jinx' would remain inside the successful trap and inhibit its future power, thus rendering it no trap at all.[37]

Tricksters habitually remove themselves from the usual rules of the hunting-game, sabotage the very notion of traps themselves, and derisively mock the human hunters who set them. As Lewis Hyde asked, 'What trapper's pride could remain unshaken once he's read Coyote's commentary?'[38] And what self-respecting ghost-hunter's pride could remain unshaken likewise once he has read the poltergeist's similarly sarcastic commentary upon his own traps' utter ineffectiveness? The poltergeist, as exemplified so perfectly by Gef (AKA: Thlókunyana), will not be caught, caged, weighed, examined or photographed up close in glorious Technicolor for the newsreels. Polts are essentially protean beasts – and protean beasts cannot be netted. To do so would cause them to be tied down, to be scientifically classified, to be restricted to just the one essential form. It is not their status as the Freudian repressed that is being guarded so well by poltergeists with their shyness – it is their *liminality*, their unclear, borderline status, forever balanced upon that delicate knife-edge between apparent existence and equally apparent non-existence. In terms of the symbolic import of these narratives, this is what it really means for a poltergeist to not get caught. 'We want you to believe in us, but not *too much*,' an alien is supposed to have once told an American UFO-hunter;[39] poltergeists say something similar to their own hunters all the time.

VIII

Ridiculous Evidence

The greatest trick the Devil ever played was convincing the world
he doesn't exist.

Charles Baudelaire

During the South Shields haunting, Marc, the man of the house, once actually succeeded in recording an ornament moving around on his videophone, sending this footage to an investigator's mobile. Unhappily, the clip mysteriously deleted itself somehow. Marc was asked to send the clip again – but he could not. It had been deleted from his phone, too.[1] When this same investigator was later transferring other rare clips of the ghost at work onto his PC, he was surprised to find three media files, not two, sitting on his desktop. The third one had no title – just an odd, grey-and-black icon. He clicked on it. What launched was a blank white screen, empty but for the phrase 'HA HA' in big black letters. Before he could save the file, it suddenly vanished.[2]

To a sceptic, this will all seem rather pathetic. There *was* some evidence, but it disappeared? 'Well, they would say that, wouldn't they?' as Mandy Rice-Davies once so famously opined. What is even more Tricksterishly mischievous than evidence going missing, however, is the notion of evidence remaining, but remaining in such a way that it appears not really to *be* evidence at all. Staying at South Shields, we can consider the bizarre polt-created tableaux, made with stuffed toys and sharp kitchen implements, which appeared around the house re-enacting scenes of extreme violence. According to one eyewitness account such arrangements were 'obscene' and 'sickening.'[3]

Maybe they were ... at the time. However, the relevant photos of them may just as easily produce laughter. There is a picture of a rabbit holding a kitchen-knife over the neck of a cute little yellow duck with a bow-tie who lies comically helpless, upended with his feet in the sky and big, black-button eyes gazing upwards, for instance – and it just looks silly, like Beatrix Potter gone wrong. A photo also exists of some children's doodle-boards on which the demon has written 'Just go NOW' and 'Stop it NOW', presumably intended to horrify all concerned. But to the average person, far removed from the action, the only thing elicited is a cynical smile – and who can blame them? Best (or worst) of all is a photo of the investigator Darren W. Ritson examining a plastic table which had impossibly dissolved and then re-formed back into perfect shape again. This table:

> ... looked as if it had been melted. It had a subtle but unusual 'sheen', as if it had been highly polished ... [it] looked hot, like melted wax [like] something one may see in a Salvador Dalí painting. Its centre was sunken, as if in a semi-molten state, and had begun to collapse in on itself. One of the legs had warped outwards so that its foot was now approximately two inches from the floor. The other legs seemed to have buckled inwards, making its appearance even more bizarre.[4]

Later that night, it suddenly regained its original appearance while everyone was out of the room: 'The tabletop was now perfectly flat, the legs were perfectly straight and no one would ever have guessed that it had been through such a bizarre transformation. It was as if it had never been damaged.'[5] This is a remarkable event but, by definition, if something paranormally returns back to its original state, then what we are ultimately left with is something which hasn't actually changed in any way at all – and a photograph of a puzzled man holding up a small blue plastic table for the camera proves absolutely zilch.[6]

* * * * *

Given the generally invisible nature of the poltergeist, fake pictures are not hard to produce. Harry Price once published a photo taken at Borley Rectory after the place had burned down in a fire, which *appeared* to show a flying brick. However, this snap was taken by a *Life* magazine photographer, Cynthia Ledsham, and what it truly showed was a brick being thrown aside by a demolition worker, positioned just out of frame. On film, the brick appeared to be levitating – even though it clearly wasn't, in actuality. Accordingly, *Life* published the picture along with a jokey caption, but Price, in his book *The End of Borley Rectory*, claimed it was genuine evidence of poltergeistery! Ledsham rightly condemned this as 'the most bare-faced hocus-pocus' on Price's behalf.[7]

The photos which exist of Gef the Mongoose are more indeterminate. In contrast to the general pattern of his shyness, Gef once specifically *requested* his image be captured on film. 'I will have my photograph taken,' he said, and jumped from behind a hedge to pose on top of a gate momentarily in front of Voirrey Irving, the daughter of the house. Unfortunately, Voirrey's resultant snaps are suspicious at best.[8] Unclear, blurry, showing *something* furry for sure, but quite *what* is debatable, they are essentially anti-photographic in their nature. Appropriately enough for a Trickster, they simply show whatever it is the observer wishes them to show, being an exercise in pure visual hermeneutics. A poltergeist-animal? Fine, that's what it is, then. A real, but quite ordinary, mongoose? Could well be. An old mangy piece of fur, set up to look vaguely like a small, hairy, allegedly paranormal creature by a teenage girl playing a joke? That's what it looks like to me. Gef never agreed to be captured in clear close-up by Nandor Fodor on the kitchen scales, but rubbishy little non-pictures like these were no problem for him at all.

*****

Attempts to gain definitive physical evidence of poltergeistery seem doomed to failure. Harry Price once staked out a detached cottage near Horley in Surrey, outside which invisible footsteps were heard marching around most mornings punctually at 8.30 a. m. Like a big-game hunter, he set 'shallow trenches filled with sand and flour, cut across the path at intervals' with the idea of recording impressions of the spook's footprints, but predictably it didn't work, another trap shrewdly evaded by Thlókunyana.[9] Matthew Manning succeeded where Price had failed. In 1972, after the family polt began continually opening and slamming shut the front-door – often leaving it swinging by the hinges, so anyone could walk in, another Duchamp-esque door which was not a door – Manning's parents tried an experiment. Covering the hall floor with sheets of newspaper, a thick layer of dampened sand was then laid down. It was now impossible to walk across the hall without leaving footprints behind – and, lo and behold, two were soon found, apparently lain down by a passing poltergeist.[10] And yet, despite the crystal-clear photograph which exists of these prints, we only have the Mannings' word for it that they didn't just make them themselves. I might believe them, but thousands wouldn't.

Likewise, a bite in a sandwich is evidence only that people have teeth, and can be hungry. The Black Monk of Pontefract once left just such a bite-mark behind it, indicating the actions of some truly enormous molars.[11] At Poona, hoping to placate the ghost with an offering of food, fruit was left out for Hermes so he would scoff it and depart. The gift was accepted, and sounds of exaggerated lip-smacking heard before the rinds were thrown back, with demonic teeth-marks clearly visible. At Sandfeld, Germany, in 1722, a pancake was stolen from an oven, and a piece later thrown at a ten-year-old boy, a disembodied voice saying 'I haven't eaten it all on my own; you've got a piece again.'[12] Who would accept half-eaten food as evidence of the reality of ghosts, though?

*****

During the 1970s, the parapsychologist Dr Joel Whitton analysed recordings of spirit-raps, finding they do not follow the usual laws of sound. If you or I were to knock on a table and have its volume turned into an acoustic graph, we would see a curve; it would rise then fall like a hill. Our bare ears cannot tell it, but mapped across milliseconds the rap will begin more quietly than it ends up at the point of our hardest knocking, then start to fall away as we stop. Recorded poltergeist raps are not like this, according to Whitton; they begin and end instantly, with vertical or near-vertical lines rising up to an effectively flat peak, a characteristic not of natural sounds, but of artificial ones.[13]

A similar analysis, performed by Dr Barrie Colvin in 2010, seems to partially confirm and deny Whitton's findings; polt raps have their loudest part very *near* the beginning, but not right at the start of this acoustic 'hill',

Colvin said, providing visual read-outs to prove it. Colvin also discovered evidence suggesting spirit-raps originate from *within* the material that makes the sound rather than upon the surface of the material, as is the case with natural knockings.[14] This is either evidence or it isn't. To a believer, the fact the sounds aren't natural means a human being *can't* be producing them. To them, 'not natural' means supernatural. To a sceptic, the fact the sounds aren't natural means a human *must* be producing them. To them, 'not natural' means fake. What you make of this data depends more upon your own *a priori* assumptions about whether ghosts are real or not than it does upon the data itself.

Experiments performed by the parapsychologist Dr Julian Isaacs during the early 1980s proved even weirder. These involved the use of 'mini-labs'; hermetically-sealed (but not to Hermes) transparent containers, filled with small objects. These were placed in front of triggered cameras in the hope polts could be induced to transport the target objects through the mini-lab walls. The poltergeists courteously obliged. There were only two problems. The first was that the cameras malfunctioned whenever anything odd occurred. The second issue was that, upon opening the mini-labs for inspection, new objects were found inside which had not been there before – notes bearing jokey messages like 'FOOLED YA!' apparently written by the spooks themselves. Thus, as *Fortean Times* commented perceptively, 'The joke is that if the effects were indeed psychically produced, the evidence is made to look like a cynical joke.'[15] Evidence with the poltergeist is not always actually evidence; and the common arbiter of scientific reality is evidence. If poltergeists are real, then they do, via this fact, undermine the whole notion of verifiable scientific reality itself. It is no wonder they are so profoundly taboo. They almost appear to wish to remain so...

*****

According to George P. Hansen, the sceptical mockery of mainstream materialist science is just a more modern method of reinforcing the ancient magical concept of taboo:

> Early peoples understood that the supernatural was dangerous. It needed to be hedged off from the mundane world. There were rules, prohibitions, and taboos surrounding it. The process continues today, but at an unconscious level.[16]

One way in which this process does indeed continue today at an unconscious level is through the laughter and disbelief of scientists in the paranormal – this functions as a means through which society as a whole can discourage our active engagement with such taboo realms; persons who believe in ghosts are often derided as stupid, gullible or mentally ill. I recall arch-sceptic Richard Dawkins once gibing that anyone who thought they'd encountered a poltergeist needed to be 'introduced to their friendly neighbourhood psychiatrist' – and he didn't mean Nandor Fodor. According to Charles Fort, 'knowledge is ignorance surrounded by laughter'.[17] What Fort meant is that scientists very often simply laugh at the anomalous in order to dismiss it, instead of actually bothering to *disprove* it (which, of course, they frequently cannot do).

By generally producing only ambiguously ridiculous evidence of their own existence, poltergeists themselves aid this process of jeering dismissal; thereby maintaining their own taboo, it might be said. We will recall that the Trickster is a liminal being which operates best at boundaries; boundaries which they often then redraw, thus reshaping our world in an imaginative sense. They would, perhaps, be unable to do this if operating from within the centre of mainstream thought or science. You can view this in two ways. Either poltergeists really are literally real, and derive some incomprehensible enjoyment or power from concealing definite proof of this fact from us or, on the other hand, these stories (even if true!) function as myths which simultaneously fulfil an important psychological function for those who believe in them. After all, that word 'belief' is central; by consistently refusing to leave unequivocal, solid proof behind after themselves, poltergeists can only ever become objects *of* belief. As such, they suggest an alternative imaginative possibility to the Dominant of cold and supposedly objective scientific proof which now utterly governs the allowed margins of what is deemed to be consensus-reality within our modern world. You can either laugh *with* poltergeist evidence, therefore, or laugh *at* it.

*****

Even hardened parapsychologists themselves can choose to scoff. In 1981, at the annual meeting of the Parapsychological Association in New York State, the investigator W. E. Cox presented some videos he had made, apparently proving the reality of poltergeists. The problem was these films were simultaneously too-good-to-be-true and too-awful-to-be-true. Cox's audience openly laughed at him, accusing him of falling prey to the whims of a trickster with a lower-case 't' – a human prankster with stage-conjuring skills.[18] But should that 'trickster' actually have borne a capital 'T'?

Cox was involved with a mediumistic circle named SORRAT (SOciety for Research on RApport and Telekinesis), founded in 1961 by the respected poet and professor, John G. Neihardt. Following the death of his wife in 1958, Neihardt encountered poltergeistery around his home, so formed a séance-circle to investigate. Ghosts quickly began communicating via intelligent rappings emanating from within the floor, with one spirit to appear being Black Elk, a celebrated North Dakota Sioux medicine man whom Neihardt had befriended in life, recording his visions and beliefs in a 1932 book, *Black Elk Speaks*.[19]

Black Elk was a *heyoka*, a specific type of sacred clown who acts as a jester and satirist for his tribe – a classic Trickster. The *heyoka* is a master of inversion, riding horses back-to-front, speaking his words in reverse, wearing his clothes inside-out, walking heels-first, or wandering around naked in cold weather complaining how hot it is. One famous *heyoka*, known as 'Straighten-Outer' would attack any round item such as a wheel with a hammer, trying to straighten it. Chosen to be a Trickster by undergoing a vision of sacred

Thunder-Beings (the original *Heyókȟa* was a Tricksterish thunder-god), by inverting the usual rules of life, a *heyoka* uses clownish satire to make people question the basic underlying assumptions of their society, even down to why wheels must be round or walking should be done facing forwards.[20] After death, the ghost of Black Elk continued this tradition by providing W. E. Cox with some rather lunatic 'evidence' that only undermined the case for his own existence, thus bringing the very idea of scientific parapsychology itself into severe question.

After Neihardt's own death, one of his students, Tom Richards, took over SORRAT and W. E. Cox went out to inspect. By now, the spirits had progressed to producing extreme poltergeist phenomena, including flying tables and impossibly localised mini-earthquakes within the Richards' basement.[21] Like Dr Julian Isaacs, Cox set up a series of supposedly hermetically-sealed mini-labs around the Richards' household, taking elaborate precautions to make them tamper-proof, challenging the SORRAT spooks to manipulate various items left inside. Locks to which only Cox had the key, sealed with special tamper-proof threads, were employed, but still the polts rose to the challenge; Hermes can transform into mist to pick any lock.[22] Or, if he prefers, he can cheat. Dared to transport an item into a mini-lab whose locks were totally sealed with glue, the ghosts subverted the rules of the game by simply throwing a bunged-up lock through the glass walls.[23]

Cox's mini-labs took the form of fish-tanks – the poltergeists rapped out a parodic song, *The Age of Aquariums*, to skit this fact![24] – which, being see-through, provided great scope for being filmed. However, nothing would happen if anyone stood there in the room watching over the haunted fish-tank. Why not? The ghosts spouted something nonsensical about alpha-waves and beta-waves from human observers becoming 'mixed like tripe in a pail' and stopping them;[25] sceptics said it might have something to do with any films being faked by human hands when nobody was around. Leave the room for a while, though, and the spooks were happy to co-operate.

Inside the mini-lab, cards would jump from sealed boxes, sort themselves into order, then jump back inside again, in open display of matter-through-matter; tied-up balloons would inflate and deflate by themselves; toy knights

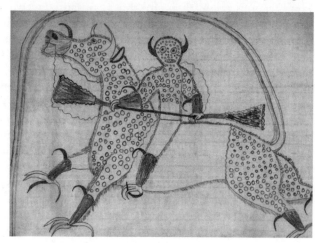

A drawing of a 'thunder-being'; an encounter with one would mark a person out as a future *heyoka*.

would dance and model cars move around 'as if pushed by an invisible child'; objects would leap through the solid glass walls without smashing them; paper would blow around with no wind; fires would light and extinguish; pens would lift themselves up and write messages such as 'RETHINK TIME', which would then fly inside waiting envelopes and vanish only to turn up later, delivered to parapsychologists' home addresses; there was no end to the wonders Cox caught on film. The trouble was ... it all looked completely fake, as you can judge for yourself by looking up the footage on YouTube. As objects would teleport from one point of space to another instantaneously, or move around in a jerky fashion, it looked like the whole thing had been produced via stop-motion animation, as though episodes of *Morph* had been remade by Spiritualists.

One sceptic produced his own copy-cat films, successfully reproducing many of the SORRAT phenomena via ordinary means; he explained you could easily bypass all the locks on the fish-tanks simply by removing a glass panel. Hoping to counter this accusation, Cox placed clocks inside the mini-labs to exhibit he hadn't been cheating; but the ghosts, for a joke, turned them to face away from the camera, thus defeating their entire purpose.[26] When presenting his evidence to the world, Cox came across less as an objective scientist, more as a stage-illusionist, full of Barnumesque patter:

> Now look at this. It should be impossible to link two leather rings without cutting one of them. Such a cut could be detected easily. Here you see two [such] leather rings. They are rising [in the air] in front of the mini-lab. Look! Here they link. They remain linked. And look, here they break apart; one falls to the table on the outside, and the other hangs on the edge of the aquarium. I have carefully examined these rings. They have not been cut. How can you explain this? Isn't this the best case of matter passing through matter you have ever seen?[27]

Abracadabra – just like that! Like many parapsychologists, Cox had some conjuring training; if he didn't, sceptics might just say he was being fooled by people who did. But, likewise, as he *did* have such training, these same sceptics could then cite this very same fact to accuse him of fraud: Catch-22! It's no wonder nobody believed him. It's also no wonder George P. Hansen's *The Trickster and the Paranormal* was dedicated to Cox's memory; he was either one of the greatest Trickster-figures of all time or the unwitting dupe of one.

It would have been better for Cox's reputation had the poltergeists stayed off-camera entirely. By encouraging him to show these films to his peers, they just made him look mad, becoming an object of mockery, pity and scorn. Was this their intention? Cox subsequently discovered some object-movements looked relatively normal to the human eye, but when examined frame-by-frame showed clear qualities of stop-motion animation, as if the ghosts were hoping to provide evidence of fraud under later analysis.[28] On some footage, self-writing pens would appear with needless strings attached, to make it seem they were operated through puppetry.[29] Solid leather rings would link through themselves, providing permanent proof of matter-through-matter's reality; but then spontaneously combust, destroying such evidence forever.[30] Separate wooden squares were similarly linked; but in order for a lab to prove this had really happened, it would be necessary to take the squares apart, thus destroying the only evidence that it *had* ever happened.[31] When a better, more foolproof mini-lab was introduced by outsiders, the polts refused to have anything to do with it and laid low for a while.[32] The ghosts claimed to be teleporting letters from their fish-tank not only through space but also through time, but it later transpired they were simply getting them stamped with false post-marks to make it appear as if they had been mailed from the future. Their excuse was that they *could* control time and space via the US Postal Service if they wanted to, but it was a big effort and they preferred to conserve their psychic energy.[33]

It appears the ghosts desired to frame themselves, and be caught cheating. We are left with a situation akin to that of 'Deepfakes' today, the imminently looming era in which easily faked computer-manipulated film and audio footage placed online can make politicians appear to be taking bribes, when in reality they are not. Contrariwise, a politician caught taking a bribe in reality could easily then just turn around and say the footage is a Deepfake. Probably, if you support the politician, then you believe him; if you don't, then you won't. And, with Cox's films, if you already believe in ghosts, then you might believe in the films, too; but if you don't, then you won't. Under such conditions, the traditional world of 'objective' or 'empirical' scientific proof vanishes away into nothing, to be replaced only with 'belief' or 'non-belief' as the grounds for acceptance, as opposed to concrete evidence as such. These were post-modern poltergeists indeed!

* * * * *

If the *heyoka* Black Elk was truly returning from the Happy Hunting Grounds, then the above acts of paradoxical inversion are just what you might expect. But, if you were a living human Trickster who wanted to act like a *heyoka* for obscure satirical or philosophical purposes, then these are just the kind of tricks you might be expected to pull too. As one assessment has it, the SORRAT films seem to say to us that 'It is possible to break the rules governing reality.'[34] Imparting such a message was also the key function of the *heyoka* with his crazy, inverted ways. But, if ghosts rather than humans really were responsible for all this exceedingly Tricksterish madness, then why?

A number of potential explanations have been advanced, many of them positively byzantine. One SORRAT member, confronted with a photo of a 'levitating' table which was clearly just being held up by human hands, said the image was deliberately framed by the ghosts to look that way, and 'Maybe they [did] it to make the sceptics leave us alone.'[35] If so, mission accomplished. There is a school of fringe thought which holds that reality itself is inherently psychically malleable, and that, when believers are gathered together, their RSPK powers will facilitate poltergeist phenomena, whereas when sceptics congregate, they will cancel this out, suppressing it. Or alternatively, non-believers might subconsciously cause a poltergeist to deliberately produce fake-looking phenomena, to reinforce their own pre-existing non-belief. Or, if polts feed off believers' psychic energy and are drained by sceptics' non-belief, maybe spooks produce fraudulent evidence of fraud to make the sceptics go away, thus keeping their psychic batteries safely topped-up? If so, then for poltergeists to maintain their sense of liminality is only for them to maintain their life-force. The more reliable or high-status the observer, it has been proposed, the less likely it is poltergeists will deign to perform for them, thus accounting for Cox being able to make his films; when scientists from a more prestigious laboratory tried to do so, nothing was recorded. A sceptic would say this is because they were less gullible and better prepared than Cox was. A believer might agree, but from a directly oppositional perspective.[36]

In subatomic physics, continuous human observation of certain non-stable particles has been shown to stall their decay, something known as the 'Zeno Effect'; maybe continuous observation of poltergeists retards their own actions in a reverse-parallel fashion? If so, then the better and more evidentially a case is documented, it has been guessed, the weaker it will become. Psychic powers are supposed to operate independently of time, and the better documented a haunting is, the more it will be publicised in the media, and the more people will come to know of it. But among these people, due to the prevailing materialistic outlook of our day, the majority will be sceptics. These spoilsports might inadvertently use their latent psychic abilities to make their minds travel back through time and affect the original haunting negatively with their disbelief, thereby lessening its effects and making it appear more fraudulent than it really was. Hence, the SORRAT experiments could have been more real at the time, but are less real now, because of sceptics subsequently reading about them.

As you, dear reader, ingest the head-spinning implications of this proposal and, most probably, reject it with amused laughter, possibly you are making those SORRAT ghosts fade away even more at this very moment. So, it's a good job most such hauntings do remain fairly obscure, otherwise they might never even have happened in the first place. However, there is a further paradox. The more obviously fake such hauntings appear, the *less* they will be written about, thus exposing them to less subsequent future critical scepticism by unbelievers like you. This will therefore make them more real again. Ah, but *then*, if they appear more real once more ... you can see where this is going, can't you? That is to say, around and around in a series of supernaturally interlinked leather rings, again and again, forever.[37] Those interested in contributing to this particular futile exercise in citizen-science should read US sociologist James McClenon's fascinating 2018 book about SORRAT, *The Entity Letters*, in order to determine whether or not, by doing so, the text will end up one day disappearing from your shelf because it was no longer ever actually written any more anyway.

* * * * *

SORRAT-style fraud of the kind once practised by Eusapia Palladino could even sometimes be *necessary* to induce poltergeistery, it has been proposed, a process known as 'artefact induction', an idea formulated by the inventive parapsychologist K. J. Batcheldor. By surreptitiously pushing a table around and saying a ghost is moving it during a séance, you might fool other sitters into thinking this is true, thereby unleashing their RSPK powers to make the table jig around by itself in actuality.[38] There may be something to Batcheldor's notion; one 1905 Swedish case was triggered by a neurotic young woman being woken in the night by loud hammering on a bedroom door. It was a guest at the wrong room. Irrationally, she thought it was a poltergeist – and, lo and behold, just such an entity soon appeared, banging on doors like the guest had.[39]

SORRAT stood for SOciety for Research on *RApport* and Telekinesis, we will recall, and by faking phenomena and thereby encouraging more belief in the reality of spirits, it has been guessed that the SORRAT leaders encouraged such strong psychic rapport among their gullible co-members that, basically, miracles began happening. According to James McClenon, this might be how ancient religions first formed; 'a group's ideology need not be valid for miracles to occur', he says, simply their levels of RSPK-unleashing belief strong enough.[40] And the belief-levels of SORRAT members *were* strong. When the entities provided one sitter with detailed instructions for creating a magical crystal-powered harp for travelling through time with, she went away and made one.[41]

By humouring the spirits, the sitters made them pleasingly good-humoured, another suggestion of Batcheldor. Their moving table would begin 'jumping about rhythmically in merriment' and rapping out the tune to *Yes Sir, We Have No Bananas*, while its human friends chanted 'Two-four-six-eight/ Come on table levitate!'[42] The polts would then deliberately mis-teleport SORRAT members one another's letters, forcing them to get in contact to exchange them, thereby building up their personal rapport further.[43] They teased one sitter about his crush on another member by causing two porcelain figurines, male and female, to move closer to one another and touch, thereby playing rapport-enhancing match-maker.[44] And all this simply from some blatant Trickster or other pushing a table about one day and saying a ghost did it!

* * * * *

Could it really be that, when it comes to poltergeists, the stronger the evidence they are not real, the stronger the evidence this actually is that they *are* real? I find many of the ideas discussed above hard to believe, although I suspect that might be rather their point. However unlikely-sounding they may be, I do find them quite delightfully paradoxical, and they certainly made me think closely about things whose nature I had previously taken wholly for granted, such as what precisely it is that constitutes such a thing as scientific evidence. In which case, all I can say is – well done, Black Elk! You are indeed a most skilful *heyoka*.

IX

False Promises

Since I gave up hope I feel so much better.

John Osborne

Ghosts do not like performing on-cue, particularly in public or within a laboratory – another factor tending to increase their liminal status as objects of mere belief. One of the most famous hauntings of all time was 'The Great Amherst Mystery', a particularly nasty case from 1870s Nova Scotia centring upon a young girl named Esther Cox. Here, all manner of wonders were performed and yet, when an impressed visiting stage-magician called Walter Hubbell declared that Esther really should be on the stage herself, the spook stubbornly refused to embrace the limelight. This is despite the fact that, beforehand, the polt had specifically promised to knock and move objects when Esther was displayed in a theatre. Once she and Hubbell were standing up on the boards, however, the spook got stage-fright. The audience demanded their money back, an angry mob tailing Cox and Hubbell outside and performing acts of human lithobolia in their general direction, a spectacle which only helped undermine the credibility of the whole affair for many.[1]

This is also humour; a sort of bathos, or disappointment of expectations. Many a poltergeist has promised devoutly to provide definite proof of itself to the world, or implied some great revelation is at hand, only for it all to fizzle out into an embarrassingly damp squib. In 1947, a Mrs Priestly of Brighton was plagued by strange lights, the disturbance of bedding and blows from an invisible hand. Matters appeared coming to a head when the ghost repeatedly called her by telephone, saying 'Wait 'til October the fifth'. She waited as told, but nothing happened. Soon, the voice was reduced to phoning in such banalities as 'Mind how you go', like some disembodied Dixon of Dock Green.[2] Nowadays, polts can even disappoint by text-message. At South Shields, by temporarily departing, the ghost lulled its victims into a false sense of security – until it then cruelly sent a text to their mobile saying 'I'M BACK' in overly melodramatic fashion.[3] Ghosts often like to lie low, then spring irritatingly back into action again as soon as their victims think they are safe. During a Scottish haunting of 1707, a servant working in a field thanked God the local lithobolic spook had not tormented him that night ... whereupon he was instantly struck hard with yet another pebble.[4]

A mediumistic circle operating in the Norfolk village of Scole during the 1990s received innumerable messages, supposedly relayed by a crack group of polt-like entities who wished to open up permanent channels of communication between our 3-D world and their own 4-D realm. Objects moved, writing formed from bright points of dancing light in thin air, and some truly bizarre photographs, purporting to show life in other dimensions, were obtained. Everything was building up to some great cosmic revelation – only for the sitters to be solemnly told at the crucial point that their experiments had to be aborted forever because they were causing time-travel difficulties for intelligent aliens from another galaxy![5] This was the actual apology delivered by the ghosts: 'I have some troubling news ... A personality from the future is interfering with the interdimensional doorway every time we open it. He is experimenting with a crystalline time-probe and his motives are not entirely benevolent.'[6] I hate it when that happens.

There is an account of a humorously disappointing – and rather macabre – poltergeist *hermaion* on record, too, said to have been presented by the Bell Witch to a woman nicknamed 'Pots'. Late one afternoon, this lady was sitting in her yard peeling an apple. She was about to leave town for pastures new, so the Witch decided to deliver her a goodbye gift. 'Pots, I have brought you a present to keep in remembrance of me when you go to your far away new home; will you accept it?' the Witch asked, sweetly. Pots, pleased, said she would. Suddenly, 'a small roll, neatly wrapped in paper' fell into Pots' lap. It contained a pair of stockings – which, the Witch said, she could wear at her own funeral. They were splattered with odd stains. 'That is blood,' explained the Witch. 'They killed a beef [cow] ... this morning, and the blood spattered on the stocking.'[7] How very thoughtful!

It's hardly surprising that, when the Witch did tell the truth, not everyone believed her. John Bell, one of the haunted family's sons, was once about to travel to North Carolina on business, when the Witch strongly advised him not to go. If he left now, he would miss the passing through town of a beautiful, wealthy young lady 'possessing forty negroes and considerable money', who would agree to be his wife. John ignored her prophecy, thinking this yet another typical lie – only to find that, in his absence, the promised rich young beauty did indeed arrive in town, and had since left.[8]

Another disappointingly ineffective poltergeistic prediction was delivered in the haunted seventeenth-century Flintshire farmhouse of one Rose-Mary Gower, where apparitions of a Black Monk and a Blue Lady have been sighted, as well as weird frog-eyed faces showing up on photographs of windows. Phenomena began in 1997 when an Irish couple saw the Virgin Mary in an adjoining field. The site then became a minor place of pilgrimage, with religious symbols appearing spontaneously upon walls.[9] In November 2005, Rose-Mary's husband teased the spook that it would be useful if it could daub the National Lottery numbers on their plasterwork instead of the usual crosses. A little while later, said Rose-Mary, the polt obliged:

> ... we discovered six numbers on the wall of the lounge. We got a little excited and decided that we would ... put the numbers on the next Saturday's lottery draw ... The phrase 'as sick as a parrot' described our

feelings when we discovered that the 'spooks' had indeed obliged with the jackpot numbers, but they were for that evening's draw, so we missed out! When my husband remonstrated with the 'spooks' for not giving us a chance to buy a ticket, they appeared to take umbrage and the wall erupted in lottery numbers, so now we are spoilt for choice![10]

Never will a ghost make anyone rich.

The Bell Witch was a truly excellent con-artist. It assumed many different false guises in its time, including that of 'the spirit of an early emigrant, who brought a large sum of money and buried my treasure for safekeeping until needed', but who had died before being able to spend it.[11] The Witch told the haunted family and their neighbours this treasure lay hidden beneath a particular boulder, which it described in such detail it was easily found the next morning. Eagerly, the treasure-hunters raised the rock, a job which took half a day. No gold was found … but the soil beneath was mixed with small pebbles, leaves and twigs, sure signs it had been disturbed previously. Tantalised, the men dug and dug, ending up with a hole nearly as deep as they were tall; but still no riches. Eventually, they gave up and went home. That night the lying Witch revisited, laughing gleefully and regaling the men with deeply unflattering descriptions of their exertions. To their credit, the poor dupes saw the funny side; and the Witch adopted the tale as a favoured comic anecdote, repeating it 'with equal zest' to all new-comers to the Bell property for the next month.[12]

When the seventeenth-century French ghost known as the Devil of Mascon told François Perrault, the Protestant Minister whose home it was haunting, that 6,000 valuable coins were concealed somewhere about the place one day, he sensibly refused to believe it. In his view, there was no such hoard present, it was merely Satan trying to tempt him into sinfully desiring money – 'this is why the Devil is called Mammon', he wisely opined.[13] If only those greedy folk on John Bell's farmstead 200 years later had been equally as suspicious, they could have saved themselves a lot of bother.

* * * * *

In October 1975 a violent criminal known as the 'Black Panther' kidnapped the heiress Lesley Whittle, murdered her and dumped the body. He also killed three people during a series of armed raids upon Post Offices. The Panther's identity was a total mystery, so it was with great interest that the author Colin Wilson, as a prominent expert upon both criminal and supernatural matters, received a letter claiming to know who he was. Wilson immediately travelled to a village near St Ives where he met up with the local postman and his wife, who had sent him the letter, in their cottage. They had a very odd story to tell. Every night at 8.00 p. m. a poltergeist began rapping on their bedroom wall, they claimed. It was the ghost of none other than Lesley Whittle herself!

This ghost was trying to help the couple solve her own murder. The wife had repeated Hermes-sent dreams of a pair of park gates which she had never seen before; the husband found a picture answering their description in a book. His wife recognised them – those *were* the gates! Rather like the Bell Witch, the spook then rapped out that the Black Panther had buried his gun under a particular stone in this park. It sent the wife a vision of just where the stone was; it was so detailed she could draw a map. The postman gave this map to the police – and the rock really was there, in exactly the place where the ghostly vision said it would be. Disappointingly, though, there was no trace of any gun beneath it. This didn't dishearten the couple. They obtained further information from the spirit that the Black Panther was a man called W. E. Jones who lived in a caravan in the Worcestershire village of Baynhall. Colin Wilson, impressed, wrote a long letter to Sir Robert Mark, a high-ranking police commissioner with whom he was acquainted, asking him to check the matter out. Sir Robert agreed, yet nothing came of it. Two months later, in December 1975, the Black Panther was finally apprehended – his name was Donald Nielsen and he lived in a house in Bradford, not a caravan in Baynhall. The poltergeist had, quite simply, been a very convincing liar.[14]

* * * * *

We would expect poltergeists to be good liars if they were also Tricksters; mythological Tricksters like Odysseus were, after all, liars *par excellence*, and Hermes, it is said, actually invented the art of deceit.[15] In the *Homeric Hymn*, once Hermes has made up with Apollo, his sunnier brother grants him one specific gift of prophecy as a sign of renewed friendship. However, it appears this is actually a trick of the solar god's own. Apollo is the god of clearly phrased, reliable predictions, like those provided by scientific laws – if you want to work out the elasticity of a spring, then Hooke's Law will not lead you astray, for instance. As such, Apollo is probably quite eager to give away one of his more minor and untrustworthy oracles, that of the Bee Maidens, to his Tricksterish little brother.

Primitive Greek soothsayers used to get high on drinking fermented honey and then enjoy visions, sent to them, so it was said, by the Bee Maidens, three winged virgin sisters and spirits of the beehive. However, being alcohol-induced, these predictions were really just hallucinations or delusions, not genuine precognitive psychic visions, so the Bee Maidens who sent them down from the heavens were depicted as being rather capricious in nature. According to Apollo, they like to tell the truth when they have eaten honey and 'the spirit is on them', but 'if they've been deprived of that divine sweetness they buzz about and mumble lies'.[16] Such erratic prophetesses would only give Apollo a bad name, so presumably he is glad to get rid of them. Hermes the Liar, however, would find them sweet as honey.

* * * * *

It would be more confusing for Hermes to mix truth in with his honeyed lies whenever he makes predictions, rather than simply sticking to a diet of pure untruths. This can be observed in the case of Donald the Battersea poltergeist, a ghost with a proudly inconsistent record of correctly predicting a string of deaths, disasters and accidents, and incorrectly foreseeing others which never came to pass at all. Donald was obsessed with the obscure British film star Jeremy Spenser, who he claimed was destined for an early grave by dying in an automobile accident. 'PLEASE … HELP JEREMY SPENSER' Donald once pleaded. 'PLEASE I IMPLORE – YOU HAVE EXCALLY TWENTY-TWO HOURS – PLASE – YOU WOULD NOT WANT HIM TO DIE – I TOLD YOU SATAUDAY WHERE HE IS – WEE – HELP.' Efforts were actually made to contact Spenser courtesy of Pinewood Studios, but the warning didn't get through … with the end result that the actor was indeed then involved in a car-crash, although not a fatal one thankfully, as Donald had implied. The polt got the original date for the misfortune wrong too, but the very day that Spenser really did overturn his car in Hampshire, Donald left a prescient note warning that 'JEREMY WILL HAVE HIS AXEDENT'.[17]

This was no one-off. On 9 December 1956, Donald left another note saying 'THEY HAVE ACCENDANT – PAULA'. As the shocked Hitchings family watched TV later that night, they heard the sad news that a young actress named Paula Marshall really had died in a car-wreck that very morning.[18] On 23 February 1957, the ghost even predicted that misfortune was about to befall Hollywood's favourite cowboy John Wayne: 'DO YOU KNOW … JOHN WAYNE – THE ONE WE SAW [on TV] TONIGHT … IS GOING TO HAVE A ACEDENT – DO WHAT YOU LIKE ABOUT IT'. Not much could be done about it, however, as on 25 February 'Big John' kept his appointment with destiny, tripping over on a film set and tearing ligaments in his foot.[19] It appears Donald was psychic … but only erratically.

Among the polt's dud tips, some were self-evidently false from the moment they were made, particularly the assertion that Britain's 1950s arch-enemy Colonel Nasser, the Arab nationalist President of Egypt, was planning to drop a nuclear bomb on London during the height of the Suez Crisis: 'I KNOW HE FIRE … AND OLD NAZZA NEWS HE GOING TO DROP A BOMB – BUT DON'T PANIC – LAY DOWN FACE ON FLOOR.'[20] Duck and Cover indeed – but, as even the slightest acquaintance with the historical record shows, there was no need for 1950s Londoners ever to do so. More plausible were Donald's advance warnings of a plane-crash; on 25 June 1957, he woke everyone in the house and urged via rapping-code that his focus-figure Shirley be evacuated to safety, as a light aircraft was about to fall from the sky into the street. Donald actually pushed Shirley out of her room and locked the door to encourage her exit. By around 8.15 a. m. the polt had determined it was a false alarm, unlocked the door, and allowed Shirley access to her quarters once more.[21]

On 25 February 1958, he predicted another such disaster and moved all of Shirley's dolls down into the coal cellar to protect them, transforming it into a makeshift air-raid shelter. Once again, no plane came down – at least not in Battersea. Headlines were actually made that very same day when an aircraft crashed at Winter Hill near Bolton, Lancashire, killing thirty-five people. When asked where the catastrophe would occur, Donald had correctly replied 'UP NORTH' – so why put all the dolls in the coal cellar?[22] Given the ghost's previous track record of correctly divining motoring accidents, it was not unreasonable to believe he might possess powers to forecast aviation disasters too, but, as per usual, Hermes preferred to stir lies in with his truths, to create as strange a concoction as possible. At Battersea, it seems as if the Bee Maidens and their overlord had once again got themselves very, very drunk upon the heady brew of precognition. If the poltergeist is indeed a kind of resurfacing of the Trickster archetype, then it is only to be expected that he is frequently fluent in falsehoods of such kinds. It is yet another reason we should not fall into the trap of taking either him or his disguises too literally. Many a false word can be wrongly discerned amid the buzzing of bees.

The Three Witches or Weird Sisters from Shakespeare's *Macbeth*, who gave out deliberately misleading prophecies. (Yale Center for British Art)

X

Funny Disguises

Do I contradict myself? Very well then, I contradict myself. I am large,
I contain multitudes.

Walt Whitman

The Trickster is, by definition, a shape-shifter; and so, to judge by the various
weird apparitional masks he has worn down the centuries, is the poltergeist.
Often, a *series* of different spectres are witnessed during any given haunting, a
problem long acknowledged as one of the more puzzling aspects of ghost-lore.
A polt infesting Tyneside's Willington Mill during 1834–37 was, according
to inhabitants of the building, fond of appearing in the contrasting forms of
a semi-transparent glowing priest, a girl wearing a lavender dress, an old,
grey-haired man, the disembodied head and hands of an old woman, a boy
in a suit, a figure clothed in a shroud, and several small animals, including a
ghost-monkey which pulled a child's shoe strap then disappeared under a bed![1]
    The Willington Mill spook also appeared as an entire menagerie of
non-existent animals, as at Skinwalker Ranch, not simply known zoological
specimens such as monkeys. One was a big white cat-like creature with an
elongated snout and the capacity to walk through closed doors and solid walls
while 'wriggling like a snake'.[2] Once, someone tried to kick it – but his foot
passed through the non-solid spectre. Vanishing, the apparition then hopped
back as a rabbit! Kicked again, the rabbit grew as large as a sheep and 'quite
luminous'.[3] Also witnessed was 'a strange-looking donkey … quite small with
short hair of a sand colour' with a nose which did 'bow upwards in the middle,
like a bump'.[4] The ghost also appeared as an animated white sheet, one witness
seeing 'a white pocket-handkerchief knotted at the four corners, which kept
dancing up and down, sometimes rising as high as the first floor window.'[5]
One time, 'a white towel' was seen lying on the floor. It rose into the air and
escaped under the door, before a 'heavy step' began treading down the stairs.[6]
    Some polts seem to go out of their way to appear in the most ridiculous
guises imaginable, yet again allowing themselves to be very easily dismissed
into a state of surpassing liminality. When a spook materialises at someone's
bedside in the shape of a strange man offering out several useless 'pieces of
tin' for no apparent reason,[7] or an apparitional dog comically pops up and

rings a dinner-gong,[8] then you have to ask how seriously it is possible to take such reports. Many witnesses are children, whose testimony may prove easy to dismiss. During one haunting, a small boy claimed to have seen a polt in the shape of a man with 'blue skin' with 'bubbles on it',[9] while one young lad nicknamed his resident spook 'Postman Pat' because he thought he dressed like him.[10] Another infant polt-focus accounted for her doll being ripped apart by having seen 'a queer animal with a green head, green eyes, and a big bushy tail' pulling her toy to shreds with its paws. A hallucination, obviously ... except that the little girl's sister shared this vision of a green devil simultaneously.[11]

* * * * *

Words cannot do justice to how silly the apparitions seen during a haunting at Sandfeld, Germany, during 1722 were; it is hard to accept they were literally real, in the sense of being corresponding visual representations of any actual existing invisible entities. And yet, they really do seem to have been witnessed by several people at once – all of them children. The visions began when a 'plague' of cats were perceived running about the haunted house, together with an odd, short-eared dog. That dog was not half as odd as the gigantic yellow one which then surprised the kids playing in the attic. This had 'a huge ugly head, with eyes as big as a child's head, a cow's snout, and only three legs' and it placed large barrels in front of the attic-door so their parents were unable to rescue their screaming offspring. Then, the spook appeared in the garden disguised as an angel called Nörcken. It sought an apron, which it tore into four pieces. A nearby adult could see no angel, but *did* see the apron moving through the air by itself. Later, this 'angel' gave the kids advice on how to exorcise the infesting demons – with the end result that the gullible parents ended up running about with pitchforks, seeking to stab their invisible assailants!

Reputedly, several small children were seen by adults to JOTTle away into thin air 'in the twinkling of an eye.' Later returned to our world, they said they had been apported to a subterranean realm inhabited by a race of 'little crooked people' who offered them coins to stay in fairy-land. The kids said no, being promptly apported back to the Earth's surface. The children also saw 'a cavalcade of strange rough things almost like calves, but smaller' fly up from a shed, flogged onwards by 'a big man with a great whip.'[12] Surely these were complete visual delusions; but delusions deliberately induced by the ghost, or not?

Just as incoherent was the poltergeist which haunted the Dagg family, of Clarendon, Quebec, in 1889.[13] The children of the house reported seeing the spirit appear 'at one time as a tall, thin man with a cow's head, horns, tail and a cloven foot, at another time as a big black dog [with 'hair like tails'], and finally as a man with a beautiful face and long white hair dressed in white, wearing a crown with stars in it.' One little girl even saw the polt as 'something in the shape of a man, but with horns and cloven hooves ... dressed in white, putting sugar in the oven', an appliance into which it also liked to JOTTle Bibles. This satanic cow-man turned to the kid and asked her if she'd like to visit Hell with him. Another time, it was perceived as 'a big black thing pulling off the bedclothes'. Adults couldn't see it, but they could hear it 'squealing like a pig' when they whipped out towards thin air under infant direction.

This loquacious spirit at first sounded like a gruff old man with a taste for obscenities, eventually becoming a beautiful, flute-throated being who sang hymns. Initially, the voice – which, unlike the apparitions, could be detected by both adults and children – manifested in the woodshed. When asked who it was, the spook spat back in horrible tones 'I am the Devil. I'll have you in my clutches. Get out of this or I'll break your neck.' Later, though, so eager was the polt to prove it was really an angel that it appeared in the yard dressed in shining ribbons, took two of the Dagg children in its arms, declaring how 'fine' it felt the baby boy to be, and sang hymns. It played a small harp before ascending into the sky engulfed by a bright red fire and vanishing forever.

Near the end of its career, after turning into a sweet-tongued spirit and publicly declaring it was about to leave Earth for good that Sunday, the ghost's astonishing reformation of character was remarked upon. The voice explained the entity they were speaking to now was 'not the person who had used that filthy language; I am an angel from Heaven sent by God to drive away that fellow.' This seemed demonstrably untrue as the polt quickly began contradicting itself, lost its temper and resumed swearing, 'saying many things quite out of harmony with his supposed heavenly origin'. It also claimed only to have ever spoken in harsh, rough tones because 'otherwise people would have believed that Dinah [the Daggs' adopted daughter] was doing it.' Perhaps the polt was suffering from a case of Multiple Personality Disorder, or MPD? After being asked by George Dagg, the father of the family, why it was persecuting them, the polt replied 'Just for fun.' It wasn't much fun when it had set the house on fire, replied Dagg. 'I didn't,' it protested. Then, the ghost *immediately* added, 'The fires always came in the daytime and where you could see them. I'm sorry I did it.'

Recall the Enfield poltergeist's complaint that 'I DON'T KNOW WHO I AM'; many poltergeists' personalities seem in a state of constant flux. Perhaps the Dagg devil and the Dagg angel were, at root, one and the same thing, but each aspect was so dissociated from its opposing counterpart that neither ever really knew what the other was doing. Thereby, the poltergeist could effectively play tricks upon *itself*, like Wakdjunkaga's warring hands killing the buffalo. According to Jung, the Trickster-figure 'is not really evil, he does the most atrocious things from sheer unconsciousness and unrelatedness',[14] rather like the Dagg poltergeist starting its fires.

MPD is a rare (and controversial – some medics don't believe in it) personality disorder where several 'people' appear to be living within one head, swapping around at random. Often, each personality has no knowledge whatsoever of the other personalities and their actions. On occasion, some 'people' know what the other 'people' inside the same head are doing, but the same is not true in reverse. When this happens, the personality with the mental advantage can play some rather cruel tricks upon the others. Take the celebrated case of Christine Beauchamp, a rather dull woman who found herself periodically 'taken over' by three other personalities. One, named Sally, was everything Christine wasn't; vivacious, mischievous and outgoing. Sally knew all about Christine; for example, that she was terrified of spiders. When in control of their shared body, Sally went out, gathered six of the largest arachnids she could find and placed them inside a box which she wrapped as a present in Christine's room. When Christine regained possession of her body, she saw the package and opened it before screaming and dropping the box, thus releasing the huge bugs to scurry all over her bedroom.[15] Another time, when Christine was travelling to New York to take up a respectable office job, Sally made her body get off the train and accept a lowly position as a waitress instead.[16] Did some rascally aspect of the Dagg poltergeist once pull a similar prank upon that better, more rarified aspect of it which manifested as an angel, in relation to the fires it lit?

An alternative viewpoint would be that the MPD belonged not to the Dagg polt *per se*, but to the case's focus-figure, Dinah McLean, a Scottish orphan who had been adopted by the Daggs aged eleven. According to the RSPK-promoter Iris M. Owen, Dinah was only adopted as a probable source of free labour, and unconsciously used the initial 'demonic' voice as an outlet to criticise her harsh guardians. Giving vent to her feelings must have made Dinah feel a little better, says Owen, leading on to the 'more amiable and conciliatory personality' of the angel later emerging, expressing her desire to move on and make up. Owen makes much of how the voice initially accused a neighbour, Mrs Wallace, of using her supposed 'Black Art' of witchcraft to conjure it up. Indignant, Mrs Wallace engaged in debate with the entity and got the better of it, causing it to make several self-contradictory statements. When the incoherence of its answers was pointed out, the voice lost its temper, growling 'Oh, don't bother me so much – you make me lie!' According to Owen, this outburst was the inevitable result of the inability of the less intelligent child's subconscious to handle the more sophisticated arguments of the adult Mrs Wallace.[17]

Direct parallels with the 'Dagg Demon' can be found at Battersea, where the spook claimed not only to be called Donald, but also a wide range of other dubious characters of an explicitly fire-raising nature. 'DONALD IS NOT AWARE OF ME', one particular alter-ego once informed the young focus-figure Shirley Hitchings, warning her not to tell her father about his existence either, lest 'I BE ANGRY AND SET FIRE'.[18] These were no idle threats. Donald commanded Shirley to summon a journalist he wanted to talk to, warning 'I WILL SET HOUSE AFIRE IF YOU DON'T … SO TAKE CARE'. Later that night, a floating match struck itself in mid-air, fell down and singed Shirley's eyebrow. 'I JUST GIVEN YOU TASTE OF WHAT I AM GOING TO DO … SO DO AS I SAY – GET HIM – OBEY – IT IS YOUR MASTER', warned the ghost – Donald wears the trousers. Soon, green flashes and smoke were being seen and bedclothes found aflame, necessitating the presence of the fire-brigade.[19]

Many of Donald's fiery threats were rather comic: 'YOU MADE ME ANGRY – I SET FIRE – YOU CAN'T STOP ME – YOU ALL MUST DIE – NO ESCAPE NOW – I DO NOT KID – GET OUT OF HOME – FOR TONIGHT I SET ATOMIC GAS OFF'.[20] Donald was generally a pleasant, humorous character, though, not a murderous arsonist or atomic terrorist, and, to account for such discrepancies, later began claiming he had not set any fires at all. If Shirley didn't do what he said, Donald once warned her that 'THEY' would 'BE NAULTY [naughty] TONIGHT'[21] – but who were 'THEY', precisely? Another pair of arsonist spooks called Miky and Dopy were now haunting the house too, threatening to leave a 'TIME BOMB HIDDEN' within it, until Donald 'GOT RID OF THEM', so he said. These twin entities fed off Donald's power, though, so he could not guarantee to ward them off forever. However, Donald at other times carelessly warned under his own name that 'I AM GO TO BE BAD TONIGHT – HA ... SET FIRE UNDER FLOOR'.[22] The best explanation Donald could devise for such inconsistency was that he had a short temper. 'I HUMBERLY OPLAJISE [humbly apologise] FOR [setting more fires] LAST NIGHT', he once rapped out, sheepishly, 'BUT YOU MADE ME ANGRY'.[23] You wouldn't like Donald when he was angry – like Bruce Banner, he became an entirely different person. He also became green; upon one occasion, Shirley suddenly found herself engulfed within emerald-hued 'blazes of fire' but, shamaness-like, emerged unharmed and unburnt from this ordeal.[24]

To complicate matters, other unpleasant polts then arrived on the scene too, Donald cautioning of one that 'IT IS BAD MAN', most unlike himself.[25] One particularly 'BAD MAN' hanging out in the Hitchings' home was Shaggy Roots, named after the wispy hairs emanating from the chin of the family's live-in grandmother, from whom he allegedly drew his psychic RSPK energy. 'I WARN YOU, HE POWERFUL' advised Donald, and, even worse, 'LIKES TO PLAY WITH FIRE', possessing the ability to turn the gas on, cut the pipe then ignite it, blowing the house up. 'I WARN YOU IT IS NO GAME BELEAVE ME – I AM HERE TO GUARD YOU', said Donald.[26] Shaggy lived in that classic liminal zone of the attic, where a candle and paraffin-lamp were JOTTled, and poured rat-poison over beds, irritating skin when people touched it.[27] Donald liked to give the impression of a young and valiant warrior battling against his malevolent rival,[28] once pledging to organise a meeting of the other household familiars 'FOR SHAGY ROOTS DISMISSAL OUT OF THE HOUSE'.[29]

Evicting Shaggy wouldn't do too much good, though – another spook would be along to replace him in a minute, such as Moaning Jim, a disembodied voice which spent its days lamenting mournfully 'Oh Ethel, Ethel' over and over again.[30] Worse, the house might even end up being invaded by aliens instead of ghosts. Knowing the case's chief investigator was interested in UFOs, Donald proclaimed that 'I WILL DO HARM TO ANYONE WHO DON'T BELIEVE IN FLYING SAUCERS', and promised to reveal many secrets about life in outer-space, such as the astonishing knowledge that there were 'THINGS' living on other planets, some of which were 8 feet tall. Donald knew this as 'I COME FROM THE ATMOSPHERE', but when it came to space-travel, we puny living humans 'GOT A LONG WAY TO GO', even though acquiring true knowledge of the cosmos was 'CHILD'S PLAY'. To prove this, Donald began speaking in a language called 'MARSON' (or Martian, in Earth-spelling): 'GILBOARTEMNRYLCHETYMARESASRIS IEFDRDKAPLAIETOEKEERKIM'. Sounds more like Welsh to me. In supposed contact with a being called Monga the Martian, Donald was quite the cunning interplanetary linguist, claiming proficiency in both Venusian and Saturnian, too. On Saturn, he said, the ETs 'TALK LIKE US' – that is to say, a lot of nonsense, presumably.[31]

* * * * *

With the hauntings of the Dagg and Hitchings families, we have ghosts which not only suffer from MPD, but also seek to evade responsibility for their own actions by saying that other ghosts pulled their tricks, not them, like when a child muddies a carpet then says 'It wasn't me, it was my invisible friend Trevor' (or Shaggy, Miky or Dopy, maybe). There is another parallel for this from within Trickster-lore, taken from the Bible. Some commentators have claimed that God Himself – in the shape of the Jehovah/Yahweh of the Old Testament, anyway – is yet another Trickster-god, as can be seen in episodes such as his *Candid Camera*-style persuasion of Abraham to brutally sacrifice his son to him as a murderous offering, only to step in at the last moment and say 'Only joking!'

In his book *Answer to Job*, C. G. Jung retells the story of another victim of Jehovah's pranks, namely Job, the ultimate man of faith. Satan makes the taunt that the rich man Job only worships God because of his fortunate station in life, so, to test Job's faith, Jehovah kills his servants, makes his family abandon him, lays waste to his cattle and empowers Satan to smite Job 'with sore boils from the sole of his foot unto his crown.'[32] The innocent Job protests he does not deserve this punishment – yet tempers this by praising Jehovah's justice, despite the evident fact he is presently receiving none. According to Jung, this demonstrates that Job 'clearly sees that God is at odds with Himself – so totally at odds that he, Job, is quite certain of finding in God a helper and an 'advocate' against God. As certain as he is of the evil in Yahweh, he is equally certain of the good.'[33]

Just as Wakdjunkaga's right arm found a protestor against itself in his left arm, so God contains an 'advocate' within Himself against his own immoral actions, as if He too has a split personality, like the Daggs' angel-demon. But Jehovah is no mere Jekyll and Hyde; he is every other potential Tom, Dick and Harry, too. To Jung, Jehovah's mentality is inherently that of 'an *antinomy* – a totality of inner opposites – and this is the indispensable condition for his tremendous dynamism, his omniscience and omnipotence.'[34] If God is truly omnipotent, then He is *everything*, all of Creation, all at once; He must be evil *as well* as good, simultaneously. In this view, Satan himself is not actually a separate entity, simply a limited and personified aspect of Jehovah, escaped from his parent soul and given temporary shape of character, like Shaggy Roots and Moaning Jim branching out from Donald.

As Jung says, Yahweh 'is too unconscious to be moral. Morality presupposes consciousness … He is everything in its totality; therefore, among other

Job endures his torments, as imagined by William Blake. Many poltergeist victims have had to demonstrate similar levels of fortitude down the years.

257

things, He is total justice, and also its total opposite ... [but these opposites] are not sufficiently related to one another, with the result that they fall apart into mutually contradictory acts'.[35] To Jung, the Old Testament God exists only in infinite internal opposition to Himself as a series of competing 'God Archetypes' including Satan, whose advice He acts upon in the Book of Job, but rejects elsewhere. Satan, in this reading, is nothing more than a convenient personification of some of Yahweh's more ungodly desires, in the same way Shaggy Roots was a convenient personification of Donald's wish to raise fires.

The root personality of Jung's God would be just as incoherent as the mind of the poltergeist; if God is Yahweh *and* Satan all in one, then we are back at Battersea, but on a much larger scale. To Jung, Yahweh existed as a coherent entity only in the minds of men who were able to conceive of Him as such. He only began to be known when man began to know Him: 'Such dependence on the object [the person who believes in Him] is absolute when the subject is totally lacking in self-reflection and therefore has no insight into Himself. It is as if He existed only by reason of the fact that He has an object which assures him He is really there.'[36] The disembodied consciousness of the poltergeist – incoherent, self-contradictory and full of a series of potential identities – is very much like that of the Trickster-God of the Old Testament. Both need to be observed, interacted with and believed in if they are ever to develop any perceptible form or depth of character. Possibly this is the reason why polts react so inconsistently to exorcisms – because, being a vast Yahweh-like *pleroma* of possible identities themselves, they are both God and the Devil at the same time. But, like all MPD patients, they are also so much more ...

*****

On 14 September 1612 a French Huguenot Minister, François Perrault, returned to his home in Mâcon to find the place in utter disarray.[37] Weird bee-buzzing noises were heard, blankets were pulled and objects thrown around. The poltergeist – the infamous 'Devil of Mascon' – soon developed a voice, which it abused to tell blatant lies about its own identity. According to Perrault, the spirit on one occasion 'did offer to transform himself into an angel of light, saying of his own accord and very loud, the Lord's Prayer, the Creed, the morning and evening prayers and the Ten Commandments.' Another time, he sang 'profane and bawdy songs', which is not *too* angelic. When Perrault gave vent to harsh biblical invective against the ghost, it replied, rather anguished, 'Thou liest; I am not cursed; I hope yet for salvation by the death and passion of Jesus Christ.' It mockingly told Perrault to send for a priest to exorcise it as an evil spirit ('don't let him forget to bring the holy water!'), whereas it later claimed to have silenced the noisy barks of Perrault's dog by having 'made the sign of the cross over its head' as if *it* were the holy exorcist. It also claimed to come from a region called the Pays de Vaud, a notorious centre of French sorcery, thus implying it was a witch-conjured Hell-beast ... then denied the fact. Sometimes the spook joked good-naturedly about being called a demon by its unwilling host, at others it seemed extremely angry, threatening to pull Perrault from bed by his feet for slander.

As the haunting progressed, the MPD-addled polt claimed he was not the same spirit who had spoken before, merely the previous entity's servant. When told he was talking nonsense, the demon replied most politely, like all good manservants should: 'I beseech you, sir, to pardon me. You are mistaken in me; you take me for another. I never was in this house before. I pray, sir, what is your name?' The ghost now seemed to think he was a living person, saying 'in a faint and moaning tone' that he had to go to the town of Chambéry to pursue a lawsuit but feared he might die on the way, so requested he be allowed make his will; it was while absent pursuing this important legal case that he sent his valet to stand in for him. The servant-ghost, being poorly paid by its demonic master, offered to leave the house too in return for some suitable gift or other, perhaps money. 'I wouldn't give you my nail-clippings,' said Perrault. 'You're not very charitable,' replied the spirit.

Soon, a further ghostly valet appeared, denying he was the previous disembodied servant (who was merely 'one of my pals') and bemoaning the absence of his master in Chambéry. Away in that same town of Chambéry, meanwhile, a loquacious polt had indeed recently taken up residence in the home of a local legal official, one Monsieur Favre, saying it had come from Mâcon on a visit! It didn't demand any legal advice, merely asked lashings and lashings of food be prepared for the imminent arrival of its 'master', before bursting into a series of rude songs and impressions of street-hawkers. Given its behaviour, we can presume the spirit in Chambéry was really that very same one simultaneously pretending to be its own servants, back in Mâcon.

Even more outlandish, the ghost claimed to have appeared at the table of Perrault's elder brother in physical, flesh-and-blood human form and taken a drink with him; a stranger had indeed recently joined the other brother's table, though presumably this was really just an ordinary human traveller. The ghost knew of various events which had happened in distant places and times so could easily have been aware of the elder Perrault's recent visitor. Having the ability to create radio play-like sound effects from thin air – croaking like a frog, or causing the ringing of bells to emerge from people's purses when they opened them – the spook could assume any verbal identity it wished. The protean being even offered to appear to Perrault in whatever visual form he liked, whether man, woman, lion, bear, dog or cat. Sensibly, Perrault replied he'd rather not have to see it at all!

Having exhausted its full range of impressions, the spook tore up its script upon 25 November 1612, taking its final bow thus: 'Ha ha! I shan't speak any more!' This time, it told the truth – the Devil of Mascon spoke not another word. It kept up its other forms of whimsy, tying ropes to bedposts in inextricable knots and making objects JOTTle, but no longer while claiming to be anything other than an ordinary, common-or-garden poltergeist. At last, this was an honest soul. Finally, on 22 December, the spirit quit Perrault's house for good – and, the very next day, a very large (and very real) viper was observed slithering out and proclaimed to be Satan vacating the premises by superstitious locals, who captured it with tongs and took it to an apothecary for closer examination. Given the other false forms the demon shaped itself into, you can hardly blame them.

* * * * *

Another poltergeist in two minds about whether it was Satan or Yahweh was the 'Wizard Clip', a spook which, as we saw earlier, gained its name from its habit of cutting out shapes in clothing with a pair of invisible scissors.[38] Disturbances began in the district of Middleway, West Virginia, sometime in the late 1700s on the farmstead of Adam Livingstone and family. Phantom horse-hooves were heard, objects moved around, fires erupted (one destroying a barn) and clothes were shredded. An Episcopalian Minister tried his hand at exorcism, only for his prayer-book to be thrown into a chamber-pot. A Methodist was then chased out of the house, pelted with lithobolic stones. A travelling Irish pedlar suggested a Catholic priest was the only flavour of clergyman with enough gumption to deal with such a powerful demon and, despite the Protestant Livingstones' initial reluctance, a Father Dennis Cahill did in the end arrive and drive the spirit out.

So impressed was Adam Livingstone that he quickly converted to Rome, despite his wife's misgivings. It was not too long before the Wizard then returned – but in a new, much more Pope-friendly guise. A blinding light filled the house at nights, while a disembodied voice talked about the necessity of conversion to the Catholic faith; loud and horrible screams were heard around the property, coming, so the voice claimed, from sinners trapped in purgatory. The first wail was so disturbing Adam collapsed when he heard it; the ghost's instructions for the family to pray for the release of these tortured souls was doubtless obeyed. The voice later sang beautifully in Latin and English, while a phantom hand appeared, making the sign of the cross. Upon one occasion Adam attempted to grab this holy hand – only to have it punch him in the face. The spook then forcibly imparted moral lessons to its victims via the medium of poltergeistery, with a shattered mirror illustrating the follies of vanity, for instance.

Punching people and smashing mirrors don't seem terribly Christian things to do, and sure enough Beelzebub soon turned up on the scene too. When a cradle containing a neighbour's baby began rocking violently, the angelic voice told Adam the Devil was trying to get at a child who would one day be his enemy (the baby grew up to be a Jesuit priest). Foretelling the future was something the polt was good at – that, and persecuting Mrs Livingstone, who resented her enforced new faith and whose every attempt at religious rebellion was stymied by the ghost. Sick of having to abstain from meat on a Friday, she locked a bowl of stew in the cellar one Thursday night, but found it replaced by a bowlful of water. Eventually, the voice, allegedly now the spirit of a dead priest, prophesied that 'Before the end of time' the Livingstone farmstead 'would become a great place of prayer and fasting and praise!' This prophecy too came true; Adam transferred ownership of 35 acres to the Church, and a chapel was built there in 1928. In 1809, the Livingstones sold up and moved to Pennsylvania. As far as is known, the Wizard Clip did not follow, in either hellish or in holy shape.

* * * * *

The notorious Bell Witch of Tennessee, who first took up acting as a career in 1817, was even more schizophrenic. Through a disembodied voice with a harsh and metallic tone, the poltergeist claimed, variously, to be 'a spirit from everywhere ... Heaven, Hell, the Earth' who was 'in the air, in houses, in any place at any time' and who had 'been created for millions of years', a ghost who 'was once very happy' but who had 'been disturbed and made unhappy', an Indian whose bones had been scattered without proper burial and whose tooth lay now beneath the Bell farmhouse keeping it from its rest, a dead child and, finally, the astral projection of a local 'witch' called Old Kate Batts who was indeed a real and eccentric local resident, but no evil sorceress.[39]

Pretending to be the 'Toothless Indian', the Witch simply laughed at John Bell, the head of the family, when, after he had dug up the floor in search of the lost molar, she admitted it was all just a joke intended to make him look a fool.[40] On another occasion, when John was 'begging' with the Witch to reveal her true identity, she took pity and swore him to secrecy; she was, she said, none other than his dead stepmother. To 'prove' this, the Witch performed a perfect vocal impression of this woman, scolding a servant. Wisely, John did not believe her.[41] Another time, the Witch said it was now visible on a particular wall. All eyes turned to the spot indicated, where a large black insect was crawling around. John immediately squashed it, whereupon the Witch began to laugh 'heartily', exclaiming 'Lord Jesus, what a fool I did make of old Jack Bell.'[42]

Later on, four *different* voices appeared, declaring themselves not the Witch herself, but her 'family': Blackdog, Mathematics, Cypocryphy and Jerusalem. Jerusalem had the voice of a boy, Blackdog sounded harsh but feminine, whereas Cypocryphy (an obscure astrological term) and Mathematics were more delicate and feminine in tone. This 'family' talked among themselves, having invisible parties around the house and causing the place to stink of whiskey. These 'exhibitions', apparently, 'opened like a drunken carousel and became perfect pandemonium, frightful to the extreme, from which there was no escape.'[43] During such revels, the voices would quarrel and fight, leaving Blackdog to referee, uttering threats of murder and violence against the others and thrashing Jerusalem most severely for his misdemeanours. At other times, when still sober, the four voices became very civil and would engage in pious hymn-singing sessions together.

The Bell Witch appears in the shape of a two-headed dog to successfully frighten a black slave.

Once, the Witch's family were actually seen – and shot at – by Bennett Porter, the husband of one of the Bell daughters, Esther. One day, Esther saw a neighbour walking up the lane. She said hello, but the woman didn't seem to hear; she just removed her bonnet and combed her hair repeatedly, appearing 'deeply absorbed or troubled'. After five minutes, she walked to a nearby grove of saplings. Then two young girls and a boy appeared and proceeded to each bend down a tree and sit on it, riding the supple young trunks up and down under their weight. Bennett Porter himself was unable to see the ghosts; but what he *could* see were the saplings, acting like see-saws. The phantoms then hid behind an old log, peeping their heads out over the top like targets at a fairground stall. Bennett determined to shoot the intruders, and Esther agreed to direct her unseeing husband where to aim his rifle. He fired and hit the log, but the ghosts just disappeared. That night, during their usual drunken cavorting, the Witch's family made great play of the fact that Bennett Porter had shot right at Jerusalem, and had succeeded in breaking his arm with the bullet.[44]

Sometimes, the Witch chose to appear not as a human being, but as an animal. John Bell once saw an odd, Skinwalker Ranch-style dog-like creature – 'unlike any he had ever seen' – sitting between some rows of corn and shot at it. A few days later, Drew Bell, one of John's children, spied a bird perching upon a fence. As the bird suddenly flapped its wings and flew away, Drew was 'mystified' to discover it was 'some unknown bird of extraordinary size'.[45] The Witch openly boasted it could assume the shape of any creature it so wished – which might be why one of the slaves on the farm claimed to have encountered it in the form of a large black dog, 'sometimes ... [with] two heads, and at other times no head.'[46] The Witch could even appear as an inanimate object. According to John Bell Jr, the family's youngest son: 'One autumn afternoon in 1828 ... a dense sulphur smoke filled the hallway from floor to ceiling, and as soon as the smoke cleared away, a black ball as large as a water bucket, seemingly composed of black wool, rolled softly across the hall floor and on into the family room to a wide open fireplace and went up the chimney.'[47] The Witch teased John Bell Sr that 'I live in the woods, in the air, in the water, in houses with people; I live in Heaven and in Hell; I am all things and anything I want to be; now don't you know what I am?'[48] Apparently he didn't; but she sounds very much like Proteus or a personification of the *anima mundi* to me!

Some of this is probably just folklore – the story of the original haunting was definitely added to down the years. What is true, however, is that Betsy Bell, John Bell's daughter and the likely focus of the whole affair, suffered certain strange medical problems, being subject to what used to be termed 'hysterical fits'. Interestingly, whenever Betsy fainted – as she often did – all the voices ceased, as her mind blanked out. This fact led Nandor Fodor to speculate that the 'Witch' therefore came purely from within Betsy's own mind. Fodor claimed (without any real evidence, as usual) that Betsy had been raped by her father and that, as such, her psyche, like that of a typical MPD patient, had fractured into several parts. These then manifested externally in the form of the poltergeist which, it is alleged, ultimately ended up killing her rapist dad with a vial of JOTTled poison. If so, then the Witch,

Cypocryphy, Mathematics, Blackdog and Jerusalem were simply fragmented aspects of Betsy herself, gaining poisonous revenge by proxy.

* * * * *

A case which holds striking parallels with the Bell Witch haunting is that of the 'Coalbaggie Bogey', which inhabited the home of a German immigrant named Peter Stein in Coalbaggie Creek, Australia, from 1891 to 1894.[49] A 'bogey' is a hairy, prank-playing, boggart-like fairy shape-shifter from old English folklore … and, evidently, from old German folklore, too. The first the Steins knew of their new home being haunted was when they heard 'strange voices, loud cooeyings and awful screamings' coming from outside at night. Then, the furniture 'became as possessed', while crockery smashed on the floor; those dishes made from tin, the spook destroyed by hammering upon them so hard they were left covered in dents. It took a particular dislike to religious paraphernalia, breaking a crucifix into little pieces before casting these shards into the Steins' faces. When the family were kneeling around a table praying one day, this same table flew up into the air to spite them.

The polt developed a voice and, just like the Bell Witch, delivered an unlikely back-story to account for its presence, claiming to be a man named George William Herbert, whose mother and sister had burned to death inside an old hut on the Steins' land years beforehand. According to George's own account, his mother had been ironing when her dress had caught fire. Dying, she handed across a gold watch and £60 to George's aunt, asking her to pass it on to him. However, George's gold-greedy uncle hit George on the head before leaving him to die out on the roadside, where he had somehow managed to regain consciousness and survive by eating weeds, a yarn which would appear untrue. Like many MPD-suffering polts, the bogey showed little consistency in its tones. Sometimes it spoke in a 'gruff manly voice' so loud 'that it ought to be heard a mile away' while at others it whispered 'as softly as a woman'. Often, the entity talked 'sensibly enough' but on other occasions it seemed 'quite mad' and swore atrociously, singing songs.

Whenever it was about to manifest, the family dogs went 'nearly wild with fear and excitement', with 'their hair standing up and their eyes bulging out of their heads', thus giving the Steins advance warning. This was useful, as the spirit made repeated attempts to burn the house down, particularly liking to singe female clothing, as if reliving the alleged circumstances of its mother's own fiery demise. This supposed tragedy had warped the poltergeist's mind; when chided for smashing so many cups and dishes, the spook pleaded it 'couldn't help it' because, when its mother caught ablaze, George had been handling crockery and had dropped it in shock, an event he felt compelled to repeat ever afterwards. The entity was capable of passing a fire-safety course if it really wanted to, however, as it once cooked itself a meal; reputedly, the polt took down a frying-pan, cracked six eggs into it, and held it over the fire to fry them with invisible hands.

As for what the bogey looked like – well, it promised never to reveal itself visually to the Steins, on the grounds that 'those who saw him would faint, for they had never seen anything like him before.' According to the testimony of the adult son of the household, Jacob Stein, the ghost did not quite keep this promise, however:

> One night … clods were pelted at us as if by some person in the fireplace. We looked and saw a strange figure. It had the body of a child, about five years old, and with a most peculiar face, with a whitish beard on it. I went to catch it and it disappeared. On another occasion I saw something like a hand coming over a box, and when I tried to grasp it there was nothing [there].

Even more bizarre were the poltergeist's appearances in animal-form:

> … on one occasion, it came in the shape of a bear, got up on the wall of the kitchen, and when we went to chase it away, it disappeared in a white smoke. On another occasion, a big mouse, about a foot long, came on the roof, and it mysteriously moved about … and another day a wallaby was near the house and it would not shift for my sisters. They tried to put the dogs on it, but [they] came back with their tails between their legs. My brother and myself put two kangaroo-dogs on it, and it ran into the creek and disappeared as if into the ground. The dogs came out on the other side looking terribly frightened … That night it talked to us and said … that it was the wallaby we were chasing. It said it could appear as a lizard or a snake or in any shape it liked.

You can see why the entity became known as the Coalbaggie Bogey; legends of shape-shifting bogey-beasts have now all-but died out, but would still have been current in rural areas during the 1890s, and a spirit appearing now as a hearth-dwelling fairy, now as a bear and now as a mouse, could more easily have been assimilated into this old tradition. In 1800s Tennessee, a similar Trickster's victims preferred to call their Proteus a 'Witch'. Nowadays, however, we try and assimilate these beings' actions under the more familiar modern umbrella of the poltergeist.

*****

Probably, many poltergeist-apparitions are merely hallucinations – whether originating from within the spirit-world, or from within the panicked human mind, we cannot tell. But, wherever they are from, why should these spectres appear as hybrid men with cow's heads and other such fantastic and implausible forms? To Patrick Harpur, the very triviality and absurdity of so many visions and apparitions are 'an essential part of them, pointing to a radical realignment of what we call reality … if these strange visitations have any purpose at all, it is to subvert the same modern worldview which discredits them.'[50] Indeed. Everybody knows such things cannot be real, so it is all the more surprising when people actually begin seeing them; it is an excellent lesson in the need not always to take things so literally. Remember! Should a Trickster ever try and introduce himself to you, he will almost certainly come wearing a mask…

XI

Theatres of the Absurd

The secret of acting is sincerity. If you can fake that, you've got it made.

George Burns

Some mask-swapping poltergeists seem intent on staging a gigantic piece of interactive comic theatre for their audiences' benefit, playing all the chief roles themselves like Alec Guinness in *Kind Hearts and Coronets*. An excellent example would be Donald the Battersea poltergeist adopting the alternative guise of the Dauphin, a deceased Revolutionary-era French prince who had supposedly escaped the guillotine only to drown in the English Channel, a tragic narrative imparted through coded raps and a flood of written notes. But this was a very media-savvy ghost. When, by coincidence, a film was released about the real-life Dauphin's adventures, named *Dangerous Exile*, his shade sneaked into a Leicester Square cinema to see it, with no ticket. The Dauphin was outraged by the movie's inaccuracies. It was 'ALL WRONG', he complained, 'EVEN MY HAIR WAS WRONG'. Furthermore, 'I DID NOT ESCAPE TO ENGLAND IN A BALLOON OR IN A LAUNDRY BASKET'. Much more plausibly, he had really fled from post-Revolutionary captivity disguised as a chimney-sweep.[1]

At other times the ghost was actively keen on imitating fictional media products. It once claimed to really be someone called 'Colly Ziber' – this turned out to be a misspelling of Colley Cibber, a Restoration-era playwright and poet associated with London's Drury Lane Theatre, about whom the BBC had broadcast a TV play on the very day that these messages from 'Ziber' had come through. It seemed Donald had read the description of the programme in the *Radio Times* and decided to play one of the figures from its cast list for himself.[2] Maybe the character of the Dauphin had similar origins; Donald enjoyed watching TV, including the 1955–56 ITV series *The Adventures of the Scarlet Pimpernel*, from which set-in-France show it later appeared he had stolen some of the general pseudo-historical details about his own latest regal role.[3]

It was in May 1956 that Donald first began pretending to be the Dauphin, scattering his communications with misspelled French (like 'CHERRY' for *'Cherie'* or 'ORAWAR' for *'au revoir'*) of a kind which suspiciously matched

Restoration playwright Colley
Cibber, whose identity was also
fraudulently adopted by the
Battersea poltergeist. (Yale Center for
British Art)

the misspellings of the focus-figure Shirley Hitchings' own poor schoolgirl
French. It is unlikely a genuine non-dyslexic Frenchman would spell out
the words to *Frère Jacques* thus: 'FAIRA SHUKER, FAIRA SHUKER,
DOM AVOW, SELEMENA DING DONG DAM'.[4] Unfortunately, the
Dauphin's back-story only sounded vaguely plausible upon first hearing it;
once specific details were looked up in reference books, it turned out the
spirit had committed innumerable historical howlers, such as not knowing
his correct name or claiming to have been born in 1798 when the French
Revolution itself had taken place nine years earlier. The Dauphin tried to
explain that the history books were mistaken, but if so then this was quite an
error for chroniclers to have made. The exposed liar engaged in toy-smashing
temper-tantrums, but then changed tack, saying he had died over a century
ago, so maybe his memory was just a bit faulty. In 2001, DNA analysis of
what turned out to be the real Dauphin's heart, preserved safe and dry in a
Paris crypt, eventually proved the polt's story about having drowned at sea
to have been false in its entirety.[5]

Undeterred, the dubious 'Dauphin' retreated further into his assumed
character, demanding he be addressed as 'HIS ROYAL HIGHNESS, PRINCE
LOUIS OF ALL FRANCE' and ordering a letter be mailed to the French
President informing him of his rightful liege's miraculous return.[6] More
strikingly, the Dauphin also began transforming the Battersea home into
a huge stage-set, reminiscent of the Palace of Versailles. He would graffiti
walls – and even Shirley's flesh – with fleurs-de-lys symbols and crossed
swords, and rearranged furniture to make it look as if he had been holding
conferences with his ghostly Ministers of State. Chairs were arrayed in circles,
books and papers left out on tables, mirrors draped over with sheets, and
the smell of half-smoked cigars lingered around the place. Shields were also
drawn on walls, and the words 'ROI LOUIS' – or 'KING LOUIS' – scrawled
out in black lead. The Dauphin actually asked Shirley to help him decorate

his throne-room; she witnessed a blue cloth fly up and pin itself to the wall 'like drop-curtains at a theatre'.[7]

By now, young Shirley had become both the female co-star and chief stage designer in her own supernatural stage play. Donald apported allegedly antique items such as crowns, signet-ring seals, sword hilts and royal ribbons around the place, but they were all just cheap modern fakes, of precisely the kind set-dressers would use.[8] Maybe Donald really was the ghost of Colley Cibber after all. He certainly made shrill demands about the treatment of his leading lady to her parents: 'THIS NOT LIKE THE PALACE IN FRANCE – SHIRLEY MUST DRESS LIKE A LADY OF COURT – GET HER DRESS, SKIRT, BLOUSE, COAT, SHOES AND DON'T WORRY ABOUT BANK MONEY – GET SOME OUT MONDAY – DO AS I SAY – SHE CANNOT LOOK LIKE A SERVANT – SHE IS MY GIRLY'.[9] It turned out she was actually the reincarnation of the Queen of Portugal: 'I REALLY WANT HER TO BE CALLED: LINGA DA SILVER – IT MEANS QUEEN OF PORTUGAL – SEE CLEAR?'[10] 'I WANT YOU TO BE MY PRINCESS', the Dauphin told Shirley, 'MY LIVING PRINCESS'. He even gave her a title, 'HER ROYAL HIGHNESS PRICNESS RENEE DE PARIS – RENEE DE FRANCE – MAIRE ANN DE SECOND DE COURT DE LOUIS'.[11]

The poltergeist planned to enrol Shirley at RADA as a trainee actress; he was sure she could 'BECOME A STAR', but needed 'A PUSH' from her handsome prince to do so.[12] But it doesn't sound as if Shirley needed *that* much of a shove to play at being a Little Princess. The spook ordered the teenage Shirley to begin playing with her childhood dolls again, and dress them up as Marie Antoinette, Elizabeth I, Anne Boleyn and Prince Louis himself. The fashion-mad Shirley gladly obliged, posing these dolls into regal scenes. 'I LIKE TO PLAY WIHT DOLLS OF MY OWN', said the Dauphin, but his real living doll was Shirley herself, or 'Renee' as he took to calling her, after her middle-name, Irene. Interestingly, Renee means 'reborn', just as Shirley was supposed to be the reincarnation of a Portuguese queen. Royal ceremonies were big news in the 1950s; 1953 had seen Queen Elizabeth II's coronation, and in 1956 Hollywood ice-queen Grace Kelly married Prince Rainier, becoming Princess Grace of Monaco. It was no wonder the ghost said things like 'TODAY LET'S PLAY YOUR DOLL TINA IS GETTING MARRIED – SHE SHALL HAVE A ROYAL WEDDING' in a 'DREAM DRESS' of the Dauphin's own design.[13]

At this point, Shirley, kept in a state of enforced unemployment by the spook, now wasted most days playing with her dolls. Possibly realising in the long-term this was unsustainable, the spirit helped persuade Shirley to attend art school to study theatrical costume design, an area in which the Dauphin had already given her much doll-related practical experience. Eventually she had to drop out from her studies, however, whereupon the polt redoubled his infantile doll-obsession, commanding Shirley to make more costumes for them, and leaving elaborate sketched instructions to her father for making miniature furniture, which were compliantly obeyed. He also resumed treating Shirley like a living mannequin herself, making demands that her mother pay for new clothes and new hairstyles to make her resemble certain TV actresses of the day.[14]

There is a circular relationship at work here, in which poltergeist and focus-figure alike are both audience and actors, and writers and readers, simultaneously, a pattern which recurs in many such tales. The suburb of Battersea had been the scene of an earlier poltergeist haunting in 1927–28, which had taken place no more than a 10-minute walk away from the Hitchings' own haunted home. This had also featured the ultra-rare trope of a ghost which wrote notes claiming to have been from a supposed historical figure. Slips of paper would float down from thin air, saying things like 'I am having a bad time here. I cannot rest. I was born during the time of William the Conqueror – Tom Blood.' Members of Shirley's family remembered this previous haunting well, and must surely have mentioned it during their own outbreak of poltergeistery, perhaps giving Donald/the Dauphin – or Shirley's own subconscious – ideas about how any such entity might choose to manifest.[15] A lying poltergeist inspired by the lies of another lying poltergeist; sometimes, it seems that all the world truly is a stage, and every haunting a kind of inescapable community theatre in the round.

* * * * *

Consider also the highly melodramatic case of Ken Webster, a schoolteacher whose centuries-old farmhouse in the Cheshire countryside was haunted during the early 1980s by a polt which staged a most elaborate charade, pretending to be a whole range of people from both the past (the 1500s) and the future (the year 2109), when futurenauts had developed the capacity for time-travel. The first sign of a Trickster at work was a trail of Hermes-style impossible six-toed footprints leading directly *up a wall* to the ceiling, into which the prints then disappeared like those of H. P. Lovecraft's Brown Jenkin/Gef the Murderous Mongoose hopping into the fourth dimension via the instant folding of a tesseract.[16] Then, tins of cat-food and bottles of lemonade piled up into pyramids in the kitchen overnight, followed by certain acts of 'very careful vandalism'[17] before a BBC Microcomputer found itself being typed on with ghostly hands. An early message left was a poem so redolent of a fragmented consciousness it could have been a lost verse from *The Waste Land*:

GET OUT YOUR BRICKs
PuSSy Cat PUSSy Cat Went TO LonDOn TO Seek
Fame aNd FORTUNE
Faith Must NOT Be LOst
For ThiS Shall Be your REDEEMER.[18]

Soon, the computer-literate ghost was claiming to be a series of mid-Renaissance country folk, one of whom had been visited by a green-glowing man from the future who, via obscure means, had installed a duplicate holographic-sounding projection of Ken's BBC Micro inside his chimney and showed him how to type on it with his mind (or by singing to it).[19] However, his secret had been discovered and the unfortunate fellow now stood accused of witchcraft when all he was really guilty of was an unorthodox method of word-processing. The poltergeist did its best to pretend to be a dweller in the past by stealing a photo of a car then returning it to Ken, charred around the edges, together with a message that, without any horse attached, it wouldn't go very far. Then it immediately undermined such fine work by making basic historical errors which seriously undermined its credibility, just like the Battersea Dauphin had three decades earlier.[20]

When pretending to hail from 2109, the polt exploited many hoary old sci-fi stereotypes. It invented comical descriptions of how to achieve time-travel by instantaneously swapping persons from two time frames around in a manner akin to teleporting pebbles from one dish to another in a pair of scales in order to achieve cosmic balance, warned of the dangers of Time Lords meeting their earlier selves and thus exploding the space–time continuum, babbled on about the significance of living within 'WHAT YOU WOULD CALL A TACHYON UNIVERSE', explained the true solution to the UFO mystery (witnesses were actually seeing through time and glimpsing future persons whizzing about in hover-ships and misinterpreting what they were, just like someone from the past misunderstanding a photo of a car), and ordered Ken to call a 'brilliant' ufologist they liked the sound of out to the haunted house – to facilitate this, the ghost provided Ken with the man's correct telephone number![21] Together with brilliant ufologists, Ken called out the SPR too, but they weren't much use. Perhaps they were spooked by the futurenauts' offer to reveal the answer to the then still-unsolved Fermat's Last Theorem in return for their immortal souls, or perplexed by their teasingly enigmatic questions like 'WHAT ARE [YOUR] THEORIES OF CAUSALITY, WHAT ANSWERER [DO YOU] HAVE FOR ITS PARADOX?'[22] I want to know that too, if you've been paying attention.

When asked to provide their names, these future-beings – who sometimes inferred they existed 'outside' of time, as Jungian archetypes like the Trickster are supposed to, rather than literally in the year 2109 as such – answered as follows: 'WHAT IS OUR NAME? TOO PERFECT THAT WE MAKE MISTAKES, AS WE MUST HAVE A CHARACTOR ... HOW CAN WE HAVE A NAME? WE ARE MANY BUT NO MORE THAN ONE IN THE TIME TO COME.'[23] Like at Enfield, the poltergeist didn't know who it was here at all. It did, however, know what a poltergeist itself was! The 1500s-dweller complained that, just as in Ken Webster's 1980s residence, 'devils turned my house upside down' after he had begun using the magic time-computer in his chimney.[24] When Ken asked the tomorrow-people to explain why their time-travel experiments were causing spooks to appear, they provided a reply suggesting they were familiar with both the RSPK hypothesis and the writings of Nandor Fodor:

POLTERGEIST PHENOMENA AS FOLLOW: - SURPLUS KENETIC ENERGY PROJECTED BY EITHER ONE OR MORE INDIVIDUALS OR BY STORAGE CHANNELS HELD WITHIN BUILDINGS AND PLACES WHERE STRONG EMOTIONS, SUCH AS FRUSTRATION, HAVE BEEN FELT MOST COMMON ENERGY CENTERED AROUND AN INDIVIDUAL. RELEASED FOR MANY REASONS. USUALLY CHILDREN OF THE AGES BETWEEN 12–19. 87.9% GIRLS. IN ALL

BUT THREE RECORDED CASE NO INJURIES INFLICTED BY THE
SOURCE – LAST CASES OF INJURIE SUSTAINED BY A FALING
BEEM IN 2006. THE FORCE IS USUALLY AN EXTREMELY FOUL
ENTITIE WHICH SEEMS TO THRIVE ON STRONGE ADVERSE
EMOTIONS MAKING LITTLE SENSE IN ITS COMMUNICATION. IT
SEEMS TO PLAY ON AN INDIVIDUALS FEER. DISLIKES LACK OF
ATTENTION – HAS BEEN THOUGHT AT ONE STAGE THAT THIS IS
THE INDIVIDUAL/S CRY TO BE NOTICED. THERE IS MORE SAID
ABOUT THIS PHENOMENA BUT IT WOULD NOT BE OF INTEREST
TO YOU ... THESE ENTITIES HAVEN'T A CONSCIOUS AS SUCH.
IT IS THE ENERGY THAT IS FORMED INTO A CHARACTOR. IT
IS SUGGESTED THAT AFTER SEVERAL SMALL P.G. [i.e. RSPK]
INCIDENTS THE INDIVIDUAL/S ATOMATICALLY IMAGINE THE
WORK OF A GHOST WHICH MOST PEOPLE ASSUME TO RESEMBLE
HUMAN FORM – THERFORE – AN IMAGE IS CREATED BY THE
PERSON/S CONCERED WHICH STRANGELY ENOUGH INFLUENCES
THE FORCES INVOLVED. AGAIN, IT SEEMS THAT THERE IS
A STRONGE CONNECTION BETWEEN THE ENTETIE/S AND THE
PERSON AS A NUCLIUS SOMETIMES IT IS CONSIDERED THAT TO
STUDY THE PERSON/S CONCERNED IS AS INFORMATIVE AS THE
PHENOMINA ITSELF ... 2109.[25]

Characteristic of communications from Hermes, this particular message
contains an inseparable jumble of truth and falsehood reminiscent of the
old 'Cretan Paradox' *koan* ('"All Cretans are liars," said the man from
Crete, truthfully'). While claiming to be a real future entity, the poltergeist
admits spooks 'HAVEN'T A CONSCIOUS [NESS] AS SUCH', being merely
RSPK-conjured thought-forms, with each 'MAKING LITTLE SENSE IN ITS
COMMUNICATION'. Thus, the poltergeist must be lying at the same time as
telling the truth, as its presumable falsities about coming from the year 2109
only serve to prove the apparent accuracy of its other comments about entities
like itself adopting purely fake disguises. Webster's 1989 book, *The Vertical
Plane*, is well worth a read if only to illustrate just how incredibly baroque and
'meta' these interactive stage-plays can often become!

*****

I have a particular interest in poltergeists that have professed to be
time-travellers, simply because I don't believe that time-travellers actually
exist; maybe they will do one day in the future, but not yet. If, a hundred
years hence, time-travel is indeed successfully invented, however, then at this
point time-travellers will turn out to have been here all along, even though
they aren't right now, but will be right now, once right now is a hundred
years older. Think about this idea, and realise its amusing paradox; the
logical inconsistency which arises when we attempt to reverse time's arrow
makes the very notion of time-travel into a further intensely Tricksterish
idea, one which has to be kept firmly taboo lest it undermine our customary
binary oppositions of past and future. What has been called 'the thin

membrane of the present' in which we all must live is yet another liminal conceptual boundary, a meniscus-like margin separating the knowable past from the unknowable future, and a natural haunt of Hermes, the bringer of precognitive dreams and dice-thrown prophecies, and the *heyoka*, he who treads every road backwards, even that of time itself.

In a recent book on what he terms 'retrocausation' – basically, the heretical psi-based idea that future events can sometimes influence or cause past ones – the science writer Eric Wargo has demonstrated how, because such ideas undermine our Dominant's most cherished assumptions about order, chronology and causality, this makes them profoundly taboo, and ridiculed even by many parapsychologists. Some psychical researchers, confronted with evidence for precognition, will try to explain it away as being down to other psi phenomena; if a psychic predicts a murder, then they might propose that, rather than seeing it happen in the future, the psychic could instead have telepathically read the murderer's prior intentions within his mind. Even reading about such things has made some sceptics feel 'physically unwell', as they are 'beyond the pale of polite discussion'.[26] Wargo himself is a very rude conversationalist, arguing that, thanks to recent discoveries in quantum physics, 'Classical causality, the one-thing-after-another billiard-ball world of Isaac Newton and his Enlightenment friends, is being revealed as a *folk causality*, a cultural construct and a belief-system, not the way things really are.'[27] And, when Trickster appears on the scene, all cultural constructs find themselves being mercilessly deconstructed via any means possible.

Retro-causation, precognition and time-travel seem like taboos even among taboos; you tend to think of parapsychologists as freethinkers, but it is actually a sphere within which the many William G. Rolls of this world have long sought mainstream scientific respectability, and there are some things that just sound so crazy and at odds with the prevailing Cartesian materialist Dominant that even Nandor Fodor wouldn't touch them with a bargepole. For example, Matthew Manning once extracted a private admission from the leading German parapsychologist Professor Hans Bender that his post-Nazi investigations into poltergeists had convinced him of the reality of life after death, but that 'it was not worth risking his reputation to state this belief publicly' – and so, Bender preferred to openly maintain they were all down to boring old RSPK.[28]

Certain Jungians have argued that ghosts, as archetypal beings, may actually exist independent of time, meaning they are not really returning from beyond the grave, just manifesting outside of the usual time frame their corresponding corporeal bodies had once physically occupied while still alive; Jung's disciple Aniela Jaffé's 1963 book *Apparitions and Precognition* would be the best example, as suggested by the very linking of these two usually separately considered phenomena in its title. In his book *Spectres of Marx*, the French deconstructionist (re: Tricksterish) philosopher Jacques Derrida argued that ghosts in Western culture manifest in a way that 'exceeds a binary or dialectic logic', as 'It is a proper characteristic of the spectre ... that no one can be sure if by returning it testifies to a living past or to a living future ... [it represents] untimeliness and disadjustment of the contemporary'.[29] Are ghosts projections from the living past, or do they live on in an eternal future in Heaven?

Is precognition a case of our present minds reaching into the future, or the future reaching back into the past of our minds, located within our present present? It is easier not to think about such things, lest our forwards-pointing non-*heyoka* brains begin to melt like clocks on a Dalí canvas – but sometimes, poltergeists' interactive stage-plays *force* us to consider them.

* * * * *

Some poltergeistic time-travellers seem very temporally confused themselves. In 1979, just such a line-fluffing actor haunted a shared 'dingy basement flat' in Edinburgh occupied by a demobbed soldier (and, later, dinosaur-hunter – talk about a liminal profession!) named Bill Gibbons. Here, disembodied voices and a crying baby would be heard, objects JOTTle into biscuit-tins and invisible furry animals leap up onto sleepers' beds at night, so a kitchen-table séance was held to see who or what was responsible. It turned out to be the ghost of a French trader named Jon; although maybe not, as the spirit then claimed to be a twenty-first century descendant of one of the flat's renters, a man from 'another time-dimension' who had become trapped in his past (but the sitters' present) after being killed by radioactive fall-out from his TARDIS' faulty 'Inter-React Drive'. This spectral futurenaut demanded the sitters 'release me from your time-zone', but didn't know how.

One sitter facetiously asked the ghost – who in a certain sense was not even really dead, not yet having been born – about the price of petrol in future aeons, whereupon the Ouija board's upturned glass shot across the table, the lights went down and the kitchen-door closed as if in anger. That night 'a tremendous crash' was heard within the room, together with sounds of things being thrown around, although when it was re-entered next morning, nothing was found broken or out of place; possibly the ghost was smashing the household crockery a few millennia hence, but loudly enough for the din to echo down through the ages. Soon, something rather non-human was being encountered around the house instead of a chronic argonaut; 'a cold, furry thing' grabbed Gibbons' wrist as he went up the stairs. Looking down, he saw 'two slitted yellow eyes staring up at me'. Exposure to future radioactivity can evidently have serious health-consequences.[30]

* * * * *

Another time-trapped entity was Robert Webbe, the spirit haunting the centuries-old childhood home of Matthew Manning. On the house's external wall was scratched the intriguing date '1731', which led Matthew to spend time in 1970 perusing the local Parish Registers, where he discovered the building had been constructed by a well-off local merchant, Robert Webbe, in that year.[31] Later hearing raps, Matthew went into the hallway, where he saw a solid-looking 'burglar' – but a burglar in eighteenth-century fancy dress, wearing a green-coloured frock coat with frilled cuffs and a lace cravat, a long brown ringlet wig, knee breeches, cream-coloured stockings and silver-buckled shoes and supporting himself unsteadily on a pair of sticks. The disabled burglar saw Matthew too, and offered his 'most humble apology' for frightening him, explaining he had trouble with his 'blessed legs', before disappearing back into the past. This was none other than Robert Webbe himself, who had died from gout not long after having built his dream-home, but refused to believe the fact.[32] The ghost seemed intent on trapping other people in time with him; as Matthew's dad lay in bed, he would see out through Webbe's eyes, experiencing his fatal illness for himself at first hand. Sometimes, the bedclothes would be disarranged as if an invisible man had been sleeping there before Mr Manning had even lain down; it appeared the two men were occupying the same point of space–time simultaneously, Mr M feeling like he was 'lying *inside* somebody who had climbed into the bed' with him.[33] Matthew himself travelled astrally back through the centuries, seeing the house as it had been in the 1700s; previously unknown structural differences he perceived later turned out to have actually existed.[34]

Via automatic writing, trance communications and ghostly graffiti, Webbe let it be known he considered himself 'A harmless lambent fire/A mistaken phantom', who sometimes realised he was dead, and other times did not. To him, the Mannings were weird spectral intrusions in his own house, as Ken Webster had also been to his own centuries-past friend. 'The dead are only Happy,' he said, but in his own eyes Webbe was generally not dead, and therefore *not* happy; and yet, at other times, Webbe said he had 'died in 1733 from my troublesome legs' and could now be found 'close to ye Church on ye southe side', in his coffin. It later turned out there were once two Robert Webbes in the house, father and son, so possibly one was aware of his own death and the other was not, or maybe the spook was just an RSPK-powered aspect of Matthew himself – 'I obey your orders', he once declared – the Trickster was typically confusing.[35]

Again sounding like Ken Webster's poltergeist, Webbe professed not to understand modern-day speech and inventions, complaining of the Mannings' 'bad tongue', use of 'unfamiliar words like carre and bulbbe' and refusing to believe their insane lies about horseless carriages. If the Mannings went around in one of those, he said, he travelled to town riding a 'tamed lion'.[36] It was interesting Webbe didn't know what an electric 'bulbbe' was, as he was only able to see things in the 1970s version of the house if similar things had existed in his own time. He admired the Mannings' modern-day paintings, but proved unable to see light-switches even when specifically pointed out to him. No such thing could ever exist, he said, 'even so longe as I sit on ye dunghill.' He could also see the Mannings' nice new smokeless modern candles, which he had his servant Beth light for him in his servery during the 1730s, something which manifested in 1971's terms as those same candles being lit in the Mannings' cloakroom and almost setting the coats on fire, the area's function having altered during the intervening centuries. Such paradoxes worked both ways around; when Matthew's mum varnished the 1970s floorboards, Webbe got his 1700s feet glued on this same backwards-time-travelling 'sticksome boarding'![37]

As an offering, Webbe once apported Matthew a freshly baked loaf – freshly baked in the 1700s, that is, by the time Matthew got his hands on it the thing had become a rock-hard bread fossil, 'as hard as concrete and about as heavy', which emitted 'an electric shock' when he touched it.

Webbe said it was 'bakered specially' for him by his cook.[38] Matthew now found other gifts left out for him, too, like antique coins in mint condition, while items of his own, like scarves and paintings, went missing. It appeared Webbe was pilfering the Mannings' property then leaving them random payments, either of money or goods, in return; their entire house had become a Hermes-haunted cairn at the crossroads of time, where gift-exchange was taking place on an epic scale. But it got even weirder. Some of the JOTTled *hermaions* were not from Webbe's own day, but the intervening centuries between the 1730s and the 1970s, such as cigarettes of discontinued brand, soiled nylon gloves, plastic beads and a typewritten letter from 1948 regarding insurance premiums. It appeared Webbe was stealing from other prior occupants of the home (from Matthew's perspective; they were *future* ones to him) too, and leaving them arbitrary apports from other time-frames in return ... which presumably means that, sometime in the Victorian era, a very puzzled 1800s family may have been receiving free lava-lamps and Spacehoppers as presents from the 1970s![39]

The whole thing was as colossally confusing as one of those modern-day episodes of *Doctor Who,* which no longer make sense to anyone other than their pointy-headed script-writers; maybe Webbe had an advantage here, as he stole one of two manuscript copies of Manning's 1978 book *The Strangers*, which tells the entire tale of the haunting, from within a closed drawer one day, thus putting him in the same position as an author holds over his own characters, having already plotted out the arc of their story.[40] Manning concluded the materialistic Webbe was 'stuck in some sort of post-mortal nightmare' unable to leave the expensive home he had so proudly constructed immediately prior to his death, becoming a living (or at least undead) gramophone record which kept on getting its needle stuck in its grooves, sometimes playing forwards, sometimes backwards, sometimes jumping around at random. But the thing is, if Webbe's poltergeist had stolen the future story of his life in the 1970s and then taken it back to his own corporeal self living in the 1700s, and physically read it, then might the time-traversing Trickster not have simply been acting out this same scripted part, thus rendering his entire fate a self-fulfilling prophecy?[41]

'This sore vexes me not to knowe mine owne time,' said Webbe, whether of his own volition or at *The Strangers*' prompting 300 years later, I am unable to decide.[42] Thinking about the whole thing 'sore vexes' my brain too. The polt tried to stop Matthew from writing his account in the first place by producing 'an overpowering smell of sewage' and tinkling an annoying invisible bell at his desk when he was hard at work on it.[43] Might preventing his story from being written have been the only way for Robert Webbe to escape his own horrible future fate? Might the book itself have been a kind of post-modern (and pre-modern) literary prison inadvertently constructed for Webbe's spirit by Matthew? I doubt it, but the story certainly raises many interestingly unanswerable 4-D questions. The ghost seemed to know the issues it raised were paradoxical to the point of parody, copying out a saying of the Greek philosopher Zeno of Citium onto a wall to the effect that the reason a man was born with two ears but only one tongue was that they should always listen twice as much as they should speak – that is, don't even *try* and solve this mystery, just sit back and enjoy it.[44] Webbe even posed one temporal head-spinner of his own, arguing with Matthew:

> This is nonsense. I am alive because I am here. If you are the voyce [that Webbe could hear haunting his house and head in the past] you are the ghost and you are dead. I cannot be deade else I would not be here … I am no ghoste. I am here … Where came you from? I have not sold myne house [to new occupants] … Now you jeste. It is only 1726 and you say 'tis [after] 1968 [when the Mannings bought the house]. 'Tis a joke. Are you a ghoulle of tomorrow?[45]

Well, *was* Matthew a 'ghoulle of tomorrow'? If time does not really work as we think it does, then how do *any of us* know that we are not the ghosts of tomorrow from some other poor soul's perspective? 'I am here and I am me,' Webbe once reassured himself, inadvertently mirroring the *cogito ergo sum* of Descartes himself.[46] But if our world is not actually Cartesian in its nature, then does this supposition even really hold? Webbe's unanswerable query is simply another form of Zen *koan*, along the lines of 'What is the sound of one hand clapping?' The final sentence in *The Strangers* was, appropriately enough, a question: 'Are we already ghosts to somebody else?'[47]

* * * * *

Ostensible chronology-subverting Time Lords also beamed down from Planet Paradox during the SORRAT experiments, with many other fictional characters. Chief investigator W. E. Cox, committed as many parapsychologists are to the RSPK hypothesis, refused to believe that any 'ghosts' as such were responsible for the phenomena: 'A true scientist would not make that assumption.'[48] As an ironic result, an entity calling itself '3x3' appeared on the scene, christened after its habit of knocking out three sets of three raps to announce its arrival. Questioning it, other SORRAT members gathered that 3x3, by its own admission, had emerged from within Cox's own subconscious in order to help him better pursue his pet theories; a case of a poltergeist-personality literally admitting it has no personality of its own.[49]

And yet, at other times, the SORRAT entities *did* have a real sense of personality. The letters they wrote possessed a lively sense of humour, teasing the views of RSPK-fans like Cox ('It upsets their *zeitgeist* to think that *zeit* might also contain some *geists*') and making parapsychological in-jokes ('The molecular friction during a botched apport is a real bitch'). They also spoke of a 'pervasive anti-dead prejudice' present among mankind, asking sitters to stop beginning their communications with quasi-racist phrases like 'Dear Spirit Friends', asking whether they would ever dream of addressing a letter to an African with 'Dear Black Man'. Often, their letters would bear punning postmarks from significant-sounding locations like Tombstone, Arizona or Deadwood, North Dakota, and contain labels from steak-slices reading 'MEDIUM', denoting both the meat's cooked status and the SORRAT sitters' status as spirit-mediums.[50]

One of the main purported communicants was John King, a seventeenth-century Welsh ghost-pirate who filled in a SORRAT questionnaire about his post-mortem existence thus:

Age: *347*
Marital Status: *Merrie Widower*
Occupation: *Freebooter, govt. clerk (no real difference)*

When asked to describe his greatest after-death experiences, King replied, with comic understatement, 'Meeting God would probably be the most important', described living people as 'those on the meat-level' and spoke of having 'scared the urine out of two old women' when he appeared to them one day having accidentally forgotten to materialise his eyes.[51] Although decrying 'the dogs of Spain', Mr King did not use language terribly characteristic of a late-Renaissance buccaneer, and many of his letters contained spelling errors of the exact same kind frequently made by SORRAT's leader Tom Richards, strongly suggesting fraud.[52]

John King had previously been a known spirit-guide to several famous Victorian Spiritualist mediums such as Eusapia Palladino, slate-writing Henry Slade and the Davenport brothers, all of whom had been exposed as exploiting conjuring tricks to create some of their miracles by sceptical stage-magicians such as John Nevile Maskelyne, who later made a good career from simulating and exposing such frauds on-stage. The very idea of ghosts writing letters also appears to have been pilfered from the notoriously dotty European nobleman Baron de Guldenstubbé, who caused laughter during the 1850s by claiming to have left paper and pencils around the tombs of famous dead people and then received signed, hand-written notes from their statues in return.[53] SORRAT's John King boasting of his association with such Tricksterish figures is akin to a man assuring you his twelve-pound note is genuine by dint of his several prior convictions for forgery.

Strangest of all were the entities' Jungian-tinged claims to exist outside time. Their letters bore return addresses consisting of drawings of clocks without any hands, and the standard mathematical symbol for infinity, an elongated horizontal '8'.[54] The apparent reason they existed outside time was because they were time-travellers – perhaps from the year 2109? UFOs were sighted during the SORRAT experiments, and Tom Richards' son Ivan became convinced these were really a time-travel craft from the future named 'The Lynx', upon which he would eventually be reincarnated as a crew-member. To confirm this, the entities sent Ivan letters containing technical drawings of The Lynx's time-engine. However, it later transpired that Ivan's father, who had long been a creative writer, had plotted a time-travel story about just such a craft while a young man. According to Ivan, the ghosts had 'built on that story ... as if ... using his mind.'[55]

The obvious solution is that Tom was writing the letters himself, recycling old material. At one point the entities claimed to be Merlin, who was really no wizard at all but a time-traveller from the twenty-fifth century. He was currently sleeping beneath England's Cadbury Tor in a special sanctum dubbed a 'vivitorium', and needed SORRAT members to awaken him with magical incantations, thereby averting some hideous global catastrophe.

One credulous sitter crossed the Atlantic and did his best to revive the sage; but would he have bothered had he known that, during his teens, Richards had penned his own Merlin-related sci-fi tale which bore almost exactly the same plot? Tom guessed the entities had read his mind, allowing them to use his youthful scribbling as the basis for their own fictional fantasies.[56] Richards later transformed his real-life experiences with SORRAT into a series of fictionalised tales about the ghosts' exploitation of his own fictions, thus making the whole thing even more like a weird literary experiment undertaken by Jorge Luis Borges rather than the standard idea most people would have of the narrative shape a poltergeist haunting should take.

But, if these stage plays are indeed pure fiction – whether penned by ghostly Tricksters or human ones – then what is their purpose? Well, what is the purpose of fiction anyway? For one thing, it is meant to be entertaining, and I think the above tales are certainly that. Other common purposes of fiction, particularly the science-fiction so many of these narratives very strongly resemble, would be to create new realms and new ways of seeing things, to raise questions about the world we inhabit; questions like, for example, how do we know we *are not* really ghouls from the future, as Robert Webbe once so eerily proposed? In other words, these stories possess the very same purposes possessed by all Trickster-legends, always. It is in this sense that these tales of timeless spirits are truly timeless.

* * * * *

One man who has considered the issue of puzzling paranormal narratives closely in recent years is Jeffrey J. Kripal, an American Professor of Religion whose main expertise lies in the field of what he accurately calls 'really weird shit'.[57] His 2016 book *The Super Natural*, co-authored with the prominent alien abductee (or modern-day shaman) Whitley Strieber contains a sensible plea for anomalous experiences to be interpreted in a hermeneutic, rather than an overly literalistic fashion. For example, Strieber himself has been plagued throughout his life by bedroom visits from gangs of little blue men and an odd, ET-like woman with a glowing vagina who compels him to go down on his knees and perform cunnilingus on her, entities which the book's authors, unlike many so-called 'nuts and bolts' ufologists, do not consider likely to be literal flesh-and-blood extra-terrestrial beings but ... well, some really weird shit. To Strieber, such shamanic visions – like those similarly outlandish apparitions seen by poltergeist victims – are essentially 'living hieroglyphs' or animated symbols, signifying ... well, yet more really weird shit.[58]

Strieber and Kripal's book suggests that paranormal events resemble a form of spontaneously authored real-life poetry more than literal encounters with ghosts and aliens, calling this liminal, borderland realm the 'symbolic imaginal', full of images which cannot be explained, merely read in a subjective fashion, like great poems which contain an infinite number of potential meanings encoded away within them, not like factual newspaper reports which can only be read in one single possible legitimate way. 'Maybe the unexplained remains unexplained because explanation is the wrong way to think about such events,' proposes Kripal, rather Tricksterishly.[59]

Kripal suggests that interactive supernatural narratives represent attempts at communication with us by some other order of reality which is so different from our own that our human brains simply cannot properly decode what it means to say, so it all comes across as jumbled-up nonsense, a code impossible to crack; a real-life playing out of Ludwig Wittgenstein's famous remark that, even if a lion could talk, we would never understand what it was saying. One poltergeist-person, Lance Sieveking, was followed 'all my life' by 'sudden, queer sounds – quite inexplicable thumps and clangs'. Whenever he heard them, Sieveking said that 'I always address my poltergeist very severely and tell it to shut up; I point out that I haven't any idea of what it *means* by the noise.'[60] He's not the only one; whenever anyone hears such inchoate dins, we all begin uselessly talking with lions.

This all reminds me of the Victorian folklorist and SPR member Andrew Lang, who in his short story *Castle Perilous* had 'an affable sprite' explain that, in the after-life, many spooks suffered from the post-mortem equivalent of aphasia, that sad disorder of brain function in which a person continually produces cross-wired malapropisms, saying 'Pass me my banana' instead of 'Pass me my hat', for example, mis-speakings which resemble nonsensical, non-interpretable variants of Freudian slips, complete *hermaion* red-herrings. Possibly, hypothesised Lang, this is what happens during poltergeist hauntings:

We urge that the ghost cannot, as it were, express himself as plainly as he would like to do, that he suffers from aphasia. Now he shows as a black dog, now as a Green Lady, now as an old man, and often he can only rap or knock, or display a light, or tug the bed-clothes ... [A Reverend F. G. Lee once recited some psalms to help lay a poltergeist to rest] and was greeted with applause, 'a very tornado of knocks' ... was the distinct and intelligible response. Now on our theory, the ghost, if he could, would have said 'Thank-you very much,' or the like, but he could not, so his sentiments translated themselves into thumps. On another occasion, he might have merely shown a light, or he might have sat on Dr Lee's chest ... or pulled his blankets off, as is not unusual. Such are the peculiarities of spectral aphasia, or rather *asemia*: the ghost can make signs, but not the *right* signs.[61]

Kripal suggests something similar, using the metaphor of standing before a mirror whose glass both separates and connects two radically different orders of being, leading to us 'imagining a presence that is imagining us'. Possibly, when we see cow-headed men, or radioactive futurenauts begin transforming into yellow-eyed werewolves and throwing invisible temper tantrums in Edinburgh kitchens, therefore, 'the imagination is intuiting or sensing something Other or Alien and then translating, mediating or picturing ... [a message] to a human psyche, but always in code ... absurdity [being] a necessary function of the translation across the border or threshold.'[62]

This is actually how the unconscious itself works within dreams, the natural realm of Hermes; for all his flaws, Freud demonstrated how dreams operate via symbols, and how their apparent nonsense functions as a visual code between our deep and surface minds. Dreams are full of puns, both verbal and visual, in which, for example, a missing melon is really an amputated breast, just like JOTTles in the view of Nandor Fodor. Poltergeist narratives and visions, also being sent to us by Hermes, just like our dreams, could operate similarly. If so, says Kripal, then it could be that scientific instruments are rather useless in such fields, and that instead 'reading and writing are the most powerful paranormal technologies that we possess, if only we knew what and how to read'.[63] Strieber himself has guessed the way that his own anomalous encounters – like most poltergeist phenomena – refuse to be recorded on film could be because they actually unfold somehow within 'a space that cameras cannot record, an inner space that relates to the physical but is not part of it.'[64]

That sounds like an admission Strieber has just been imagining things, but this is not quite the case; we don't simply *imagine* our dreams, they really *do* take place, but never anywhere they can actually be recorded. If hauntings do function more as dream-like story narratives than as events *per se*, then you would not go to the sciences to truly grasp such things, but to the humanities. The very word 'narrative' is derived from the Greek word '*gnosis*', meaning 'to know', Gnosticism being a traditional school of mysticism which holds that matter is somehow evil or unreal, and that true reality and knowledge lie within the inner soul. Paranormal experiences, as physically enacted stories, act to reunite the material and psychic realms, making 'material events ... behave like mental events and vice-versa', says Kripal; the stage set of a poltergeist haunting thus becomes truly a re-enactment of the Jungian state of *pleroma*, or original unity of all things, both mental and material, in which mind and the world become 'mirror in mirror mirror'd', to use a phrase of W. B. Yeats.[65] The proper guide to this strange land is not the scientist with his measuring-stick, but Hermes with his magic staff. But, when Hermes waves this wand at us, he is also waving it at himself:

> Sometimes the hermeneut finds himself in a paradoxical 'circle' or 'loop' in which the reading transforms both the read and the reader. It is very much like the mind-bending understanding of quantum physics ... in which the act of observation really and truly changes the behaviour and expression of the observed, which of course then changes the reality of the observer. Again, there is no stable 'subject' looking at or interpreting a stable 'object' in such moments. In hermeneutics, as in quantum physics, there is a single process that co-creates both the subject and the object *at the same time* ... it is not your fault that you do not understand these hermeneutical paradoxes ... It is confusing being a [living] novel.[66]

No doubt Ken Webster, Shirley Hitchings, Matthew Manning, Bill Gibbons, Robert Webbe (x2), Donald, the Dauphin, 2109, 3x3, John King, W. E. Cox, Merlin and the many other good folk at SORRAT, whether living, dead or yet to be born, would all agree. All were in many respects just yet more characters in search of an author ... that author, in some incomprehensible, Trickster-like sense, being themselves.

XII

Verbal Humour

The words of Mercury are harsh after the songs of Apollo.
William Shakespeare

If verbal humour is sometimes used by the poltergeist, then this is generally dependent upon the manifestation of a voice. Characteristically, these disembodied accents enjoy insulting people; in 2003 a pensioner from Calcutta called the police to report a rude male spirit who was constantly criticising his wife's wrinkly looks, as reflective of her advanced age.[1] Gef the Mongoose was particularly good at dishing out abuse. Whenever Mr Irving was examining his mail, the creature would shout 'Read it out, you fat-headed gnome!' – the unfortunate farmer looked a bit like one. Gef had a gift for comic caricature. According to him, a half-witted visitor 'had a face like a frizzled onion' while others had 'ears like an elf' and 'ears like corn-scoops'.[2] When asked if he had a message for a lady who was about to fly back to South Africa, he amusingly replied: 'Yes. Tell her I hope the propeller drops off.'[3]

Other polts are not quite as verbally inventive. 'So Hans from Eyrar is come now and wishes to talk with me, the ------- idiot,' once cursed the Devil of Hjalta-Stad, an Icelandic ghost of the 1700s, when confronted with an unwelcome visitor.[4] We may fill in the blank here as we desire, deploring as we do so the crude predictability of the slur. St John Vianney, the famously holy nineteenth-century Frenchman known as the Curé d'Ars, was a great ascetic for God. Perhaps this was why a disembodied demonic voice he called *grappin* used to taunt him with accusations of secretly indulging in sybaritic activities, shouting 'Vianney, Vianney, you truffle-eater, you! Are you still alive; haven't you died yet? I'll get you!'[5] This gibe would have been particularly insulting, as Vianney actually lived exclusively off a diet of boiled potatoes – which he imagined, for some reason, is what Christ would have wanted.[6]

Some polts, like that which once haunted Killakee House in Ireland in the shape of an oversized demonic black cat, can apparently understand the concept of words having double meanings. Killakee House was in need of modernisation, and did not as late as 1970 possess a refrigerator.

The milkman just left bottles standing in a shallow stream which ran through the grounds each morning to keep them cool – until at length the foil caps started going missing, though the milk inside was left untouched. Magpies were blamed, so a stone 'box' was constructed in the stream, with a heavy slate lid to prevent birds from pecking the bottles. Despite this, the silvery caps still vanished. While pondering this mystery, the milkman's customers became compensated for their loss by a different type of 'cap' appearing in large numbers around the house overnight; Derby hats, opera hats, straw sun-hats and children's knitted hats with woolly pom-poms on top apported all over the place. A nineteenth-century lady's linen cap with fetching drawstrings was hailed as the pride of the collection.[7] I suppose the householders must at some point have said they wanted their caps back?

A 1654 haunting in Glenluce featured a polt similarly keen on word-play. When the local Protestant Minister turned up, the ghost wasn't too impressed; as soon as he walked through the door, the uncouth Scottish spook exclaimed loudly 'You are a dog, sir!' The Minister was outraged – only to realise an actual dog was walking through the door directly behind him.[8] This reminds me of that ever-popular childhood joke of calling a girl a bitch before pointing immediately at the nearest canine, claiming you were actually talking about that. It also reminds me of old tales told about Hermes in which, for instance, he wilfully and over-literally misinterprets a female antagonist's cry that 'I shall not be moved!' as an invitation for him to magically transform her into a doorstop.[9]

Occasionally, we even encounter reports of talking electronic children's toys being manipulated by polts for humorous purposes. At South Shields, both a Scooby Doo figure and a Bob the Builder toy either said things they were not meant to, or spontaneously emitted factory-programmed phrases during situations which seemed curiously appropriate. When a TV crew were interviewing the ghost's victims about the time their small son had gone missing at the polt's hands, Bob piped up with the phrase 'Ha, ha! Can you find me?'[10] This not being one of the things the toy had been manufactured to say, this should have been impossible – especially as it was turned off at the time! A Scooby Doo figure also repeatedly spouted off about 'solving a mystery'; but, considering that *is* actually what he had been built to do, perhaps this isn't quite so strange. Another talking toy scared a researcher called Malcolm Robinson in 1995. When he went to investigate poltergeistery at a house in Stirlingshire, this bird suddenly squawked 'What are you doing here?' at him. This, said Robinson, gave him the biggest fright of his life.[11]

* * * * *

Polts may also enjoy making snide reference to the titles of books and other such items which possess some sarcastic relevance to the situation at hand. William G. Roll tells us of a home in which a conflict between mother and child was playing out, wherein two phonograph records shattered into pieces of their own accord. Their titles? *My Mother* and *At*

Home With Me.[12] At an unquiet house named 'Beth-oni' in Oxfordshire in 1907, a polt-related apparition was seen to remove a certain volume from a shelf before replacing it. A distinct mark was found in the dust where the book had been shifted, and two finger marks were even left atop of it. The title was *In Strange Company.*[13]

A haunted office in the City of London was in 1901 the scene of a similar event. An issue of *Pearson's Magazine* fell to the floor, the pages being 'drawn together at the lower end, as if held together by someone's finger and thumb' until they arrived at an illustration of a spectre throwing a man over a precipice, with the heading 'Real Ghost Stories'.[14] In 1977, a couple from Holloway were teased by a polt that loved to mess up their book collection, arranging them neatly on the floor around a pouffe when no-one was in. One volume in particular, *Modern Cake Decorating* by Audrey Ellis, was especially favoured, sailing from its shelf to lie open at the same page each and every time – a page bearing the recipe for a dish called 'American Devil's Food'.[15] A Donald McGill-style picture postcard which once plopped onto a séance table at Scole in Norfolk, meanwhile, bore the suitably punning caption 'If living, please write – if dead, don't bother!'[16]

In the house of a Mr Beecham, the rector of Stockerson in Leicestershire some time during the 1600s, a tobacco-pipe would repeatedly float to the other end of the room. A Mr Mun, visiting, set out to observe this curious motion. Instead, a Bible flew into his lap and opened itself at Genesis 3:15, reading 'Come Satan, I'll show thee thy Doom: The Seed of the Woman shall break the Serpent's Head. Avoid Satan.'[17] Don't tempt the Devil to play his tricks on you was the moral being pointed out verbally here, I think. During a séance held at Russian Hill, a book was hurled at one female sitter, striking her 'severely' on the head. It then jumped into the air, a page being turned down during the process. Opening it up, a quote from the Bible – the only one in the entire text, it actually being a history of Central America – was found pointed at by the folded-down corner. 'Can ye not discern the signs of the times?' it asked those present, ominously.[18]

One day, written in soap on the bathroom mirror, the Enfield poltergeist left a one-word message: 'QUILIT'. Nobody knew what it meant; the nearest word in the dictionary was found to be 'quillet', a term now long-obsolete. Its meaning? A trick or a jest. The dictionary gave a most appropriate illustrative usage of the word, from Shakespeare: 'Some tricks, some quillets how to cheat the Devil.'[19] One almost wonders how good the erudite spook would have been at the cryptic crossword. At other times, however, the Enfield entity appears to have been rather inept in its command of language. Here are the run-together contents of two scrawled messages, the second of which was left behind by the ghost on a scrap of paper *immediately* after it had left the first; you can decide for yourself whether or not the bathos evoked here is deliberate. 'I WILL STAY IN THIS HOUSE. DO NOT READ THIS TO ANYONE ELSE OR I WILL RETALIATE ... CAN I HAVE A TEA BAG?'[20] This is, in my view, quite funny, both dastardly and motley at once ... but was it *meant* to be?

Likewise, some of the more grandiloquent verbal pronouncements of Gef the Trash-Talking Mongoose come across as being nothing more than endearing but nonsensical bluster:

> Thou wilt never know what I am ... I am a freak. I have hands and I have feet. And if you saw me you would be paralysed, petrified, mummified, turned into a pillar of salt ... I am the fifth dimension, I am the eighth wonder of the world, I can split the atom![21]

Did Gef *know* how funny he sounded here, like the rodent reincarnation of P. T. Barnum? Similarly, when he refused to believe a teenage visitor who said he could drive a steamroller, saying 'You young bugger, you would put it over the hedge' before threatening him with the dread words 'I'll wet on your head!' did he not see how comical his words could later appear? Or was he deliberately trying to make his audience laugh?[22] Verbal dexterity is a sign of demonstrable intelligence, as well as one of the key characteristics of a good comedian. But verbal humour can also be derived from another source – namely, the fact that a person's utterances can, on occasion, reveal them as being an absolute idiot. From time to time, the poltergeist does both – but then, as a Trickster, the ultimate 'cunning fool', perhaps we should expect no less. If Hermes invented language, then he at the very same time also invented the exquisite comic art of talking absolute rot.

An early e-fit of our friend Gef.

XIII

Defying Authority and Blasphemy

He turns revolt into style.

Thom Gunn

In May 1922 a Mr D. Neaves, of Roodepoort, South Africa, made an official complaint about the long-term lithobolic bombardment of his property. The police were little help; hardly had officers arrived than another stone hit the roof. Mr Neaves' house was an isolated building, and constables were at a loss to explain where the missiles originated. Phenomena centred upon a 'Hottentot' housemaid, who was made to stand outside under close observation – whereupon more stones showered down vertically around her, from thin air. An Inspector Cummings now ordered the entire household to remain indoors under guard. All around the house he stationed underlings, gazing out over flat, open fields. Still stones fell on the roof. The quarantined family needed water, so the police escorted the maid to the nearest well. A large stone fell beside her. She ran back inside, and another stone fell on the roof. Convinced she must be responsible, the Inspector tied her hands. Yet another stone fell on the roof. Inspector Cummings was being made fun of.[1] Read symbolically, it is not just Inspector Cummings being mocked here, but what he represents in a wider sense. The police are perhaps the most visible symbol of authority in our society, embodying the forces of law and, importantly, of order. Neither concept is respected by the poltergeist or the Trickster, though, as we saw with the persecution of Magistrate Mompesson by the Drummer of Tedworth. No matter what Inspector Cummings did, the polt was one step ahead. 'Why should I obey your laws?' the spook seemed to say. 'They're nothing to do with me.' All societal laws are temporary and contingent; and yet they are what we use to help us shape our world. But the poltergeist is above them all. He represents a state of chaos where the laws – apparently so rigid and so clear to us mere mortals who have to obey them – are revealed as being malleable and plastic.

Similar cases abound. A hut on the outskirts of Hyderabad, India, was once infested by an invisible arsonist. The local police-chief went to investigate; and, as soon as he entered, his trousers promptly caught fire! He ordered the place be abandoned and sealed up.[2] Comparable things bothered German cops called out to investigate a polt at Kiel during the 1920s. Their clothing spontaneously combusted or was torn from their bodies by invisible hands, while a police-car suffered three flat tyres and two crashes inside a mile on the way to the scene.[3] A house in the Rue des Noyers in Paris was in 1860 being systematically demolished by heavy missiles. Constables stationed on watch could find no visible assailants; worse, they themselves were soon being rudely hit with lithobolic objects.[4] In 1849 in another Paris street, the Rue des Grès, a poltergeist undertook to demolish an entire building by throwing paving-stones at it. Policemen dispatched to keep order could do nothing. Neither could the Inspector of the Paris Police, who investigated personally. Even the head of the French secret service failed to bring about an end to the affair.[5]

We might ask why it is that police-forces get involved in poltergeist cases in the first place. In England, constables first began investigating hauntings during the early 1800s when, in an age of little mass entertainment, 'ghost-hunts' became popular after-dark activities among the urban poor. A spirit would allegedly be sighted wandering inside an abandoned house and, before long, gangs of youths and thrill-seekers would congregate, ready to barge inside or hurl rocks through windows. Needless to say, the damage done to both property and public decorum were not looked upon kindly by the powers that be. Therefore, officers were required both to prevent breaches of the peace and also to inspect the ghosts, in the hope they would turn out to be little more than rumour. As social historian Owen Davies puts it, the police could thereby 'perform a dual function of debunking ghosts and maintaining public order'. If there was no spectre there to be seen in the first place, there would also be no subsequent slum children running around after it raising riot for fun.[6]

*****

What happens when police are called to investigate an apparently genuine spook, though? Usually, a debunking 'explanation' still has to be provided for public consumption, no matter how spurious. At the end of the 1922 Roodepoort case, Inspector Cummings claimed suddenly to have found somebody skulking around on the farm throwing rocks after all. This vandal was not named to the Press, nor did Cummings reveal whether he had brought charges against him or her; and nor, most importantly, did he explain how exactly the miscreant had managed to make showers of stones appear from thin air then drop down in an entirely straight line from above.[7] The official falsity of ghosts is reasserted here by the Inspector, with his alleged 'arrest', but in a manner that is only superficial. That is the police's main role *vis-à-vis* poltergeistery; to say 'as you were' to a relieved public, and thereby free them of the awkward necessity of modifying their pre-existing world-view.

Occasionally, though, officers are honest enough to admit they have witnessed events which are inexplicable. When called out to what her radio described rather inadequately as a 'disturbance' at the haunted house in Enfield, WPC Carolyn Heeps saw, with her own eyes, a chair wobbling from side to side before sliding towards the kitchen of its own volition. She examined the chair immediately afterwards, and was at a loss for any possible explanation. However, she then admitted there wasn't much she could do about the matter because 'Nobody was breaking the law, and if something invisible was breaking the laws of Nature, then that was a job for the scientists.'[8]

* * * * *

Learned men, academics and scientists represent a different kind of authority. They can't arrest a ghost but they *can* say with even more Dominant-sanctioned clout that they don't exist … even when they do. A nineteenth-century German academic theologian named Professor Schuppart was eventually forced to confront the reality of spooks. Initially, the Professor was persecuted by self-propelled stones smashing all his windows. Then, he was slapped in the face by unseen hands, day and night, while ropes tied themselves around his throat and feet, and those of his wife. Two constables were sent to guard the Schupparts in their bed, but they were slapped too. Such torments continued for *six years*, leaving Schuppart with a collection of several thousand lithobolic stones to call his own. The demon had a real disdain for the Professor's studies. When reading, his lamp would fly away so he couldn't see the words, his texts of learning were shredded and thrown at his feet or covered with spilled ink, and when Schuppart was lecturing, the page he was reading from would be torn from his lecture-notes.[9] This was nothing less than an assault upon the very authority of academic knowledge itself; no matter what it said in all those learned books, whatever physical or spiritual laws were laid down within, the ghost could disregard them. 'You know nothing, Herr Doktor,' it said; then demonstrated this fact, in public, before his students.

An equally unfriendly ghost at a Vienna blacksmith's was investigated in 1906 by a scientifically-minded local member of the SPR called Wärndorfer. The SPR during this period placed great emphasis upon the need for a scientific approach towards investigations, to lend them as much credibility as possible. During Wärndorfer's visit, he saw tools, coals and pieces of iron flying around in the presence of two teenage apprentices. Intrigued, he produced a small copper plate with which he hoped to perform hypnotic experiments upon the boys, to see what effect this would have. The result was not a positive one; Wärndorfer was hit in the back of his hand by a flying screw, making it bleed and swell. He wondered if this had anything to do with his experimental plate:

> On being hit it struck me that many of the flying objects had dropped near it [the plate], and that on its being held in my hand, my hand had been struck. I then laid it on the smithy, and in a very short time an iron piece flew with a thundering noise against the corrugated iron roof of the smithy. I gave it to one of the boys to hold, and something dropped quite near him … A neighbour came in and asked to have a try. He stood opposite me, leaning against the turning lathe, with his back against the wall; nobody was behind him … He was struck in the back by a handle off the lathe.[10]

Evidently, the poltergeist did not want to be empirically examined, and set out to play merry havoc with the piece of analytical apparatus: yet again, it defied scientific authority.

Poltergeists also particularly disrespect sceptics. People arrive at a haunted house, profess self-righteously that it's all just so much rot and rubbish in the name of the prevailing Dominant, and then come a cropper. A haunted French farmhouse was, sometime during the 1800s, visited by one Saturnin Tinel, then aged ten, his grandfather, and a brigadier, all keen to see what was going on. Apparently, nothing; they waited two hours with nary a peep. 'Well … here is a bad bit of humbug,' the brigadier said sarcastically, as they were about to leave. As soon as he uttered these words, all the furniture and crockery in the kitchen broke into a mad dance, Tinel was hurled against the front door, and his grandfather's cap was thrown into the fire.[11]

When an eighteen-year-old French maidservant named Germain Maire expressed disbelief in ghosts in 1910, she was quickly subjected to pieces of bread, stones and nails falling around her in the yard. She publicly declared she was not scared, as it was all clearly just a practical joke, and went down to the cellar for a bottle of wine. Re-emerging, an 'enormous pebble' whizzed from nowhere and smashed it in her hand.[12] Particularly tragic for a French person, we might presume. In 1888, a group of Australian cattle-drivers were bothered by swarms of supernaturally-thrown twigs. Initially scared, the men later laughed at the silliness of the whole affair, beginning to dismiss it as just imagination, when all of a sudden another flying stick thrust itself down one incipient sceptic's throat, choking off his laughter mid-chuckle.[13] Best of all, an 1856 report of an old haunted Spanish mission near Los Angeles featured the slapstick detail of a sceptical visitor challenging the 'non-existent' spooks to 'do something to astonish him', whereupon he was 'instantly drenched' by a volume of cold water teleporting directly above him.[14]

Gef the Mongoose particularly detested sceptics, shouting 'Doubter, Doubter,' at them in a 'shrill' voice both 'malevolent and full of venom'.[15] If one particular non-believer came to the haunted farmhouse, he warned, he would 'blow his brains out' with a shotgun. This Saducee did dare to visit, however, and was kept up all night by Gef playing poltergeist. When asked what he had done to deserve this, Gef replied 'You're a doubter'. The man was a doubter no more, though; looking under the bed, he saw 'a pair of piercing eyes' staring back at him. 'Now do you believe?' asked Gef, spitting. 'Don't you dare to upset Jimmo [Mr Irving] with any sceptical remarks!' The next day the visitor apologised to his host for ever having distrusted him.[16]

Harry Price was another who hesitated to believe in Gef's existence, once scoffing that his story 'rivals the *Arabian Nights*' in its 'fantastic impossibilities'. It was no wonder Gef said he despised Price, amusingly calling him 'the man who puts the kybosh on the spirits' and deriding him as a self-publicising 'newspaper man' and media-whore. Knowing of the penchant one of Price's assisting 'spook-men' had for employing Nandor Fodor-type Freudianism, 'He's damned well not going to get to know *my* inferior complex', Gef vowed.[17] Price – while occasionally a faker himself – could be a merciless debunker of fake hauntings when in the mood,[18] and Gef did not wish to receive similar treatment, so stubbornly refused to manifest at all when he was there investigating.[19] If Price saw nothing happening, then how could he say fakery was taking place? Fakery of what, precisely? Fakery of nothing at all going on? Wouldn't that mean there *was* something going on? The ghost would 'not talk to a doubting Thomas' and frequently disappeared temporarily even when sympathetically curious visitors arrived, only to reappear immediately afterwards in classic Trickster fashion.[20] But, of course, in such a self-defeating way he only gave those much-hated sceptics further reason not to believe in his existence, the cunning idiot ...

* * * * *

Sometimes, people who *do* believe in polts attempt to play the expert by making supposedly authoritative pronouncements about what such entities can and cannot do – authoritative pronouncements which are then immediately rendered null and void. When William G. Roll investigated a Newark poltergeist of 1961, he reassured those present that 'It doesn't hit people.' Immediately, a flying bottle whacked him 'squarely on the head'.[21] In the California home of one T. B. Clarke in April 1874, heavy furniture began moving around by itself. When Clarke's daughter was walking up the stairs, her father indicated towards an object that had almost hit her the night before, joking 'Nellie, look out for your head!' Equally jocular, she replied 'Oh! It is not time for them to begin yet,' as the phenomena had, so far, only occurred after a certain hour. Instantly, a large chair went spinning across the stairs, blocking her path as if purposely to contradict her.[22]

At Amherst, the investigator Walter Hubbell, glancing at the family cat one day, remarked idly that it was curious how the ghost never bothered it – whereupon the moggy was lifted 5 feet into the air and dropped down onto a young girl's back, before rolling across the floor and running from the house as quickly as it could.[23] At Humpty Doo, just as a Maori visitor was explaining how, according to the traditional beliefs of her own culture, polts had no power to physically harm their victims, a pair of pliers appeared in mid-air and hit her hard on the wrist, leaving a purple swelling.[24] Tricksters care not for authority of any kind, even that of those who believe in them.

* * * * *

During the famous haunting of Epworth Parsonage in Lincolnshire in 1716–17, the spook, dubbed 'Old Jeffrey', liked to disrupt prayers said for King George. In the words of Epworth's parson, Samuel Wesley, Jeffrey 'would make a great noise over our heads constantly' whenever this was done. Eventually, Samuel tried an experiment; he omitted the references to George from his prayers and found the knocking stopped, leading some to joke the spirit was a Jacobite.[25] But why did it act so? Those who favour the RSPK hypothesis may enjoy the following passage, written by John Wesley (Samuel's son, the founder of Methodism) and printed in an issue of the *Arminian Magazine* in 1784:

As both my father and mother are now at rest, and incapable of being pained thereby, I think it my duty to furnish the serious reader with a key to this circumstance. The year before King William died, my father observed my mother did not say Amen to the prayer for the king. She said she could not; for she did not believe the Prince of Orange was king. He vowed he would never cohabit with her till she did. He then took his horse and rode away, nor did she hear any thing of him for a twelvemonth. He then came back, and lived with her as before. But I fear his vow was not forgotten before God.[26]

John Wesley felt the poltergeist was a punishment sent from Heaven to persecute his father for not keeping his word. However, another way of interpreting these disrespectful incidents would be as a rebellion not only against the reigning monarch, but also against the authority of the paterfamilias of the house, with Mrs Wesley being the cause of the phenomena, her suppressed resentment over her husband's intransigent attitude festering away until it found eventual rowdy expression in the figure of Old Jeffrey. The polt-fancying poet Sacheverell Sitwell, noting Mrs Wesley was pregnant when Samuel left, speculated her unborn baby picked up on these tensions in the womb before later, in subconscious collusion with her mother, the child took supernatural revenge upon her dad![27]

Defying the authority of the father figure of a private household is one thing; ridiculing the father figure of an entire nation quite another. How many people realise that a real life President of the United States, no less, was once allegedly baited by a poltergeist? The tale of Andrew Jackson and the Bell Witch is an intriguing one, if true (which, as research has shown, it regrettably isn't). The yarn goes that Jackson, not yet then President but still a General in the army, came along on a wagon to investigate the Witch. Several of the General's men went so far as to declare that they would 'do up' the Witch, if it dared play any pranks on them. The demon begged to differ. When Jackson's wagon was travelling over a 'smooth level piece of road',

Epworth Rectory, once haunted by a disrespectful poltergeist.

it halted and stuck fast. No matter how hard the horses pulled, the wagon stayed 'welded to the earth'. The General ordered his men to dismount and push, but to no avail. The wheels were even taken off and examined, but looked fine. Eventually, Jackson reached the only conclusion possible. 'By the eternal boys,' he yelled, throwing up his hands, 'it is the Witch!' Now a 'sharp metallic voice' spoke from some bushes, declaring enough was enough. 'All right General, let the wagon move on, I will see you again tonight,' the Witch conceded. At this, the future President admitted publicly his impotence. 'By the eternal boys, this is worse than fighting the British!' he exclaimed, in equal parts awe and vexation.[28]

Historically, poltergeists have most enthusiastically baited the authority of the Church, as ably demonstrated by the Naples poltergeist of 1696–97, a most unholy ghost. Phenomena focused upon a sixteen-year-old novice, Carlo Maria Vulcano, who joined the Order of the Hieronymites in December 1693. As well as splattering Vulcano with stinking excrement, the demon also insultingly placed a chamberpot full of shit before an image of Saint Anastasio before invading the monks' refectory and replacing the soft centres of their loaves with horse-dung for them to bite into. When Vulcano was expelled from the monastery in January 1697, his room was fumigated with incense to dispel the spirit along with him. It fought back by apporting another chamberpot full of turds above which was written the inscription 'For such a deity, such a perfume', a particularly offensive erasure of binary opposites. Worse, when asked why it had come, the entity replied that it only sought 'to do what God has ordained for me ... To ceaselessly torment that novice,' thereby blasphemously implying that *God Himself* was behind all this evil, as in the Book of Job![29]

In Christopher Marlowe's *Tragical History of Doctor Faustus*, there is a scene in which the demon Mephistopheles confers upon Faust the covering of invisibility, and takes him to see the Pope and his Cardinals in Rome. It is a parody of Papal extravagance and cruelty; and Faust plays the role of invisible court-jester to it all. He snatches meat from the hands of the Pope, steals his glass as he is about to drink from it and lands him a box on the ear. The holy men think that Faustus is a poltergeist and fetch bell, book and candle to exorcise him, to no avail; once their ineffective ceremony is concluded, 'FAUSTUS and MEPHISTOPHILIS beat the FRIARS, fling fire-works among them and exeunt.'[30] Have things really changed all that much since?

*****

As already shown, exorcisms are particular objects of poltergeistic scorn. An Indian spook of the 1870s was warned off with the stern words 'I defy anything to touch this cross', uttered by a religious visitor bearing a large crucifix. The polt quickly picked up the cross and hurled it right back at its owner. A priest was then called to perform a blessing, but his vestments were pulled and his exorcism book 'immediately taken up to a corner of the roof' where it stayed stuck with its pages 'fluttering as though a great wind was fanning the leaves.' Before another priest, an egg stood up on its smaller end for no reason. The priest tried to right it, but failed; yet once he removed his

The Bell Witch frightens off some Shakers, the nineteenth-century American equivalent of Jehovah's Witnesses, by setting the dogs on them.

hand, it did so of its own accord, the man taunted as being too weak to even be able to budge a tiny little egg.[31] During the early days of her persecution by Dracu the Devil, a stone was lobbed through Eleonore Zugun's kitchen window. A priest blessed the pebble, marked it with a cross, and threw it into the nearby River Seret. Swiftly, the same stone, recognisable due to the holy mark the priest had placed upon it, was thrown back through the window once again.[32]

At Humpty Doo, exorcists had pistol cartridges and knives hurled at them by the ghost. A description of what happened when one priest arrived to bless the house is typical: 'The polt … went ape, smashing windows, hurling Father Tom's crucifix and Bible around the house, banging and scraping on and inside walls and keeping the occupants awake and thoroughly spooked all night.' A Greek Orthodox priest later set up an altar on the kitchen table, blessing each room and reading 'arcane passages' from a big black book, but fared no better: 'he was assaulted by an invisible force that repeatedly tried to wrench the book from his grasp and to twist his right arm behind his back. Ashen-faced, he finally sat down, declaring his adversary to be tougher than the average spook.'[33]

The Bell Witch was also tougher than the average spook. When some Shakers came to combat the unclean spirit one day, she shouted for three large guard dogs to run out and attack their horses, which the fierce animals obediently did. The Witch repeated the tale to callers as a favoured anecdote, particularly pleased with the detail that the Shakers, while fleeing on their terrified steeds, had to hold on to their 'big hats'.[34] During a 1942 Czech haunting in which a cow teleported inside a house, water poured from a boy's clothes and an old man was struck below the eye with a fork, an exorcising priest found himself with a wet cloth being pressed down firmly over his mouth. It sounds comical; until you consider that this is essentially waterboarding.[35]

* * * * *

Poltergeists furthermore display frequent disrespect towards the Bible, as demonstrated by the experience of the Van Reenen family of Plettenberg Bay, South Africa, who in 1975 had to flee their home, eight children and all, as more than a hundred items inexplicably burst into flames over the course of three horrible months, particularly Bibles. According to Mrs van Reenen: 'Our two family Bibles began showing scorch-marks … They got worse day by day, until both Bibles caught fire at the same time.' Understandably, the family concluded they were under assault from something 'evil'.[36]

In Seattle's Bothell Hell House, Bibles were also repeatedly targeted for abuse. The Good Books would be found lying on the floor 'engulfed in flame' with their pages 'blackened and curled', or even teleport impossibly into the washing-machine in the middle of its cycle. Sometimes Bibles simply burned on their shelves – while other books around them remained wholly untouched. The house's owner possessed so many Bibles not because he was especially religious, but to protect himself from the polt, which had taken to leaving death threats such as '666 DIE' scrawled all over his walls. His plan didn't work, with protective crucifixes and angel statues also being broken, singed or turned upside-down by the spook. A classic Trickster, the ghost enjoyed inverting things; not just crosses, but the traditional Native American pictogram for 'man' which was found drawn all over the walls too, and which, when turned upside-down, became transformed into actually meaning 'dead man'. Other ghostly graffiti used techniques akin to customary Indian methods of decorating pottery. Recalling the old 'house built on a Native American burial ground' trope from the film *Poltergeist*, traditional Indian 'smudge-sticks' were brought in to perform an exorcism ritual … but themselves spontaneously ignited while the ceremony was taking place.[37]

The Irish Derrygonnelly case of 1877 involved a family of Methodist farmers who were advised to place an open Bible on top of a bed to dispel the evil fairy – to no initial effect. According to Sir William Barrett, 'This they did in the name of God, putting a big stone on the top of the volume, but the stone was lifted off by an unseen hand, and the Bible placed on top of it. After that, "it" … moved the Bible out of the room and tore seventeen pages right across.'[38] An 1866 haunting from Philadelphia became so annoying that two local Baptist pastors were summoned. One suspected it was nothing but trickery. However:

> Soon after he entered the parlour a hymn book was projected from a table and thrown with violence against the door. With his own hands he picked up the book and replaced it. Before his eyes the volume was seized by an invisible force and for a second time thrown across the room, and a Testament sent to keep it company. Again the books were replaced, and again sent whirling around the room, at times making the entire circuit of the apartment; then they would fly off at a tangent and come to a full stop violently against the walls.[39]

This could all be interpreted as the ghosts attacking a book that they are, due to its godly power, somehow scared of, but with equal validity as being a visible sacrilegious mockery of the Bible's utter uselessness against them.

When Gef the Mongoose saw Mr Irving reading his Bible one day, he just jibed him: 'Look at the pious old atheist, reading the *Bible*; he will swear in a minute.'[40] Gef doesn't sound scared of the Good Book here. Instead, he dismisses it as pure cant – a tool of showy hypocrisy, not of holy exorcism. It was the same with the spook which haunted the most famous of all Victorian spirit-mediums, D. D. Home, while a young man living with his religious aunt in America during the late 1840s. Disturbed by the polt moving furniture, she placed a Bible very firmly down on top of one wandering table, exclaiming 'There! That will soon drive the devils away!' It didn't; still the table walked. The woman then climbed up on top of it to hold it down with her weight. As soon as she did so, the table – with her and the Bible still on it – levitated up into the air to defy her.[41]

We also get prayers and Bible-readings being disrupted by poltergeistery. During the 1830s haunting of Willington Mill in Tyneside, an elderly Quaker gentleman once came to stay. When he produced his Bible, his candle began to jump up and down and vibrate in its holder so he could not see the pages properly. Whenever he stopped reading, it was fine; but as soon as he started up again, the candle resumed its delinquency.[42] At France's haunted Calvados Castle, the resident Abbé was once sat quietly reading his breviary when a sudden mass of water – in the midst of a spell of beautiful weather – fell down the chimney into the fireplace, scattering ashes right into his face and eyes, leaving him temporarily blinded by wet soot.[43] The Scottish Ringcroft poltergeist of 1695 had a particularly virulent aversion to the saying of prayers. Repeatedly, when the haunted family gathered around to praise God, the spirit cried 'Hush! Hush!' at the end of every sentence, causing the household dog to bark loudly. The polt also liked to whistle, groan and throw mud and lumps of burning peat around, while pulling prayer-sayers backwards and forwards, hoisting them up from their knees and shouting 'Bo, Bo, Kick, Cuck!' at them. It also made several attempts to burn down the building.[44]

A haunting at a nunnery in northern France in 1940 featured some spectacular outbreaks of anti-religious poltergeistery, centring upon a nineteen-year-old maid, Josiane. Windowpanes, crucifixes and images of the Virgin Mary would break by themselves, while books upon sacred subjects were ripped to pieces when she was in the same room. One night, her clothing was torn to shreds in a matter of seconds. To put a stop to such sacrilege, the Mother Superior placed a blessed relic on Josiane's bedside table. The table then sprang to life, rushed into the shocked nun's room, threw the relic down onto her bed and waltzed back around to its original position.[45]

A Russian poltergeist of 1853 had scant respect for holy water. Three Russian Orthodox priests brought sacred icons and a basin full of this blessed liquid around to cleanse the haunted residence of a local government official, Captain Jandachenko, but the polt took no notice. Instead, it threw stones and smashed a window. A rock was then dropped right into the container filled with holy water itself, thereby visibly demonstrating the substance's lack of potency. Defeated, the priests slunk away, their faith very sorely tested.[46] When Eleonore Zugun was taken to the Romanian Convent of Suczava in an attempt to exorcise Dracu, she was brought before an icon of

St Johannes to seek divine aid. As soon as this saint's name was pronounced, a rock was thrown against the icon, destroying it, hurled with such force it lodged itself into the wall.[47]

Provocatively, some poltergeistery actually takes place within churches. When Esther Cox, the young girl at the centre of the infamous 'Great Amherst Mystery', visited her local Baptist Church, escapades such as the following were not unknown:

> ... during the first singing, the ghost, which had been quiet for some days, again manifested itself by knocking on ... the pew in front. When told to stop by Miss Cox, it would cease the noise for a moment, but then break out worse than ever. Throughout the prayer it continued; and when the organ began for the second singing, the noise became so distinct and disturbing that Miss Cox and party were forced to leave the church[48] ... [During a later trip] every time the Minister said anything about Satan or the Holy Ghost, this demon ... would knock on the floor or the back of the pew, and, finally, he upset the kneeling-stool and commenced to throw the hymn-books about. Esther became crimson with mortification; the congregation was greatly disturbed ... and we left the church.[49]

A parallel is found in the case of Abby Warner, a spirit-medium from Cleveland, who on Christmas Eve 1851 attended a sermon, only for it to be repeatedly interrupted by spirit-rappings. The Minister made clear his desire that 'those knockings might cease', whereupon a single rap 'of remarkable force and vibratory power' rang out, followed by the noises increasing in both number and volume by way of refusal. Abby was subsequently placed on trial for creating a public outrage. However, as it could not be proven that Warner was physically making the knockings herself the case was dismissed, much to the chagrin of the presiding judge who expressed 'sincere regret' that nobody should be prosecuted for such an outrageous show of civic indecency.[50]

* * * * *

We will recall one possible critical interpretation of the Trickster-figure is that he is a personified parody of the holy shaman or high-priest. If so, then perhaps the most cutting such satirist was Donald the Battersea poltergeist, who went so far as to construct an entire blasphemous spoof religion based upon worshipping the Hollywood teen-idol and 'live fast, die young' car-crash victim James Dean, and his now-forgotten 1950s British equivalent Jeremy Spenser whom, as we saw earlier, he falsely predicted was destined to die in a tragic vehicle-smash of his own some day.

During the 1950s, the quasi-religious way in which that curious new species known as 'the teenager' began to worship pop singers and stars of the silver screen was becoming an obvious feature of post-war consumer-culture. Shirley Hitchings, the Battersea focus-figure, was no different, with one of her favourite demi-gods being Jeremy Spenser, star of *The Prince and the Showgirl* – Shirley clearly desired to be the princess of Spenser's heart. Donald realised this, and tried to set them up, regardless of the fact that Shirley was still legally a child. 'DO YOU LIKE JEREMY?' he asked one day, '[I think] HE IS SWEET', as did Shirley. The polt went on to swooningly admire Spenser's 'HAIR DARK', 'EYES BROWN' and 'COMPLEXION TAN'. 'I WANT JEREMY SPENSER'S PICTURE', Donald then declared ... but what did he want it for?[51]

Donald intended it to become a religious icon, to be worshipped by Shirley in lieu of a more standard wall-mounted image of Jesus Christ. Donald snipped a magazine-photo of Spenser, glued it onto cardboard, hung it above Shirley's bed and ordered her to 'ALLWAYS KEEP HIS PICTURE BY YOU – NEVER LET IT OUT OF YOUR SIGHT'.[52] As Donald fibbed that Spenser had fallen madly in love with her from afar, maybe he expected Shirley to kneel down before the actor's sacred image and, like a teeny-bop Bride of Christ, pray for the blessing of their future union. Following his car-crash, Donald purportedly visited Spenser's hospital ward and heard him moaning Shirley's name; Donald had been penning Jeremy gushing letters about his potential underage-lover, and (so Donald lied) he liked the sound of what he had read.[53] Indeed, Spenser's very soul subsequently spoke to his acolyte from thin air, saying 'Hello, Shirley! Come to me. You don't know me, but I know you, Jeremy.'[54]

Donald later JOTTled Christmas cards and letters supposedly bearing messages from Spenser and his associates around the haunted house for Shirley to find; one allegedly came from Spenser's brother, asking her to phone him.[55] Then, the culminating sacrilege of all – like a phenomenal icon of the Virgin Mary, Shirley's wall-mounted Spenser photograph began to weep miraculous tears! They tasted 'salty', apparently.[56] Shirley started referring to Spenser as her lovely 'cry-baby' and wrote a song (or hymn?) in his honour with her good friend Doreen.[57] Donald soon provided Shirley with yet more holy relics; a magic locket containing Jeremy's photo which would keep him from all harm for as long as Shirley wore it around her neck, and a special jewel which induced visions of Spenser if you stared into it for long enough.[58] Donald then began stalking the man, so he claimed, following him and his brother around in their homes and at film-studios.[59] He even JOTTled away what he said was the front-door key to the flat of one of Jeremy's friends and left it out to be pocketed.[60] Donald also wrote fan-mail to Spenser and other screen-stars, and sent applications trying to get Shirley a job as an actress on TV show *The Adventures of Sir Lancelot*, where she would no doubt one day bump into her desired beau (Donald would write out these letters, put them in addressed envelopes, then the family would affix stamps and post them out).[61]

Another letter was delivered to the case's chief investigator, Harold 'Poltergeist' Chibbett, informing him of Shirley's true level of devotion to Jeremy, for love of whom she would lie on her bed and weep. Donald basically admitted he was lying about Spenser being in love with Shirley in return, but still thought it worth engineering a meeting between them as 'WHO KNOWS? HE MAY LIKE HER.'[62] Tragically, he did not. Chibbett contacted Spenser's brother and agent, telling them what was going on. For a long time, Spenser himself did not respond. Eventually, one of the actor's representatives called around at the Hitchings' Battersea home in person – it was apparently his brother's solicitor, and he ordered them to stop constantly sending the Spensers weird love-letters and warnings about car-crashes supposedly penned in the hand of a 'ghost'. That night, Donald threw a major tantrum, throwing Shirley out of bed, smearing Vaseline on walls and tossing around lit matches.[63]

Maybe this was for the best, as Shirley's religious symptoms were becoming increasingly morbid, as if the cult had really been designed not by any poltergeist, but by J. G. Ballard. While fretting about Spenser's possible car-crash, Shirley developed Eleonora Zugun-type stigmata on her face, a small wound appearing there in the same position it was anticipated Jeremy's own face would be sliced open by flying glass or twisted metal. Donald also used a pen to mark out on a doll where the scars would appear once the catastrophe had taken place, like a plastic-surgeon.[64] Following Spenser's rejection of Shirley, however, a new tack was necessary. Another of Shirley's teen-idols was James Dean, by whose own automobile-related death on 30 September 1955 she had been greatly shaken, keeping a file of newspaper clippings about the tragedy as a memento.[65] Shirley could not be rebuffed by Dean, as he was dead, so Donald now apported a photo of him onto her bed, with marks drawn across his face and hands too, indicating the Christ-like wounds sustained in his fatal collision.[66]

James Dean himself then turned up at Battersea in spook-form, giving Shirley helpful advice on how to become a film-star, using risible US teen-speak. He even utilised a typewriter to provide Shirley with a kind of holy text, detailing his basic biography like one of the Lives of the Saints.[67] Donald actually became jealous of Dean's ghost, imitating his Americanisms – 'SEE YOU LATER, ALLIGATOR' – to win back Shirley's favour, but also calling him 'A PEST' and complaining 'THAT JAMES DEAN IS GOT A CHEEK – I DO NOT MIND HIM HELPING BUT HE IS NOT CUTTING ME OUT'.[68] Dean in turn felt threatened by Donald and Shirley's love for Jeremy Spenser, and this caused tension between the two ghosts, before eventually Dean agreed to step aside in favour of Donald and 'this guy Jeremy': 'please help him – look – before I came, yer was full of Don – look – I feel I'm cutting him out – and beleave me, brother – I don't want to be on the wrong side of him'.[69]

If James McClenon was right, and many religions really are formed in a spate of excited paranormal enthusiasm surrounding the eruption of miraculous-seeming poltergeistery among early gurus and worshippers, then Shirley Hitchings' abortive James Dean/Jeremy Spenser cult was one such potential creed that never quite worked out. The Hermes-haunted dividing line between blasphemy and sanctity is perhaps not quite as clear-cut and binary in its nature as mainstream religious authorities would like to have us think.

XIV

Poltergeists at Play

We don't stop playing because we grow old, we grow old because
we stop playing.

G. B. Shaw

Poltergeists, as we saw at the start of this book, have often been dismissed as merely little children playing games. This might not be true, but they have certainly frequently played games *with* little children. During the haunting of Epworth Parsonage, Keziah Wesley, the youngest of the haunted family's brood, used to love chasing 'Old Jeffrey' around from room to room, following the sound of his rappings, playing 'catch-chase'.[1] The Amherst spook played a different game. It piled seven chairs on top of one another, making a pile 6 feet in height, then pulled out the one nearest the bottom, causing the others to fall to the floor with 'a terrific crash' as if playing supernatural Jenga.[2] The Bell Witch could be equally infantile. While several of the Bell children were sitting on a sledge, the Witch screamed out 'Hold on tight!' and then paranormally pulled them around the room on it, several times, at impossibly fast speed.[3] A fairy-like poltergeist called Malekin haunting a manor house in the Suffolk village of Dagworth during the early 1200s would shout 'Play again! Play again!' after pulling its many characteristically childish tricks, so it is said.[4] Gef the Mongoose was an equally light-hearted soul; he enjoyed playing hide-and-seek with the daughter of the Irving household, Voirrey, and her dog, and encouraged people to go outside and use skipping ropes and tennis racquets while he looked on enthusiastically. As Voirrey grew older, Gef's appetite for such childish things waned along with hers.[5]

Another ludic poltergeist played up during the family holiday of a teenage boy named Tom Ross at the California resort of Mammoth Mountain in 1982. Tom would challenge the spook to move various objects, close the door and leave the master bedroom. When the lights flickered, this was a signal the challenge was complete. Going back inside, the named objects would indeed have been successfully moved around – even if not present in the room in the first place. The spook enjoyed this game as it left a smiley face lying on the bed, formed from elaborately folded towels. Tom soon decided to 'increase the difficulty' for the ghost by being present in the 'games-room' with it. Placing a cloth on a curtain-rod, he dared the polt to move it. Nothing happened, so Tom kept turning away and quickly looking back again to catch it in the act. He failed, but one time found the towel gone anyway. Where was it? In his own back-pocket! 'It was like a magic trick' said Tom and, while the outcome to the game scared him a bit, he had to admit it was also kind of 'funny'.[6]

A particular poltergeist favourite is playing 'fetch' – another sign of their half-animal consciousness? John Mompesson described the Drummer of Tedworth's interaction with one of his servants thus:

> The fift of November in the morning, it kept a mighty noise and one of my men observing ... that there was two boards stood edge long and did seem to move, he said to it Give me that board, [and] the board came within a yard of him, he said againe, Nay, Let me have it in my hand; it came home to his very foot, he shuft it back again to him, and so from one to another at least twenty times, but I forbad such familiarity.[7]

A 1950 spook haunting a Dutch couple living in Indonesia liked to play fetch with their adopted daughter. Mr Krom watched the girl throw a stick over a wall into an empty courtyard. He heard it hit the ground. And yet, 'a fraction of a second afterwards', it lay back at her feet again.[8] Ivan T. Sanderson, the famed fortean investigator, played a game of fetch with an outdoor poltergeist at a Sumatran rubber plantation in 1928. While he and some guests were sitting on the veranda one evening, they observed small stones fly in from the jungle beyond and roll gently to a halt against the wall behind them. Sanderson's host, used to the lithobolia, said they could easily play a game by marking the stones, then throwing them into the undergrowth. Lipstick, chalk and pencils were used; almost all the marked pebbles came back, most within seconds. Yet nobody was visible in the tangled vegetation, ready to return them.[9]

In 1837 a German house near a mountain stream was being subjected to yet another lithobolic attack. As an experiment, it was suggested some pebbles be marked with a cross and thrown into the water. Within less than a minute, they were falling back inside the house, dripping wet.[10] At a haunted house in Salamanca, Spain, around 1570, one witness picked up a pebble and examined it carefully, making precise note of its appearance. Then he tossed it over the nearest house, saying 'If this came from a devil or a fairy, then throw the same stone back at me!' The polt obeyed, the very same stone striking the man just above his eyes.[11] The Bell Witch used to wait for the Bell children to pass by a certain thicket upon their return home from school, whereupon stones and sticks were gently thrown at them. The children turned this into a little game, cutting notches on the sticks, tossing them back into the bushes and waiting for them back.[12]

Guessing-game contests are another perennial favourite. Gef the Talking Mongoose always knew whether a tossed coin had landed heads or tails – or even when the penny hadn't really been tossed at all.[13] In 1877, Sir William Barrett found the Derrygonnelly polt equally as skilled. He challenged it to knock the same number of times as the digit he was thinking of in his head; it did so successfully. Then, he held his hands in his pockets and extended a certain number of fingers; could the poltergeist guess this, too? It certainly could – right every time.[14] The Amherst poltergeist was able to correctly indicate, by rapping, how much money visitors had inside their pockets.[15]

Given their invariable accuracy, presumably none of these mind-reading ghosts were actually just guessing at all – but their activities were certainly framed by their human percipients as being a kind of game.

* * * * *

Other spooks make use of ludic paraphernalia. At Thornton Heath, Mrs Forbes was dusting one day when she heard a whizzing sound go past her. Looking up, she saw three darts embedded in her husband's dartboard – all scoring perfect doubles.[16] In his book *Invizikids*, Michael J. Hallowell, one of the investigators of the South Shields case, tells us how, while small, he liked rolling a red plastic ball back and forth with his imaginary friend Elizabeth; until, one day, Hallowell's grandmother walked in and saw, to her astonishment, the ball being pushed back to him by an unseen force.[17] At the 300-year-old clubhouse of the West Bowling Golf Club in Bradford in 1974, where doors locked themselves and apparitions were sighted, games of snooker would be played out on the tables with unseen cues.[18] In 1998, Deirdre Morris of Tunbridge Wells claimed her dead husband David was playing chess with her. David having been an ardent chess fan, she had left his board set up on a table in tribute, but, upon coming downstairs each morning, repeatedly found one of the pieces had been moved, as though David was making his next move from the afterlife.[19]

A remarkable instance of a poltergeist providing people with game-playing equipment is detailed in a pamphlet from 1592, concerning a haunting in the Oxfordshire village of North Aston. Here, one William Whing lost his initial fear of the spirit and addressed it in 'pleasant jesting tearmes', saying 'if thoue bee a good fellow, fling us downe a quoit or two, that my companyon and I may go play'. Immediately, there fell down 'a thinne broad stone, in just forme and proportion of a round quoite, such as commonly men use to play with'. Sensing his luck was in, Whing asked for another; again, one appeared. Whing then requested enough quoits that he might be able to play a full game, and Hermes was only too happy to apport them.[20]

Sometimes, ghosts delight in interacting with children's toys, as during a haunting at a London community centre where paper aeroplanes were thrown by invisible hands and toy 'sit-in' cars drove around unoccupied.[21] In 2006, crowds in the Argentinean town of Firmat were so disturbed by an apparent haunted swing in a children's playground that they called in police. This swing would sway backwards and forwards forcefully despite there being nobody near it, while all the other swings would remain perfectly still. This happened constantly, for ten whole days and was captured on film. No explanation was forthcoming.[22] Usually when polts play with toys, dead children are blamed, a position with which I have already stated I do not necessarily agree. During a haunting in Pittsburgh in 1971–72, a couple felt 'a small body' crawl into bed between them one night; the husband kicked it and a kind of 'wave-body', like shimmering heat-haze, appeared, followed by the sound of objects being knocked over and childish laughter. It was concluded a ghost-baby was at play, something supposedly backed up by a rocking horse moving to and fro of its own accord.[23]

* * * * *

Presuming they are not all dead children, why *do* poltergeists like to play? Several people have ventured explanations. Iris M. Owen's Philip liked to 'possess' a certain table and then chase one of the sitters around the room until he was forced to jump cowering up onto a chair as if fleeing a mouse, something the other sitters present laughingly encouraged the spook to do.[24] One of Owen's colleagues, Dr Joel Whitton, had the idea that these games only occurred because the members of the circle were regressing back to a state of childlike creativity and joy. According to him, 'The adult in such a situation says, 'These things cannot happen.' But the child says, 'I want them to happen, so they *will* happen.'' And then, of course, they do – via RSPK. During the sittings, Whitton claimed, the participants became like a family of siblings, feeling more relaxed, as one naturally would be with one's own family, and more psychologically open to engaging in child-like emotions and actions, as did the ghost.[25]

Another theory appears in Max Freedom Long's classic work, *The Secret Science Behind Miracles*. Long, an American, arrived in Hawaii in 1917 and became interested in the island's native priests, the *kahunas*. These *kahunas* believed man had three different souls, one of which, the 'lower self', corresponded broadly to our ideas of both the subconscious, and the poltergeist. According to Long, these 'lower selves' could find themselves cut off from a man's other two souls after death, should that man die suddenly from accident or illness. This kind of spirit, he said:

> ... is illogical, having only animal-like deductive reason. It responds to hypnotic suggestion. It is like a child and is often a playful 'poltergeist' or noisy ghost. It loves to attend séances and make tables tip. It tries to answer questions, and usually gives such answers as make it appear to be a liar or worse. It loves to imitate one's deceased relatives.[26]

The Hawaiian *kahunas*, said Long, could manipulate these confused entities for their own ends. By chanting a death-prayer over some food which would then be left out for the ghosts to 'eat', the *kahuna* could charge up these spirits with enough *mana*, or vital energy, to make them deadly against his enemies. Letting them loose, these fully-charged beings could then suck the life-force from the *kahuna*'s foe after being given a hair or piece of clothing belonging to the person so they could pick up his 'psychic scent'. First the victim's feet would grow numb, and then the rest of his body, by steps, until the ghosts reached his heart and he died.[27] However, once this process has ended, the *kahuna* is left with something of a problem; namely, a series of idiotic poltergeistic lower-selves, charged up with enough energy to cause mayhem. Therefore, when the lower-selves had returned from a successful mission, the *kahuna* would order them to play wildly until they had burnt out all their vital force. And what form did this rumbustious play take? According to Long, the spooks would 'move or throw objects, make loud noises and create a bedlam of some proportions.'[28]

*****

Maybe it is pointless to even ask the question of why poltergeists play. After all, when you think back to your own childhood, do you really know why

A Hawaiian *kahuna*, who could send his pet polts out to play with you – although not very nicely.

it was that *you* played? Perhaps we would be better off trying to play along with Trickster rather than attempting to endlessly analyse his games; he plays by different rules each time he manifests, in any case. Analysts of Trickster tales have often pointed out that the paradoxical-sounding concept of 'serious play' is at work within them; many Trickster-figures' activities seem logically pointless and rather random, and are in fact a sort of play themselves, in which the most solemn rules of normal social behaviour are deconstructed, laughed at and re-examined humorously, later to be reordered and reborn anew, in a kind of productive chaos.[29] As one critic has put it, 'The Trickster incarnates in every culture the oxymoronic imagination at play, literally "fooling around" to discover new paradigms and even new logics.'[30]

Outside of formal sporting competitions, play is essentially an end in itself. There may be no point in looking for reasons why children and adults – or indeed ghosts – play, as there *is* no real reason for it other than to experience the joy of play as an end in itself. Play cuts at the very roots of causality, as we have no idea why it is, ultimately, that we do play, other than that it is fun. There is no pre-defined goal at the end of it all beyond, perhaps, the winning of the game itself. Many games, however, have no winner – or no rules. A happy child, frolicking on the family lawn contentedly, pointlessly, oblivious to the world around them ... and a poltergeist, also quite happy, childishly playing fetch or stacking up chairs. Is there much difference between the two, in the end? Poltergeist play is yet another reminder to us not to look for any definite answers; sometimes, most likely, polts play simply because they *just do*. If we are unable to understand this, then perhaps the problem is ours, not theirs. The real question should not be why do poltergeists play, so much as why *shouldn't* they play?

XV

Threats of Violence

We're bringing violence back where it belongs – in the home.

Alfred Hitchcock

It is a stereotype of polteregistery that ghosts may frequently threaten to harm someone but generally stop just short of doing them any actual injury; it is almost as if, many commentators have guessed, they are somehow not allowed to.[1] Again and again, lithobolic missiles miss their targets by a matter of inches, or else strike their victims so lightly the impact does them no harm whatsoever. A 1718 haunting in a Lutheran parsonage at Gröben, Germany, featured a very considerate spook indeed. While it liked to smash windows with rocks, if anyone was standing in front of the pane being destroyed, the stones would fall perpendicularly to the ground in an unnatural fashion after they had gone through the glass so the person wouldn't get hit. Once, a stone was falling right down on top of a man's head until a maid screamed and the rock swerved aside at full pelt, throwing itself through a window-pane and out into the courtyard.[2]

Guy Lyon Playfair reports that, during one Brazilian case, a stone floated around, tapped three people very gently upon their heads, and then fell down lifeless to the floor. According to those being 'assaulted', the stone felt like a 'ball of compressed air' not a hard rock.[3] There are certain affinities with slapstick here. When people in comedy films are smashed over the head with chairs or bottles, they tend to be made of cardboard or sugar, no matter how realistic they might appear. The actors feel very little; it just looks as though they do. In poltergeist cases, the materials involved *are* real – and yet they too still don't hurt. Maddalena Rimassa, a thirteen-year-old girl from Genoa, was in 1865 attacked in a way which appeared more violent than it actually was. Whenever she passed a window, a 'shower of missiles' would immediately strike her head, but despite these volleys looking quite violent, they did not produce so much as a bruise.[4]

During the 1682 New England haunting after which the very term 'lithobolia' was originally coined, one witness found himself sprinkled with glass from a devil-smashed window. However, the shards did not hurt him as the polt had unexpectedly caused the glass to be broken down into blunt and 'regularly marked-out ... even squares', as if done by a workman, 'to the end some of these little pieces might fly in my face ... and give me a surprise, but without any hurt.'[5] During a Czech case of 1928, it was noticed that stones materialised but a few feet away from their human targets and, as soon as fully solidified, dropped straight to the ground. It was only while still merely *semi*-solid that they continued their trajectory on towards their victims. Thus, when people were hit with rocks, they 'felt no more substantial than being hit by a ball of paper.'[6]

* * * * *

The use of knives and other sharp implements is another standard tactic of terror. At Humpty Doo a priest was confronted by a kitchen-knife flying right at his chest, before stopping just short to fall innocuously at his feet. Claiming to be used to such experiences, the holy man carried on with his exorcism as though nothing had happened. Another Australian polt once stabbed a knife into the corpse of a dead pig.[7] At Töttelstedt, Germany, in 1581, axes, hatchets and oven-forks were thrown at a farmer named Schiel, along with less harmful but still unpleasant excrement. No sharp items at any point actually hit him, though.[8] The Enfield polt, as usual, was more inventive, warning Mrs Harper to dispose of a bag of knives from a kitchen drawer; it seemed worried that 'Tommy', the spirit of a five-year-old boy who it claimed was now living in the house, might get hold of them. 'HE CAN BE DANGEROUS WITH A KNIFE' the ghost said. Not long after, a floating knife followed the teenage Janet from room to room, 'dancing around on its own' and pointing at her.[9]

The 1878–79 haunting of Esther Cox at Amherst, Nova Scotia, was rather different. Sometimes, dangerous projectiles just missed Esther – a large carving-knife went 'whizzing through the air' inches over her head as she exited the pantry one day.[10] At other times the missiles did find their mark, though. Once, a knife was snatched from a man's hand while he was whittling wood and then stabbed into Esther's back, leaving the weapon sticking out of a large wound with Esther 'bleeding profusely'. The man retrieved the knife and hid it away – only for Hermes to pick his pocket and hurl the thing back into Esther's same wound with an uncanny accuracy![11] After Esther wrote out protective Bible verses on slips of paper, the polt took umbrage by cutting a 'triangular gash' in her forehead with a steak-bone, stabbing her in the head with a fork and trying to cut her throat with a pair of shears.[12]

An Italian poltergeist of 1909 once succeeded in hitting a man on the forehead with a dung-covered rock so hard that he suffered 'a sharp pain' and a bump 'the size of an almond', so even usually harmless lithobolia can *sometimes* turn nasty.[13] One of the most disturbingly violent hauntings I know of occurred in Daly City, California, where people were slapped, hurled around and choked, with one victim actually being knocked unconscious by the spook. Objects were painfully thrown too, and attempts made to smother people with sheets and pillows. Bizarrely, a baby had a crucifix teleported inside its nappy and its chain entwined excruciatingly tight around its genitals; the child's cot was also repeatedly set on fire, with pieces of paper reading '*he, child, die, baby*' found littered around the haunted home before bursting into flames too.[14]

* * * * *

As this implies, some polts prefer to issue verbal threats rather than (or alongside) physical ones. The South Shields spook repeatedly sent menacing text messages to its victims, producing such misspelled phrases as 'Get you bich' and 'You're dead.'[15] In 1991, a ghost haunting the premises of a Cornish brassware company used a computer to intimidate employees, writing things like 'I have you, I have you, Ha, Ha, Ha' on-screen.[16] A 2008 case from Dundee featured lurid details about a knife being placed within a baby's cot and various items being slashed up, while warnings like 'You must go' and 'Gonna hurt you' appeared scrawled on notepads and across walls.[17] This sounds not unlike the Amherst entity which, infamously, carved the phrase 'ESTHER COX YOU ARE MINE TO KILL' on a bedroom wall – one moment the wall was clear, then the ominous graffiti was there. Apparently, the ghost was 'neither an elegant nor an accomplished penman.'[18] A 1999 Colombian polt went one further, scratching the stigmatic taunts 'you will not live' and 'Eva deserves to die forever' on the body of a sixteen-year-old girl.[19] Despite these messages, none of the people involved *were* murdered by ghosts, though; such threats just sound like yet more rather sick jokes.

A series of hostile notes left behind by a 1928 Irish ghost were even more infantile. They read 'We will work it on you while the three of you are there', 'It is a pity I cannot work it harder' and then, quite marvellously, 'I will come down the chimney to-night and take Nana's glasses'.[20] It is hard to see how this final, genuinely babyish, communication could have produced any response other than laughter. Likewise, Matthew Manning's childhood poltergeist kept on writing the words 'Matthew Beware' in a juvenile hand around his house, but according to Matthew, 'The warnings did not tell me what to beware of, and I ignored them as much as possible. It was as though there was a child causing many of the disturbances, because so many … displayed a childish mentality.'[21]

* * * * *

Some poltergeists seem (appropriately enough) in two minds about whether or not they will bring any physical harm. The Scottish Ringcroft ghost of 1695 suspended a huge tree-branch over some children in their bed one night, growling that 'If I had a commission [permission from God] I would brain them'; but surely if the spirit had really wanted to smash their skulls in, it could have done so?[22] At other times the same spook claimed it *did* have a commission from God to haunt the victimised family, saying it had been 'sent to warn the land to repent, for a judgement is to come if the land do not quickly repent.' The nature of this judgement, it said, was that a hundred far worse poltergeists would be dispatched by God Almighty to persecute every home in the nation, a threat which went wholly unfulfilled.[23] Gef the Mongoose was equally as vacillating, saying: 'I am not evil. I could be if

I wanted. You don't know what damage or harm I could do if I were roused. I could kill you all, but I won't.'[24] A French poltergeist of 1850 was similarly schizophrenic; after it had caused the village mayor to 'howl' with pain after striking him violently on the thigh, the ghost immediately gave him a 'gentle caress' with an invisible hand which 'alleviated all the pain in an instant'.[25]

And yet, in spite of the general stereotype, other ghosts *do* follow through on their threats; as usual, Tricksters are consistently inconsistent. A poltergeist from Georgia, USA, perpetrated the following harrowing assault upon a Mr Surrency in the family sitting room in 1879, as described by the victim's brother:

> Just as I entered ... I saw one of the huge andirons lift itself from the fire and begin to move across the room. It gathered momentum as it went, and rose swiftly in the air till it reached the level of my brother's head when it dealt him a heavy blow on the temple. He sprang to his feet, stunned and bleeding, while I grasped the andiron in my hands, trying thus to shield my brother; but I may as well have essayed to hold a thunderbolt, for it wrenched itself free from my grasp and struck my brother again in the head. 'Run,' I called to my brother, 'run for your life! If you stay here you will be killed, and I cannot help you.' The poor boy did run out of the room and the andiron followed, striking him heavy blows, till the victim, covered with blood, fell unconscious at our mother's feet. Then the andiron moved slowly across the hall and resumed its accustomed place on the hearth.[26]

During one 1920s case a cook became so irritated by the pranks a poltergeist played that she cursed the thing openly. No sooner had she done so than a 'sharp hissing sound' was heard, whereupon the cook fled the room with both hands clasped over her head, which was then found to be swelled and bleeding as if she had been hit by a sharp and heavy object; and yet no such object had been seen to strike her. She left the haunted home immediately, not even packing her clothes.[27]

Blessed Christina of Stommeln had to endure various horrible physical torments from her poltergeistic persecutor alongside the cavalcade of disturbing shit-based phenomena we examined earlier. If you believe her hagiography, then the Devil in polt form would steal her pillow, making her bump her head, beat her so hard that 'it could almost be heard in the local market-place', burn her clothes while she was still wearing them, throw her against walls, press red-hot stones against her skin, stab her with nails and 'gnaw at her flesh like a dog'. The Devil also tore off her shoes, with the skin from her feet, and cut the shoes into little pieces; her dresses, too, became ribbons. Once, it smashed down Christina's door, hurled stones and bones, and bit several priests who tried to protect her. On another occasion, Christina's sister was seen by several witnesses to be stabbed in the back by a floating sword. Weirdest of all, the ghost brought a flayed cat into the house and thrust its head down Christina's throat to choke her, before making a human skull float in and begin mocking her from within the grinning rictus of its mouth. One day, she was found buried up to her neck in mud outside. Another time, she was discovered bound to the side of a tree; according to

The poison given to John Bell by the Bell Witch was tested out on a handy nearby cat – which then promptly died. Happily for animal lovers, the story appears to be largely untrue.

her, Satan had visited her in bed, thrust willow twigs right through her ankles to act as bloody manacles, then dragged her outside. A religious hysteric who was tormented by the irrational fear that, while swallowing the Communion Host one day, Beelzebub might sneakily swap it for a live toad or ball of squirming maggots, we may well suspect Christina of having inflicted some of her wounds upon herself – either literally, or by proxy via the RSPK-fuelled figure of the demonic poltergeist.[28]

The most well-known ghostly wounds were those bites and scratches imposed upon the Romanian poltergeist-focus Eleonore Zugun during the early 1920s by her attendant spirit Dracu; film footage of this actually exists. Zugun is sat at a table before a drawing of Dracu, given a hammer, and told to hit the ghost's image. As she does so, large welts begin rising up on her body.[29] A Dr Walther Kröner smeared layers of grease over Zugun's face and arms to determine whether, when the scratches occurred, the grease itself was displaced too, or whether they simply appeared upon her skin spontaneously from within, like stigmata. He discovered the grease was indeed being 'ploughed aside'; occasionally, the grease alone would bear scratches, as though the invisible claws of Dracu didn't always have the strength to penetrate this protective barrier. The teeth marks in Zugun's skin were also often covered with malodorous spittle. When analysed, this substance was found to have 'swarmed with staphylococci'.[30] Considered from the perspective of shamanism, these sound rather like the ordeals of cutting and physical dismemberment at the hands of spirits once endured by adolescent initiates during their rites, but taking place within actual physical reality.

* * * * *

Accounts of poltergeists actually killing people are scarce indeed. The sad case of Maria José Ferreira of the Brazilian town of Jabuticabal, for example, may or may not have been murder. When it first appeared in 1965, the ghost seemed friendly – Maria could request sweets and flowers, and the spirit would happily drop them at her feet, gifts from Hermes placed to-order. However, it was not long until stones were falling onto her plate while she was trying to eat, or hard apples being pelted at her in the yard. Soon, Hermes was stealing things, not gifting them; when she asked for a guava to be plucked from a tree, the fruit simply vanished from sight instead. Then the ghost became violent, slapping and biting her face, placing cups over her mouth and nostrils while she was asleep to suffocate her, sticking needles into her flesh and setting her clothes on fire. It even attempted rape. Maria's story reached a premature end when, in 1970, aged thirteen, she downed a soft drink laced with formicide and died.[31] Was this suicide, or the most malevolent *hermaion* of all time?

The case of Maria José Ferreira may be ambiguous, but that of the Bell Witch poisoning John Bailey Bell certainly was not. John was the head of the household, whom the Witch disliked immensely, persecuting him day and night. Eventually, he took to his bed ill and didn't get back up again; the Witch had switched John's usual medicine for what was described as being 'a smoky-looking vial ... about one-third full of dark-coloured liquid.' Supposedly, the Witch admitted to having placed the new 'medicine' in the cabinet, saying that: 'It's useless for you to try to revive Old Jack, I have got him this time; he will never get up from that bed again ... I put it [the poison] there, and gave Old Jack a big dose out of it last night while he was asleep, which fixed him.' To test the liquid, some was placed into a cat's mouth through a straw; the animal, so we are told, 'jumped and whirled over a few times, stretched out, kicked and died very quick.' The bottle and its contents were then thrown into the open hearth, whereupon a 'blue blaze' shot up the chimney 'like [gun] powder.'[32]

That's the story, anyway – we've already mentioned how it was actually a fabrication – but there is one apparently reliable parallel for a polt causing a similar quantity of potion-like liquid to appear on record, so I suppose you never know. This strange fluid – described by the spook specifically as being a 'potionne' – appeared in an antique drinking-glass in Matthew Manning's parents' bedroom one evening. According to Matthew, the 'potionne' was 'a brown liquid which looked heavy, with a deposit of sediment in the bottom' that smelled of port. Manning poured the drink into a screw-top jar. Within an hour it had gone deep purple. An hour and a half later, it was inky-blue, then the next morning a bright green like grass. It stayed on the family's window-sill for several days until one morning the jar was found empty. Nobody was foolish enough to actually drink from it, though – they didn't even give any to a cat.[33]

* * * * *

These accounts of poltergeist murders are but two in number, and strike me as being either unlikely or speculative. What most polts' assaults remind me of ultimately is that kind of play which a cat engages in with a captured mouse or bird, prior to offing it with a well-aimed bite to the neck. Take this description of the fate of a twelve-year-old boy called Harry during a US haunting of 1850–51:

> At times he was violently caught up from the ground until his head nearly struck the ceiling; once he was thrown into a cistern of water, and once also he was tied up and suspended from a tree. Under the eyes of a clergyman visitor the boy's trousers were rent from the bottom upwards, higher than the knee, and were literally torn to ribbons an inch or more wide.[34]

One gets the clear impression that the ghost could, if it so wished, have torn poor Harry to ribbons at any moment, too – likewise with Eleonore Zugun, Esther Cox and their own spooks. That the spirits did not suggests to me that these assaults were all essentially a very rough form of play-violence more than genuine homicidal aggression. Indeed, some reported physical assaults do seem simply strange or playful rather than sinister. Harry Price gives an account of a medieval convent whose noisy ghost insisted upon dragging the nuns from their beds at night and tickling them 'nearly to death'.[35] At a haunted Oxfordshire house named 'Beth-Oni', similarly, a child complained of being tickled by unseen hands in her bed.[36] Just as absurdly, there have been a few polts who found it funny to throw cats into people's faces. This happened at La Constantinie in France during the late 1800s,[37] and during the haunting of a pair of Northern Irish sisters named Frances and Elizabeth Dixon during the late 1700s.[38] Occasionally, polts have also transferred objects into people's mouths as a bizarre form of jokey assault. The Bromley Garden Centre poltergeist once JOTTled a flower-bulb into a man's mouth; he nearly choked on it.[39] At Enfield, the spook once shoved a digestive biscuit into Janet's mouth. It appeared 'just out of nowhere.'[40]

Maybe we should start considering polts that bite, scratch and choke as being similar to that annoying class of children who, meaning no essential harm, still think it amusing to push other kids down stairs or throw stones at them? I distinctly remember having fistfuls of grass shoved down my throat by another boy when I was a small child and nearly choking on it, thinking I was going to die. Afterwards, he said he was only playing; but it didn't seem that way to me at the time. Possibly a similar dynamic exists between some poltergeists and their victims?

* * * * *

Play-fighting is just another kind of play-acting. In his book *Straw Dogs*, the philosopher John Gray explains that 'Language begins in the play of animals and birds. So does the illusion of self-hood.'[41] By playing, and by play-acting, we learn first to lie, and then learn to lie about ourselves. For Gray, the self is a mere construct which doesn't truly exist, with its roots lying in the childhood act of playing. The language Gray means here is that of body language. This begins in play-fights during which, he says, young humans and animals both have fun and learn to lie. Gray quotes the anthropologist Gregory Bateson to the effect that the nips animals give each other during play:

> ... do not denote what those actions for which they stand [i.e. genuine, aggressive adult biting] would denote ... Not only does the playful nip not denote what would be denoted by the bite for which it stands, but in addition, the bite itself is fictional. Not only do the playing animals not quite mean what they are saying, but they are usually communicating about something which does not exist [i.e. the 'real' bite].[42]

The next step from such play, suggests Gray, is play-acting, which can also be a form of deliberate deception. He talks of ravens – those archetypal Trickster-birds – which have been observed play-acting the making of a cache in which to hide food, but not actually leaving any food there in order to fool other animals away from raiding their real, hidden stores. Maybe rough poltergeist play is also a form of deception and their supposed 'identities' merely yet another elaborate performance of play-acting, another way of distracting us away from their own hidden caches of secret true identity. How, one could ask, could a poltergeist best go about adopting the apparent but fraudulent guise of an evil spirit or demon? Well, by means simply of play-acting – even if that does not always mean playing nicely. Like Gregory Bateson's animals, when Dracu bites, is it even really a bite at all?

XVI

Rewriting Physical Laws

The law is an ass.

Charles Dickens

Perhaps the most common way in which poltergeists remake our world is in their repeated rewriting of the known laws of physics. In the real world, objects don't move or fly around of their own accord without the application of any direct motive force – except, of course, when a polt is present. A classic example came from the haunted Victorian carpenter's shop at Swanland where, as we saw earlier, pieces of wood fluttered around as though alive. As described by one witness:

> From time to time a piece of wood just cut and fallen upon the floor jumped up on the benches and started a dance amidst the tools ... They seemed animated and intelligent. I remember a piece which jumped from the bench on to an easel standing three yards away, whence it bounded on to another piece of furniture, then into a corner of the shop, where it stopped. Another traversed the shop like an arrow ... Immediately afterwards a piece took flight with a wavy motion. Another went in a slanting line and then alighted quickly at my feet.

Sometimes these objects flew in a straight line, but often their motion was 'undulating, rotatory, spiral, serpentine, or jerky.' Even stranger, they fell without any noise; even though 'they came at such a speed that in normal conditions they would have produced a fairly loud clatter.'[1] So, not only do objects fly around, they do so in a variety of highly unnatural and inconsistent flight patterns.

We also read of objects still adhering, as though with superglue, to flat surfaces when tilted at an angle which, really, means they should fall off. According to Iris M. Owen, one characteristic of her fake ghost Philip's fictional personality was his notorious sweet-tooth; a piece of candy was left out for Philip at the start of each séance-session. A sitter once teasingly made an attempt to grab this, saying Philip had better hold on to it if he wanted it for himself. At this point, the table tilted away at a 45 degree angle, as if Philip was guarding his treat, with the candy still clinging to its surface. This experiment was tried again, successfully, with other sweets – none of which were sticky.[2]

Such actions can be read as another form of play; a play with laws which are meant to be eternal and immutable, but which, apparently, are actually anything but. In these tales, polts quite literally defy the laws of physics – and, indeed, the subsequent attempts of witnesses to get them to conform to those laws. At Calvados Castle a cupboard heavily laden with books and linen once rose up 20 inches into the air and, though it was pressed down upon by a priest, the thing simply would not fall back down to the ground.[3] In 1987, the entire small Brazilian city of Itapeva was – according to newspapers, anyway – subjected to a plague of flying furniture, rocks and dustbins. Policemen witnessed stones pulling themselves out of soil and flinging themselves against houses. A special prayer-session was held at the local cathedral to restore the laws of gravity to their usual order ... but was rudely interrupted when a one-kilo rock tore a hole through the roof.[4]

*****

One habitual method of poltergeists rewriting the laws of Creation is when they cause solid objects to pass through other solid objects; matter-through-matter is the technical term for this, as we saw earlier. During a 1952 case from Neudorf, Germany, nails – kept in a locked kitchen cupboard – suddenly appeared a few inches below a bedroom ceiling before falling to the floor. Even weirder, various objects were then seen *falling out of a wall* at great speed. Picked up, they felt warm to the touch.[5] At Humpty Doo, two journalists backed themselves up right against a wall to avoid flying objects ... only to have a shower of gravel hurled at them from behind, as if the wall itself was not even there.[6] In the village of Little Burton in 1677, a 15-foot pole from a garden was tossed onto a bed. It was impossible for the householders to take it back outside again, as it was too large to fit through any doorways! They had to remove a pane from the window to get it out – but the polt had to do no such thing to get it in.[7] Matthew Manning was once having a bath when he saw the plug rising into the air and shooting towards the window at top speed; the item simply passed through the glass, leaving the pane wholly unscathed.[8]

Things being placed inside closed boxes and then escaping again, quite impossibly, are another staple trope of poltergeistery. This happened at Sandfeld in 1722, when a flying tablecloth and blue apron were placed inside a box which two people then sat down upon – only for these same items to fly back into the room without the lid being opened.[9] During the Poona haunting, toys kept emerging from a toy box and chucking themselves at a boy in his bed, even behind his 'secure' mosquito net. A heavy dictionary was used to weigh the lid down, but to no avail; the toys were passing directly through the wood itself, a spinning-top exiting the closed chest to whack the lad in his bed.[10] During a 1948 case from Bavaria, a family were bombarded by a rain of stones and tools. These tools were carefully gathered up and

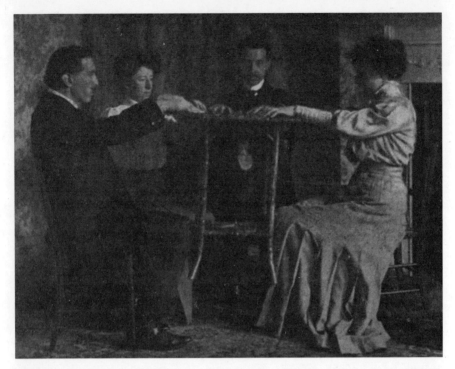

Objects flatly refuse to obey the normal laws of physics when in the presence of a polt.

returned to their box by the family's mother, who then sat down on top of it, only for them to all reappear, one by one, in different parts of the room to spite her.[11]

The Black Monk of Pontefract could pull identical pranks. One evening, as the haunted Pritchard family sat in their lounge, an egg floated into the room, poised itself 'very carefully' in the air and fell to the floor, exploding with an overpowering scent of flowers. Another egg then followed, so Mrs Pritchard ran to the fridge, removed all the eggs, placed them inside a wooden box, and sat on the lid – but again the trick was repeated. Mrs Pritchard looked into the box; one egg was missing. She closed it up again and sat back down on top of it. Still eggs kept on appearing and smashing like scent-bombs until, eventually, the box was empty.[12]

Best of all, during the Naples case of 1696–97, a certain Father Felippo found his doubloons and silver coins stolen from his room one day. Towards evening he went for a walk and passed by a peach-tree. Felippo pulled down four peaches; cutting the first open, he found one of his missing doubloons inside. Cutting open a second, he found another coin. Slicing open a watermelon later that night, he discovered all but five of his missing silver pieces apported inside there, too.[13] Do these still count as *hermaions* if it was Hermes who stole away the treasure in the first place?

*****

Even more profoundly damned are accounts of matter spontaneously reassembling itself. At South Shields, a lottery scratch-card kept reappearing inside the house after being thrown out. A note of its serial number was made and the card torn up 'into little pieces' and put in the bin. It was then found, 'perfectly intact', sitting in the kitchen later that day.[14] During the Naples case, the haunted monastery was shaken by earthquake-like forces before, in one room, the ceiling collapsed. A monk ordered the demon to replace it. Immediately, 'Then was seen by all … the stones and wood of the ceiling to unite themselves and go up in the air like something carried, and to unite with the remainder that had not fallen, leaving, however, a sign of the junction.'[15]

Another reverse-temporal experience was reported by a Londoner named Graham Pouncy in 1982. He spoke of how, when a child, he had accidentally smashed a vase at a friend's house. Bending down to pick it up, he surprisingly found it whole again. At this point the temperature dropped, the room darkened, and a green hand crawled across the window. Graham and his pal fled, the doors slamming behind them.[16] At Thornton Heath, a brass bowl once flew into a wall with such force that it crumpled up 'like a concertina'. 'What a pity,' said a friend of Mrs Forbes, 'you've looked after that so well.' As she spoke, the bowl straightened itself back out again noiselessly, becoming as good as new.[17] During one 1960 Brazilian case of lithobolia, a wristwatch had its glass knocked out and its wristband stretched out of place; but, the next morning, was found fully intact again.[18] Such blatant retro-causality can only have been the work of backwards-walking *heyoka*-spirits.

Curiously, sometimes poltergeists enjoy keeping up with current paranormal fashions in their defiance of physical laws. Following widespread media publicity surrounding the Israeli psychic Uri Geller in the 1970s, several accounts emerged of spooks engaging in Geller's patented spoon-bending acts. At Enfield, Guy Lyon Playfair asked Janet if she would have a go at bending spoons held in her hand, having seen Geller do so on TV. By directing Janet's RSPK energies into this task, Playfair hoped to divert the polt away from engaging in more destructive activities. It transpired Janet could indeed bend spoons – without even touching them. She got a headache while concentrating, and it was soon discovered why; spoons had bent within drawers, and the lid of a metal teapot twisted utterly out of shape in the kitchen.[19] During an American case of 1850–51, spoons were similarly bent double by unseen hands and thrown at those sitting around a dinner-table.[20] There's nothing much new under the sun when it comes to poltergeistery, it seems.

*****

Sometimes objects act with physical characteristics other than those they would ordinarily possess. During the Naples outbreak, a book was hurled to the floor by the demon, causing it to break into little shards *as if it were made of glass!*[21] Stones more like magnets than rocks were reported during one Brazilian case. A stone appeared from thin air and,

4 feet above ground, split into two pieces. They fitted like two parts of a jigsaw, and snapped together as if magnetised.[22] During another case, a small and light matchbox fell from a mantelpiece, landing with a loud and booming noise 'like a bar of iron.'[23] Contrariwise, during another haunting a displaced picture in a glazed frame fluttered down through the air 'like a piece of paper' instead of behaving like the heavy(ish) object it actually was.[24] During one 1870 Russian haunting, objects tossed at a female victim would strike her 'like straw or a feather' if ordinarily heavy, or 'like strokes of a hammer' if normally of the lightest weight, in acts of wilful physical perversity.[25] Equally anomalous sounds are also reported, as in the following rather inexplicable testimony:

> I was standing at the kitchen door on the outside and I couldn't hear a thing. I stepped into the kitchen and there was a horrible pounding that [was so loud it] was shaking the lamp ... And yet you step back into the hallway and nothing. Not one sound.[26]

Compare this to a 1920s Australian haunting in which a series of gigantic bangs shook a haunted house 'to its foundations' – but to those inside the house, they seemed to come from *outside* it, while to those outside it they seemed to come from *inside*.[27] Did they come from both – and neither – simultaneously?

Contradictory heat or fire-related phenomena also appear, as when a bucketful of cold water bubbled and boiled at Amherst.[28] Guy Lyon Playfair details a 1972 case of poltergeist arson from Paraguay wherein the first object to catch fire was a *damp* shirt.[29] That's odd enough; but a *cold fireball* is even worse. In 2003, it was reported that the house of a Chilean couple, the Ulloa Veras, was haunted by a 'massive ball of fire, the size of a football' which made 'the things it touched turn as cold as ice.' This bizarre property didn't prevent the couple's home from burning to the ground in its entirety, however.[30] One Turkish poltergeist somehow managed to start a fire inside a cold refrigerator – where it burned not food, but JOTTled clothes.[31] An object refusing to burn or catch alight when it really should is another standard motif; during a Scottish case of 1718 a Minister's Bible was thrown onto a blazing fire, but failed to be blackened by the flames.[32] So, sometimes things burn when they shouldn't, and don't burn when they should ... the only pattern possible to discern is one of deliberate Trickster-style contrariness.

Certain physical effects are quite simply bizarre one-offs. Dust jumping from a vacuum cleaner and spelling out words;[33] gravity being interfered with so that soap powder pours from a box in a horizontal fashion;[34] every bottle of milk in an apartment turning sour overnight;[35] a TV set repeatedly making the sound of a door bell;[36] all have been reported down the years, but for one night only, as they say. Some hauntings include a number of unique one-offs, as with a 1980s Norwegian case in which an ordinary electric light suddenly began emitting 'a rainbow of colours', cushions started unzipping themselves with movements like those of 'invisible mice' being observed within, and a flagpole splintered itself into pieces 'as if struck by lightning'.[37] Undoubtedly the weirdest one-off phenomenon I ever heard of came from a haunted Welsh farmhouse where it is said all the petals fell from a bouquet one day ... then spontaneously transformed into a pile of dead wasps.[38]

* * * * *

Some polts like to suggest that there might be certain consistent physical patterns or laws present behind them. But do such instances really demonstrate the existence of any genuine laws, or merely false imitations? No matter what physical or energetic patterns you might detect in one case, you will not find them present in *all* poltergeist outbreaks. While the Italian medium Eusapia Palladino used to lose weight whenever tables were levitating in her presence, an Irish medium named Kathleen Goligher was found to *gain* weight during such performances – a weight corresponding directly to that of the table floating.[39] The ordinary laws which govern the motion and behaviour of objects do not vary in this wildly contradictory way. Nor, indeed, are they selective. A. R. G. Owen used this fact to argue against the adoption of any 'general poltergeist field-theory', saying that:

> The 'poltergeist force' differs from electromagnetic forces in that it seems independent of the material composing the body on which it acts ... [and] is selective in a way which the gravitational field is not. Two pebbles may be side by side, and one taken and the other left. Thus there is a rather refined localisation of the region of application of the force ... that militates against a field explanation.[40]

It has been noted that the heyday of physical mediumship – the high Victorian era – was, ironically, also the heyday of scientific materialism.[41] However, the dead world of matter, in the presence of powerful Spiritualist mediums like Eusapia Palladino, suddenly seemed alive as objects leapt around and musical instruments played by themselves in the séance-room. That which seemed most stable, most reliable and predictable, instead became a very visible manifestation of the capricious and the unpredictable. It was like a gigantic practical joke being played upon the doctrines of Maxwell and Darwin by a world which they had allegedly shorn once and for all of its every spiritual underpinning. The poltergeist is a contemporary resurfacing of that joke. Like the Trickster Mercurius, polts mediate between matter and spirit, infusing both with aspects of one another, and thus remaking our world in the most wonderful, magical – and, frequently, humorous – way possible. The poltergeist thus does not simply break the laws of physics when it makes objects float or pass through solid walls; as I keep on saying, it breaks our entire prevailing worldview.

XVII

Unusual Conjunctions

Only connect.

E. M. Forster

Below is a bizarre parody of the song *Windmills of Your Mind*, taken from the mid-1990s BBC television sketch-show *The Smell of Reeves and Mortimer*:

Like a shrimp in a suitcase on a window ledge
Like a pair of tartan slippers underneath a hedge
Like a scoutmaster at daybreak putting peanuts in his glove
Like a specially formed ice-arch for climbing over doves
Like a sardine with a hairnet staring at a priest:
These things we always find
In the windmills of your mind.[1]

Such comedy, of a type often termed 'surreal', was once defined by the comedy duo Reeves and Mortimer themselves thus: 'True surrealism produces either shock, or laughter, by the juxtaposition of events and ideas.'[2] Hence their lyrics; with the shrimp in the suitcase, say, it is hard to say precisely why this is an amusing image. There just seems to be something inherently absurd in the combination of these objects that provokes a burst of laughter in weird people like me.

Poltergeists themselves enjoy rearranging objects into unusual combinations or patterns, some of which provoke amusement when seen. Occasionally, this can be as elaborate as deliberately dressing people – or even animals – up in inappropriate clothing. During a 1909 Italian haunting, two goats were comically clad in men's clothes, for example.[3] According to a 1650 English pamphlet called *The Strange Witch at Greenwich*, a fairy-like spook found it amusing to repeatedly place his victim's trousers upon his wife's head,[4] while a haunted eighteenth-century German theologian named Professor Schuppart had to suffer the indignity of having his wig stolen and arranged upon his own spouse's skull.[5] They must all have looked quite ridiculous.

* * * * *

More characteristic are cases wherein ordinary, everyday objects are moved around and placed in strange arrangements and patterns. Two particularly odd examples involved cabbages, of all things. A polt-like brownie haunting the home of a French Lord in 1615 spent an entire evening transporting cabbage-leaves in from the garden and inserting them into tapestries or placing them within vases like inept floral displays,[6] while in 1699 a demon in the Hertfordshire village of Burton enjoyed pulling cabbages from their soil after dark, then lining them all up in the shape of crosses and fleurs-de-lys.[7] A 1967 Norfolk polt gained real joy from creating several apparently pointless combinations of objects. Potatoes were found in the garage, a packet of razor blades was placed in a hearth, a twelve-bore shotgun was dismantled and its parts left scattered in random rooms, airing cupboard doors were placed ajar with a clock balanced across them, and a wallet discovered burning atop a sack of wheat.[8] A Glasgow polt of 1974–75 removed drawers from a sideboard and replaced them with cushions from armchairs and vice-versa, an excellent instance of creative inversion.[9]

At Calvados Castle, a bed was found turned on its side with a table shoved under it – another time, this same table was placed right in the middle of the same bed. An armchair was also balanced upon a desk, a couch turned upside down, cushions lined up in rows on a windowsill, shoes displaced from wardrobes and candlesticks arranged atop lamps.[10] One 1990s Australian polt loved making every last coffee mug vanish overnight from inside a mess hall. Again and again, they were later spied standing upright on the roofs of surrounding huts or perching precariously atop tall posts; some were 'filled to the very top' with dry coffee-powder.[11] The following elaborate incidents were described as occurring inside one polt-infested New England household in 1682:

> A cheese hath been taken out of the press and crumbled all over the floor.
> A piece of iron … stuck into the wall and a kettle hung thereon. Several cocks
> of English hay, mowed near the house, were taken and hung upon trees; and
> some made into small whisps, and put all up and down the kitchen.[12]

Of course, human beings *could* have performed such tasks … but why?

* * * * *

Other poltergeists display a real sense of regimented precision and order in their object-arrangements. A woman named Kerry Barnfield entered her kitchen one morning in May 2002 only to find every tin removed from its cupboard and arrayed in a perfect circle on her mat, some piled two cans high.[13] A polt infesting a corner-shop in Hyde between 1989 and 1991 showed similar levels of OCD-like behaviour. The owner would return home only to find all her saucepans removed from their shelves and lined up across the kitchen, running in systematic order from smallest to largest.[14]

A striking photograph exists of two serried ranks of objects laid out on the floor of the kitchen at Enfield. One is a row of five small potted plants; directly opposite is a row of five tea-mugs, each placed down exactly parallel with a corresponding pot-plant, almost as if waiting to engage in some form of battle.[15]

Also at Enfield, 'a most elaborate construction' one day appeared on the kitchen table, 'consisting of two cups, a glass, the sugar-tin, the tea-caddy, the butter-dish, a flannel and a dishcloth all piled on top of each other.' The ghost announced 'I DONE THAT', so must have been proud of its creation.[16]

A woman named Gail Baird returned home to her haunted Edinburgh flat one day to find her large collection of fluffy animal toys arranged 'in a pyramid' in the middle of her bed. Another time, she found all the pictures from the living-room walls placed in a 'neat pile' in the centre of the carpet by her polt.[17] Another Edinburgh poltergeist once tipped a vase full of flowers into a sink – then reshaped them all perfectly into a much nicer new display in the plughole; this same spook also stole books before hiding them inside a fridge and oven.[18] A ghost haunting a York bed shop used the repeating carpet-pattern of the premises as inspiration for its art, pedantically lining up various objects on the floor according to its pre-existing template.[19]

* * * * *

It would be odd to attribute all this to spirits of the dead for the simple reason that, in life, most people don't actually enjoy performing such actions, so it is hard to see why they might suddenly adopt the hobby once deceased. A rare exception was the disturbed son of Bishop James Pike who, prior to his suicide, had developed 'a persistent interest in the balancing of patterns of lines and objects' leading to him arranging 'all four of the identical coffee tables in the living room … out from the fireplace as if for some particular aesthetic effect.' When Bishop Pike later found clothing rearranged in a way 'not only orderly, but unusually so' in one half of a closet, and 'in complete disarray' in the other, you can see why he thought his child might have returned from the grave.[20]

But, presuming you don't suddenly develop OCD after you die, why might poltergeists repeatedly do such things? Maybe they are intended as jokes. I remember, as a teenager, being taken on a residential trip to a Scottish island with the Geography Department. While there, we went out to observe so-called 'erratics' in the field – big boulders, deposited down in odd locations like the middle of a meadow, by the action of glaciers. That night, a friend had a good idea. For a joke, he transported a large rock into our teacher's room and tucked it up inside his bed. When later confronted about this, he pleaded ignorance, saying it must have been just another 'erratic'.

This exact same joke has been played by several polts down the years, probably the most persistent placer of bedroom erratics being the 1914 Vodable poltergeist, which continually concealed objects as varied as turnips, pincers, plates and thistles beneath people's sheets before they went to sleep at night. Repeatedly, it placed a bust of the house's former owner inside one of the beds, looking quite snug, with 'its head on the pillow and the bedclothes tucked in round its chin.'[21] The Drummer of Tedworth contented itself with emptying chamber pots into people's beds before strewing them thoughtfully with ashes,[22] while the Woodstock spirit of 1649 once caused three dozen trenchers of wood to be 'laid smoothly' beneath a servant's quilt.[23]

* * * * *

Over the years, *Fortean Times* magazine has reported plenty of strange conjunctions of items which were nothing to do with polts, apparently just because they were funny. In October 1999 residents of Trinity Street in Norwich awoke to find digestive biscuits – some of them half-eaten – taped to street-signs and the walls and windows of every house. This was strangely similar to a 2001 incident in Cheltenham when the window of a Vauxhall Nova was smashed open and the interior of the vehicle filled entirely with broken biscuits. A Mini parked nearby was also found covered in biscuits by persons or beings unknown.[24] I'd blame human weirdos, not spooks, myself. However, I would also argue these tricks are in some ways indistinguishable from certain related poltergeist actions. Is filling cars with biscuits really that different, in essence, from putting turnips into beds or rearranging cabbages in funny patterns?

But are these things really jokes, or are they art? The proto-Surrealist writer Lautréamont, in his peculiar anti-novel *Les Chants de Maldoror* famously spoke of the 'chance meeting of a sewing-machine and an umbrella on a dissecting table', which came to stand as the classic illustration of the apparently arbitrary conjunctions of random objects which are the very essence of Surrealist art. But where does the art here come from? The artistic beauty of the conjunctions is surely not inherent within the objects themselves – but, rather, is *perceived* somehow within the human mind. It is exactly the same with their apparent humour. A 1992 interview with Doc Shiels, the rather wonderful 'surrealchemist' magician and artist, is very revealing upon the

The Comte de Lautréamont, perceiver of the strange beauty to be found when an umbrella meets a sewing-machine on a dissecting-table.

usefulness of discordant connections in humour, art and the conjuring up of the paranormal alike (Shiels claimed to be able to magically summon sea-monsters via surrealchemist means).[25] According to him:

> Humour, with or without laughter, is often linked, psychologically, with incongruity. Surrealchemy is concerned with what is usually thought of as incongruous, discordant stuff ... we put things into situations where those things are normally thought of as wrong, or inappropriate ... Its effect can be seen simultaneously as distasteful, shocking and funny. Fortean events are often absurd, ridiculous, and at the same time profoundly disturbing. A surrealchemical shaman – a magician dealing with so-called fortean happenings – combines and uses all these disparate elements. Humour helps us to invoke things [like sea-monsters] where those things are not 'normally' expected to be.

Teddy bears are not *normally* supposed to be arranged in elaborate pyramids in the middle of people's beds or cabbage-leaves in vases either. Our perception of the oddness of these conjunctions of object and place – their utter 'wrongness' – is what creates the humour, or the art, of the whole situation. The bizarre conjunctions of objects that polts so often throw up could be seen as another breaking down of the barriers of normal social discourse, just like much good art is. By effacing the liminal borderline between such concepts as 'rational' and 'irrational', or 'in-place' and 'out-of-place', the poltergeist symbolically undermines the underlying assumptions of our well-ordered and logical modern society itself.

* * * * *

It is an anthropological commonplace that dirt is merely 'matter out of place', as shown by the anthropologist Mary Douglas in her influential book *Purity and Danger*. To Douglas, this definition:

> ... implies two conditions: a set of ordered relations and a contravention of that order ... Dirt is the by-product of a systematic ordering and classification of matter ... It is a relative idea. Shoes are not dirty in themselves, but it is dirty to place them on the dining-table; food is not dirty in itself, but it is dirty to leave cooking utensils in the bedroom, or food bespattered on clothing.

We therefore condemn as dirty 'any object or idea likely to confuse or contradict cherished classifications.'[26] According to Douglas, all peoples create a Dominant-like model through which to see the world, a kind of anticipated order for things, which we expect to see upheld; we *do* expect to see tin-cans piled up in our cupboards, but *not* in strange little circles on the kitchen floor. Usually, Douglas says, we deal with such ambiguous events simply by 'ignoring or distorting' them, 'so that they do not disturb our established assumptions'. In this sense, poltergeists themselves could be considered as socially 'dirty', as, according to mainstream science, they are not really supposed to exist. However, as Douglas then says, 'it is not always an unpleasant experience to confront ambiguity ... There is a whole gradient on which laughter, revulsion and shock belong at different points and intensities.'[27] Pollution, when defined as matter out of place, 'is like an inverted form of humour. It is not a joke for it does not amuse. But the structure of its symbolism uses comparison and double-meaning just like the structure of a joke.'[28]

If you smile at some poltergeist rearrangements of objects, probably you are amused by the sense of odd creative imagination that seems to lie behind them. You are reading the event as being, essentially, a joke expressed in the form of art – not the worst definition you could come up with for surrealism itself. If you react with terror, however, then you are reacting to the rearrangement of objects as an *actual literal event*, rather than seeing the more entertaining wider symbolism which lies present behind it. The sense of disorder evoked has provoked not a pleasant reaction but an unpleasant one within you. Why, though? Not merely because of the actual physical reordering of items that has taken place, surely – a pile of cuddly teddies lying in a heap on a bed isn't actually *that* scary in and of itself, after all – but because of what that same reordering implies in terms of the whole expected model through which you normally view reality.

* * * * *

Nonetheless, the fact remains that most people who encounter such ghostly rearrangements do indeed react to them with fear. An aura of liminal disgust and danger has been built up around these matters within the modern world. Why? According to Mary Douglas, 'anomalous events' of all kinds 'may be labelled dangerous' by society as a whole because: 'Attributing danger is one way of putting a subject above dispute. It ... helps to enforce conformity ... [because] a rule of avoiding anomalous things both affirms and strengthens the definitions to which they do not conform.'[29]

By labelling the paranormal as metaphorically 'dirty' and worthy of nothing but derision, the 'safe' and 'ordered' version of the currently prevailing materialist scientific Dominant is preserved. Not only are poltergeists dismissed as being 'dangerously unscientific', that category, in and of itself, reinforces the idea that science itself must forever remain the ultimate arbiter of actual reality in the world around us. However, as Douglas adds: 'Any given system of classification [like that of science] must give rise to anomalies, and any given culture must confront events which seem to defy its assumptions. It cannot [always] ignore the anomalies which its scheme produces, except at risk of forfeiting confidence.'[30]

Most people unquestioningly give our approved scientific Dominant their assent; and yet, when poltergeist reorderings of objects occur within your own home, you are forced to change your allegiance to another way of looking at the universe. This is why I think such events really provoke such terror and unease; because people have been conditioned, since early childhood, to react to the supernatural in that way. They fear much more for the health of their wider *Weltanschauung* than for their physical safety when they see a pyramid made of teddy-bears, or some small tea-cups placed along the kitchen floor in a row, surely.

* * * * *

Are people right to fear this radical reordering of their world? In practical terms, yes; nobody *wants* a demon messing up their soft-furnishings. However, it is possible to view such poltergeistery more positively. Any system of existing order can potentially become fossilised and hide-bound, and any ordered system, whether of knowledge or of household objects, must have made initial use of a set of materials that were, originally, arranged only within a state of chaos. Certain things were chosen to then be ordered in a certain way, and thus the pattern of order in a given system was created. In fact, however, other potential systems of ordering could just as easily have been created from the initial chaos of potentiality. Once a system of order was placed upon the chaos of our world by religion, and all was explained and classified in terms of that. Now, that same potential material has been reordered, reclassified and reinterpreted through the lens of science. It was still the same original potential material which both world-views sprung up from, though. Two contrasting Dominants, one original set of potential materials; both simply included and excluded certain things from their mental picture to ensure their way of seeing the world made nice, neat, ordered sense. Mary Douglas argued that disorder:

> ... provides the material of pattern. Order implies restriction; from all possible materials, a limited selection has been made and from all possible relations a limited set has been used. So disorder by implication is unlimited, no pattern has been realised in it, but its potential for patterning is indefinite. This is why, though we seek to create order, we do not simply condemn disorder. We recognise that it is destructive to existing patterns; also that it has potentiality. It symbolises both danger and power.[31]

The Trickster is often referred to by academics as a 'sacred *bricoleur*'. This definition is related both to the art of *bricolage* (making something using a mixture of materials, as in a Surrealist painting/collage) and to the idea of the Trickster being a creative tinkerer, who uses whatever materials he has at hand to improvise the solution to whatever problem he currently faces.[32] When the A-Team fashion a heat-seeking anti-aircraft missile from nothing but a cardboard-box, some plasticine and a tube of old toothpaste, then that's being a *bricoleur*; when poltergeists transform ordinary household odds and ends into works of creative art, then that also is being a *bricoleur*.

A different way of viewing matters, therefore, would be to say not that the poltergeist's reordering of objects is a purely destructive act perpetrated against the old world-order but instead an act of creativity which may one day enable us to recognise the potential birth of a new one. This creativity can be clearly seen when the poltergeist moves an object around in such a way that its function changes – in effect, transforming it from being one object, with one associated definition and one only, into quite another. An iron weight being stuck into the wall and then used as a hook to hang a kettle upon is one instance; cabbage-leaves being turned into floral displays within vases by a French brownie, or drawers being used as cushions by a 1970s Glasgow poltergeist, are others.

*****

During a haunting in the home of an Italian museum-worker in 1903, three flower-vases and a lamp were once carefully arranged on the floor in the form of a cross.[33] You can read your own hermeneutic meaning into these objects once they have been repatterned thus. Beforehand, they would have simply been three vases and a lamp, signifying nothing. Their recombination, however, seems to ask us to speculate about their new function – was this improvised cross some message from God, for instance? A religiously-minded observer may have guessed so; however, had these items simply stayed put in their ordinary original position, then not even the most fanatical of religious zealots would have been minded to see anything holy whatsoever in them.

This transformation of an object from one meaning or way of usage into another has traditionally been one of the main mythological functions of the Trickster-figure, inherent within his role as sacred *bricoleur*. During the legend of Hermes' theft of his brother Apollo's sacred cattle, Hermes transforms them from living animals into dead food, or burnt sacrifices to the gods. According to Lewis Hyde:

> … so long as the cattle cannot be moved from their unmown meadow they cannot mean anything. Conversely, the moment at which they may be butchered and eaten is the moment at which their earlier state acquires its significance. Their meat means one thing on the hoof, another in the fire, and yet another hung in the barn. Hermes-the-Thief moves the meat from one situation to another and by such substitutions it comes to have its [new] significance.[34]

Similarly, cabbage-leaves stored in a kitchen are simply food; their function is obvious. Taken from the kitchen and placed in vases by Puck, they become decoration, and gain a new function – both to decorate, and to open the possibility of a new way of considering the world. So do Hermes' inventive cattle mutilations. It may be wrong to view the poltergeist's reordering of objects as an exercise purely in the production of pointless disorder. In the world of the Trickster, there is no such thing as *pointless* disorder, as Paul Radin explained:

> Disorder belongs to the totality of life, and the spirit of this disorder is the Trickster. His function in an archaic society, or rather the function of his mythology, of the tales told about him, is to add disorder to order and so make a whole, to render possible, within the fixed bounds of what is permitted, an experience of what is not permitted.[35]

By breaking the order of the world with his various bizarre recombinations of objects, the poltergeist actually makes it in a sense more whole, opening the path to new ways of viewing reality. The mess he so often creates is thus not really a mess at all, but a kind of humorous and creative chaos.

XVIII

Machines in the Ghosts

There never was an explanation that didn't itself have to be explained.

Charles Fort

What is the causal mechanism which lies behind the poltergeist? One paradoxical answer may well be that there are so many potential ones that in effect there are actually none at all. According to Harry Price, poltergeistery was sometimes preceded by a noise like 'the winding up of a jack' or the 'winding of a big clock', as though the ghosts were busily accumulating kinetic energy.[1] At Epworth, for example, the ghost's arrival was presaged by a noise from near the roof, sounding like 'a winding or cranking, like the turning or winding of clockwork, of a windlass or of some machine' which lasted for around 15 minutes.[2] During a Swiss case of 1862, 'a perfect imitation of a watch being wound' was heard.[3] Other suggestive sounds appeared at Calvados Castle; a 'heavy elastic body of some kind rolling down the stairs'[4] and 'a large and heavy ball descending from the second floor to the first, jumping from step to step.'[5] A similar din was heard at Sauchie in 1960–61; a '"thunking" noise, like a bouncing ball' followed the focus-figure around at times.[6]

At Skinwalker Ranch, the Gormans heard metallic clangs, as if from heavy machinery, emanating from underground – leading some to speculate about top-secret subterranean US military equipment causing the haunting as part of a psi-warfare experiment.[7] During a UFO-related poltergeist outbreak on another Utah farm in 1969, electronic beeping sounds were heard, together with a noise resembling 'a metallic post-driver hammering a post, over and over, into the ground'. Whenever anyone went out to see what it was, it would stop temporarily, only to resume minutes later.[8] Speaking of such noises, the poet and polt-enthusiast Sacheverell Sitwell guessed that such ghosts' 'pranks and manifestations could not begin ... until this power had been stored, this clock wound up, or the process, whatever it may have been, had been brought to the necessary pitch of readiness.'[9] But why would spirits need to use such clearly *artificial* mechanisms to generate their outbursts? Are we to conclude that they are made of invisible clockwork?

This kind of logic reached its natural conclusion in the work of a Canadian inventor named John Hutchison who, in 1981, helped found Hathaway Consulting Services with the aim of developing a machine for the artificial generation of poltergeist phenomena. Placing a jumbled array of Tesla Coils and other electromagnetic devices in a small room, Hutchison claimed to be able to make objects move, float and spontaneously combust, no matter what they were made of – E-M forces shouldn't be able to flip wood, or cause fires inside concrete, but Hutchison said his 'poltergeist machine' could. He was never able to develop it into a commercially viable device, though. For one thing, it only worked erratically, at random; you may have to wait hours or days for any poltergeistery to actually occur. For another, it was potentially dangerous; Hutchison could not guarantee it would not rip users' dental fillings out, fuse their sockets or burn their houses down. Finally, the machine, being full of spooks, had a tendency to destroy itself when switched on![10] I am reminded of the Surrealist André Breton's notion of soluble fish, or the proverbial chocolate teapot here ...

* * * * *

Other alleged mechanisms have been actually seen at work, not just heard, as at Epworth and Calvados Castle. It has often been wondered how polts can make their loud rapping sounds. A visual answer to this conundrum was helpfully provided by a spirit from Daventry, Northamptonshire, in 1658. Here, knockings were seen being physically made by a disembodied hand which stopped at the wrist; it was carrying a hammer, which it dropped when challenged.[11] This 'explanation' actually explains precisely nothing, though; for flying disembodied fists cannot be accounted for by our current world-view any more than flurries of unnatural rappings can. The mysterious hammer-wielding hand is thus more of an *imitation* of an explanation than a real one.

I can only find one other example of a poltergeist using a hammer, from the 1677 haunting at Little Burton. There, sounds like thunder came from a bedroom. Rushing up, the men of the house found a large hammer upon the bed, and the bedstead itself much damaged, bearing 'near a thousand prints' from the implement. Another night, 'a Hand with an Arm-wrist' was spied using the hammer to repeatedly bang against this same bedstead. As the witnesses approached it, 'the Hand and Hammer fell down behind the Bolster and could not be found'. As soon as they went downstairs, the ghost hurled the tool into the middle of the room.[12] But was that hand really necessary? A. R. G. Owen's guess was that 'the mind [of the percipient] supplies the phantom hand that beats on the bed-head, perhaps in an effort to fill the gap in the chain of cause and effect.'[13]

* * * * *

If so, the human mind has great distaste for gaps in causality; disembodied hands are encountered in as many as 7 per cent of cases, according to one study.[14] There is even an account of phantom feet being seen to account for the appearance of phantom footsteps,[15] and evidence of some phantom hands leaving decidedly non-phantom handprints behind after them. This might sound like conclusive evidence that such hands possess objective physical existence, but not necessarily. They could still simply be conjured up temporarily via RSPK. 'If the image used by the mind to move ... [an object] was that of a hand, would the resultant imprint not resemble one even if it were only internally generated and externally projected?' it was once asked.[16]

One chilling hand-related tale was detailed in a letter to Harry Price from a Mrs Violet L. Salmon in 1943: 'My grandmother, when in an upstairs room, saw the door open a little way, a hand come round the door, almost immediately withdraw, and the door close. No one was there and she left the house the next day.'[17] Meanwhile, a victim of the Ringcroft poltergeist of 1695 attested that:

> ... it pull'd me off the side of a Bed, knock'd upon the Chests and Boards, as People do at a Door, And as I was at Prayer, leaning on the side of a bed, I felt something thrusting my Arm up, and casting my eyes thitherward perceived a little white Hand and an Arm, from the Elbow down, but it vanished presently.[18]

A black hand bothered an apprentice in the French village of Cideville in 1850; he said it came down the chimney and smacked him in the face (nobody else present saw this hand, although they *could* hear the slap it made ...)[19] At Rerrick in Scotland at the end of the 1700s, 'the appearance of a hand moving up and down' was seen but, when snatched at, 'it quietly vanished, and we felt only cold air.'[20] Another Scottish demon of 1654 once manifested as 'a naked forearm and hand which beat violently upon the floor'.[21] During an 1870 Russian case, 'a small and delicate pink hand like that of a child' was observed drumming on a window-pane and making a racket, and witnessed 'spring[ing] up from the floor' before disappearing beneath bedsheets.[22]

Phantom hands don't always have to be human. The first sign of a poltergeist at work during a 1974 haunting in the Brazilian town of Guarulhos was the appearance of 'large parallel cuts' in furniture. The apparitional arm of 'a wild beast' with 'sharp-ended claws ... black, shiny and curved' was soon seen to account for this. Maybe this was the very same hand which then began tossing stones around and scratching people's faces, legs and arms. This was then followed by the sighting of 'something horrible with a face in fire and big teeth', and various other animal-like apparitions.[23] From Ripperstone Farm in Wales in 1977, we have a silver hand drifting through the bedroom of the woman of the haunted house and touching her on the arm. When she awoke this arm was massively swollen and effectively useless, a condition lasting for weeks.[24] Perhaps the earliest phantom hand on record was observed in 1349 in Cyrenbergh in the Landgrave of Hesse, where a 'small and gracious human hand' was both seen and felt. This hand, even though it had no mouth, developed a voice; it said it belonged to a man (or elf) named Reyneke who lived inside a hollow mountain.[25]

Such instances pale into insignificance by comparison to the accounts of spirit-hands allegedly encountered during Victorian Spiritualist séances.

One such gathering in the presence of the famed medium D. D. Home in 1853 featured a gleaming silvery self-luminous hand appearing on a table, attached to an arm up to the elbow. This was actually held by a witness, before dissolving then rematerialising in his grasp. It felt, he said, like a real hand, with fingernails, knuckles and all the rest. The spirits asked if the sitters would like to see a black man's ghost-hand, whereupon a rather shadowy, grey-coloured one appeared in view. One hand then picked up a pencil and tried to write.[26] During another of Home's séances, when a self-playing accordion was examined, some sitters claimed they could see a ghostly hand pressing its fingers on the keys, while others could see only the keys being fingered with no hand there to do so at all.[27] Best of all was the phantom hand conjured out of pure ectoplasm by the female medium Mina Crandon – it crawled straight out of her vagina, like Thing from the Addams Family taking a horrible liberty with Morticia.[28]

*****

Often, such hands are icy-cold, a traditional sign they belonged to the dead.[29] One such hand appeared to Fazio, the father of the Renaissance writer Girolamo Cardano, sometime during the 1480s. Fazio was a doctor, called out to attend a dying patient. He heard knocking from the walls of his lodging-room, but was told not to worry – it was only the resident *follet*, or folly-filled household fairy. In bed, Fazio then felt a thumb pressing down on his head. Opening his eyes, he saw a little hand, 'like that of a boy of ten ... and so cold that it was extremely unpleasant'. It crawled over his forehead and down to Fazio's mouth – which it then tried to enter! It slipped two fingers inside before the doctor could throw it off.[30]

At Amherst, Esther Cox was whacked by her unseen polt so hard that 'the marks of fingers could be plainly seen just exactly as if a human hand had slapped her face.'[31] When people encounter such phantom hands it tends to alter their perception of poltergeist activities, making witnesses prone to interpret them almost in crude, materialistic terms. Certainly, the notion of an invisible hand being present at Amherst influenced the investigator Walter Hubbell's interpretation of events. Notice how he speaks as though the spook physically went through a series of discrete stages of action in order to start a fire, using its hands to do so:

> I never fully realised what an awful calamity it was to have an invisible monster, somewhere within the atmosphere, going from place to place about the house, gathering up old newspapers, rags, clothing, and in fact all kinds of combustible material, and after rolling it up into a bundle and hiding it in a basket of soiled linen or in a closet, then go and steal matches out of the match-box in the kitchen or somebody's pocket.[32]

According to the Renaissance Jesuit Martín del Rio, there was quite a dispute among scholars during his day about the precise 'sort of pact' entered into by witches which would allow 'demons to throw stones and do other things of this kind, which would appear to require [the use of] hands and physical implements', so evidently such literalistic thinking has had a long history behind it.[33]

*****

There is no real consistency in these cases, though, as the perceptible mechanisms apparently used have differed from haunting to haunting. How, for example, do ghosts throw stones? During the Humpty Doo case, someone briefly caught what was called 'a unique glimpse of a polt reloading'. One witness saw 'a strange object' flying down the gravel driveway at incredible speed. It was 'spherical, jet-black and smaller than fist-size' and trailed a 2 foot stream of gravel behind it.[34] This is fascinating; but again explains nothing. What *was* that flying black ball, after all? The 'explanation' actually provides us with nothing more than a whole new mystery to ponder. An even greater non-explanation for lithobolia came from a seventeenth-century haunting at Spreyton, Devon, where one victim claimed that a bird 'flew in at the window with a great force, and with a stone in its mouth flew directly against' his forehead. Actually, it subsequently turned out not to be a stone but 'a weight of brass or copper' which just makes the whole thing even more bizarre.[35]

More traditionally, during the original 1682 New England case of lithobolia 'the appearance of a hand' was observed tossing pebbles.[36] A Scottish lithobolia case of 1680–81 was preceded by a sighting of a local dead woman's spirit walking around gathering stones in her lap – the obvious implication being that she later went on to throw them.[37] Australia's celebrated 'Guyra Ghost' of 1921 was preceded by a twelve-year-old girl being chased home one afternoon by a mysterious man who threw stones at her for no apparent reason. That very night, bombardment of her home with rocks began – but was it this same mystery man throwing them, in unseen form?[38]

When it comes to visible mechanisms causing knockings, meanwhile, it's not just hammer-wielding hands that have occasionally been witnessed. During an 1862 Swiss haunting, a servant-girl, in addition to hearing a disembodied voice groaning 'pity me', was also startled by the sight of 'a transparent, grey little cloud, which floated in through the partly open kitchen window, crossed the room, and pounded on the door to the bedroom.'[39] But was a small hidden hand floating along inside the rapping cloud too? During the same haunting, people did come into contact with an invisible but 'frozen' hand and its fingertips.[40] Another tactile cloud appeared during a 1695 haunting in Scotland, when 'a black thing' appeared in the corner of a barn:

... which increased gradually as if it would have fill'd the whole House; [witnesses] could not discern any distinct Form it had, but only that it resembled a black Cloud; it was very frightening to them all, and threw Barley-Chaff and Mud in their Faces. It did also gripe some of them by the Middle Arms, and other Parts, so hard, that for five days after they thought they felt those Gripes.[41]

So, some apparent polt mechanisms appear to be unique to individual cases; bad news for theorists!

* * * * *

The confusing poltergeistic vandalism of a house at Canvey Island in 1709 sums up our present problem in microcosm. On one occasion, *nothing* was seen destroying the house's windows, they just collapsed in of their own accord: 'the Windows of the Hall, against his back as he sat, were, with a more forcible Dash and Clatter than ever, broken; tho' the other Person, that stood right against the Window ... saw nothing strike against it; and the Glass not to shatter out, but fall down on the Ledge.' Another time, missiles were seen to be responsible for the breakages: 'they plainly saw the Glass broken ... from within, and a piece of Stone or Brick to come thro' and fall on the outside.' Another time, a makeshift weapon was observed to shatter the panes: 'Mr James' Son said he plainly discern'd a white Stick; the rest did not apprehend anything it was done with, only heard the blow, and saw the Glass broken.' After this, a servant-girl spotted an apparition open the parlour door. Pale and ghastly-looking, he wore a grey coat and a pale hat ... and carried a white stick.[42]

Which of these accounts represents the *real* mechanism by which the vandalism was perpetrated? *Any* of them? And, if so, how can we tell which one? Perhaps the ultimate mechanism of the poltergeist will never be found – indeed, if it operates acausally, as I have tentatively proposed, then it would be impossible to ever detect one. Instead, these things are, in themselves, mere ghosts of explanations; a Tricksterish reminder that there are some mysteries which may never be solved.

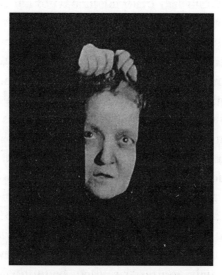

The horror! Ghostly hands materialise
above the head of Eusapia Palladino and
tug at her hair.

NON-CONCLUSION

Agents of *Aporia*

TV INTERVIEWER: Very briefly, can you tell us what a poltergeist is?
GUY LYON PLAYFAIR: Very briefly, no.

The poltergeist is the perfect paranormal personification of perplexity. As yet, any attempt to fully explain them has failed miserably, as I hope this book has shown. I for one actually rather hope that the mystery of the poltergeist *is* never solved – because, if it is, then the subject's appeal would be unutterably reduced. The supernatural would become 'just science'. Goodbye grimoires, hello textbooks.

There are massive and seemingly intractable problems inherent within the field of lab-based parapsychology as a whole. Experimenters have produced findings apparently demonstrating that psychic powers are non-energetic, independent of space and time and, furthermore, are what is termed 'goal-oriented', that is to say, not affected by the complexity of the task at hand. If this is indeed so, then it seems impossible for their observers ultimately to distinguish between them, and thus to tell what kind of psychic power is actually in play during any particular instance. If a psychic successfully guesses which designs are shown on a randomly-shuffled deck of Zener cards, then is he demonstrating deliberate telepathy by reading the mind of the other person looking at them, or did he quite unknowingly use precognition to discern how they would all be shuffled beforehand? This sounds silly, but is a recognised problem; if psi events are, to all intents and purposes, acausal and non-energetic processes to their observers, how can they ever hope to discern what is truly going on during them? As George P. Hansen put it, things like clairvoyance, telepathy, precognition and RSPK are 'only labels, they do not designate mechanisms'.[1]

Poltergeists are even worse. If they, too, are ostensibly non-energetic in nature, as I have argued, then it would be impossible to distinguish, in practice, whether a lithobolic stone has been thrown by an invisible demon, or by personified RSPK forces from within the human brain. You may consider one of these two possibilities to be the more likely, but you cannot actually *prove* it, if no detectable energetic processes are involved. It may be

Participants within the ancient Eleusinian Mysteries knew better than we do that mysteries properly speaking are something to be entered into, not 'solved' like crimes against logic.

objected that, as with the Miami warehouse case, there are some hauntings on record wherein coherent energetic processes *are* apparently observed, but as shown earlier, the physical 'laws' deduced from such hauntings do not apply uniformly to other cases. There is also the problem that, if ideoplastic polts tend to adopt the identities suggested by their observers, then, in the presence of a scientifically-minded researcher like William G. Roll, might one not choose to appear (falsely) as an energetic process, in response to his own logical desires?

We can only detect the *effects* of the poltergeist, not its ultimate *causes*. When we speak of its actions, we actually do so using metaphors, albeit unknowingly. I just spoke of psychic 'forces' coming from within the human brain to try and account for a stone being thrown – and yet, if the event was acausal in nature, no forces as such would actually have been used (or at least, not any forces that we humans could hope to perceive). Indeed, it may not even be the case that the stone was actually *thrown* at all, in the sense we usually use that word! The paranormal is just not terribly well-suited to being studied by conventional science.

* * * * *

Now this book is approaching its end, I appreciate some readers may be hoping I am about to draw all my material together into some kind of grand, over-arching explanation. Well, not really. Sorry. This is about the best I can do. Possibly, I would very hesitantly propose, somewhere within the human brain lurk still the archaic and archetypal Trickster-elements of our race, the personality elements of undeveloped, uncivilised, undifferentiated early man (or of our early childhood selves, the two often being much the same thing). Normally, these seeds remain buried, still and dormant. Sometimes, though, through whatever process – maybe RSPK, maybe not – these race-memories which usually lie sleeping deep within our civilised, modern, adult minds, can externalise themselves within the outside world as the figure we now call 'the poltergeist'. So, when poltergeists act like the Trickster, that is simply because *we* are in fact the poltergeist, and also, somewhere deep down within ourselves, we are the Trickster as well.

Is this the idea this whole book has been leading up towards? No; it is just a thought. As with the proposals of William G. Roll, Nandor Fodor and a thousand others, it may have some merit in some individual cases, and little or no merit in others. Perhaps it has only a certain metaphorical value, or none at all; I leave that for you to judge. I don't even *believe* it myself, as such. As Charles Fort once said, 'I believe nothing of my own that I have ever written. I cannot accept that the products of minds are the subject matter for beliefs.'[2] Nor can I. At best, I hope my idea is at least interesting and worth considering, if you are inclined to do so. If not, then fine. Even if my hypothesis – or, let's be honest, wild guess – should prove to be 100 per cent true, in 100 per cent of cases (which I'm 100 per cent certain it won't), then how could I hope to prove it?

*****

When asked if he had reached any conclusions about poltergeistery after many years spent studying it, the American academic Christopher Laursen replied 'Inconclusions, if anything.'[3] So, what is the point of studying a topic which can probably never end up being fully understood by the human mind? I would answer that it is worthy of study precisely *because* it cannot be fully understood in this way. Contemplation of the poltergeist serves its own inherent purpose because it can give us a sense of contact with some sort of hidden, subconscious, and not-quite expressible world. In short, it leads us on to what Socrates called the *aporia* – a sense of unsolvable paradox. The more hermeneutic scrutiny we place it under, the more the phenomenon reveals to us that, in an ultimate sense, we know nothing. The more we examine its specific details, the less we can explain its overall nature, and vice-versa. Study of the phenomenon is therefore a means of Zen-style enlightenment through disenlightenment, of education through paradox. In reconnecting us to the unknowable the poltergeist reconnects us also with the numinous. Whether you consider these *koan*-like stories true or fictional, they do this either way. According to Charles Fort:

> ... all wisdom is partly idiocy. The seeker of wisdom departs more and more from the state of the idiot, only to find that he is returning. Belief after belief fades from his mind: so his goal is the juncture of two obliterations. One is of knowing nothing, and the other is of knowing that there is nothing to know.[4]

We should stop seeking definite explanations for the poltergeist; it is a futile exercise. When asked what exactly it was trying to prove, the Enfield poltergeist once replied with a single word: 'DUNNO.'[5] At least it was honest. In the final analysis of the ever-wise ghost-scholar Father Herbert Thurston, 'nothing could be considered more purposeless or irrational than the vagaries of the poltergeist.'[6] How right he was; but then, he was a man of God and so knew all about unseen entities that moved in mysterious ways, their wonders to perform.

We need to return to respecting, not rejecting, *aporia* – not wherever science has a justifiable and necessary role to play, but in areas, such as poltergeistery, where it can do next to nothing. In Greek times an encounter with something that did not make sense – a genuine anomaly, something apparently paranormal – did not indicate a violation of Nature and its laws as we have been trained to think today, but, rather, revealed some obscure underlying unity present beneath it. Being a revelation of divine or archetypal patterns underpinning Nature, they were not truly *super*natural, just natural.[7] Nature is at some level inherently anomalous, and unresolvable conundrums like those produced by poltergeists forcibly remind us so. For Patrick Harpur, such anomalies cannot ever be fully fathomed. They are, quite simply, mysteries that are insoluble – and, as he wisely says:

> It is a modern error to take mysteries literally; that is, to turn them into problems which then have to be solved. We cannot solve mysteries – we can only enter into them; and then it is we who are solved or dissolved, transformed in such a way that we see the 'problem' quite differently, as a delightful paradox for instance.[8]

Approached like this, we do not try to *solve* the mystery of the poltergeist; we *experience* it, as something beneficial to the soul, a free *hermaion* from the universe itself. Once we accept the phenomenon has no ultimate, fixed meaning, once we accept we cannot hope to fully explain it – in short, once we reach a state of *aporia* in relation to it – then that is the point at which the poltergeist's most valuable significance emerges; namely, a sense of wonder. As Jung once said, 'It is only ingrained belief in the sovereign power of causality that creates intellectual difficulties and makes it appear unthinkable that causeless events exist or could ever occur.'[9] Many people wonder what the poltergeist is. I think they are misguided. They should just *wonder*. This book is dedicated to all those who are *tetelesmenoi Hermei* – fully initiated into the Mysteries of Hermes.

'CREDO QUIA ABSURDUM EST'
(I believe because it is absurd)

* * * * *

The comedy is ended.

François Rabelais

Hermes flies again!

Bibliography

NOTE: Editions listed are ones I personally consulted, not necessarily original publishers or publication dates.

Ashford, Jenny, *The Unseen Hand: A New Exploration of Poltergeist Phenomena* (USA: Bleed Red Books, 2017)

Ashford, Jenny & Mera, Steve, *The Rochdale Poltergeist: A True Story* (USA: Bleed Red Books, 2015)

Ashford, Jenny & Mera, Steve, *House of Fire and Whispers: Investigating the Seattle Demon House* (USA: Bleed Red Books, 2016)

Ashford, Jenny & Ross, Tom, *The Mammoth Mountain Poltergeist* (USA: Bleed Red Books, 2015)

Aubrey, John, *Miscellanies Upon Various Subjects* (USA: BiblioBazaar, 2006)

Barrington, Mary Rose, *JOTT: When Things Disappear ... and Come Back or Relocate – and Why It Really Happens* (USA: Anomalist Books, 2018)

Bord, Janet, *Fairies: Real Encounters with Little People* (UK: Michael O'Mara, 1997)

Bord, Janet & Bord, Colin, *Alien Animals* (UK: Granada/Panther, 1985)

Briggs, Katharine, *The Fairies in Tradition and Literature* (UK: Routledge Classics, 2002)

Brookesmith, Peter (Ed.), *Marvels & Mysteries: Ghosts* (UK: Parallel Publishing, 1995a)

Brookesmith, Peter (Ed.), *Marvels & Mysteries: Marvels of the Mind* (UK: Parallel Publishing, 1995b)

Brown, Norman O., *Hermes the Thief: The Evolution of a Myth* (USA: Lindisfarne Press, 1990)

Budden, Albert, *UFOs: Psychic Close Encounters – The Electromagnetic Indictment* (UK: Blandford, 1996)

Carrington, Hereward & Fodor, Nandor, *Haunted People: The Story of the Poltergeist Down the Centuries* (USA: E. P. Dutton, 1951)

Carter, Angela, *Burning Your Boats: Collected Short Stories* (UK: Vintage, 1996)

Cassirer, Manfred, *The Persecution of Mr Tony Elms – The Bromley Poltergeist* (UK: self-published, 1993)

Chambers, Dr Paul, *Sex & the Paranormal* (UK: Blandford, 1999)

Clarke, Roger, *A Natural History of Ghosts: 500 Years of Searching for Proof* (UK: Particular Books, 2012)

Clarkson, Michael, *The Poltergeist Phenomenon* (USA: New Page, 2011)

Crowe, Catherine, *The Night Side of Nature* (UK: Wordsworth Editions, 2000)

Crudden, Michael (Trans.), *The Homeric Hymns* (UK: Oxford World's Classics, 2001)

Davies, G. L., *Horror of Haverfordwest* (UK: Sixth Books, 2018)

Davies, Owen, *The Haunted: A Social History of Ghosts* (UK: Palgrave Macmillan, 2007)

Dingwall, E. J., *Very Peculiar People* (UK: Rider, 1950)

Douglas, Mary, *Purity and Danger* (UK: Routledge Classics, 2002)

Du Plessis, I. D., *Poltergeists of the South* (South Africa: Howard Timmins, 1966)

Eliade, Mircea, *Shamanism: Archaic Techniques of Ecstasy* (USA: Princeton University Press, 2004)

Evans, Dr Christopher & Wilson, Colin, *The Giant Book of the Unknown* (UK: Magpie Books, 1991)

Evans, Hilary, *Gods, Spirits, Cosmic Guardians* (UK: Aquarian Press, 1987)

Evans, Hilary & Bartholomew, Robert E., *Outbreak! The Encyclopedia of Extraordinary Social Behaviour* (USA: Anomalist Books, 2009)

Evans-Wentz, W. Y., *The Fairy-Faith in Celtic Countries* (USA: BiblioBazaar, 2008)

Feuerstein, Georg, *Holy Madness: Spirituality, Crazy-Wise Teachers and Enlightenment* (USA: Hohm, 2006)

Finucane, R. C., *Ghosts: Appearances of the Dead and Cultural Transformation* (USA: Prometheus Books, 1996)

Flammarion, Camille, *Haunted Houses* (UK: T. Fisher Unwin, 1924)

Fodor, Nandor, *On the Trail of the Poltergeist* (UK: Arco, 1959a)

Fodor, Nandor, *The Haunted Mind: A Psychoanalyst Looks At the Supernatural* (USA: Garrett Publications, 1959b)

Fort, Charles, *The Book of the Damned* (UK: John Brown, 1995)

Fort, Charles, *New Lands* (UK: John Brown, 1996)

Fort, Charles, *Lo!* (UK: John Brown, 1997)

Fort, Charles, *Wild Talents* (UK: John Brown, 1998)

Frazer, Sir J. G., *The Golden Bough* (UK: Oxford World's Classics, 1998)

Freedom Long, Max, *The Secret Science Behind Miracles* (UK: Wildside Press, 2009)

Gauld, Alan & Cornell, A. D., *Poltergeists* (UK: Routledge & Kegan Paul, 1979)

Gooch, Stan, *The Origins of Psychic Phenomena* (USA: Inner Traditions, 2007)

Goss, Michael, *Poltergeists: An Annotated Bibliography of Works in English, c. 1880–1975* (USA: Scarecrow Press, 1979)

Gray, John, *Straw Dogs: Thoughts On Humans and Other Animals* (UK: Granta, 2003)

Green, Andrew, *Our Haunted Kingdom* (UK: Fontana, 1974)

Hall, Michael J., *The World's Most Haunted House: The True Story of the Bridgeport Poltergeist on Lindley Street* (USA: New Page Books, 2014)

Hallowell, Michael J., *Invizikids: The Curious Enigma of 'Imaginary' Childhood Friends* (UK: Heart of Albion Press, 2007)

Hallowell, Michael J. & Ritson, Darren W., *The South Shields Poltergeist: One Family's Fight against an Invisible Intruder* (UK: Sutton Publishing, 2008)

Hallowell, Michael J. & Ritson, Darren W., *The Haunting of Willington Mill* (UK: History Press, 2011)

Hallowell, Michael J. & Ritson, Darren W., *Contagion: In the Shadow of the South Shields Poltergeist'* (UK: Limbury Press, 2014)

Hansen, George P., *The Trickster and the Paranormal* (USA: Xlibris, 2001)

Hardinge, Emma, *Modern American Spiritualism* (USA: New York Printing Company, 1870)

Harold, Clive, *The Uninvited* (UK: Star Books, 1979)

Harpur, Patrick, *Daimonic Reality: A Field Guide to the Otherworld* (USA: Pine Winds Press, 2003)

Harpur, Patrick, *A Complete Guide to the Soul* (UK: Rider, 2010)

Healy, Tony & Cropper, Paul, *Australian Poltergeist: The Stone-Throwing Spook of Humpty Doo and Many Other Cases* (Australia: Strange Nation, 2014)

Henderson, Jan-Andrew, *The Ghost that Haunted Itself* (UK: Mainstream, 2008)

Hitchings, Shirley & Clark, James, *The Poltergeist Prince of London: The Remarkable True Story of the Battersea Poltergeist* (UK: History Press, 2013)

Holder, Geoff, *Poltergeist Over Scotland* (UK: History Press, 2013)

Hopton, Andrew (Ed.), *Anomalous Phenomena of the Interregnum* (UK: Aporia Press, 1991)

Hough, Peter & Randles, Jenny, *Mysteries of the Mersey Valley* (UK: BCC, 1999)

Hubbell, Walter, *The Great Amherst Mystery* (USA: Brentanos, 1916)

Hyde, Lewis, *The Gift: How the Creative Spirit Transforms the World* (UK: Canongate, 2007)

Hyde, Lewis, *Trickster Makes This World: Mischief, Myth and Art* (UK: Canongate, 2008)

Hynes, William J. & Doty, William G. (Eds.), *Mythical Trickster Figures: Contours, Contexts and Criticisms* (USA: University of Alabama Press, 1997)

Bibliography

Jaynes, Julian, *The Origin of Consciousness in the Breakdown of the Bicameral Mind* (USA: Mariner, 2000)

Jorjani, Jason Reza, *Prometheus and Atlas* (UK: Arktos, 2016)

Josiffe, Christopher, *Gef! The Strange Tale of an Extra-Special Talking Mongoose* (UK: Strange Attractor Press, 2017)

Jung, C. G., *Psychology and the Occult* (UK: Ark, 1993)

Jung, C. G., *Memories, Dreams, Reflections* (UK: Harper Perennials, 1995)

Jung, C. G., *Answer to Job* (UK: Routledge Classics, 2002)

Jung, C. G., *Four Archetypes* (UK: Routledge Classics, 2006)

Jung, C. G., *Synchronicity: An Acausal Connecting Principle* (UK: Routledge, 2010)

Jung, C. G. & Kerényi, Karl, *The Science of Mythology* (UK: Routledge Classics, 2002)

Keel, John, *UFOs: Operation Trojan-Horse* (UK: Abacus, 1976)

Kelleher, Colm A. & Knapp, George, *Hunt for the Skinwalker: Science Confronts the Unexplained at a Remote Ranch in Utah* (USA: Paraview Pocket Books, 2005)

Kerényi, Karl, *Hermes Guide of Souls* (USA: Spring Publications, 1996)

Kurlander, Eric, *Hitler's Monsters: A Supernatural History of the Third Reich* (USA: Yale University Press, 2017)

Lang, Andrew, *Cock Lane and Common Sense* (USA: BiblioBazaar, 2006)

Lebling, Robert, *Legends of the Fire Spirits: Jinn and Genies from Arabia to Zanzibar* (UK: IB Tauris, 2010)

Lecouteux, Claude, *The Secret History of Poltergeists and Haunted Houses: From Pagan Folklore to Modern Manifestations* (USA: Inner Traditions, 2012)

Lecouteux, Claude, *The Tradition of Household Spirits* (USA: Inner Traditions, 2013)

Lombroso, Cesare, *After Death – What? Researches in Hypnotic and Spiritualistic Phenomena* (UK: Aquarian Press, 1988)

Lovecraft. H. P., *The Classic Horror Stories* (UK: Oxford World's Classics, 2016)

Mackay, Charles, *Extraordinary Popular Delusions and the Madness of Crowds* (UK: Wordsworth, 2006)

MacManus, Dermot, *The Middle Kingdom* (UK: Colin Smythe, 1979)

Manning, Matthew, *The Link* (UK: Colin Smythe, 1987)

Manning, Matthew, *The Strangers* (UK: Colin Smythe, 1995)

Maxwell-Stuart, P. G., *Poltergeists* (UK: Amberley, 2011)

McClenon, James, *The Entity Letters* (USA: Anomalist Books, 2018)

McGovern, Una (Ed.), *Chambers Dictionary of the Unexplained* (UK: Chambers, 2007)

Melechi, Antonio, *Servants of the Supernatural: The Night Side of the Victorian Mind* (UK: Arrow, 2008)

Monnin, Alfred, *Life of the Curé d'Ars* (UK: Burns & Lambert, 1862)

Moretti, Nick (Ed.), *The Bell Witch Anthology* (USA: no publisher listed, 2006)

Owen, A. R. G., *Can We Explain the Poltergeist?* (USA: Helix Press/Garrett Publications, 1964)

Owen, Iris M., *Conjuring Up Philip: An Adventure in Psychokinesis* (Canada: Fitzhenry & Whiteside, 1976)

Owens, Susan, *The Ghost: A Cultural History* (UK: Tate Publishing, 2017)

Paul, Philip, *Some Unseen Power: Diary of a Ghost-Hunter* (UK: Robert Hale, 1985)

Perry, Michael (Ed.), *Deliverance: Psychic Disturbances and Occult Involvement* (UK: SPCK, 1996)

Pike, Bishop James A., *The Other Side: An Account of My Experiences with Psychic Phenomena* (UK: W. H. Allen, 1969)

Playfair, Guy Lyon, *The Flying Cow: Research into Paranormal Phenomena in the World's Most Psychic Country* (UK: Souvenir Press, 1975)

Playfair, Guy Lyon, *The Indefinite Boundary: An Investigation into the Relationship Between Matter and Spirit* (UK: Souvenir Press, 1976)

Playfair, Guy Lyon, *This House Is Haunted: The Investigation into the Enfield Poltergeist* (UK: Sutton Publishing, 2007)

Plotinus, *The Enneads* (UK: Penguin Classics, 1991)

Price, Harry, *Poltergeist Over England* (UK: Country Life, 1945)

Radin, Paul, *The Trickster: A Study in American Indian Mythology* (USA: Schocken Books, 1988)

Reeves, Vic & Mortimer, Bob, *The Smell of Reeves and Mortimer* (UK: Fantail, 1993)

Rickard, Bob & Michell, John, *Unexplained Phenomena: A Rough Guide Special* (UK: Rough Guides, 2000)

Rogo, D. Scott, *The Poltergeist Experience* (UK: Aquarian Press, 1990)

Rogo, D. Scott, *On the Track of the Poltergeist* (USA: Anomalist Books, 2005)

Roll, William G., *The Poltergeist* (USA: Paraview Special Editions, 2004)

Roll, William G. & Storey, Valerie, *Unleashed: Of Poltergeists and Murder, the Curious Story of Tina Resch* (USA: Paraview Pocket Books, 2004)

Rosenthal, Eric, *They Walk in the Night: True South African Ghost Stories and Tales of the Supranormal* (South Africa, Dassie Books, 1951)

Roud, Steve, *London Lore* (UK: Random House, 2008)

Roy, Archie E., *The Eager Dead: A Study in Haunting* (UK: Book Guild, 2008)

Sagan, Carl, *The Demon-Haunted World: Science as a Candle in the Dark* (USA: Ballantine, 1997)

Screeton, Paul, *Quest for the Hexham Heads* (UK: CFZ Press, 2012)

Sitwell, Sacheverell, *Poltergeists: An Introduction and Examination Followed by Chosen Instances* (USA: University Books, 1959)

Skrbina, David, *Panpsychism in the West* (USA: MIT Press, 2017)

Solomon, Grant & Solomon, Jane, *The Scole Experiment: Scientific Evidence for Life After Death* (UK: Campion Books, 2006)

Spencer, John & Spencer, Anne, *The Encyclopedia of Ghosts and Spirits* (UK: Book Club Associates, 1992)

Spencer, John & Spencer, Anne, *The Poltergeist Phenomenon: An Investigation Into Psychic Disturbance*' (UK: Headline, 1997)

Steiger, Brad, *Otherworldly Affaires: Haunted Lovers, Phantom Spouses, and Sexual Molesters from the Shadow World* (USA: Anomalist Books, 2008)

Steinmeyer, Jim, *Charles Fort: The Man Who Invented the Supernatural* (UK: William Heinemann, 2008)

Strieber, Whitley & Kripal, Jeffrey J., *The Super Natural: Why the Unexplained Is Real* (USA: Tarcher Perigree, 2017)

Thurston, Father Herbert, *Ghosts and Poltergeists* (USA: Henry Regnery, 1954)

Vallee, Jacques, *Passport to Magonia: From Folklore to Flying Saucers* (UK: Tandem, 1975)

Warner, Marina, *Phantasmagoria* (UK: Oxford University Press, 2006)

Wargo, Eric, *Time Loops: Precognition, Retrocausation and the Unconscious* (USA: Anomalist Books, 2018)

Webster, Ken, *The Vertical Plane* (UK: Thorsons, 2018)

Welsford, Enid, *The Fool: His Social and Literary History* (UK: Faber & Faber, 1968)

Wilson, Colin, *Poltergeist! A Study in Destructive Haunting* (UK: Caxton, 2000)

Yeats, W. B., *The Major Works* (UK: Oxford World's Classics, 2001)

Zöllner, Johann, Transcendental Physics (USA: W. J. Schofield, 1881)

References

Introduction

1. Mackay, 2006, pp.498–501; Owen, 1964, pp.33–45
2. Finucane, 1996, pp.140–1
3. Healy & Cropper, 2014, pp.101–7
4. MacManus, 1979, pp.88–9
5. Lecouteux, 2012, p.55
6. Ibid., p.139
7. Vallee, 1975, p.58
8. Cited in Gooch, 2007, pp.25–26
9. Flammarion, 1924, pp.162–3; *see* pp.159–68 for more
10. Frank Podmore, 'The Worksop and Wem Poltergeists' in Sitwell, 1959, p.402
11. Ibid., pp.403–4
12. Ibid., p.408
13. Ibid., p.414
14. Ibid., pp.410–12
15. Ibid., p.414
16. Maurice Grosse, 'How to Investigate Poltergeists' in Spencer & Spencer, 1992, p.366
17. William Barrett, 'Poltergeists in Ireland and Elsewhere' in Sitwell, 1959, pp.329, 352
18. Wilson, 2000, p.363
19. Gauld & Cornell, 1979, p.109
20. Davies, 2007, p.176
21. Jim Schnabel, 'The Münch Bunch', *Fortean Times* 70, pp.23–9
22. Davies, 2007, pp.174–5
23. Owen, 1964, p.70; some sources have Kidner as twelve years old
24. Thurston, 1954, p.121; *see* pp.119–22 for more
25. Crowe, 2000, pp.314–15
26. Fort, 1998, p.21
27. Fort, 1997, pp.37–41
28. Holder, 2013, pp.206–7
29. Spencer & Spencer, 1997, pp.60–5, 151–2, 221; Alan Murdie, 'Ghostwatch' column, *Fortean Times* 381, pp.18–20
30. Cited in Flammarion, 1924, pp.206–8
31. Roy, 2008, p.79
32. Ashford & Ross, 2015, pp.57, 76–8
33. Owen, 1964, p.386; A. R. G. Owen himself doesn't actually use the specific term 'RSPK'
34. Perry, 1996, p.22
35. Owen, 1976, pp.107–8
36. Ashford, 2017, pp.147–9
37. Rogo, 2005, pp.96–7
38. Joel Whitton, 'The Psychology of the Poltergeist Reaction' in Owen, 1976, pp.178–9
39. Ibid., pp.181–2
40. Ashford & Mera, 2015, p.195
41. Kim B. Chaffin, 'The Stone-Throwing Spook of Little Dixie', *Fortean Times* 79, pp.29–32
42. Hyde, 2008, p.121
43. Charles Boer, 'Preface' in Kerényi, 1996, p.20
44. *Fortean Times* 80, p.19
45. Paul, 1985, pp.110, 112, 117

Caveat Lector

1. Lang, 2006, p.19
2. McGovern, 2007, pp.182–3
3. Price, 1945, p.45
4. Owens, 2017, pp.42–3; Welsford, 1968, pp.282–4
5. Owens, 2017, pp.103–6
6. Clarkson, 2011, pp.220–4

7. Hansen, 2001, pp.182–3
8. Roger Clarke, 'An American Haunting', *Fortean Times* 360, pp.52–7; Ashford & Mera, 2016, pp.42–3, 46–7, 156–8
9. Davies, 2007, pp.213–14
10. Sagan, 1997, pp.174–5
11. Steiger, 2008, pp.138–43
12. Holder, 2013, pp.155–8
13. Ibid., pp.183–4
14. *The Times*, 16 September 2014, p.36
15. Clarkson, 2011, pp.120–1
16. Christopher Laursen & Paul Cropper, 'The Baldoon Mystery', *Fortean Times* 315, pp.30–9
17. Hough & Randles, 1999, pp.31–3
18. Welsford, 1968, p.317
19. Radin, 1988, p.xxiv
20. Feuerstein, 2006, pp.359–60

PART ONE

I. The Haunted Mask

1. Thurston, 1954, p.68; *see* pp.61–79 for more
2. Owen, 1964, p.253
3. Hansen, 2001, pp.35, 433; Hyde, 2008, p.355
4. Some would dispute Satan's inclusion in this list (Hyde, 2008, p.10) whilst others approve (Jung, 2006, p.159)
5. Cited in Hynes & Doty, 1997, p.47
6. Ibid., pp.34–5; Hansen, 2001, pp.46–7
7. Hansen, 2001, pp.35–6
8. Radin, 1988, pp.xxiii–iv
9. Spencer & Spencer, 1997, p.104

10. Christine Wood, 'Fortean Bureau of Investigation', *Fortean Times* 117, pp.24–5
11. Hall, 2014, pp.40, 65, 78, 82–3, 99
12. Hitchings & Clark, 2013, p.76
13. Ibid., p.217
14. Josiffe, 2017, p.167
15. Ibid., pp.44–5
16. Ibid., pp.151–4
17. Ibid., p.179, 180, 185
18. Ibid., pp.184–5
19. Ibid., pp.67, 129
20. Ibid., p.164
21. Ibid., p.164
22. Ibid., pp.126–7
23. Ibid., p.124, 133
24. Ibid., p.187
25. Ibid., pp.171, 175–6
26. Ibid., p.176
27. Ibid., pp.51–3
28. Ibid., pp.124, 126, 156
29. Ibid., p.145
30. Ibid., p.149
31. Ibid., pp.149, 155
32. Ibid., p.215
33. Brookesmith, 1995a, pp.70–73; *Fortean Times* 15, p.4–5; Screeton, 2012, pp.38–9
34. Healy & Cropper, 2014, p.285
35. Ibid., pp.287–8
36. Cited in Playfair, 1976, p.125
37. Playfair, 2007, p.viii
38. Maxwell-Stuart, 2011, p.7
39. Christopher Josiffe, 'Gef the Talking Mongoose', *Fortean Times* 269, pp.32–40
40. Hyde, 2008, p.54
41. Ibid., p.45
42. Radin, 1988, p.168
43. Ibid., p.168
44. Budden, 1996, pp.60–1
45. Cited in Hansen, 2001, p.42
46. Ibid., p.401
47. Harpur, 2003, pp.155–6
48. Warner, 2006, p.13
49. Hansen, 2001, p.215

50. Steinmeyer, 2008, pp.211–12, 276–7
51. Fort, 1995, p.25
52. Ibid., p.3
53. Fort, 1998, pp.158–9
54. Fort., 1995, p.2
55. Bill Love, 'Shock to the System', *Fortean Times* 171, pp.48–53
56. Crowe, 2000, pp.274–91
57. Finucane, 1996, pp.106–9
58. Fort, 1995, p.97
59. Ibid., p.228
60. Fort, 1997, pp.32–3
61. Davies, 2007, pp.131–2
62. Peter Bander cited in Manning, 1987, p.11
63. McGovern, 2007, p.569
64. Roll, 2004, p.10
65. Ibid., p.159
66. Cited in Manning, 1987, p.6
67. Roll, 2004, p.163
68. Rogo, 1990, pp.110, 231
69. Rogo, 2005, pp.146–7
70. Ibid., p.151
71. Cited in Pike, 1969, p.136
72. Gauld & Cornell, 1979, p.319
73. Ibid., pp.320–1
74. Roll, 2004, pp.165–6
75. Cited in Gauld & Cornell, 1979, pp.328–9

II. The Living Dead

1. Hyde, 2008, p.213
2. *Morning Post* (n.d.) cited in Crowe, 2000, p.300
3. *An Authentic, Candid and Circumstantial Narrative of the Astonishing Transactions at Stockwell...* cited in Crowe, 2000, p.296; *see* pp.293–9 for more
4. Price, 1945, p.145
5. Aubrey, 2006, p.112
6. Fort, 1998, p.96
7. Owen, 1964, p.118
8. Flammarion, 1924, pp.85, 128

9. *Fortean Times* 156, p.14
10. *Fortean Times* 21, p.4
11. Carrington & Fodor, 1951, p.58
12. *Fortean Times* 50, p.10
13. Thurston, 1954, pp.107–8
14. Gauld & Cornell, 1979, pp.151–2
15. Ibid., p.74; *see* pp.72–6 for more
16. Price, 1945, p.339; see pp.337–43 for more
17. Gauld & Cornell, 1979, p.166; see pp.161–6 for more
18. Cited in Owen, 1964, p.241
19. Hyde, 2008, p.6
20. Hynes & Doty, 1997, p.48
21. Brown, 1990, pp.16–17
22. Hyde, 2008, p.208
23. Thurston, 1951, pp.178–80; *see* pp.177–81 for more
24. Ludovicus Sinistrari de Ameno, *De Daemonialitate, et Incubus, et Succubis* cited in Vallee, 1975, pp.120–3
25. Flammarion, 1924, p.78
26. Ibid., p.75
27. Hynes & Doty, 1997, p.64
28. Rogo, 1990, p.140
29. *Fortean Times* 375, p.22
30. Cited in Thurston, 1954, p.125; *see* pp.125–35 for more
31. Ibid., pp.29–30
32. F. W. Grottendieck, 'The Case of Mr G----------- in Sumatra' in Sitwell, 1959, pp.381–3
33. Flammarion, 1924, pp.277–8
34. Thurston, 1954, pp.90–4; Rogo, 1990, pp.158–60
35. Barrington, 2018, pp.107–8

36. Rogo, 1990, p.162
37. Jung, 2006, p.167
38. Kerényi, 1996, p.97
39. Rogo, 1990, pp.152–8
40. Ashford, 2017, p.41; Clarkson, 2011, pp.84–5
41. Skrbina, 2017, pp.23–8
42. Ibid., pp.91–2
43. Ibid., pp.102–3
44. John Nicholson, 'The Politics of Prodigies', *Fortean Times* 48, pp.52–3; C. Demont, 'Joseph Glanvil and the Ghosts of Wessex' in *Fortean Times* 48, pp.55–6; Price, 1945, pp.43–4
45. Clarkson, 2011, p.85
46. Hynes & Doty, 1997, p.54
47. Radin, 1988, p.7
48. Roll & Storey, 2004, pp.17, 26–35, 164, 172, 214–16, 223–4
49. Ibid., pp.206–8
50. Ibid., p.223
51. Ibid., pp.19–20, 53, 63
52. Ibid., p.92
53. Ibid., p.221
54. Fort, 1998, p.191

III. Breaking Down Barriers

1. Brookesmith, 1995a, p.68
2. Christopher Josiffe, 'Gef the Talking Mongoose', *Fortean Times* 269, pp.32–40
3. Hallowell & Ritson, 2011, p.119
4. Roud, 2008, p.293
5. Du Plessis, 1966, pp.33–8
6. Ashford & Mera, 2016, p.21
7. Ashford & Ross, 2015, p.35–6
8. Healy & Cropper, p.259
9. Perry, 1996, pp.22–3
10. Bil Love, 'Shock to the System', *Fortean Times* 171, pp.48–53
11. Rickard & Michell, 2000, p.8

12. Hubbell, 1916, p.114
13. Cited in Roll, 2004, p.37; *see* Thurston, 1954, pp.146–51 for more
14. Owen, 1964, p.119
15. Hynes & Doty, 1997, p.64
16. Healy & Cropper, 2014, p.77
17. Perry, 1996, p.34
18. Clarke, 2012, pp.73, 81–2
19. Ashford & Mera, 2016, pp.5, 13
20. Hitchings & Clark, 2013, pp.176–7, 262
21. Hyde, 2008, p.71
22. Ibid., p.72
23. Ibid., p.263
24. Hynes & Doty, 1997, p.59
25. Playfair, 1975, p.249
26. Hynes & Doty, 1997, p.58; Kerényi, 1996, p.141
27. Brown, 1990, pp.5–7, 9–11, 18, 23
28. Spencer & Spencer, 1997, p.170
29. Rogo, 1990, pp.129–32
30. Josiffe, 2017, p.168
31. Zöllner, 1881, pp.53–4, 66, 92–3, 190–1
32. Ibid., pp.34–5, 41, 82–3, 86, 103–4
33. Ibid., pp.58, 63–4
34. Ibid, pp.86, 89
35. Ibid., pp.89–90
36. Wargo, 2018, pp.102, 147–8
37. Lovecraft, 2016, pp.291, 479–80; Josiffe, 2017, p.360
38. Zöllner, 1881, p.70
39. Ibid., pp.135–6
40. Melechi, 2008, pp.217–31
41. Hansen, 2001, pp.130, 137–8
42. Price, 1945, p.55
43. *Daily Mail*, 28 May 1906, cited in Price, 1945, p.30
44. Kelleher & Knapp, 2005, p.67
45. Ibid., p.69
46. Ibid., p.8

47. http://magoniamagazine.blogspot.com/2014/01/trickster.html
48. Jorjani, 2016, pp.384–5
49. Kelleher & Knapp, 2005, pp.85–6
50. Ibid., p.118–119
51. Ibid., pp.63–5, 144–7
52. Ibid., pp.34–50
53. Ibid., p.50
54. Ibid., pp.3–6, 26–7, 191–2
55. Fort, 1997, p.120
56. Radin, 1988, p.15
57. Carrington & Fodor, 1951, p.181
58. Green, 1974, p.301
59. Brown, 1990, p.85
60. Hyde, 2008, p.210
61. Ibid., pp.313–14
62. Price, 1945, p.54
63. Barrett in Sitwell, 1959, pp.341–2
64. Fodor, 1959a, p.19
65. Flammarion, 1924, pp.159–61 & 167
66. Harpur, 2007, p.94
67. Hynes & Doty, 1997, p.48
68. Barrett in Sitwell, 1959, p.344
69. Clarke, 2011, p.103

IV. Keys to Meaning
1. Flammarion, 1924, pp.129–30; *see* pp.128–31 for more
2. Ibid., p.115
3. Ibid., p.105
4. Thurston, 1954, p.35
5. Price, 1945, p.286
6. Cited in Price, 1945, p.293; *see* pp.279–302 for more
7. Healy & Cropper, 2014, p.271
8. Thurston, 1954, pp.122–3
9. Hynes & Doty, 1997, p.59
10. Kerényi, 1996, pp.122–5
11. Brown, 1990, pp.32–6, 107–9
12. Hyde, 2008, p.11
13. Brown, 1990, pp.39–40

14. Spencer & Spencer, 1997, p.53
15. Brown, 1990, pp.39–40; Kerényi, 1996, pp.59–60
16. Clarkson, 2011, p.123
17. Barrington, 2018, pp.17, 22, 23, 80–1
18. Ibid., p.75
19. Brookesmith, 1995b, pp.13, 15; Kerényi, 1996, pp.24–5
20. Pike, 1969, pp.138–9, 151, 172–3
21. Hynes & Doty, 1997, p.60
22. Ashford & Mera, 2016, pp.72–3
23. Hyde, 2008, pp.134–5, 139
24. Barrington, 2018, pp.30–1
25. Ibid., pp.47–9
26. Spencer & Spencer, 1997, pp.69–79
27. Fodor, 1959b, pp.3–9, 13–14, 90–1
28. Ibid., pp.71–2
29. Ibid., p.78
30. Perry, 1996, pp.21–2
31. Spencer & Spencer, 1997, p.221
32. Hynes & Doty, 1997, pp.48, 50–4, 56
33. Ibid., p.62
34. McGovern, 2007, p.260
35. Fodor, 1959b, pp.92–7; Carrington & Fodor, 1951, pp.215–22
36. Fodor, 1959a, pp.207–11; Carrington & Fodor, 1951, p.132
37. Fodor, 1959b, p.80–3; Carrington & Fodor, 1951, p.129
38. Carrington & Fodor, 1951, p.129
39. Ibid., p.132
40. Fodor, 1959a, p.209
41. Fodor, 1959b, pp.86–8
42. Fodor, 1959a, p.210
43. Ibid., pp.211, 13–14
44. Ibid., p.217
45. Ibid., p.132
46. Ibid., pp.218–19

47. See Barrington, pp.36, 38–9, 44, for more typical key-related JOTTS
48. Green, 1974, p.91
49. Spencer & Spencer, 1997, p.66
50. Playfair, 2007, pp.15–22
51. Barrington, 2018, pp.69–71
52. Patrick Harpur, 'The Problem of Pixilation', *Fortean Times* 209, pp.54–5
53. Hyde, 2008, pp.101–7
54. http://www.spr.ac.uk/expcms/index.php?section=74
55. Hansen, 2001, p.22

V. Borderline Personalities
1. Perry, 1996, pp.12, 19–20
2. Ibid., p.13
3. Rogo, 2005, pp.149–51
4. Hansen, 2001, pp.48–51
5. Ibid., p.129
6. Ibid., p.84
7. Davies, 2018, p.49
8. Ibid., p.15
9. Hansen, 2001, p.84
10. Ibid., p.51
11. Ibid., p.149
12. Hallowell & Ritson, 2014, p.116
13. Ibid., pp.140–3
14. Josiffe, 2017, pp.1–6, 86
15. Ibid., pp.199–201
16. Ibid., p.135
17. Hansen, 2001, p.38
18. http://www.tricksterbook.com/ArticlesOnline/GhostsAndLiminality.html
19. Lecouteux, 2012, p.23
20. Briggs, 2002, p.286
21. Josiffe 2017, pp.76–7, 150
22. Ibid., pp.366–8
23. Jorjani, 2016, p.43
24. Hansen, 2001, p.210
25. Jorjani, 2016, p.45
26. Hansen, 2001, p.196
27. Ibid., pp.189–90

28. Ibid., p.38; http://www.tricksterbook.com/ArticlesOnline/GhostsAndLiminality.html
29. Gauld & Cornell, 1979, p.226; Davies, 2007, p.177
30. Brookesmith, 1995a, p.105; Gauld & Cornell, 1979, pp.27, 140; Hubbell, 1916, p.80; Owen, 1964, p.162; Price, 1945, pp.373–4; Steiger, 2008, pp.165–6
31. Frazer, 1998, pp.702–703
32. Ibid., p.703
33. Ibid., 1998, p.703
34. Fort, 1998, p.178
35. Ibid., pp.177–8
36. https://mysteriousuniverse.org/2018/04/poltergeists-and-phds-an-interview-with-dr-christopher-laursen/
37. Roll & Storey, 2004, p.225
38. Ibid., pp.26–35, 104–5, 226–9
39. Ibid., pp.36–8, 41, 55, 198
40. Ibid., p.56
41. Ibid., pp.120–2
42. Ibid., pp.96–7
43. Ibid., pp.242–3, 254–6, 271–4
44. Davies, 2007, pp.176–7
45. Gooch, 2007, p.27; Lecouteux, p.2013
46. Ashford, 2017, pp.86–9
47. Barrington, 2018, pp.103–4
48. Ashford & Ross, 2015, pp.24–5
49. Bord, 1997, p.17
50. Ashford, 2017, pp.119–22;Clarkson, 2011, pp.99–103; Roll, 2004, pp.100–103;Rogo, 1990, pp.127–9; Rogo, 2005, pp.56–7
51. Green, 1974, pp.322–3
52. Rogo, 2005, pp.55–63
53. Hitchings & Clark, 2013, p.14
54. Ibid., p.16
55. Ibid., p.22
56. Ibid., pp.246, 256
57. Ibid., pp, 224, 246
58. Ibid., p.301
59. Ibid., pp.73, 79
60. Ibid., pp.17, 33, 66, 142, 178
61. Ibid., pp.77, 80
62. Ibid., pp.191, 271
63. Ibid., p.190
64. Ibid., pp.153–4, 241, 183, 207–8
65. Ibid., p.105
66. Ibid., pp.21–2, 63
67. Ibid., pp.103–4, 108–10
68. Ibid., pp.178, 251
69. Ibid., pp.218–9
70. Ibid., pp.27–8, 78, 80, 98–9, 263
71. Ibid., p.217
72. Ibid., p.30
73. Ibid., pp.49–51, 61
74. Ibid., p.31
75. Ibid., pp.46–8
76. Ibid., p.95
77. Ibid., p.57
78. Ibid., pp.234–5
79. Ibid., pp.285–9

VI. Shamans Without the Shamanism

1. Fodor, 1959b, p.72–4
2. Strieber & Kripal, 2017, p.196
3. Lombroso, 1988, pp.39–71, 90–102, 111–12, 123, 171, 305; Dingwall, 1950, pp.178–214; McClenon, 2018, p.76
4. Ashford & Mera, 2015, p.108
5. Rogo, 1990, pp.184–5
6. Ashford, 2017, pp.160–5
7. Rogo, 1990, pp.164–8
8. Ibid., pp.173–5; Ashford, 2017, pp.187–9
9. Eliade, 2004, p.206
10. Healy & Cropper, 2014, p.273
11. McGovern, 2007, pp.619–20
12. Hansen, 2001, pp.86–7
13. Ibid., pp.93–4
14. Mark Pilkington, 'The Trickster', *Fortean Times* 175, pp.40–1
15. Gooch, 2007, pp.46–8
16. Eliade, 2004, pp.19, 47, 17–9, 256, 257
17. Ibid., pp.15–16; Hynes & Doty, 1997, pp.89–90
18. Hansen, 2001, p.87
19. Eliade, 2004, p.18
20. Owen, 1964, p.199
21. Lang, 2006, p.39
22. Eliade, 2004, pp.27–8
23. Ibid., p.36
24. Ashford, 2017, pp.160–5
25. Ibid., p.159
26. Ibid., pp.178–9
27. Hansen, 2001, pp.56–7
28. Hitchings & Clark, 2013, pp.45, 71
29. Hansen, 2001,, pp.54–6
30. Hynes & Doty, 1997, p.92
31. Hansen, 2001, p.87
32. Ibid., p.87
33. Hynes & Doty, 1997, pp.94–9
34. Ibid., p.87–8
35. Hansen, 2001, pp.88–9
36. Ibid., pp.89–93
37. Ibid., pp.101–8
38. Cited in Price, 1945, pp.5–6
39. Sitwell, 1959, p.54
40. Kurlander, 2017, pp.132–3, 139–41; Roll, 2004, p.100
41. Ibid., p.101
42. Kurlander, 2017, p.132
43. Jorjani, 2016, pp.xvii, 30–2, 49–50
44. Ibid., pp.84–5, 104–5, 109
45. Ibid., pp.27, 41, 55–6
46. Hansen, 2001, pp.340–1
47. Ibid., p.425

VII. Traps of Logic

1. *Fortean Times* 32, pp.40–1
2. Barrington, 2018, p.11
3. Fort, 1997, pp.23–4
4. Carrington & Fodor, 1951, p.48
5. Fort, 1997, p.21
6. Ibid., p.31
7. Ibid., p.225
8. Rickard & Michell, 2000, pp.201–2
9. Jung, 2010, p.7
10. Ibid., pp.22–5
11. Hansen, 2001, pp.325–9
12. Jung, 2010, p.25
13. Fort, 1998, p.6
14. Hyde, 2008, pp.97–100
15. Steinmeyer, 2008, pp.12, 180–1, 275
16. Fort, 1995, p.2
17. Fort, 1997, p.5
18. McGovern, 2007, p.240
19. Plotinus, 1991, p.263 [IV.3.9]
20. Thurston, 1954, p.47; *see* Maxwell-Stuart, 2011, pp.97–122 for more
21. Hyde, 2008, pp.48–9

VIII. Our Minds Playing Tricks on Us

1. Hyde, 2008, p.18
2. Radin, 1988, pp.25–8
3. Ashford, 2017, pp.321–2
4. Hallowell & Ritson, 2008, p.33
5. Ibid., pp.200–1
6. Ibid., pp.106–7
7. Ibid., p.207
8. Jung, 2006, p.160
9. Jung & Kerényi, 2002, p.86
10. Douglas, 2002, pp.104–5
11. R. B. Onians, *Origins of European Thought About the Body and the Mind*, cited in Douglas, 2002, p.104
12. Cited in Owen, 1964, pp.154–5
13. Ibid., p.149

14. Rogo, 1990, p.87
15. Owen, 1976, p.147
16. Ibid., p.22
17. Ibid., p.32
18. Ibid., p.214
19. Solomon & Solomon, 2006, p.48
20. Ibid., p.36
21. Hardinge, 1870, pp.334–5; see pp.334–45 for more
22. Ibid., p.338
23. Price, 1945, p.270
24. Ibid., pp.260–2
25. Hyde, 2008, p.101–2

IX. Loki Unbound

1. Hyde, 2008, p.187; Welsford, 1968, pp.200–3; Jung, 2006, p.162
2. Price, 1945, p.1
3. Lecouteux, 2012, p.18
4. Price, 1945, p.1
5. Lecouteux, 2012, p.18
6. Rickard & Michell, 2000, p.10
7. Playfair, 1975, p.248
8. Cassirer, 1993, pp.24–5
9. Ibid., p.6
10. Ibid., p.6
11. Wilson, 2000, pp.153–5; *see* pp.137–71 for more
12. Ibid., p.157
13. *Fortean Times* 112, p.21
14. Wilson, 2000, p.158
15. Ibid., pp.162–3
16. Playfair, 1975, p.250
17. Gauld & Cornell, 1979, pp.297–8
18. Spencer & Spencer, 1997, p.249
19. Ibid., 1997, p.54
20. Owen, 1964, p.40
21. Thurston, 1954, p.194
22. Owen, 1964, p.68
23. Barrett in Sitwell, 1959, p.344
24. Flammarion, 1924, p.108
25. Spencer & Spencer, 1997, pp.249–51
26. Hallowell & Ritson, 2008, pp.313–5
27. Ashford & Mera, 2015, pp.98–9

28. Hallowell & Ritson, 2014, p.172

X. The World Turned Upside-Down

1. Jung, 2006, p.168
2. Playfair, 2007, p.152
3. Ibid., p.157
4. Ibid., p.147
5. Ibid., pp.152–3
6. Roll, 2004, p.32
7. Cited in Rickard & Michell, 2000, p.7
8. Hall, 2014, pp.60–1
9. Lecouteux, 2012, p.180
10. Henry Lovel, *Horrid and Strange News from Ireland ...* in Hopton, 1991, pp.6–14
11. Ibid., p.10
12. Owen, 1964, p.33
13. Playfair, 2007, p.146
14. Ibid., pp.130–1
15. Ibid., p.251
16. Hyde, 2008, pp.177–80
17. Douglas, 2002, pp.201–2

XI. Identity Crisis

1. Playfair, 2007, p.145
2. Ibid., p.140
3. Ibid., pp.185, 138, 137, 184
4. Peter Hough, 'Wet Wet Wet', *Fortean Times* 89, pp.23–6; Ashford & Mera, 2015, pp.17, 19–20, 21–2, 24–5, 33–4, 36, 48, 55, 60–1, 64, 72–3, 77 (in the book, 'Geoffrey' is called 'John')
5. Hyde, 2008, p.206, Brown, 1990, p.60
6. Carrington & Fodor, 1951, p.143
7. Wilson, 2000, p.144
8. *Fortean Times* 6, pp.7–9
9. Evans, 1987, p.139
10. Harpur, 2003, p.99
11. Evans, 1987, p.226
12. Gauld & Cornell, 1979, p.98
13. *Fortean Times* 235, p.8

14. Finucane, 1996, pp.106–8
15. Jung, 1993, p.55
16. F. W. H. Myers, *Automatic Writing*, cited in Jung, 1993, pp.55–6
17. Jung, 1993, p.56
18. Playfair, 2007, p.147
19. Ashford & Ross, 2015, pp.75–6
20. Josiffe, pp.183–4
21. Hallowell, 2007, pp.59–68
22. Ibid., p.61
23. Ibid., p.63; Josiffe, pp.268–78
24. Gauld & Cornell, 1979, pp.36–7
25. Crudden, 1991, pp.45–6
26. Hyde, 2008, p.50
27. Ibid., pp.50–1

XII. Motives Unknown

1. Radin, 1988, p.8
2. Ibid., pp.17–18
3. Ibid., p.135
4. Carrington & Fodor, 1951, pp.180–1; see pp.175–212 for Fodor's summary of Gef
5. Ibid., p.183
6. Jung, 2006, p.160
7. Ibid., p.170
8. Ibid., p.170
9. Carrington & Fodor, 1951, pp.184–5
10. Manning, 1987, p.37
11. Evans-Wentz, 2008, p.554
12. William Barrett, 'Poltergeists Old and New' cited in Owen, 1964, p.313
13. Owen, 1964, pp.313–14
14. Rogo, 1990, pp.251–2
15. Fodor, 1959a, p.67

XIII. Poltergeist Art

1. Carrington & Fodor, 1951, p.206
2. Josffe, 2017, p.186
3. Christopher Josiffe, 'Gef the Talking Mongoose', *Fortean Times* 269, pp.32–40
4. Carrington & Fodor, 1951, pp.210–11

5. Ibid., pp.85–6; *see* pp.85–91 for more
6. Thurston, 1954, p.11; *see* pp.10–13 for more
7. Alexander Telfair, *A New Confutation of Sadducism...* cited in Price, 1945, p.76; *see* pp.75–80 for more
8. Flammarion, 1924, pp.84–6
9. Holder, 2013, p.163; *see* pp.158–66 for more
10. Ashford & Ross, 2015, pp.69–70
11. *Fortean Times* 143, p.51
12. Gauld & Cornell, 1979, p.110; *see* pp.99–115 for more
13. Cited in Holder, 2013, p.13; *see* pp.12–15 for more
14. Rosenthal, 1951, pp.129–30
15. Gauld & Cornell, 1979, p.8; see pp.5–18 for more
16. Crowe, 2000, p.319; *see* pp.318–20 for more
17. Jack Romano, 'Spanish Eyes', *Fortean Times* 157, pp.36–40
18. Hyde,1998, p.254
19. Yeats, 2001, p.431
20. Gary Lachman, 'The Occult World of C. G. Jung', *Fortean Times* 264, pp.40–5
21. Jung, 1995, p.216
22. Clarkson, 2011, pp.84, 234; Rogo, 1990, pp.257–60
23. Fodor, 1959a, p.145
24. Hyde, 2007, p.54
25. Rogo, 1990, pp.255–6
26. Manning, 1987, p.6
27. Ibid., p.63
28. Ibid., pp.65–6
29. Gooch, 2007, p.121
30. Ibid., p.74
31. Kerényi, 1996, pp.138–41
32. Hyde, 2008, pp.306–7
33. Hansen, 2008, p.62

34. Rickard & Michell, 2000, p.46

PART TWO

I. Practical Jokes

1. *Fortean Times* 7, p.5
2. Playfair, 2007, p.198
3. Maxwell-Stuart, 2011, p.105
4. Healy & Cropper, 2014, p.272
5. Kelleher & Knapp, 2005, p.239
6. Ibid., pp.39, 238–40
7. *Fortean Times* 87, p.8
8. Cited in Monnin, 1862, pp.107–8
9. Flammarion, 1924, pp.156–7; *see* pp.155–8 for more
10. Ibid., pp.160–1
11. Price, 1945, pp.164–9
12. Flammarion, 1924, p.129
13. Price, 1945, p.168
14. Gauld & Cornell, 1979, p.68; *see* pp.68–71 for more
15. Alan Murdie, 'Ghostwatch' column, *Fortean Times* 245, p.26
16. Crowe, 2000, p.310
17. Lang, 2006, p.82
18. Owen, 1964, p.137
19. Flammarion, 1924, p.131
20. Lecouteux, 2012, pp.38–9
21. Cassirer, 1993, pp.5, 12, 17–18, 17
22. Finucane, 1996, p.221
23. Steiger, 2008, p.135
24. Playfair, 2007, p.138

II. Vandalism

1. Alan Murdie, 'Ghostwatch' column, *Fortean Times* 244, p.17
2. Fort, 1998, p.115
3. Gauld & Cornell, 1979, pp.214–15; *see* pp.211–19 for more
4. Cited in Flammarion, 1924, p.279; *see* pp.278–80 for more

5. Price, 1945, pp.65–7
6. *See* Holder, 2013, p.46 for ghosts doing just this
7. Owen, 1964, p.21
8. Maxwell-Stuart, 2011, p.144
9. Lecouteux, 2012, pp.89–93 & Maxwell-Stuart, 2011, pp.126–9
10. Lecouteux, 2012, p.52
11. Ibid., p.129
12. Healy & Cropper, p.261
13. Green, 1974, p.126
14. Paul, 1985, p.89
15. Ibid., p.107
16. Hardinge, 1870, p.453; *see* pp.444–53 for more
17. *Fortean Times* 25, p.13
18. *Fortean Times* 6, p.9
19. Owen, 1964, p.108; Flammarion, 1924, pp.233–5; Lecouteux, 2012, pp.194–8; Wilson, 2000, pp.14–17
20. Holder, 2013, pp.154–5
21. Brookesmith, 1995a, pp.94–7
22. Playfair, 1976, pp.257–8
23. Flammarion, 1924, pp.71–2
24. Lecouteux, 2012, pp.157–60
25. Lecouteux, 2013, p.143
26. *Daily Telegraph* (London), 8 April 1942, cited in Price, 1945, pp.244–5
27. Price, 1945, pp.240–6; Holder, 2013, pp.112–16
28. Lecouteux, 2012, p.139
29. Robert Damon Schneck, 'Holy Geist!', *Fortean Times* 228, pp.48–52
30. Holder, 2013, p.53
31. Cited in Davies, 2007, p.30
32. *Fortean Times* 47, pp.20–1
33. *Fortean Times* 29, p.25
34. Thurston, 1954, pp.192–3
35. Roll, 2004, pp.99–100
36. Carter, 1996, pp.305–6

III. Slapstick

1. Price, 1945, pp.256–7
2. Roll, 2004, p.41
3. *Fortean Times* 30, p.17
4. Dwight Whalen, 'Stoned on Annie Taylor', *Fortean Times* 45, pp.62–6
5. Holder, 2013, p.34
6. Report from Mr Bristow in Volume VII of the *Proceedings* of the SPR cited in Sitwell, 1959, pp.70–1; *see* pp.70–3 and Flammarion, 1924, pp.256–60 for more
7. Du Plessis, 1966, pp.39–44
8. Davies, 2007, p.212
9. Cited in M. V. Ingram, *An Authenticated History of the Famous Bell Witch*, in Moretti, 2006, p.212
10. Flammarion, 1924, p.161
11. Ingram in Moretti, 2006, p.204
12. Gauld & Cornell, 1979, p.133
13. Price, 1945, p.289
14. Ibid., p.209; *see* pp.204–12 for more
15. Price, 1945, p.352; *see* pp.350–3 for more
16. Harriet Parks Miller, *The Bell Witch of Middle Tennessee*, in Moretti, 2006, p.267; *see* pp.266–70 for more
17. Owen, 1964, p.395
18. Lecouteux, 2012, pp.128–30
19. Gauld & Cornell, 1979, pp.161–6
20. Hubbell, 1916, p.109
21. Owen, 1964, p.137
22. Ashford & Mera, 2015, p.22
23. Podmore in Sitwell, 1959, p.406
24. Gooch, 2007, p.32; *see* pp.28–33 for more

IV. Sick Jokes

1. Tony Healy and Paul Cropper, 'Stone Me!', *Fortean Times* 116, pp.34–9; Healy & Cropper, 2014, pp.9–55
2. Thurston, 1954, pp.172–5
3. Price, 1945, p.344
4. Roger Clarke, 'Adams Family Values', *Fortean Times* 359, pp.44–9
5. Ingram in Moretti, 2006, p.214
6. Richard Williams Bell, *Our Family Trouble*, in Moretti 2006, p.35
7. Ibid., pp.35–6
8. Ibid., pp.36–7
9. Hardinge, 1870, pp.449 & 451
10. Ibid., pp.452–3
11. Laura Makarius, *The Crime of Manabozo*, cited in Hansen, 2001, p.67
12. Playfair, 2007, p.145
13. Hansen, 2001, p.45
14. Ibid., p.45

V. Toilet Humour

1. Hansen, 2001, p.45
2. Stewart Lee, 'Bizarre Cabaret', *Comedy Review* 4, pp.58–61
3. Playfair, 2007, p.196
4. Ibid., p.217
5. Thurston, 1954, p.163; see pp.162–71 for more
6. Carrington & Fodor, 1951, p.78
7. Gauld & Cornell, 1979, pp.109–10
8. Lecouteux, 2013, p.149

9. Gauld & Cornell, 1979, p.118; see Crowe, 2000, p.304 for more
10. Ibid., p.40; see Thurston, 1954, pp.193–4 for more
11. Thurston, 1954, p.194
12. *Fortean Times* 95, p.51
13. Playfair, 2007, p.218
14. Lebling, 2010, p.149
15. Hynes & Doty, 1997, p.42
16. Ibid., p.42
17. Ibid., p.127
18. Ibid., p.136
19. Ibid., pp.44–5
20. Maxwell-Stuart, 2011, pp.51–5; *Fortean Times* 190, p.22; Owen, 1964, pp.398–400
21. Monnin, 1862, p.115
22. Thurston, 1954, pp.63–4
23. Lecouteux, 2012, pp.15–18
24. Chambers, 1999, p.79
25. Maxwell-Stuart, 2011, p.80
26. Hansen, 2001, p.77
27. Ibid., pp.76–7
28. Ibid., p.80
29. Hallowell & Ritson, 2014, p.88
30. Hansen, 2001, p.81; see Evans & Bartholomew, 2009, pp.555–61 for more
31. Carrington & Fodor, 1951, pp.196–7
32. Ibid., p.188
33. Gooch, 2007, p.31
34. Douglas, 2002, p.142
35. Ibid., p.150

VI. Absurdity of Location
1. *Fortean Times* 7, p.5
2. *Fortean Times* 10, p.3
3. Wilson, 2000, p.328
4. Alan Murdie, 'Ghostwatch' column, *Fortean Times* 212, p.19
5. *Fortean Times* 104, p.6
6. *Fortean Times* 150, p.23

7. *Fortean Times* 378, p.24
8. Hallowell & Ritson, 2008, pp.298–9
9. *Fortean Times* 38, pp.24–5
10. Green, 1974, back cover
11. Spencer & Spencer, 1997, p.109
12. *Fortean Times* 271, p.12
13. Roll, 2004, p.36
14. *Fortean Times* 161, p.8
15. Review in *Fortean Times* 170, p.62; Healy & Cropper, 2014, pp.101–7
16. Davies, 2007, p.178
17. Hansen, 2001, p.42

VII. Hide-and-Seek
1. Tony Healy & Paul Cropper, 'Stone Me!', *Fortean Times* 116, pp.34–9; Healy & Cropper, 2014, pp.18–19
2. Ashford & Mera, 2016, pp.70, 88, 90, 102, 116–17, 153, 174
3. Ibid., pp.11–12
4. Playfair, 2007, p.9
5. Playfair, 1975, p.266
6. Playfair, 2007, p.193
7. Roll & Storey, 2004, p.79
8. Gooch, 2007, p.32
9. Kelleher & Knapp, 2007, p.126
10. Ibid., pp.188–9
11. Rogo, 2005, p.176
12. Cited in Maxwell-Stuart, 2011, p.58
13. Healy & Cropper, 2014, p.65
14. Cited in Thurston, 1954, p.151
15. Ashford & Ross, 2015, pp.17, 40, 50
16. Cited in Flammarion, 1924, pp.258–9
17. Cited in Fodor, 1959a, p.25
18. Ibid., p.33
19. Ibid., p.40
20. Price, 1945, p.19

21. Cited in Cassirer, 1993, p.28
22. Thurston, 1954, p.98
23. Healy & Cropper, 2014, p.77; see pp.56–88 for more
24. Owen, 1964, p.116
25. Manning, 1995, pp.21–2
26. Carrington & Fodor, 1951, p.116
27. Ibid., p.193; Josiffe, 2017, p.157
28. Ibid., p.212
29. Ibid., p.184
30. Josiffe, 2017, p.196
31. Ibid., p.156
32. Owen, 1964, p.146
33. Price, 1945, p.69; see pp.67–70 for more
34. Hardinge, 1870, p.447
35. Cited in Hyde, 2008, p.21
36. Carrington & Fodor, 1951, p.181
37. Hyde, 2008, p.21
38. Ibid., p.22
39. Strieber & Kripal, 2017, p.128

VIII. Ridiculous Evidence
1. Hallowell & Ritson, 2008, p.318
2. Ibid., pp.98–9
3. Ibid., p.151
4. Ibid., p.178
5. Ibid., p.186
6. Ibid., plates section
7. Brookesmith, 1995a, p.46
8. Carrington & Fodor, 1951, p.177; Josiffe, 278–88
9. Price, 1945, p.26
10. Manning, 1995, pp.83–5
11. Wilson, 2000, p.152
12. Gauld & Cornell, 1979, p.106
13. Wilson, 2000, p.221; Owen, 1976, pp.212–13
14. *Fortean Times* 265, p.5
15. 'Fortean Times Random Dictionary of the Damned: The Cosmic Joker', *Fortean Times* 185, p.55

16. Hansen, 2001, p.155
17. Fort, 1995, p.17
18. McClenon, 2018, pp.105–6
19. Ibid., pp.202–3
20. https://en.wikipedia.org/wiki/Heyoka
21. McClenon, 2018, pp.58–9, 377
22. Ibid., pp.16, 33
23. Ibid., pp.94–5
24. Ibid., p.43
25. Ibid., p.107
26. Ibid., pp.16–17, 132, 206
27. Ibid., p.12
28. Ibid., p.120
29. Ibid., p.220
30. Ibid., p.101
31. Ibid., p.223
32. Ibid., p.131
33. Ibid., pp.120–1
34. Ibid., p.93
35. Ibid., p.212
36. Ibid., pp.171–2, 256
37. Ibid., pp.227–8, 244–9
38. Ibid., pp.93, 218–19
39. Rogo, 1990, pp.70–2
40. McClenon, 2018, p.241
41. Ibid., p.210
42. Ibid., pp.43, 44, 47
43. Ibid., p.73
44. Ibid., p.217

IX. False Promises
1. Hubbell, 1916, pp.96–8
2. Alan Murdie, 'Ghostwatch' column, *Fortean Times* 239, p.28
3. Hallowell & Ritson, 2006, p.253
4. Holder, 2013, p.51
5. Roy, 2008, p.561
6. Solomon & Solomon, 2006, p.235
7. Bell, R. in Moretti, 2006, pp.47–8
8. Ibid., p.25
9. Rose-Mary Gower, Janet Bord and Tristan Gay Hulse, 'Bless This House', *Fortean Times* 113, pp.26–7
10. Letter in *Fortean Times* 217, p.75

11. Bell, R. in Moretti, 2006, p.37
12. Ibid., p.28
13. Maxwell-Stuart, 2011, p.105
14. Wilson, 2000, pp.316–19
15. Hyde, 2008, p.17
16. Ibid., pp.290–1
17. Hitchings & Clark, 2013, pp.134–5, 150–1
18. Ibid., p.152
19. Ibid., p.163
20. Ibid., p.133
21. Ibid., p.188
22. Ibid., p.219

X. Funny Disguises
1. Gauld & Cornell, 1979, p.196; *see* Price, 1945, pp.170–91 for more
2. Hallowell & Ritson, 2011, pp.139 & 142
3. Ibid., pp.141–142
4. Ibid., pp.142–143
5. Ibid., p.143
6. Ibid., p.174
7. Paul, 1985, p.84
8. Spencer & Spencer, 1997, p.102
9. Hallowell & Ritson, 2014, p.114
10. Spencer & Spencer, 1997, p.251
11. Alan Murdie, 'Ghostwatch' column, *Fortean Times* 315, p.19
12. Gauld & Cornell, 1979, pp.112–15
13. Thurston, 1954, pp.162–71; Paul Cropper & Tony Healy, 'Dagg's Demon', *Fortean Times* 344, pp.30–6
14. Jung, 2006, p.178
15. Gooch, 2007, p.167; *see* pp.166–71 for more
16. Wilson, 2000, p.67
17. Owen, 1976, pp.113–14
18. Hitchings & Clark, 2013, p.49
19. Ibid., pp.62–3
20. Ibid., p.68
21. Ibid., p.78

22. Ibid., p.72
23. Ibid., p.87
24. Ibid., pp.229–30
25. Ibid., p.85
26. Ibid., pp.88–9
27. Ibid., pp.141, 143
28. Ibid., p.144
29. Ibid., p.133
30. Ibid., p.131
31. Ibid., pp.66–7, 78, 86–7
32. Job 2:7
33. Jung, 2002, p.6
34. Ibid., p.7
35. Ibid., p.10
36. Ibid., p.10
37. Compiled from Thurston, 1954, pp.39–50 & Maxwell-Stuart, 2011, pp.97–122
38. Robert Damon Schneck, 'Holy Geist!', *Fortean Times* 228, pp.48–52
39. Bell, R. in Moretti, 2006, pp.25–33
40. Ibid., p.26
41. Ingram in Moretti, 2006, p.225
42. Ibid., p.217
43. Bell, R. in Moretti, 2006, p.33
44. Ibid., pp.51–2
45. Ingram in Moretti, 2006, p.138
46. Bell, R. in Moretti, 2006, p.35
47. Parks Miller in Moretti, 2006, p.283
48. Ingram in Moretti, 2006, p.224
49. Healy & Cropper, 2014, pp.158–66
50. Harpur, 2003, p.xvi

XI. Theatres of the Absurd
1. Hitchings & Clark, 2013, pp.210–11
2. Ibid., pp.74–5, 91–2
3. Ibid., pp.115–16
4. Ibid., pp.84, 100
5. Ibid., pp.102, 110–11, 128, 159, 173, 291–2
6. Ibid., pp.166, 123–4
7. Ibid., pp.106, 114, 126–7, 134
8. Ibid., pp.129, 194, 209, 223–4, 278

9. Ibid., p.80
10. Ibid., pp.173–4
11. Ibid., p.124
12. Ibid., p.172
13. Ibid., pp.106–7, 114, 120, 132
14. Ibid., pp.264–5, 270–1
15. Ibid., p.45; Price, 1945, pp.229–39
16. Webster, 2018, pp.14–15
17. Ibid., pp.16–70
18. Ibid., pp.20, 133–4
19. Ibid., p.312
20. Ibid., pp.29, 50
21. Ibid., pp.217, 224, 235, 236, 290, 326–8
22. Ibid., pp.34, 237–8
23. Ibid., p.136
24. Ibid., p.314
25. Ibid., pp.214–16
26. Wargo, 2018, pp.6, 106–7, 109–10, 175–6, 198–9
27. Ibid., p.4
28. Manning, 1995, p.3
29. Cited in Jorjani, 2016, pp.25–7
30. Bill Gibbons, '25a Regent Terrace, Edinburgh', Fortean Times 55, pp.56–8
31. Manning, 1995, pp.4–5
32. Ibid., pp.11–15
33. Ibid., pp.75–81
34. Manning, 1987, p.61
35. Manning, 1995, pp.28, 31, 34, 128
36. Ibid., pp.61–2
37. Ibid., pp.39–42
38. Ibid., pp.48–9
39. Ibid., pp.49–5
40. Ibid., p.59
41. Ibid., p.66
42. Ibid., p.64
43. Ibid., p.89
44. Ibid., p.23
45. Ibid., p.123
46. Ibid., p.122
47. Ibid., p.125
48. McClenon, 2018, p.62
49. Ibid., p.28
50. Ibid., pp.69, 71, 73, 119
51. Ibid., p.111
52. Ibid, pp.111, 122

53. Ibid, pp.75–6; Melechi, 2008, pp.200–3, 207–11, 217–18
54. Ibid., p.68
55. Ibid., pp.224–5
56. Ibid., pp.138–9
57. Strieber & Kripal, 2017, p.4
58. Ibid., p.66
59. Ibid., p.192
60. Lance Sieveking, 'Bittering Hall', Fortean Times 55, p.55
61. Lang, 2006, pp.113–14
62. Strieber & Kripal, 2017., pp.119–20, 125–7
63. Ibid., p.229
64. Ibid., p.65
65. Ibid., pp.204–5
66. Ibid., p.113–14

XII. Verbal Humour

1. Fortean Times 183, p.10
2. Carrington & Fodor, 1951, pp.184–5
3. Josiffe, 2017, p.196
4. Owen, 1964, p.241
5. Rickard & Michell, 2000, p.128
6. Monnin, 1862, p.73
7. Evans & Wilson, 2001, p.387
8. Maxwell-Stuart, 2011, p.127
9. Doty & Hynes, 1997, p.57
10. Hallowell & Ritson, 2008, p.262
11. Alan Murdie, 'Ghostwatch' column, Fortean Times 239, p.29
12. Roll, 2004, p.175
13. Gauld & Cornell, 1979, p.186; see pp.183–6 for more
14. Thurston, 1954, p.102; see pp.96–105 for more
15. Playfair, 2007, pp.203–4
16. Solomon & Solomon, 2006, p.82
17. Owen, 1964, p.23
18. Hardinge, 1870, p.447

19. Playfair, 2007, p.242
20. Ibid., p.84
21. Carrington & Fodor, 1951, p.183
22. Ibid., pp.199–200; Josiffe, 2017, pp.225–6

XIII. Defying Authority and Blasphemy

1. Fort, 1997, pp.24–5
2. Keel, 1976, p.238
3. Steiger, 2008, p.45
4. Flammarion, 1924, pp.69–70
5. Ibid., pp.71–2
6. Davies, 2007, pp.93–4
7. Fort, 1997, p.25
8. Playfair, 2007, p.6
9. Crowe, 2000, p.304; Lecouteux, 2012, p.94
10. Cited in Roll, 2004, pp.33–4
11. Flammarion, 1924, pp.214–15
12. Ibid., p.221
13. Healy & Cropper, 2014, pp.190–2
14. Hardinge, 1870, pp.439–40
15. Josiffe, 2017, p.134
16. Ibid., pp.240–1
17. Ibid., pp.80–4, 99
18. Ibid., p.59
19. Ibid., pp.88, 92
20. Ibid., pp.66, 106
21. Roll, 2004, p.43; see pp.43–55 for more
22. Roll, 2007, pp.28–9
23. Hubbell, 1916, p.119
24. Healy & Cropper, 2014, p.14
25. Price, 1945, pp.95–6
26. Cited in Ibid., p.106
27. Sitwell, 1959, pp.82–3
28. Ingram in Moretti, 2006, pp.198–9
29. Gauld & Cornell, 1979, pp.161–6
30. III.iii
31. Thurston, 1954, pp.178–9
32. Price, 1945, p.256
33. Tony Healy and Paul Cropper, 'Stone Me!', Fortean Times 116, pp.34–9
34. Bell, R. in Moretti, 2006, pp.43–4

35. *Fortean Times* 259, p.5
36. *Fortean Times* 16, p.5
37. Ashford & Mera, 2016, pp.6–7, 42–3, 46–7, 59–61, 108, 238–9
38. Barrett in Sitwell, 1959, p.341
39. Thurston, 1954, p.118
40. Carrington & Fodor, 1951, p.208
41. Maxwell-Stuart, 2011, p.201
42. Gauld & Cornell, 1979, p.198
43. Flammarion, 1924, p.110
44. Price, 1945, pp.77–8
45. Roll, 2004, p.38
46. Thurston, 1954, p.88; *see* pp.87–90 for more
47. Price, 1945, p.256
48. Hubbell, 1916, p.92
49. Ibid., p.140
50. Hardinge, 1870, pp.299–301
51. Clark & Hitchings, 2013, pp.133–4
52. Ibid., p.140
53. Ibid., p.151
54. Ibid., p.154
55. Ibid., pp.155–6
56. Ibid., p.155
57. Ibid., p.158
58. Ibid., pp.168, 169
59. Ibid., p.158
60. Ibid., pp.252–3, 255
61. Ibid., pp.146–9
62. Ibid., p.162
63. Ibid., pp.175–6
64. Ibid., pp.136, 138
65. Ibid., p.165
66. Ibid., pp.138–9
67. Ibid., pp.160–1, 164–5
68. Ibid., pp.161–2, 165
69. Ibid., p.168

XIV. Poltergeists at Play

1. Price, 1945, pp.107–8; *see* pp.81–110 for more
2. Hubbell, 1916, p.110
3. Wilson, 2000, p.112
4. Alan Murdie, 'Ghostwatch' column, *Fortean Times* 381, pp.18–21
5. Josiffe, 2017, p.161
6. Ashford & Ross, 2015, pp.45–7
7. Cited in Gauld & Cornell, 1979, p.47
8. Roll, 2004, p.39
9. Ibid., p.42
10. Carrington & Fodor, 1951, p.35
11. Owen, 1964, pp.48–9; Lecouteux, pp.123–4
12. Bell, R. In Moretti, 2006, p.42
13. Carrington & Fodor, 1951, p.199
14. Barrett in Sitwell, 1959, p.343
15. Hubbell, 1916, p.71
16. Fodor, 1959a, p.69
17. Hallowell, 2007, pp.8–9
18. *Fortean Times* 3, p.13
19. *Fortean Times* 112, p.21
20. Gauld & Cornell, 1979, p.35; see pp.32–8 for more
21. Spencer & Spencer, 1997, p.161
22. *Fortean Times* 231, p.22
23. Gauld & Cornell, 1979, pp.357–9
24. Owen, 1976, p.60
25. Ibid., pp.86–7
26. Freedom Long, 2009, p.65
27. Ibid., pp.58–61
28. Ibid., p.56
29. Hynes & Doty, 1997, pp.30, 210, 214–15
30. Ibid., p.212

XV. Threats of Violence

1. For typical examples, *see* Gauld & Cornell, 1979, p.116; Playfair, 1976, p.259; Sitwell, 1959, p.147; Thurston, 1954, p.27; Wilson, 2000, p.116
2. Thurston, 1954, pp.36–7
3. Playfair, 1976, p.244
4. Thurston, 1954, p.129
5. Ibid., p.134
6. Barrington, 2018, p.106
7. Tony Healy and Paul Cropper, 'Stone Me!', *Fortean Times* 116, pp.34–9; Healy & Cropper, 2014, p.29
8. Gauld & Cornell, 1979, p.30; *see* pp.27–32 for more
9. Playfair, 2007, pp.193–4
10. Hubbell, 1916, p.100
11. Ibid., p.74
12. Ibid., pp.128–9
13. Lecouteux, 2012, p.144; *see* pp.140–55 for more
14. Rogo, 1990, pp.189–95
15. Hallowell & Ritson, 2008, p.205
16. Spencer & Spencer, 1997, p.142
17. Holder, 2013, pp.211–12
18. Hubbell, 1916, pp.46–7
19. *Fortean Times* 239, p.28
20. Thurston, 1954, p.183
21. Manning, 1978, pp.37–8
22. Holder, 2013, p.36
23. Sitwell, 1959, p.84
24. Christopher Josiffe, 'Gef the Talking Mongoose', *Fortean Times* 269, pp.32–40
25. Lecouteux, 2012, p.114; *see* pp.113–17 for more
26. Parks Miller in Moretti, 2006, p.268
27. Thurston, 1954, p.35
28. Maxwell-Stuart, 2011, pp.51–5
29. Rogo, 1990, p.78
30. Gauld & Cornell, 1979, p.136
31. Playfair, 1976, pp.244–5; see pp.243–6 for more
32. Bell, R. in Moretti, 2006, pp.56–7
33. Manning, 1995, pp.56–8

34. Thurston, 1954, p.12
35. Price, 1945, p.13
36. Ibid., p.327
37. Flammarion, 1924, p.122; *see* pp.118–26 for more
38. Owen, 1964, p.21
39. Cassirer, 1993, p.11
40. Playfair, 2007, p.197
41. Gray, 2003, p.76
42. Gregory Bateson, *A Theory of Play and Fantasy*, cited in Ibid., pp.76–77

XVI. Rewriting Physical Laws

1. Cited in Flammarion, 1924, pp.257–9
2. Owen, 1976, p.69
3. Flammarion, 1924, p.114
4. *Fortean Times* 49, p.29
5. Roll, 2004, p.98
6. Healy & Cropper, 2014, pp.44–5
7. Price, 1945, p.69
8. Manning, 1987, p.99
9. Gauld & Cornell, 1979, p.107
10. Ibid., p.108
11. Roll, 2004, p.97
12. Wilson, 2000, p.156
13. Gauld & Cornell, 1979, p.165
14. Hallowell & Ritson, 2008, p.222
15. Gauld & Cornell, 1979, p.164
16. Letter in *Fortean Times* 37, p.63
17. Fodor, 1959a, p.24
18. Playfair, 1975, pp.260–3
19. Playfair, 2007, p.120
20. Sitwell, 1959, p.48
21. Gauld & Cornell, 1979, p.166
22. Playfair, 1976, p.243
23. Sitwell, 1959, p.48
24. Ibid., p.357
25. Ibid., p.74
26. Cited in Rogo, 2005, p.110
27. Healy & Cropper, 2014, p.140
28. Hubbell, 1916, p.54
29. Playfair, 1975, p.257

30. *Fortean Times* 182, p.9
31. Healy & Cropper, 2014, p.272
32. Holder, 2013, p.53
33. Hallowell & Ritson, 2014, p.97–8
34. Hall, 2014, p.101
35. Pike, 1968, p.82
36. Hall, 2014, p.56
37. Spencer & Spencer, 1997, pp.127–8
38. Ashford, 2017, p.247
39. Owen, 1976, pp.154–5
40. Owen, 1964, p.423
41. Playfair, 1976, p.87; Harpur, 2003, p.61

XVII. Unusual Conjunctions

1. Reeves & Mortimer, 1993, p.6
2. Stewart Lee, 'Bizarre Cabaret', *Comedy Review* 4, pp.58–61
3. Lecouteux, 2012, p.142
4. Maxwell-Stuart, 2011, p.25
5. Lecouteux, 2012, p.94
6. Ibid., p.129
7. Maxwell-Stuart, 2011, p.144
8. Gauld & Cornell, 1979, pp.298–9
9. Holder, 2013, p.163
10. Flammarion, 1924, p.105
11. Healy & Cropper, 2014, pp.28–9
12. Increase Mather, *An essay for the recording of Illustrious Providences ...* cited in Thurston, 1954, p.127
13. Letter in *Fortean Times* 169, p.55
14. Peter A. McCue, 'Renovation Hauntings', *Fortean Times* 268, pp.30–5
15. Playfair, 2007, plate section
16. Ibid., p.225
17. Henderson, 2008, pp.96–7
18. Holder, 2013, p.209

19. Spencer & Spencer, 1997, p.124
20. Pike, 1968, pp.78, 80
21. Flammarion, 1924, p.130
22. Gauld & Cornell, 1979, p.58
23. Owen, 1964, p.38
24. *Fortean Times* 131, p.10 & *Fortean Times* 152, p.11
25. 'The FT Interview: Doc Shiels', *Fortean Times* 62, pp.48–53
26. Douglas, 2002, pp.44–5
27. Ibid., pp.46–7
28. Ibid., p.151
29. Ibid., p.49
30. Ibid., p.48
31. Ibid., p.117
32. Hynes & Doty, 1997, p.42
33. Flammarion, 1924, pp.212–13
34. Hyde, 2008, p.61
35. Radin, 1988, p.185

XVIII. Machines in the Ghosts

1. Price, 1945, p.40
2. Sitwell, 1959, pp.81–2
3. Flammarion, 1924, p.282; *see* pp.281–3 for more
4. Ibid., p.103
5. Ibid., p.102
6. Owen, 1964, p.133
7. Kelleher & Knapp, 2005, p.224
8. Ibid., p.179
9. Sitwell, 1959, p.82
10. Albert Budden, 'Poltergeist DIY', *Fortean Times*, pp.23–26
11. Finucane, 1996, p.139
12. Price, 1945, pp.67–8
13. Owen, 1964, p.268
14. Gauld & Cornell, 1979, p.228
15. Rogo, 1990, p.277
16. Spencer & Spencer, 1997, p.185
17. Cited in Price, 1945, p.347; *see* pp.346–8 for more
18. Alexander Telfair, *A New Confutation*

of Sadducism ... cited in Price, 1945, p.77

19. Lang, 2006, p.189; Lecouteux, 2012, p.115
20. Lang, 2006, p.241
21. Maxwell-Stuart, 2011, p.128
22. Lecouteux, 2012, p.165; *see* pp.160–2 for more
23. Spencer & Spencer, 1997, pp.53, 54
24. Harold, 1979, p.60
25. Lecouteux, 2012, p.166
26. Hardinge, 1870, p.106
27. Thurston, 1954, p.42
28. McClenon, 2018, p.121
29. Lecouteux, 2012, p.166

30. Maxwell-Stuart, 2011, p.69
31. Hubbell, 1916, p.109
32. Ibid., pp.110–11
33. Maxwell-Stuart, 2011, p.97
34. Tony Healy and Paul Cropper, 'Stone Me!', in *Fortean Times* 116, pp.34–9
35. Aubrey, 2006, p.113
36. Thurston, 1954, p.127
37. Holder, 2013, pp.29–31
38. Healy & Cropper, 2014, p.137; *see* pp.136–57 for more
39. Gauld & Cornell, 1979, p.11
40. Lecouteux, 2012, p.166
41. Alexander Telfair, *A New Confutation of Sadducism* ... cited in Price, 1945, p.79

42. Gauld & Cornell, 1979, pp.216–18

Non-Conclusion

1. Hansen, 2001, p.425
2. Fort, 1997, p.17
3. https:// mysteriousuniverse. org/2018/04/ poltergeists-and-phds- an-interview-with-dr- christopher-laursen/
4. Fort, 1997, p.127
5. Playfair, 2007, p.164
6. Thurston, 1954, p.202
7. Peter M. Rojcewicz, 'Between One Eye Blink and the Next: Fairies, UFOs and Problems of Knowledge' in Narváez, 1997, p.503
8. Harpur, 2010, p.30
9. Jung, 2010, p.142